Computational Frameworks
for the Fast Fourier Transform

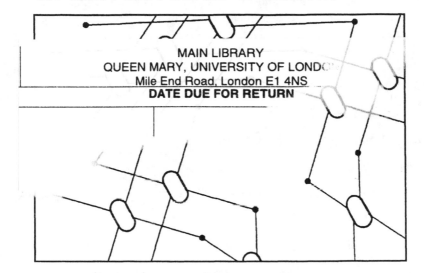

FRONTIERS IN APPLIED MATHEMATICS

The SIAM series on Frontiers in Applied Mathematics publishes monographs dealing with creative work in a substantive field involving applied mathematics or scientific computation. All works focus on emerging or rapidly developing research areas that report on new techniques to solve mainstream problems in science or engineering.

The goal of the series is to promote, through short, inexpensive, expertly written monographs, cutting edge research poised to have a substantial impact on the solutions of problems that advance science and technology. The volumes encompass a broad spectrum of topics important to the applied mathematical areas of education, government, and industry.

EDITORIAL BOARD

BOOKS PUBLISHED IN FRONTIERS IN APPLIED MATHEMATICS

Computational Frameworks
for the Fast Fourier Transform

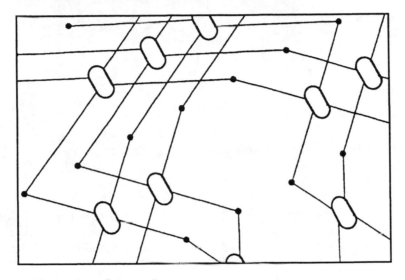

Charles Van Loan

Cornell University
Ithaca, New York

siam

Society for Industrial and Applied Mathematics
Philadelphia

Library of Congress Cataloging-in-Publication Data

Van Loan, Charles.
    Computational Frameworks for the fast Fourier transform / Charles Van Loan.
       p. cm. -- (Frontiers in applied mathematics : 10)
      Includes bibliographical references and index.
      ISBN 0-89871-285-8
      1. Fourier transformations. I. Title. II. Series.
    QA403.5.V35 1992
    515'.723 -- dc20
                                       92-4450

Dedicated to
Marian, Ted, and Elizabeth

Contents

Preface   ix
Preliminary Remarks   xi

Preface

The fast Fourier transform (FFT) is one of the truly great computational developments of this century. It has changed the face of science and engineering so much so that it is not an exaggeration to say that *life as we know it would be very different without the FFT*.

Unfortunately, the simplicity and intrinsic beauty of many FFT ideas are buried in research papers that are rampant with vectors of subscripts, multiple summations, and poorly specified recursions. The poor mathematical and algorithmic notation has retarded progress and has led to a literature of duplicated results. I am convinced that *life as we know it would be considerably different if, from the 1965 Cooley-Tukey paper onwards, the FFT community had made systematic and heavy use of matrix-vector notation!* Indeed, by couching results and algorithms in matrix/vector notation, the FFT literature can be unified and made more understandable to the outsider. The central theme in this book is the idea that different FFT algorithms correspond to different factorizations of the discrete Fourier transform (DFT) matrix. The matrix factorization point of view, so successful in other areas of numerical linear algebra, goes a long way toward unifying and simplifying the FFT literature. It closes the gap between the computer implementation of an FFT and the underlying mathematics, because it forces us to think well above the scalar level.

By approaching the FFT matrix/vector terms, the algorithm can be used as a vehicle for studying key aspects of advanced scientific computing, e.g., vectorization, locality of reference, and parallelization. The FFT deserves to be ranked among the great teaching algorithms in computational science such as Gaussian elimination, the Lanczos process, binary search, etc.

I would like to thank a number of colleagues and students for helping to make this book possible. This manuscript began as a set of class notes for a vector-parallel FFT course taught at Cornell in the spring of 1987. The contributions of all the students, especially Clare Chu, Yi-Zhong Wu, Anne Elster, and Nihal Wijeyesekera, are gratefully acknowledged. Clare Chu went on to write a beautiful thesis in the area that has been of immense help to me during the writing of §§1.4, 3.5, 4.3, and 4.4.

Sid Burrus's March 1990 visit to Cornell rejuvenated my interest in the manuscript, which at that time had been dormant for a number of years. I arranged to give a second edition of the FFT course during the fall of that year. Among the attendees who put up with my revisions and expansions of the earlier manuscript, Richard Huff, Wei Li, Marc Parmet, and Stephan Parrett deserve special mention for their contributions to the finished volume. I am also indebted to Dave Bond, Bill Campbell, Greg Henry, Ricardo Pomeranz, Dave Potyondy, and Dean Robinson.

I also wish to thank Chris Paige and Clement Pellerin of McGill University and Lennart Johnsson of Thinking Machines for reading portions of the text and making many corrections and valuable suggestions.

In addition, I would like to acknowledge the financial suppport of the Army Re-

search Office through the Mathematical Sciences Institute (MSI) at Cornell. With
the help of the MSI, I was able to organize a workshop on the FFT during the spring
of 1987. More recently, I was supported during the summer of 1990 by grants to the
Cornell Computational Optimization Project from the Office of Naval Research and
the National Science Foundation. During this time, the manuscript was considerably
refined.

Finally, I am indebted to Cindy Robinson–Hubbell at the Advanced Computing
Research Institute at Cornell for overseeing the production of the camera-ready copy
and to Crystal Norris at SIAM for a superb job of copyediting and managing the
whole project.

Preliminary Remarks

References

Annotated bibliographies are given in each section and a master list of references is supplied at the end of the book. We offer a few general bibliographic remarks here at the outset, beginning with the following list of good background texts:

R.E. Blahut (1984). *Fast Algorithms for Digital Signal Processing*, Addison-Wesley, Reading, MA.

R.N. Bracewell (1978). *The Fourier Transform and Its Applications*, McGraw-Hill, New York.

E.O. Brigham (1974). *The Fast Fourier Transform*, Prentice-Hall, Englewood Cliffs, NJ.

E.O. Brigham (1988). *The Fast Fourier Transform and Its Applications*, Prentice-Hall, Englewood Cliffs, NJ.

C.S. Burrus and T. Parks (1985). *DFT/FFT and Convolution Algorithms*, John Wiley & Sons, New York.

H.J. Nussbaumer (1981b). *Fast Fourier Transform and Convolution Algorithms*, Springer-Verlag, New York.

The bibliography in Brigham (1988) is particularly extensive. The researcher may also wish to browse through the 2000+ entries in

M.T. Heideman and C.S. Burrus (1984). "A Bibliography of Fast Transform and Convolution Algorithms," Department of Electrical Engineering, Technical Report 8402, Rice University, Houston, TX.

A particularly instructive treatment of the Fourier transform may be found in

G. Strang (1987). *Introduction to Applied Mathematics*, Wellesley-Cambridge Press, Wellesley, MA.

The books by Brigham contain ample pointers to many engineering applications of the FFT. However, the technique also has a central role to play in many "traditional" areas of applied mathematics. See

J.R. Driscoll and D.M. Healy Jr. (1989). "Asymptotically Fast Algorithms for Spherical and Related Transforms," Technical Report PCS-TR89-141, Department of Mathematics and Computer Science, Dartmouth College.

M.H. Gutknecht (1979). "Fast Algorithms for the Conjugate Periodic Function," *Computing* 22, 79–91.

P. Henrici (1979). "Fast Fourier Methods in Computational Complex Analysis," *SIAM Rev.* 21, 460–480.

T.W. Körner (1988). *Fourier Analysis*, Cambridge University Press, New York.

The FFT has an extremely interesting history. For events surrounding the publication of the famous 1965 paper by Cooley and Tukey, see

J.W. Cooley (1987). "How the FFT Gained Acceptance," in *History of Scientific Computing,* S. Nash (ed.), ACM Press, Addison-Wesley, Reading, MA.

J.W. Cooley, R.L. Garwin, C.M. Rader, B.P. Bogert, and T.G. Stockham Jr. (1969). "The 1968 Arden House Workshop on Fast Fourier Transform Processing," *IEEE Trans. Audio Electroacoustics AU-17*, 66–76.

J.W. Cooley, P.A. Lewis, and P.D. Welch (1967). "Historical Notes on the Fast Fourier Transform," *IEEE Trans. Audio and Electroacoustics AU-15*, 76–79.

However, the true history of the FFT idea begins with (who else!) Gauss. For a fascinating account of these developments read

M.T. Heideman, D.H. Johnson, and C.S. Burrus (1985). "Gauss and the History of the Fast Fourier Transform," *Arch. Hist. Exact Sci. 34*, 265–277.

History of Factorization Ideas

The idea of connecting factorizations of the DFT matrix to FFT algorithms has a long history and is *not* an idea novel to the author. These connections are central to the book and deserve a chronologically ordered mention here at the beginning of the text:

I. Good (1958). "The Interaction Algorithm and Practical Fourier Analysis," *J. Roy. Stat. Soc. Ser. B, 20,* 361–372. Addendum, *J. Roy. Stat. Soc. Ser. B, 22,* 372–375.

E.O. Brigham and R.E. Morrow (1967). "The Fast Fourier Transform," *IEEE Spectrum 4,* 63–70.

W.M. Gentleman (1968). "Matrix Multiplication and Fast Fourier Transforms," *Bell System Tech. J. 47,* 1099–1103.

F. Theilheimer (1969). "A Matrix Version of the Fast Fourier Transform," *IEEE Trans. Audio and Electroacoustics AU-17,* 158–161.

D.K. Kahaner (1970). "Matrix Description of the Fast Fourier Transform," *IEEE Trans. Audio and Electroacoustics AU-18,* 442–450.

M.J. Corinthios (1971). "The Design of a Class of Fast Fourier Transform Computers," *IEEE Trans. Comput. C-20,* 617–623.

M. Drubin (1971a). "Kronecker Product Factorization of the FFT Matrix," *IEEE Trans. Comput. C-20,* 590–593.

I.J. Good (1971). "The Relationship between Two Fast Fourier Transforms," *IEEE Trans. Comput. C-20,* 310–317.

P.J. Nicholson (1971). "Algebraic Theory of Finite Fourier Transforms," *J. Comput. System Sci. 5,* 524–527.

A. Rieu (1971). "Matrix Formulation of the Cooley and Tukey Algorithm and Its Extension," *Revue Cethedec 8,* 25–35.

B. Ursin (1972). "Matrix Formulations of the Fast Fourier Transform," *IEEE Comput. Soc. Repository R72-42.*

H. Sloate (1974). "Matrix Representations for Sorting and the Fast Fourier Transform," *IEEE Trans. Circuits and Systems CAS-21,* 109–116.

D.J. Rose (1980). "Matrix Identities of the Fast Fourier Transform," *Linear Algebra Appl. 29,* 423–443.

C. Temperton (1983). "Self-Sorting Mixed Radix Fast Fourier Transforms," *J. Comput. Phys. 52,* 1–23.

V.A. Vlasenko (1986). "A Matrix Approach to the Construction of Fast Multidimensional Discrete Fourier Transform Algorithms," *Radioelectron. and Commun. Syst. 29,* 87–90.

D. Rodriguez (1987). *On Tensor Product Formulations of Additive Fast Fourier Transform Algorithms and Their Implementations*, Ph.D. Thesis, Department of Electrical Engineering, The City College of New York, CUNY.

R. Tolimieri, M. An, and C. Lu (1989). *Algorithms for Discrete Fourier Transform and Convolution*, Springer-Verlag, New York.

H.V. Sorensen, C.A. Katz, and C.S. Burrus (1990). "Efficient FFT Algorithms for DSP Processors Using Tensor Product Decomposition," *Proc. ICASSP-90*, Albuquerque, NM.

J. Johnson, R.W. Johnson, D. Rodriguez, and R. Tolimieri (1990). "A Methodology for Designing, Modifying, and Implementing Fourier Transform Algorithms on Various Architectures," *Circuits, Systems, and Signal Processing 9*, 449–500.

Software

The algorithms in this book are formulated using a stylized version of the Matlab language which is very expressive when it comes to block matrix manipulation. The reader may wish to consult

M. Metcalf and J. Reid (1990). *Fortran 90 Explained*, Oxford University Press, New York

for a discussion of some very handy array capabilities that are now part of the modern Fortran language and which fit in nicely with our algorithmic style.

We stress that nothing between these covers should be construed as even approximate production code. The best reference in this regard is to the package *FFTPACK* due to Paul Swarztrauber and its vectorized counterpart, *VFFTPACK* due to Roland Sweet. This software is available through netlib. A message to netlib@ornl.gov with a message of the form "send index for FFTPACK" or "send index for VFFTPACK" will get you started.

Chapter 1

The Radix-2 Frameworks

A fast Fourier transform (FFT) is a quick method for forming the matrix-vector product $F_n x$, where F_n is the discrete Fourier transform (DFT) matrix. Our examination of this area begins in the simplest setting: the case when $n = 2^t$. This permits the orderly repetition of the central divide-and-conquer process that underlies all FFT work. Our approach is based upon the factorization of F_n into the product of $t = \log_2 n$ sparse matrix factors. Different factorizations correspond to different *FFT frameworks*. Within each framework different *implementations* are possible.

To navigate this hierarchy of ideas, we rely heavily upon block matrix notation, which we detail in §1.1. This "language" revolves around the Kronecker product and is used in §1.2 to establish the "radix-2 splitting," a factorization that indicates how a $2m$-point DFT can be rapidly determined from a pair of m-point DFTs. The repeated application of this process leads to our first complete FFT procedure, the famous Cooley–Tukey algorithm in §1.3.

Before fully detailing the Cooley–Tukey process, we devote §§1.4 and 1.5 to a number of important calculations that surface in FFT work. These include the butterfly computation, the generation of weights, and various data transpositions. Using these developments, we proceed to detail the *in-place* Cooley–Tukey framework in (§1.6). In-place FFT procedures overwrite the input vector with its DFT without making use of an additional vector workspace. However, certain data permutations are involved that are sometimes awkward to compute. These permutations can be avoided at the expense of a vector workspace. The resulting *in-order* FFTs are discussed in §1.7,

1

where a pair of *autosort* frameworks are presented. A fourth framework due to Pease is covered in §1.8.

Associated with each of these four methods is a different factorization of the DFT matrix. As we show in §1.9, four additional frameworks are obtained by transposing these four factorizations. A fast procedure for the inverse DFT can be derived by conjugating any of the eight "forward" DFT factorizations.

1.1   Matrix Notation and Algorithms

The DFT is a matrix-vector product that involves a highly structured matrix. A description of this structure requires the language of block matrices with an emphasis on Kronecker products. The numerous results and notational conventions of this section are used throughout the text, so it is crucial to have a facility with what follows.

1.1.1   Matrix/Vector Notation

We denote the vector space of complex n-vectors by $\mathbb{C}^n$, with components indexed from zero unless otherwise stated. Thus,

$$x \in \mathbb{C}^2 \quad \Rightarrow \quad x = \begin{bmatrix} x_0 \\ x_1 \end{bmatrix}.$$

For m-by-n complex matrices we use the notation $\mathbb{C}^{m \times n}$. Rows and columns are indexed from zero, e.g.,

$$A \in \mathbb{C}^{2 \times 3} \quad \Rightarrow \quad A = \begin{bmatrix} a_{00} & a_{01} & a_{02} \\ a_{10} & a_{11} & a_{12} \end{bmatrix}.$$

From time to time exceptions to the index-from-zero rule are made. These occasions are rare and the reader will be amply warned prior to their occurrence.

Real n-vectors and real m-by-n matrices are denoted by $\mathbb{R}^n$ and $\mathbb{R}^{m \times n}$, respectively.

If $A = (a_{kj})$, then we say that a_{kj} is the (k, j) entry of A. Sometimes we say the same thing with the notation $[A]_{kj}$. Thus, if α is a scalar then $[\alpha A]_{kj} = \alpha a_{kj}$.

The *conjugate*, the *transpose*, and the *conjugate transpose* of an m-by-n complex matrix $A = (a_{kj})$ are denoted as follows:

$$\begin{aligned} \bar{A} &= (\bar{a}_{kj}) & (m\text{-by-}n), \\ A^T &= (a_{jk}) & (n\text{-by-}m), \\ A^H &= (\bar{a}_{jk}) & (n\text{-by-}m). \end{aligned}$$

The *inverse* of a nonsingular matrix $A \in \mathbb{C}^{n \times n}$ is designated by A^{-1}. The n-by-n identity is denoted by I_n. Thus, $AA^{-1} = A^{-1}A = I_n$.

1.1.2   The Discrete Fourier Transform

The *discrete Fourier transform* (DFT) on $\mathbb{C}^n$ is a matrix-vector product. In particular, $y = [y_0, \ldots, y_{n-1}]^T$ is the DFT of $x = [x_0, \ldots, x_{n-1}]^T$ if for $k = 0, \ldots, n-1$ we have

$$y_k = \sum_{j=0}^{n-1} \omega_n^{kj} x_j, \tag{1.1.1}$$

where

$$\omega_n = \cos\left(2\pi/n\right) - i\sin\left(2\pi/n\right) = \exp\left(-2\pi i/n\right)\,,$$

and $i^2 = -1$. Note that ω_n is an nth root of unity: $\omega_n^n = 1$.

In the FFT literature, some authors set $\omega_n = \exp(2\pi i/n)$. This does not seriously affect any algorithmic or mathematical development. Another harmless convention that we have adopted is *not* to scale the summation in (1.1.1) by $1/n$, a habit shared by other authors.

In matrix-vector terms, the DFT as defined by (1.1.1) is prescribed by

$$y = F_n x,$$

where

$$F_n = (f_{pq}) \qquad f_{pq} = \omega_n^{pq} = \exp(-2\pi pq i/n) \tag{1.1.2}$$

is the n-by-n *DFT matrix*. Thus,

$$F_1 = [\,1\,], \qquad F_2 = \begin{bmatrix} 1 & 1 \\ 1 & -1 \end{bmatrix}, \quad \text{and} \quad F_4 = \begin{bmatrix} 1 & 1 & 1 & 1 \\ 1 & -i & -1 & i \\ 1 & -1 & 1 & -1 \\ 1 & i & -1 & -i \end{bmatrix}.$$

1.1.3   Some Properties of the DFT Matrix

We say that $A \in \mathbb{C}^{n\times n}$ is *symmetric* if $A^T = A$ and *Hermitian* if $A^H = A$. As an exercise in our notation, let us prove a few facts about F_n that pertain to these properties. The first result concerns some obvious symmetries.

Theorem 1.1.1 *The matrix F_n is symmetric.*

Proof. $[F_n^T]_{jk} = \omega_n^{kj} = \omega_n^{jk} = [F_n]_{jk}.$ $\square$

Note that if $n > 2$, then F_n is *not* Hermitian. Indeed, $F_n^H = \bar{F}_n^T = \bar{F}_n$. However, if $n = 1$ or 2, then F_n is real and so F_1 and F_2 are Hermitian.

Two vectors $x, y \in \mathbb{C}^n$ are *orthogonal* if $x^H y = 0$. The next result shows that the columns of F_n are orthogonal.

Theorem 1.1.2 $F_n^H F_n = nI_n$.

Proof. If μ_{pq} is the inner product of columns p and q of F_n, then by setting $\omega = \omega_n$ we have

$$\mu_{pq} = \sum_{k=0}^{n-1} (\bar{\omega}^{kp})\omega^{kq} = \sum_{k=0}^{n-1} \omega^{k(q-p)}.$$

If $q = p$, then $\mu_{pq} = n$. Otherwise, $\omega^{q-p} \neq 1$, and it follows from the equation

$$(1 - \omega^{q-p})\mu_{pq} = \sum_{k=0}^{n-1} \omega^{k(q-p)} - \sum_{k=1}^{n} \omega^{k(q-p)} = 1 - \omega^{n(q-p)} = 0$$

that $\mu_{pq} = 0$ whenever $q \neq p$. $\square$

We say that $Q \in \mathbb{C}^{n\times n}$ is *unitary* if $Q^{-1} = Q^H$. From Theorem 1.1.2 we see that $F_n/\sqrt{n}$ is unitary. Thus, the DFT is a scaled unitary transformation on $\mathbb{C}^n$.

1.1.4   Column and Row Partitionings

If $A \in \mathbb{C}^{m \times n}$ and we designate the kth column by a_k, then

$$A = [\, a_0 \mid a_1 \mid \cdots \mid a_{n-1} \,], \qquad a_k \in \mathbb{C}^m,$$

is a *column partitioning* of A. Thus, if $A = F_n$ and $\omega = \omega_n$, then

$$a_k = \begin{bmatrix} 1 \\ \omega^k \\ \vdots \\ \omega^{k(n-1)} \end{bmatrix}.$$

Likewise,

$$A = \begin{bmatrix} b_0^T \\ b_1^T \\ \vdots \\ b_{m-1}^T \end{bmatrix}, \qquad b_k \in \mathbb{C}^n,$$

is a *row partitioning* of $A \in \mathbb{C}^{m \times n}$. Again, if $A = F_n$, then

$$b_k^T = \left[1, \omega^k, \ldots, \omega^{k(n-1)} \right].$$

1.1.5   Submatrix Specification

Submatrices of $A \in \mathbb{C}^{m \times n}$ are specified by the notation $A(u, v)$, where u and v are integer row vectors that "pick out" the rows and columns of A that define the submatrix. Thus, if $u = [\, 0 \ 2 \,]$, $v = [\, 0 \ 1 \ 3 \,]$, and $B = A(u, v)$, then

$$B = \begin{bmatrix} a_{00} & a_{01} & a_{03} \\ a_{20} & a_{21} & a_{23} \end{bmatrix}.$$

Sufficiently regular index vectors u and v can be specified with the *colon notation*:

$$u = k{:}j \quad \Leftrightarrow \quad u = [\, k, \, k+1, \ldots, j] \qquad k \leq j.$$

Thus, $A(2{:}4, 3{:}7)$ is a 3-by-5 submatrix defined by rows 2, 3, and 4 and columns 3, 4, 5, 6, and 7. There are some special conventions when entire rows or columns are to be extracted from the parent matrix. In particular, if $A \in \mathbb{C}^{m \times n}$, then

$$A(u, :) \quad \Leftrightarrow \quad A(u, 0{:}n - 1),$$
$$A(:, v) \quad \Leftrightarrow \quad A(0{:}m - 1, v).$$

Index vectors with nonunit increments may be specified with the notation $i{:}j{:}k$, meaning count from i to k in steps of length j. This means that $A(0{:}2{:}m - 1, :)$ is made up of A's even-indexed rows, whereas $A(:, n - 1{:}{-}1{:}0)$ is A with its columns in reverse order. If $A = [\, a_0 \mid a_1 \mid \cdots \mid a_{21} \,]$, then $A(:, 3{:}4{:}21) = [\, a_3 \mid a_7 \mid a_{11} \mid a_{15} \mid a_{19} \,]$.

1.1.6 Block Matrices

Column or row partitionings are examples of matrix blockings. In general, when we write

$$
A = \left[\begin{array}{ccc} A_{00} & \ldots & A_{0,q-1} \\ \vdots & & \vdots \\ A_{p-1,0} & \cdots & A_{p-1,q-1} \end{array} \right] \begin{array}{c} m_0 \\ \vdots \\ m_{p-1} \end{array} \tag{1.1.3}
$$
$$
\begin{array}{ccc} n_0 & \cdots & n_{q-1} \end{array}
$$

we are choosing to regard A as a p-by-q block matrix where the block A_{kj} is an m_k-by-n_j matrix of scalars.

The notation for block vectors is similar. Indeed, if $q = 1$ in (1.1.3), then we say that A is a p-by-1 block vector.

The manipulation of block matrices is analogous to the manipulation of scalar matrices. For example, if $A = (A_{ij})$ is a p-by-q block matrix and $B = (B_{ij})$ is a q-by-r block matrix, then $AB = C = (C_{kj})$ can be regarded as a p-by-r block matrix with

$$
C_{kj} = A_{k0}B_{0j} + \cdots A_{k,q-1}B_{q-1,j},
$$

assuming that all of the individual matrix-matrix multiplications are defined.

Partitioning a matrix into equally sized blocks is typical in FFT derivations. Thus, if $m_0 = \cdots = m_{p-1} = \nu$ and $n_0 = \cdots = n_{q-1} = \eta$ in equation (1.1.3), then $A_{kj} = A(k\nu{:}(k+1)\nu - 1, j\eta{:}(j+1)\eta - 1)$.

1.1.7 Regarding Vectors as Arrays

The reverse of regarding a matrix as an array of vectors is to take a vector and arrange it into a matrix. If $x \in \mathbb{C}^n$ and $n = rc$, then by $x_{r \times c}$ we mean the matrix

$$
x_{r \times c} = [\, x(0{:}r-1) \mid x(r{:}2r-1) \mid \cdots \mid x(n-r{:}n-1)\,] \in \mathbb{C}^{r \times c},
$$

i.e., $[x_{r \times c}]_{kj} = x_{jr+k}$. For example, if $x \in \mathbb{C}^{12}$, then

$$
x_{3 \times 4} = \left[\begin{array}{cccc} x_0 & x_3 & x_6 & x_9 \\ x_1 & x_4 & x_7 & x_{10} \\ x_2 & x_5 & x_8 & x_{11} \end{array} \right].
$$

The colon notation is also handy for describing the columns of $x_{r \times c}^T$:

$$
x_{r \times c}^T = [\, x(0{:}r{:}n-1) \mid x(1{:}r{:}n-1) \mid \cdots \mid x(r-1{:}r{:}n-1)\,].
$$

Thus,

$$
x_{3 \times 4}^T = \left[\begin{array}{ccc} x_0 & x_1 & x_2 \\ x_3 & x_4 & x_5 \\ x_6 & x_7 & x_8 \\ x_9 & x_{10} & x_{11} \end{array} \right] = [\, x(0{:}3{:}11) \mid x(1{:}3{:}11) \mid x(2{:}3{:}11)\,].
$$

Suppose $x \in \mathbb{C}^n$ with $n = rc$. In the context of an algorithm, it may be useful for the sake of clarity to identify $x \in \mathbb{C}^n$ with a doubly subscripted array $X(0{:}r-1, 0{:}c-1)$. Consider the operation $b \leftarrow b + x_{r \times c}a$, where $a \in \mathbb{C}^c$, $b \in \mathbb{C}^r$, and "$\leftarrow$" designates assignment. The doubly subscripted array formulation

$$X(0{:}r-1, 0{:}c-1) \equiv x_{r \times c}$$
for $k = 0{:}r-1$
    for $j = 0{:}c-1$
        $b(k) \leftarrow b(k) + X(k,j)a(j)$
    end
end

is certainly clearer than the following algorithm, in which x is referenced as a vector:

for $k = 0{:}r-1$
    for $j = 0{:}c-1$
        $b(k) \leftarrow b(k) + x(jr+k)a(j)$
    end
end

Our guiding philosophy is to choose a notation that best displays the underlying computations.

Finally, we mention that a vector of length $n = n_1 \cdots n_t$ can be identified with a t-dimensional array $X(0{:}n_1-1, \ldots, 0{:}n_t-1)$ as follows:

$$X(\alpha_1, \ldots, \alpha_t) \equiv x(\alpha_1 + \alpha_2 N_2 + \cdots + \alpha_t N_t).$$

Here, $N_k = n_1 \cdots n_{k-1}$. In multidimensional settings such as this, components are indexed from one.

1.1.8 Permutation Matrices

An n-by-n permutation matrix is obtained by permuting the columns of the n-by-n identity I_n. Permutations can be represented by a single integer vector. In particular, if v is a reordering of the vector $0{:}n-1$, then we define the permutation P_v by

$$P_v = I_n(:, v).$$

Thus, if $v = [\, 0, \ 3, \ 1, \ 2\,]$, then

$$P_v = \begin{bmatrix} 1 & 0 & 0 & 0 \\ 0 & 0 & 1 & 0 \\ 0 & 0 & 0 & 1 \\ 0 & 1 & 0 & 0 \end{bmatrix}.$$

The action of P_v on a matrix $A \in \mathbb{C}^{n \times n}$ can be neatly described in terms of v and the colon notation:

$$\begin{aligned} AP_v &= A(:, v), \\ P_v^T A &= A(v, :). \end{aligned}$$

It is easy to show that $P_v^T P_v = I_n(v, :)I_n(:, v) = I_n$ and that

$$P_v = I_n(:, v) \ \Rightarrow \ P_v^T = I_n(:, w), \quad w(v) = 0{:}n-1. \tag{1.1.4}$$

1.1.9 Diagonal Scaling and Pointwise Multiplication

If $d \in \mathbb{C}^n$, then $D = \text{diag}(d) = \text{diag}(d_0, \ldots, d_{n-1})$ is the n-by-n diagonal matrix with diagonal entries $d_0, \ldots, d_{n-1}$. The application of D to an n-vector x is tantamount to the *pointwise multiplication* of the vector d and the vector x, which we designate by $d .* x$:

$$y = Dx = \text{diag}(d)x \quad \Leftrightarrow \quad y = d .* x \quad \Leftrightarrow \quad y_i = d_i x_i .$$

More generally, if $A, B \in \mathbb{C}^{m \times n}$, then the pointwise product of $(c_{kj}) = C = A .* B$ is defined by $c_{kj} = a_{kj} b_{kj}$. It is not hard to show that $A .* B = B .* A$ and $(A .* B)^H = A^H .* B^H$.

A few additional diagonal matrix notations are handy. If $A \in \mathbb{C}^{n \times n}$, then $\text{diag}(A)$ is the n-vector $[\, a_{00}, \; a_{11}, \; \ldots \; a_{n-1,n-1} \,]^T$. If $D_0, \ldots, D_{p-1}$ are matrices, then $D = \text{diag}(D_0, \ldots, D_{p-1})$ is the p-by-p block diagonal matrix defined by

$$D = \begin{bmatrix} D_0 & 0 & \cdots & 0 \\ 0 & D_1 & \cdots & 0 \\ \vdots & \vdots & \ddots & \vdots \\ 0 & 0 & \cdots & D_{p-1} \end{bmatrix}.$$

1.1.10 Kronecker Products

The block structures that arise in FFT work are highly regular and a special notation is in order. If $A \in \mathbb{C}^{p \times q}$ and $B \in \mathbb{C}^{m \times n}$, then the *Kronecker product* $A \otimes B$ is the p-by-q block matrix

$$A \otimes B = \begin{bmatrix} a_{00}B & \cdots & a_{0,q-1}B \\ \vdots & & \vdots \\ a_{p-1,0}B & \cdots & a_{p-1,q-1}B \end{bmatrix} \in \mathbb{C}^{pm \times qn}.$$

Note that

$$I_n \otimes B = \begin{bmatrix} B & 0 & \cdots & 0 \\ 0 & B & \cdots & 0 \\ \vdots & \vdots & \ddots & \vdots \\ 0 & 0 & \cdots & B \end{bmatrix}$$

is block diagonal.

A number of Kronecker product properties are heavily used throughout the text and are listed inside the front cover for convenience. Seven Kronecker facts are required in this chapter and they are now presented. The first four results deal with products, transposes, inverses, and permutations.

Kron1

If A, B, C, and D are matrices, then

$$(A \otimes B)(C \otimes D) = (AC) \otimes (BD),$$

assuming that the ordinary multiplications AC and BD are defined.

Kron2

If A and B are nonsingular matrices, then $A \otimes B$ is nonsingular and $(A \otimes B)^{-1} = A^{-1} \otimes B^{-1}$.

Kron3

  If A and B are matrices, then $(A \otimes B)^T = A^T \otimes B^T$.

Kron4

  If P and Q are permutations, then so is $P \otimes Q$.

The first property says that the product of Kronecker products is the Kronecker product of the products. The second property says that the inverse of a Kronecker product is the Kronecker product of the inverses. The third property shows that the transpose of a Kronecker product is the Kronecker product of the transposes *in the same order*. The fourth property asserts that the Kronecker product of two permutations is a permutation.

These results are not hard to verify. For example, to establish Kron1 when all the matrices are n-by-n, define $U = A \otimes B$, $V = C \otimes D$, and $W = UV$. Let U_{kj}, V_{kj}, and W_{kj} be the kj blocks of these matrices. It follows that

$$
\begin{aligned}
W_{kj} &= \sum_{q=0}^{n-1} U_{kq} V_{qj} = \sum_{q=0}^{n-1} (a_{kq} B)(c_{qj} D) \\
&= \left(\sum_{q=0}^{n-1} a_{kq} c_{qj} \right) BD = [AC]_{kj} BD.
\end{aligned}
$$

This shows that W is the conjectured Kronecker product.

The next two Kronecker properties show that matrix-vector products of the form $z = (I \otimes A)v$ or $z = (A \otimes I)v$ are "secretly" matrix-matrix multiplications.

Kron5

  If $A \in \mathbb{C}^{r \times r}$ and $x \in \mathbb{C}^n$ with $n = rc$, then

$$
y = (I_c \otimes A)x \quad \Leftrightarrow \quad y_{r \times c} = A x_{r \times c}.
$$

Kron6

  If $A \in \mathbb{C}^{c \times c}$ and $x \in \mathbb{C}^n$ with $n = rc$, then

$$
y = (A \otimes I_r)x \quad \Leftrightarrow \quad y_{r \times c} = x_{r \times c} A^T.
$$

The proofs of Kron5 and Kron6 are routine subscripting arguments. The last Kronecker property that we present in this section is a useful corollary of Kron1.

Kron7

  If A is a matrix, then

$$
I_p \otimes (I_q \otimes A) = I_{pq} \otimes A.
$$

A number of other, more involved Kronecker facts are required for some Chapter 2 derivations. See §2.2.1.

1.1.11 Algorithms and Flops

As may be deduced from the loops that we wrote in §1.1.7, we intend to use a stylized version of the Matlab language for writing algorithms. Matlab is an interactive system that can be used to express matrix computations at a very high level. See Coleman and Van Loan (1988, Chapter 4). The colon notation introduced in §1.1.5 is an integral part of Matlab and partially accounts for its success. Other aspects of Matlab notation are fairly predictable. For example, the following algorithm explicitly sets up the DFT matrix $F = F_n$ that we defined in (1.1.2):

$$
\begin{aligned}
&\textbf{for } p = 0{:}n-1 \\
&\quad \omega \leftarrow \exp(-2\pi i p/n) \\
&\quad F(p,0) \leftarrow 1 \\
&\quad \textbf{for } q = 1{:}n-1 \\
&\quad\quad F(p,q) \leftarrow \omega F(p,q-1) \\
&\quad \textbf{end} \\
&\textbf{end}
\end{aligned}
\tag{1.1.5}
$$

The computation (1.1.5) involves $O(n^2)$ complex operations.

In this text a more precise quantification of arithmetic is usually required, so we count the number of flops. A *flop* is a real arithmetic operation. Thus, a complex add involves two flops, while a complex multiplication involves six flops:

$$
\begin{aligned}
(a+ib)+(c+id) &= (a+c)+i(b+d), \\
(a+ib)(c+id) &= (ac-bd)+i(ad+bc).
\end{aligned}
$$

It is not hard to show that the execution of (1.1.5) involves $6n^2$ flops and n exponentiations.

On a simple scalar machine the counting of flops can be used to predict performance. Thus, execution of (1.1.5) on a machine that performs β_s flops per second would probably run to completion in about $6n^2\beta_s$ seconds. This assumes that a call to *exp* involves only a few flops and that n is large.

Sometimes we prefer to regard a computation at the vector level rather than at the scalar level. For example, in (1.1.5) the column $F(:,q)$ is the pointwise multiplication of the vectors $F(:,1)$ and $F(:,q-1)$; therefore we may prescribe the computation of $F = F_n$ as follows:

$$
\begin{aligned}
&F(0,0) \leftarrow 1; \ F(0,1) \leftarrow 1 \\
&\textbf{for } p = 1{:}n-1 \\
&\quad F(p,0) \leftarrow 1; \ F(p,1) \leftarrow \exp(-2\pi i p/n) \\
&\textbf{end} \\
&\textbf{for } q = 2{:}n-1 \\
&\quad F(:,q) \leftarrow F(:,q-1) \ .* \ F(:,1) \\
&\textbf{end}
\end{aligned}
\tag{1.1.6}
$$

Although (1.1.6) involves the same amount of arithmetic as (1.1.5), we have organized it in such a way that vector operations are stressed. With this emphasis it is more appropriate to say that (1.1.6) involves $O(n)$ complex vector operations of length n. In particular, there are approximately $4n$ (real) vector multiplies and $2n$ (real) vector adds associated with the vector execution of (1.1.6). *Vector computers* are able to execute vector operations such as $F(:,q-1) \ .* \ F(:,1)$ at a rate that is faster than what is realized on a sequence of scalar operations. To design efficient codes for such a machine, the programmer must have a facility with vector notation and be able to effect the kind of scalar-to-vector transition typified by our derivation of (1.1.6) from (1.1.5).

It is important *not* to exaggerate the value of flop counts and vector operation counts as predictors of performance. In some settings multiplicative flops are costlier than additive flops, in which case algorithmic design may focus on the minimization of the former. In this regard, it is sometimes useful to adopt a 3-multiply, 5-add approach to complex multiplication. For example, if we compute the three products $\alpha = (a+b)(c-d)$, $\beta = bc$, and $\gamma = ad$, then $(a+ib)(c+id) = (\alpha - \beta + \gamma) + i(\beta + \gamma)$. The point we are making here is that even for something as simple as a complex multiply, counting flops need not tell the whole story.

Another way in which simple flop counting can be misleading has to do with pipelining, a concept that we delve into in §1.4.3 and §1.7.8. Many high-performance machines with multiple functional units are able to pipeline arithmetic with the net result being a multiply-add each clock cycle. Thus, it is possible for an algorithm that involves 1000 flops to be as fast an algorithm that involves 500 flops if the multiply-add feature is fully exploited.

Flop counting does have its place, but it is almost always the case that the data motion features of an algorithm have a greater bearing on overall performance. One of the goals of this book is to make the reader aware of these issues.

Problems

P1.1.1　Show that if $y = F_n c$ and $p(z) = c_0 + c_1 z + \cdots + c_{n-1} z^{n-1}$, then for $k = 0{:}n - 1$ we have $y_k = p(\omega^k)$.

P1.1.2　Show that
$$F_n(k{:}k, 1{:}n-1) = F_n(n-k{:}n-k, n-1{:}-1{:}1)$$
for all k that satisfy $1 \le k \le n - 1$.

P1.1.3　Prove Kron5– Kron7.

P1.1.4　Suppose $A \in \mathbb{C}^{m \times m}$, $B \in \mathbb{C}^{n \times n}$, $X \in \mathbb{C}^{m \times n}$, and $Y = AX + XB \in \mathbb{C}^{m \times n}$. Show that if x, $y \in \mathbb{C}^{mn}$ are defined by $x_{m \times n} = X$ and $y_{m \times n} = Y$, then $y = [(I_n \otimes A) + (B^T \otimes I_m)]x$.

P1.1.5　Suppose $P = P_x \otimes P_y$, where P_x and P_y are permutations of order m and n respectively. This means that $P = P_z$ for some $z \in \mathbb{C}^{mn}$. Specify z in terms of x and y.

P1.1.6　Verify (1.1.4).

P1.1.7　Halve the number of flops in (1.1.5) by exploiting symmetry.

P1.1.8　Suppose $w = \begin{bmatrix} 1, \omega, \ldots, \omega^{n-1} \end{bmatrix}$ is available where $\omega = \omega_n$. Give an algorithm for setting up $F = F_n$ that does not involve any complex arithmetic.

Notes and References for Section 1.1

The mathematical and algorithmic aspects of numerical linear algebra are surveyed in

T. Coleman and C.F. Van Loan (1988). *Handbook for Matrix Computations*, Society for Industrial and Applied Mathematics, Philadelphia, PA.

G.H. Golub and C.F. Van Loan (1989). *Matrix Computations, 2nd Ed.*, Johns Hopkins University Press, Baltimore, MD.

For an intelligent discussion of flop counting in high-performance computing environments, see page 43 of

J.L. Hennessy and D.A. Patterson (1990). *Computer Architecture: A Quantitative Approach,* Morgan Kaufmann Publishers, San Mateo, CA.

Kronecker products, which figure heavily throughout the text, have an interesting history and widespread applicability in applied mathematics. See

H.C. Andrews and J. Kane (1970). "Kronecker Matrices, Computer Implementation, and Generalized Spectra," *J. Assoc. Comput. Mach. 17*, 260–268.

C. de Boor (1979). "Efficient Computer Manipulation of Tensor Products," *ACM Trans. Math. Software 5*, 173–182.

A. Graham (1981). *Kronecker Products and Matrix Calculus with Applications*, Ellis Horwood Ltd., Chichester, England.

H.V. Henderson, F. Pukelsheim, and S.R. Searle (1983). "On the History of the Kronecker Product," *Linear and Multilinear Algebra 14*, 113–120.

H.V. Henderson and S.R. Searle (1981). "The Vec-Permutation Matrix, The Vec Operator and Kronecker Products: A Review," *Linear and Multilinear Algebra 9*, 271–288.

J. Johnson, R.W. Johnson, D. Rodriguez, and R. Tolimieri (1990). "A Methodology for Designing, Modifying, and Implementing Fourier Transform Algorithms on Various Architectures," *Circuits, Systems, and Signal Processing 9*, 449–500.

P.A. Regalia and S. Mitra (1989). "Kronecker Products, Unitary Matrices, and Signal Processing Applications," *SIAM Rev. 31*, 586–613.

1.2   The FFT Idea

This book is about fast methods for performing the DFT $F_n x$. By "fast" we mean speed proportional to $n \log_2 n$. The purpose of this section is to establish a connection between F_n and $F_{n/2}$ that enables us to compute quickly an n-point DFT from a pair of $(n/2)$-point DFTs. *Repetition of this process is the heart of the radix-2 FFT idea.*

1.2.1 F_4 in Terms of F_2

Let us look at the $n = 4$ DFT matrix. Here we have

$$F_4 = \begin{bmatrix} 1 & 1 & 1 & 1 \\ 1 & \omega & \omega^2 & \omega^3 \\ 1 & \omega^2 & \omega^4 & \omega^6 \\ 1 & \omega^3 & \omega^6 & \omega^9 \end{bmatrix},$$

where $\omega = \omega_4 = \exp(-2\pi i/4) = -i$. Since $\omega^4 = 1$, it follows that

$$F_4 = \begin{bmatrix} 1 & 1 & 1 & 1 \\ 1 & \omega & \omega^2 & \omega^3 \\ 1 & \omega^2 & 1 & \omega^2 \\ 1 & \omega^3 & \omega^2 & \omega \end{bmatrix} = \begin{bmatrix} 1 & 1 & 1 & 1 \\ 1 & -i & -1 & i \\ 1 & -1 & 1 & -1 \\ 1 & i & -1 & -i \end{bmatrix}.$$

Let Π_4 be the 4-by-4 permutation

$$\Pi_4 = \begin{bmatrix} 1 & 0 & 0 & 0 \\ 0 & 0 & 1 & 0 \\ 0 & 1 & 0 & 0 \\ 0 & 0 & 0 & 1 \end{bmatrix}$$

and note that

$$F_4 \Pi_4 = \left[\begin{array}{cc|cc} 1 & 1 & 1 & 1 \\ 1 & -1 & -i & i \\ \hline 1 & 1 & -1 & -1 \\ 1 & -1 & i & -i \end{array} \right]$$

is just F_4 with its even-indexed columns grouped first. The key, however, is to regard this permutation of F_4 as a 2-by-2 block matrix, for if we define

$$\Omega_2 = \begin{bmatrix} 1 & 0 \\ 0 & -i \end{bmatrix} = \text{diag}(1, \omega_4)$$

and recall that

$$F_2 = \begin{bmatrix} 1 & 1 \\ 1 & -1 \end{bmatrix},$$

then

$$F_4 \Pi_4 = \begin{bmatrix} F_2 & \Omega_2 F_2 \\ F_2 & -\Omega_2 F_2 \end{bmatrix}. \tag{1.2.1}$$

Thus, each block of $F_4 \Pi_4$ is either F_2 or a diagonal scaling of F_2.

1.2.2 Π_n and the Radix-2 Splitting

The general version of (1.2.1) connects F_n to $F_{n/2}$, assuming that n is even. The vehicle for establishing this result is the permutation Π_n, which we define as follows:

$$\Pi_n = I_n(:,v) \qquad v = \begin{bmatrix} 0{:}2{:}n-1 \\ 1{:}2{:}n-1 \end{bmatrix}.$$

(Refer to §1.1.8 for a description of the notation that we are using here.) Note that

$$y = \Pi_n^T x \qquad \Leftrightarrow \qquad y = \begin{bmatrix} x(0{:}2{:}n-1) \\ x(1{:}2{:}n-1) \end{bmatrix}, \tag{1.2.2}$$

making it appropriate to refer to Π_n^T as the *even-odd sort permutation*. If Π_n^T is applied to a vector, then it groups the even-indexed components first and the odd-indexed components second. At the matrix level, if $A \in \mathbb{C}^{n \times n}$, then

$$A\Pi_n = [\, A(:,0{:}2{:}n-1) \mid A(:,1{:}2{:}n-1) \,]$$

is just A with its even-indexed and odd-indexed columns grouped together. The following theorem shows that copies of $F_{n/2}$ can be found in $F_n \Pi_n$.

Theorem 1.2.1 (Radix-2 Splitting) *If $n = 2m$ and*

$$\Omega_m = \mathrm{diag}(1, \omega_n, \ldots, \omega_n^{m-1}), \tag{1.2.3}$$

then

$$F_n \Pi_n = \begin{bmatrix} F_m & \Omega_m F_m \\ F_m & -\Omega_m F_m \end{bmatrix} = \begin{bmatrix} I_m & \Omega_m \\ I_m & -\Omega_m \end{bmatrix} (I_2 \otimes F_m).$$

Proof. If p and q satisfy $0 \le p < m$ and $0 \le q < m$, then

$$
\begin{array}{llll}
[F_n \Pi_n]_{pq} & = \; \omega_n^{p(2q)} & = \; \omega_m^{pq} & = \; [F_m]_{pq}, \\
[F_n \Pi_n]_{p+m,q} & = \; \omega_n^{(p+m)(2q)} & = \; \omega_m^{(p+m)q} & = \; [F_m]_{pq}, \\
[F_n \Pi_n]_{p,q+m} & = \; \omega_n^{p(2q+1)} & = \; \omega_n^p \omega_m^{pq} & = \; [\Omega_m F_m]_{pq}, \\
[F_n \Pi_n]_{p+m,q+m} & = \; \omega_n^{(p+m)(2q+1)} & = \; -\omega_n^{p(2q+1)} & = \; [-\Omega_m F_m]_{pq}.
\end{array}
$$

Here we have used the easily verified facts $\omega_n^2 = \omega_m$ and $\omega_n^m = -1$. These four equations confirm that the four m-by-m blocks of $F_n \Pi_n$ have the desired structure. We can express this block structure using the Kronecker product notation, because $I_2 \otimes F_m = \mathrm{diag}(F_m, F_m)$.   □

The term *radix*-2 means that we are relating F_n to a half-sized DFT matrix. More generally, if p divides n, then it is possible to relate F_n to $F_{n/p}$. The radix-p connection is explored in the next chapter.

The most important consequence of Theorem 1.2.1 is that it shows how to compute an n-point DFT from two appropriate $n/2$-point DFTs.

Corollary 1.2.2 *If $n = 2m$ and $x \in \mathbb{C}^n$, then*

$$F_n x = \begin{bmatrix} I_m & \Omega_m \\ I_m & -\Omega_m \end{bmatrix} \begin{bmatrix} F_m x(0{:}2{:}n-1) \\ F_m x(1{:}2{:}n-1) \end{bmatrix}.$$

Proof. From Theorem 1.2.1 we have

$$F_n = \begin{bmatrix} I_m & \Omega_m \\ I_m & -\Omega_m \end{bmatrix} \begin{bmatrix} F_m & 0 \\ 0 & F_m \end{bmatrix} \Pi_n^T.$$

The corollary follows by applying both sides to x. $\square$

Of course, this splitting idea can be applied again if m is even, thereby relating each of the half-length DFTs $F_m x(0{:}2{:}n-1)$ and $F_m x(1{:}2{:}n-1)$ to a pair of quarter-length DFTs. If n is a power of two, then we can divide and conquer our way down to 1-point DFTs.

1.2.3 An Example

Suppose $n = 16$. Corollary 1.2.2 says that $F_{16} x$ is a combination of the 8-point DFTs $F_8 x(0{:}2{:}15)$ and $F_8 x(1{:}2{:}15)$. We depict this dependence as follows:

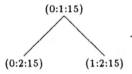

We can apply the same splitting to the $(0{:}2{:}15)$ and $(1{:}2{:}15)$ subproblems. Because the even and odd parts of $x(0{:}2{:}15) = [\, x_0,\ x_2,\ x_4,\ x_6,\ x_8,\ x_{10},\ x_{12},\ x_{14}\,]^T$ are specified by $x(0{:}4{:}15) = [\, x_0,\ x_4,\ x_8,\ x_{12}\,]^T$ and $x(2{:}4{:}15) = [\, x_2,\ x_6,\ x_{10},\ x_{14}\,]^T$, we have the following syntheses:

Thus, $F_{16} x$ can be generated from four quarter-length DFTs as follows:

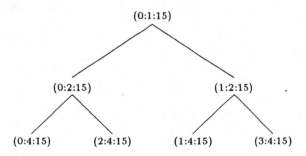

All of the 4-point DFTs at the bottom of this tree are themselves the consequence of a two-level synthesis. For example,

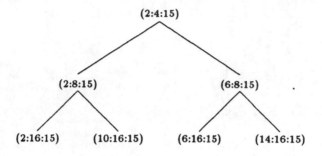

Noting that the leaves of this tree represent 1-point DFTs, we can obtain a complete tree description of the overall computation. See Fig. 1.2.1. In that schematic we write $[\,k\,]$ for $(k{:}16{:}15)$ to emphasize that at the leaves of the tree we have scalar, 1-point DFTs: $F_1 x_k = x_k$.

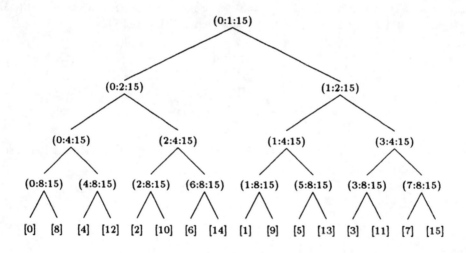

FIG. 1.2.1. *The structure of a radix-2 FFT* $(n = 16)$.

1.2.4 The Computation Tree In General

Suppose $n = 2^t$ and that we number the levels of the computation tree from the bottom to the top, identifying the leaf level with level 0. Each level-q DFT has the form $F_L x(k{:}r{:}n-1)$, where $L = 2^q$ and $r = n/L$. It is synthesized from a pair of level $q-1$ DFTs, each of which has the form $F_{L_*} x(k{:}r_*{:}n-1)$, where $L_* = L/2$ and $r_* = 2r$. We depict this operation as follows:

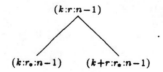

In matrix terms, the basic "gluing" operation is prescribed by Corollary 1.2.2. Suppose the DFTs $u = F_{L_*}x(k{:}r_*{:}n-1)$ and $v = F_{L_*}x(k+r{:}r_*{:}n-1)$ are available along with the diagonal elements of $\Omega_{L_*} = \mathrm{diag}(1, \omega_L, \ldots, \omega_L^{L_*-1})$. By defining $z = \Omega_{L_*}v$ we see that the computation

$$F_L x(k{:}r{:}n-1) = \begin{bmatrix} I_{L_*} & \Omega_{L_*} \\ I_{L_*} & -\Omega_{L_*} \end{bmatrix} \begin{bmatrix} u \\ v \end{bmatrix} = \begin{bmatrix} u+z \\ u-z \end{bmatrix}. \qquad (1.2.4)$$

requires $5L$ flops. (There are L_* complex additions and L_* complex multiplications.) We refer to the DFTs

$$F_L x(k{:}r{:}n-1), \qquad k = 0{:}r-1,$$

as the *intermediate DFTs of level q*. If we assemble these vectors in an array, then we obtain the *matrix of intermediate DFTs*:

$$F_L x_{r\times L}^T = F_L\left[\, x(0{:}r{:}n-1) \mid \cdots \mid x(r-1{:}r{:}n-1)\,\right]. \qquad (1.2.5)$$

Thus, as we go from level $q-1$ in the tree to level q, we are effectively carrying out the transition

$$F_{L_*} x_{r_* \times L_*}^T \quad \longrightarrow \quad F_L x_{r \times L}^T.$$

Climbing to the top of the tree in this way is typical in a *fast Fourier transform*.

1.2.5   An Assessment of Work

Ordinarily a complex matrix-vector product involves $8n^2$ flops, since there are n length-n inner products to perform. Let us see how much quicker the FFT approach is. At level q there are 2^{t-q} intermediate DFTs, each of length $L = 2^q$. Assuming the availability of the weights that define Ω_{L_*}, each of these length-L intermediate DFTs requires $5L$ flops from the above analysis of (1.2.4). It follows that the complete process involves

$$T = \sum_{q=1}^{t} 2^{t-q}(5 \cdot 2^q) = 5n\log_2 n$$

flops altogether. The difference between computing $F_n x$ conventionally and via the FFT is dramatic:

TABLE 1.2.1
Ratio of slow to fast DFT methods.

n	$\dfrac{8n^2}{5n\log_2 n}$
32	≈ 10
1024	≈ 160
32768	≈ 3500
1048576	≈ 84000

Thus, if it takes one second to compute an FFT of size $n = 1048576$, then it would require about one day to compute $F_n x$ conventionally.

Our assumption of weight availability in the above complexity argument does not undermine these observations, for it turns out that properly organized weight computations amount to an $O(n)$ overhead.

1.2.6   A Recursive Radix-2 FFT Procedure

The computation tree coupled with the synthesis rule of equation (1.2.4) characterizes what we refer to as a *radix-2 FFT*. The tree language is very descriptive, but we can state what is going on in more rigorous, algebraic terms by summarizing the process in a Matlab-style recursive function:

> **function** $y =$**fft**(x, n)
>   **if** $n = 1$
> $y \leftarrow x$
>   **else**
> $m \leftarrow n/2$
> $\omega \leftarrow \exp(-2\pi i/n)$
> $\Omega \leftarrow \text{diag}(1, \omega, \ldots, \omega^{m-1})$
> $z_T \leftarrow \textbf{fft}(x(0{:}2{:}n-1), m)$
> $z_B \leftarrow \Omega\,\textbf{fft}(x(1{:}2{:}n-1), m)$
>
> $y \leftarrow \begin{bmatrix} I_m & I_m \\ I_m & -I_m \end{bmatrix} \begin{bmatrix} z_T \\ z_B \end{bmatrix}$
>   **end**
> **end**

Here $y = F_n x$ and n is a power of two. The purpose of the next section is to express this recursive procedure in nonrecursive form.

Problems

P1.2.1 Suppose the function **fft** is applied to a problem where $n = 16$. Enumerate the nodes in the corresponding computation tree in the order of their computation.

P1.2.2 Note that no flops are required to compute products of the form $a(b + id)$ whenever $a = \pm 1$ or $a = \pm i$. Bearing this in mind, precisely how many flops are required by the function **fft** when it is applied to an $n = 4$ problem?

Notes and References for Section 1.2

The reader is urged to review any of the following articles for a survey of the fascinating history of the FFT:

J.W. Cooley (1987). "How the FFT Gained Acceptance," in *History of Scientific Computing*, S. Nash (ed.), ACM Press, Addison-Wesley, Reading, MA.

J.W. Cooley, R.L. Garwin, C.M. Rader, B.P. Bogert, and T.G. Stockham Jr. (1969). "The 1968 Arden House Workshop on Fast Fourier Transform Processing," *IEEE Trans. Audio and Electroacoustics AU-17*, 66-76.

J.W. Cooley, P.A. Lewis, and P.D. Welch (1967). "Historical Notes on the Fast Fourier Transform," *IEEE Trans. Audio and Electroacoustics AU-15*, 76–79.

M.T. Heideman, D.H. Johnson, and C.S. Burrus (1985). "Gauss and the History of the Fast Fourier Transform," *Archive for History of Exact Sciences 34*, 265–277.

Different characterizations and perspectives of the FFT are offered in

L. Auslander and R. Tolimieri (1979). "Is Computing with the Finite Fourier Transform Pure or Applied Mathematics?" *Bull. Amer. Math. Soc. 1*, 847–897.

R.N. Bracewell (1989). "The Fourier Transform," *Scientific American*, June, 86–95

W.L. Briggs and V. Henson (1990). "The FFT as Multigrid," *SIAM Rev. 32*, 252–261.

C.B. de Boor (1980). "FFT as Nested Multiplication with a Twist," *SIAM J. Sci. Statist. Comput. 1*, 173–178.

The optimality of the FFT has attracted considerable attention in the computational complexity field. See

P. Diaconis (1980). "Average Running Time of the Fast Fourier Transform," *J. Algorithms 1*, 187–208.

P. Diaconis (1981). "How Fast Is the Fourier Transform?," in *Computer Science and Statistics: Proceedings of the 13th Symposium on the Interface*, W.F. Eddy (ed.), Springer-Verlag, New York, 43–44.

W.M. Gentleman (1978). "Some Complexity Results for Matrix Computations on Parallel Processors," *J. Assoc. Comput. Mach. 25*, 112–114.

C.H. Papadimitriou (1979). "Optimality of the Fast Fourier Transform," *J. Assoc. Comput. Mach. 26*, 95–102.

J.E. Savage and S. Swamy (1978). "Space-Time Tradeoffs on the FFT Algorithm," *IEEE Trans. Inform. Theory IT-24*, 563–568.

S. Winograd (1979). "On the Multiplicative Complexity of the Discrete Fourier Transform," *Adv. Math. 32*, 83–117.

The radix-2 splitting has been established a number of times in the literature. See

D.J. Rose (1980). "Matrix Identities of the Fast Fourier Transform," *Linear Algebra Appl. 29*, 423–443.

C. Temperton (1983a). "Self-Sorting Mixed Radix Fast Fourier Transforms," *J. Comput. Phys. 52*, 1–23.

R. Tolimieri, M. An, and C. Lu (1989). *Algorithms for Discrete Fourier Transform and Convolution*, Springer-Verlag, New York.

FFT ideas extend beyond the field of complex numbers. See

M. Clausen (1989). "Fast Fourier Transforms for Metabelian Groups," *SIAM J. Comput. 18*, 584–593.

E. Dubois and A.N. Venetsanopoulos (1978b). "The Discrete Fourier Transform over Finite Rings with Application to Fast Convolution," *IEEE Trans. Comput. C-27*, 586–593.

F.P. Preparata and D.V. Sarwate (1977). "Computational Complexity of Fourier Transforms over Finite Fields," *Math. Comp. 31*, 740–751.

The FFT is but one of a number of fast transforms. The following papers offer connections between the FFT and a number of these other techniques:

B.J. Fino and V.R. Algazi (1977). "A Unified Treatment of Discrete Fast Unitary Transforms," *SIAM J. Comput. 6*, 700–717.

H.O. Kunz (1979). "On the Equivalence Between One-Dimensional Discrete Walsh–Hadamard and Multidimensional Discrete Fourier Transforms, *IEEE Trans. Comput. C-28*, 267–268.

V. Vlasenko and K.R. Rao (1979). "Unified Matrix Treatment of Discrete Transforms," *IEEE Trans. Comput. C-28*, 934–938.

Finally, and with an eye towards the future, we mention the new and exciting area of *wavelets*. Wavelet research is leading to the development of new fast algorithms for problems that were previously tackled through the use of FFTs. A nice snapshot of this emerging computational framework is given in

G. Strang (1989). "Wavelets and Dilation Equations," *SIAM Rev. 31*, 614–627.

1.3   The Cooley–Tukey Radix-2 Factorization

In this section, a nonrecursive specification of the function fft of §1.2.6 is given, and we emerge with the famous Cooley–Tukey (C–T) radix-2 FFT. Some additional block matrix notation enables us to connect the Cooley–Tukey procedure with a *sparse factorization* of the DFT matrix. We shall be making similar connections for all of the FFT techniques that we present in subsequent sections. It is a good way to unify what turns out to be a vast family of algorithms.

1.3.1   The Sparse Factorization Idea

FFT techniques are based upon sparse factorizations of the DFT matrix. Suppose that in the case where $n = 2^t$ we can write $F_n = A_t \cdots A_1 P_n^T$, where P_n is some permutation and each A_q has two nonzero entries per row. It follows that if $x \in \mathbb{C}^n$, then we may compute $F_n x$ as follows:

$$
x \leftarrow P_n^T x
$$
$$
\textbf{for } q = 1{:}t
$$
$$
\qquad x \leftarrow A_q x
$$
$$
\textbf{end}
$$

Note that this requires $O(n \log_2 n)$ flops to execute if the sparsity of the A_q is exploited. Our goal is to define the matrices A_q and the permutation P.

1.3.2   Butterfly Operators

For $L = 2L_*$ define the *radix-2 butterfly matrix* $B_L \in \mathbb{C}^{L \times L}$ by

$$
B_L = \begin{bmatrix} I_{L_*} & \Omega_{L_*} \\ I_{L_*} & -\Omega_{L_*} \end{bmatrix},
$$

where

$$
\Omega_{L_*} = \mathrm{diag}(1, \omega_L, \ldots, \omega_L^{L_*-1})
$$

and (as usual) $\omega_L = \exp(-2\pi i/L)$. Recall from (1.2.4) how the level q DFTs are synthesized from the level $q - 1$ DFTs:

$$
F_L x(k{:}r{:}n-1) = B_L \begin{bmatrix} F_{L_*} x(k{:}r_*{:}n-1) \\ F_{L_*} x(k+r{:}r_*{:}n-1) \end{bmatrix}. \tag{1.3.1}
$$

Here, $L = 2^q$, $r = n/L$, $L_* = L/2$, and $r_* = 2r$. Starting at $n = L$, we have

$$
F_n x = B_n \begin{bmatrix} F_{n/2} x(0{:}2{:}n-1) \\ F_{n/2} x(1{:}2{:}n-1) \end{bmatrix}.
$$

Descending one level in the computation tree, we find a pair of butterfly operations, namely,

$$
F_{n/2} x(0{:}2{:}n-1) = B_{n/2} \begin{bmatrix} F_{n/4} x(0{:}4{:}n-1) \\ F_{n/4} x(2{:}4{:}n-1) \end{bmatrix}
$$

and

$$
F_{n/2} x(1{:}2{:}n-1) = B_{n/2} \begin{bmatrix} F_{n/4} x(1{:}4{:}n-1) \\ F_{n/4} x(3{:}4{:}n-1) \end{bmatrix}.
$$

It follows that

$$
F_n x = B_n \begin{bmatrix} B_{n/2} & 0 \\ 0 & B_{n/2} \end{bmatrix} \begin{bmatrix} F_{n/4} x(0{:}4{:}n-1) \\ F_{n/4} x(2{:}4{:}n-1) \\ F_{n/4} x(1{:}4{:}n-1) \\ F_{n/4} x(3{:}4{:}n-1) \end{bmatrix}.
$$

In general, it looks as if we are headed for an expression of the form

$$
F_n x = A_t \cdots A_1 P_n^T x,
$$

where P_n is some permutation and A_q is a direct sum of the butterfly operators, i.e.,

$$
A_q = \mathrm{diag}(\underbrace{B_L, \ldots, B_L}_{r}) = I_r \otimes B_L \qquad L = 2^q, \ r = n/L.
$$

Let us confirm this for the case $n = 16$ before we prove the general result.

1.3.3 Preview of the C–T Radix-2 Factorization

In §1.2.3 we detailed an $n = 16$ FFT using "tree language." We now repeat the process using Kronecker product language. At the top of the tree we connect two 8-point DFTs:

$$F_{16}x = (I_1 \otimes B_{16}) \left[\begin{array}{c} F_8x(0{:}2{:}15) \\ F_8x(1{:}2{:}15) \end{array} \right].$$

Each 8-point DFT is synthesized from a pair of 4-point DFTs using the butterfly operator B_8. Thus,

$$\left[\begin{array}{c} F_8x(0{:}2{:}15) \\ F_8x(1{:}2{:}15) \end{array} \right] = (I_2 \otimes B_8) \left[\begin{array}{c} F_4x(0{:}4{:}15) \\ F_4x(2{:}4{:}15) \\ F_4x(1{:}4{:}15) \\ F_4x(3{:}4{:}15) \end{array} \right].$$

Repeating this process produces the stage-2 computation

$$\left[\begin{array}{c} F_4x(0{:}4{:}15) \\ F_4x(2{:}4{:}15) \\ F_4x(1{:}4{:}15) \\ F_4x(3{:}4{:}15) \end{array} \right] = (I_4 \otimes B_4) \left[\begin{array}{c} F_2x(0{:}8{:}15) \\ F_2x(4{:}8{:}15) \\ F_2x(2{:}8{:}15) \\ F_2x(6{:}8{:}15) \\ F_2x(1{:}8{:}15) \\ F_2x(5{:}8{:}15) \\ F_2x(3{:}8{:}15) \\ F_2x(7{:}8{:}15) \end{array} \right],$$

preceded by the stage-1 computation

$$\left[\begin{array}{c} F_2x(0{:}8{:}15) \\ F_2x(4{:}8{:}15) \\ F_2x(2{:}8{:}15) \\ F_2x(6{:}8{:}15) \\ F_2x(1{:}8{:}15) \\ F_2x(5{:}8{:}15) \\ F_2x(3{:}8{:}15) \\ F_2x(7{:}8{:}15) \end{array} \right] = (I_8 \otimes B_2) \left[\begin{array}{c} x(0) \\ x(8) \\ x(4) \\ x(12) \\ x(2) \\ x(10) \\ x(6) \\ x(14) \\ x(1) \\ x(9) \\ x(5) \\ x(13) \\ x(3) \\ x(11) \\ x(7) \\ x(15) \end{array} \right].$$

Note that $(I_8 \otimes B_2)$ "sees" a scrambled version of x, which we denote by $P_{16}^T x$. We have much more to say about this permutation later. For now recognize that we have established

$$F_{16}x = (I_1 \otimes B_{16})(I_2 \otimes B_8)(I_4 \otimes B_4)(I_8 \otimes B_2)P_{16}^T x$$

and so

$$F_{16} = (I_1 \otimes B_{16})(I_2 \otimes B_8)(I_4 \otimes B_4)(I_8 \otimes B_2)P_{16}^T. \qquad (1.3.2)$$

This is a special instance of what we call the *Cooley–Tukey Radix-2 Factorization*. Note that it is a sparse matrix factorization, for if we set $A_4 = I_1 \otimes B_{16}$, $A_3 = I_2 \otimes B_8$, $A_2 = I_4 \otimes B_4$, and $A_1 = I_8 \otimes B_2$, then $F_{16} = A_4 A_3 A_2 A_1 P_{16}^T$ and each A_q has only two nonzero entries per row. This is because each B_L has two nonzeros per row: one from I_{L_*} and one from Ω_{L_*}.

1.3.4 The Cooley–Tukey Factorization

Equation (1.3.2) suggests the existence of a factorization of the form

$$F_n P_n = (I_1 \otimes B_n)(I_2 \otimes B_{n/2}) \cdots (I_{n/2} \otimes B_2).$$

A simple induction argument establishes this result and produces a formal specification of the permutation P_n.

Lemma 1.3.1 *Suppose $n = 2^t$ and $m = n/2$. If $F_m P_m = C_{t-1} \cdots C_1$ and*

$$P_n = \Pi_n (I_2 \otimes P_m), \tag{1.3.3}$$

then

$$F_n P_n = (I_1 \otimes B_n)(I_2 \otimes C_{t-1}) \cdots (I_2 \otimes C_1).$$

Proof. From Theorem 1.2.1, $F_n \Pi_n = B_n (I_2 \otimes F_m)$ and so by hypothesis

$$F_n \Pi_n = B_n (I_2 \otimes C_{t-1} \cdots C_1 P_m^T).$$

But by Kron1

$$I_2 \otimes (C_{t-1} \cdots C_1 P_m^T) = (I_2 \otimes C_{t-1}) \cdots (I_2 \otimes C_1)(I_2 \otimes P_m^T)$$

and therefore

$$F_n \Pi_n = B_n (I_2 \otimes C_{t-1}) \cdots (I_2 \otimes C_1)(I_2 \otimes P_m^T).$$

The lemma follows, since $(I_2 \otimes P_m^T)^{-1} = (I_2 \otimes P_m^T)^T = (I_2 \otimes P_m)$. $\quad\square$

A nonrecursive specification of P_n is possible through induction.

Lemma 1.3.2 *If $n = 2^t$, P_n is defined by (1.3.3), and $R_q = I_{2^{t-q}} \otimes \Pi_{2^q}$, then*

$$P_n = R_t \cdots R_1. \tag{1.3.4}$$

Proof. The lemma holds if $t = 1$, since $P_2 = \Pi_2 = I_2$. By induction we therefore assume that if $m = 2^{t-1} = n/2$, then

$$P_m = \tilde{R}_{t-1} \cdots \tilde{R}_1,$$

where $\tilde{R}_q = I_{2^{t-1-q}} \otimes \Pi_{2^q}$. But from (1.3.3) and Kron1 we have

$$
\begin{aligned}
P_n &= \Pi_n (I_2 \otimes P_m) \\
&= \Pi_n (I_2 \otimes \tilde{R}_{t-1} \cdots \tilde{R}_1) \\
&= \Pi_n (I_2 \otimes \tilde{R}_{t-1}) \cdots (I_2 \otimes \tilde{R}_1).
\end{aligned}
$$

Using Kron7

$$I_2 \otimes \tilde{R}_q = I_2 \otimes (I_{2^{t-1-q}} \otimes \Pi_{2^q}) = I_{2^{t-q}} \otimes \Pi_{2^q} = R_q$$

for $q = 1{:}t - 1$. The proof is complete with the observation that $R_t = \Pi_n$. □

We refer to P_n as the *bit-reversing* permutation, and we discuss it in detail in §1.5. With P_n we are able to specify the first of several important sparse matrix factorizations of F_n.

Theorem 1.3.3 (Cooley–Tukey Radix-2 Factorization) *If $n = 2^t$, then*

$$F_n = A_t \cdots A_1 P_n^T,$$

where P_n is defined by (1.3.4) and

$$A_q = I_r \otimes B_L, \qquad\qquad L = 2^q, \; r = n/L,$$

$$B_L = \begin{bmatrix} I_{L_*} & \Omega_{L_*} \\ I_{L_*} & -\Omega_{L_*} \end{bmatrix}, \qquad\qquad L_* = L/2,$$

$$\Omega_{L_*} = \operatorname{diag}(1, \omega_L, \ldots, \omega_L^{L_*-1}), \qquad \omega_L = \exp(-2\pi i/L).$$

Proof. If $n = 2$, then $P_n = \Pi_n = I_n$, $F_n = B_n$, and the theorem holds by virtue of Lemma 1.3.1:

$$F_2 P_2 = F_2 = \begin{bmatrix} 1 & 1 \\ 1 & -1 \end{bmatrix} = I_1 \otimes B_2.$$

For general $n = 2^t$ we see that Lemma 1.3.1 provides the necessary inductive step if we define $A_t = I_1 \otimes B_n$ and $A_q = I_2 \otimes C_q$ for $q = 1{:}t - 1$. □

The Cooley–Tukey radix-2 factorization of F_n is a sparse factorization and is the basis of the following algorithm.

Algorithm 1.3.1 (Cooley–Tukey) If $x \in \mathbb{C}^n$ and $n = 2^t$, then the following algorithm overwrites x with $F_n x$:

$$x \leftarrow P_n^T x$$
$$\text{for } q = 1{:}t$$
$$\qquad x \leftarrow A_q x$$
$$\text{end}$$

An actual implementation of this procedure involves looking carefully at the *permutation phase* and the *combine phase* of this procedure. The permutation phase is concerned with the reordering of the input vector x via P_n and is discussed in §1.5. The combine phase is detailed in §1.4 and involves the organization of the butterfly operations $x \leftarrow A_q x$. The overall implementation of the Cooley–Tukey method is covered in §1.6.

Problems

P1.3.1 Suppose $A \in \mathbb{C}^{m \times m}$ and $B \in \mathbb{C}^{n \times n}$. Assume that $y = (A \otimes B)x$, where $x \in \mathbb{C}^{mn}$ is given. Give a complete algorithm for computing $y \in \mathbb{C}^{mn}$.

P1.3.2 In Theorem 1.3.3, describe the block structure of the product $A_q \cdots A_1$, where $q \leq t$.

Notes and References for Section 1.3

What may be called the "modern era" of FFT computation begins with

J.W. Cooley and J.W. Tukey (1965). "An Algorithm for the Machine Calculation of Complex Fourier Series," *Math. Comp.* *19*, 297–301.

A purely scalar derivation of the radix-2 splitting is given. (See §1.9.5.) An alternative proof of the Cooley–Tukey factorization may be found on page 100 of

R. Tolimieri, M. An, and C. Lu (1989). *Algorithms for Discrete Fourier Transform and Convolution*, Springer-Verlag, New York.

1.4   Weight and Butterfly Computations

As we observed in §1.3, the combine phase of the Cooley–Tukey process involves a sequence of butterfly updates of the form $x \leftarrow A_q x$, where

$$A_q = I_r \otimes B_L, \qquad\qquad L = 2^q,\ r = n/L,$$

$$B_L = \begin{bmatrix} I_{L_*} & \Omega_{L_*} \\ I_{L_*} & -\Omega_{L_*} \end{bmatrix}, \qquad\qquad L_* = L/2,$$

$$\Omega_{L_*} = \mathrm{diag}(1, \omega_L, \ldots, \omega_L^{L_*-1}), \qquad \omega_L = \exp(-2\pi i/L).$$

We now examine this calculation and the generation of the weights ω_L^j. We use the occasion to introduce various aspects of vector computation and to reiterate some of the familiar themes in numerical analysis, such as stability, efficiency, and exploitation of structure.

We start by presenting a half-dozen methods that can be used to compute the *weight vector* w_{L_*}, which we define as

$$w_{L_*} = \begin{bmatrix} 1 \\ \omega_L \\ \vdots \\ \omega_L^{L_*-1} \end{bmatrix}, \qquad \omega_L = \exp(-2\pi i/L). \qquad (1.4.1)$$

These methods vary in efficiency and numerical accuracy. With respect to the latter, it is rather surprising that roundoff error should be a serious issue in FFT work at all. The DFT matrix F_n is a scaled unitary transformation, and it is well known that premultiplication by such a matrix is stable. But because we must compute the weights, we are in effect dealing with a *computed* unitary transformation. The quality of the computed weights is therefore crucial to the overall accuracy of the FFT.

After our survey of weight computation, we proceed with the details of the actual butterfly update $x \leftarrow A_q x$. Two frameworks are established and we discuss the ramifications of each with respect to weight computation and the notion of vector stride. Finally, we set up a model of vector computation and use it to anticipate the running time of one particular butterfly algorithm.

1.4.1   A Preliminary Note On Roundoff Error

It is not our intention to indulge in a detailed roundoff error analysis of any algorithm. However, a passing knowledge of finite precision arithmetic is crucial in order to appreciate the dangers of reckless weight computation.

The key thing to remember is that a roundoff error is usually sustained each time a floating point operation is performed. The size of the error is a function of mantissa length and the details of the arithmetic. If x and y are real floating point numbers and "op" is one of the four arithmetic operations, then the computed version of the quantity x op y is designated by $\text{fl}(x \text{ op } y)$. We assume that

$$\text{fl}(x \text{ op } y) = (x \text{ op } y)(1 + \epsilon)$$

where $\epsilon \leq \mathbf{u}$ and $\mathbf{u}$ is the *unit roundoff* of the underlying machine. On a system that allocates d bits to the mantissa, $\mathbf{u} \approx 2^{-d}$. (See Golub and Van Loan (1989).)

During the execution of an algorithm that manipulates floating point numbers, the roundoff errors are compounded. Accounting for these errors in an understandable fashion is a combinatoric art outside the scope of this book. However, if we restrict our attention to the weight-generation methods of the following section, then it is possible to build up a useful intuition about roundoff behavior due to the regular nature of the computations.

1.4.2 Computing the Vector of Weights w_{L_*}

We now compare six different methods that can be used to compute the weight vector w_{L_*} that is defined in (1.4.1). Surveys with greater depth include Oliver (1975) and Chu (1988).

Some of the algorithms require careful examination of the real and imaginary portions of the computation, and in these situations we use the notation z^R and z^I to designate the real and imaginary portions of a complex number z.

Recall that the complex addition

$$a + b = (a^R + ia^I) + (b^R + ib^I) = (a^R + b^R) + i(a^I + b^I)$$

requires a pair of real additions (two flops), while the complex multiplication

$$(a^R + ia^I)(b^R + ib^I) = (a^R b^R - a^I b^I) + i(a^R b^I + a^I b^R)$$

involves four real multiplications and two real additions (six flops). We will *not* be using the 3-multiply complex multiply algorithm discussed in §1.1.11.

Perhaps the most obvious method for computing the vector w_{L_*} is to call repeatedly library routines for the sine and cosine functions.

Algorithm 1.4.1 (Direct Call) If $L = 2^q$ and $L_* = L/2$, then the following algorithm computes the vector $w = w_{L_*} = [1, \omega_L, \ldots, \omega_L^{L_*-1}]^T$:

$$\theta \leftarrow 2\pi/L$$
$$\textbf{for } j = 0{:}L_* - 1$$
$$\qquad w(j) \leftarrow \cos(j\theta) - i\sin(j\theta)$$
$$\textbf{end}$$

This algorithm involves L trigonometric function calls. If we assume that the cosine and sine function are quality library routines, then very accurate weights are produced. Typically, a good cosine or sine routine would return the nearest floating point number to the exact function value, meaning a relative error in the neighborhood of $\mathbf{u}$. However, each sine/cosine evaluation involves several flops and there is no exploitation of the fact that the arguments are regularly spaced. Can we do better by taking advantage of the equation $\omega_L^j = \omega_L\omega_L^{j-1}$?

Algorithm 1.4.2 (Repeated Multiplication) If $L = 2^q$ and $L_* = L/2$, then the following algorithm computes the vector $w = w_{L_*} = [1, \omega_L, \ldots, \omega_L^{L_*-1}]^T$:

> $w(0) \leftarrow 1;\ \theta \leftarrow 2\pi/L;\ \omega_L \leftarrow \cos(\theta) - i\sin(\theta)$
> **for** $j = 1{:}L_* - 1$
> $\quad w(j) \leftarrow \omega_L\cdot w(j-1)$
> **end**

Observe that we have essentially replaced the sine/cosine calls with a single complex multiplication. A total of $3L$ flops are involved. However, ω_L^j is the consequence of $O(j)$ operations, and so it tends to be contaminated by $O(j\mathbf{u})$ roundoff.

Our third method combines the accuracy of Algorithm 1.4.1 with the convenient multiplicative simplicity of Algorithm 1.4.2. The idea is to exploit the fact that

$$w_{L_*}(2^{j-1}{:}2^j - 1) = \omega_L^{2^{j-1}} w_{L_*}(0{:}2^{j-1} - 1)$$

for $j = 1{:}q - 1$. For example, if $q = 4$ and $\omega = \omega_{16}$, then

$$w_8(4{:}7) = \begin{bmatrix} \omega^4 \\ \omega^5 \\ \omega^6 \\ \omega^7 \end{bmatrix} = \omega^4 \begin{bmatrix} 1 \\ \omega \\ \omega^2 \\ \omega^3 \end{bmatrix} = \omega^4 w_8(0{:}3).$$

The repeated use of this idea gives the following procedure:

Algorithm 1.4.3 (Subvector Scaling) If $L = 2^q$ and $L_* = L/2$, then the following algorithm computes the vector $w = w_{L_*} = [1, \omega_L, \ldots, \omega_L^{L_*-1}]^T$:

> $w(0) \leftarrow 1$
> **for** $j = 1{:}q - 1$
> $\quad \mu \leftarrow 2^j\pi/L;\ \omega \leftarrow \cos(\mu) - i\sin(\mu)$
> $\quad w(2^{j-1}{:}2^j - 1) \leftarrow \omega\cdot w(0{:}2^{j-1} - 1)$
> **end**

This method involves $3L$ flops and $2(q-1)$ sine/cosine calls. Note however, that ω_L^j is the consequence of approximately $\log_2 j$ complex multiplications and that the factors are the result of accurate library calls. Hence, it is reasonable to assume that the computed ω_L^j is contaminated by $O(\mathbf{u}\log_2 j)$, a marked improvement over Algorithm 1.4.2.

It is interesting to characterize Algorithms 1.4.2 and 1.4.3 using Givens rotations. A *Givens rotation* is a 2-by-2 real orthogonal matrix of the form

$$G = \begin{bmatrix} \cos(\phi) & \sin(\phi) \\ -\sin(\phi) & \cos(\phi) \end{bmatrix}.$$

Set $\theta = 2\pi/L$. If a and b are complex numbers and $b = \omega_L a$, then it is easy to verify that

$$\begin{bmatrix} b^R \\ b^I \end{bmatrix} = \begin{bmatrix} \cos(\theta) & \sin(\theta) \\ -\sin(\theta) & \cos(\theta) \end{bmatrix} \begin{bmatrix} a^R \\ a^I \end{bmatrix}.$$

Thus, the complex product $\omega_L a$ is equivalent to premultiplication by a 2-by-2 Givens rotation matrix.

Algorithm 1.4.2 computes $w_{L_*}(j)$ by repeatedly applying a Givens rotation to $[1, 0]^T$:

$$\left[\begin{array}{c} w_L^R(j) \\ w_L^I(j) \end{array} \right] = \left[\begin{array}{cc} \cos(\theta) & \sin(\theta) \\ -\sin(\theta) & \cos(\theta) \end{array} \right]^j \left[\begin{array}{c} 1 \\ 0 \end{array} \right] = \left[\begin{array}{cc} \cos(j\theta) & \sin(j\theta) \\ -\sin(j\theta) & \cos(j\theta) \end{array} \right] \left[\begin{array}{c} 1 \\ 0 \end{array} \right].$$

On the other hand, if $L = 2^q$ and we define the rotations

$$G_p = \left[\begin{array}{cc} \cos(2^p\theta) & \sin(2^p\theta) \\ -\sin(2^p\theta) & \cos(2^p\theta) \end{array} \right] = \left[\begin{array}{cc} \cos(\theta) & \sin(\theta) \\ -\sin(\theta) & \cos(\theta) \end{array} \right]^{2^p}$$

for $p = 0:q - 1$, then Algorithm 1.4.3 essentially computes $w_L(j) = \omega_L^j$ from the equation

$$\left[\begin{array}{c} w_L^R(j) \\ w_L^I(j) \end{array} \right] = G_{q-1}^{b_{q-1}} \cdots G_0^{b_0} \left[\begin{array}{c} 1 \\ 0 \end{array} \right],$$

where $k = (b_{q-1} \cdots b_1 b_0)_2$ is the binary expansion of j.

The next three methods on our agenda exploit the following trigonometric identities:

$$\begin{array}{rcl} \cos(A + B) + \cos(A - B) & = & 2\cos(A)\cos(B), \\ \sin(A + B) + \sin(A - B) & = & 2\sin(A)\cos(B). \end{array} \quad (1.4.2)$$

By setting $B = \theta$ and $A = (j - 1)\theta$ in these identities and rearranging we obtain

$$\begin{array}{rcl} \cos(j\theta) & = & 2\cos(\theta)\cos((j-1)\theta) - \cos((j-2)\theta), \\ \sin(j\theta) & = & 2\cos(\theta)\sin((j-1)\theta) - \sin((j-2)\theta). \end{array}$$

Thus, $\cos(j\theta)$ and $\sin(j\theta)$ can be computed in terms of "earlier" cosines and sines, as demonstrated in the following algorithm.

Algorithm 1.4.4 (Forward Recursion) If $L = 2^q$ and $L_* = L/2$, then the following algorithm computes the vector $w = w_{L_*} = [1, \omega_L, \ldots, \omega_L^{L_*-1}]^T$:

$$\theta \leftarrow 2\pi/L$$
$$w(0) \leftarrow 1; w(1) \leftarrow \cos(\theta) - i\sin(\theta)$$
$$\tau \leftarrow 2w^{(R)}(1) \quad \{\tau = 2\cos(\theta)\}$$
$$\text{for } j = 2:L_* - 1$$
$$\quad w^{(R)}(j) \leftarrow \tau w^{(R)}(j-1) - w^{(R)}(j-2)$$
$$\quad w^{(I)}(j) \leftarrow \tau w^{(I)}(j-1) - w^{(I)}(j-2)$$
$$\text{end}$$

This method involves approximately $2L$ flops, which compares favorably to the $3L$ flops required by Algorithms 1.4.2 and 1.4.3. However, we can expect rounding errors to be magnified by $\tau = 2|\cos(\theta)|$ each step. As a result, errors of order $O(\tau^j u)$ will probably contaminate $w_{L_*}(j)$. If $L \geq 6$, then $\tau > 1$. This level of error is unacceptable. A more detailed analysis reveals that the growth rate is even a little worse than our cursory analysis shows. See Table 1.4.1.

To derive the fifth method, assume that $1 \leq k \leq q - 1$ and $1 \leq j \leq 2^k - 1$. By setting $A = 2^k\theta$ and $B = j\theta$ in (1.4.2), we obtain

$$\begin{array}{rcl} \cos((j+2^k)\theta) & = & 2\cos(2^k\theta)\cos(j\theta) - \cos((2^k-j)\theta), \\ \sin((j+2^k)\theta) & = & 2\sin(2^k\theta)\cos(j\theta) - \sin((2^k-j)\theta). \end{array}$$

Thus, if we have $w_{L_*}(0{:}2^k-1)$, then we can compute $w_{L_*}(2^k{:}2^{k+1}-1)$ by (a) evaluating $\cos(2^k\theta)$ and $\sin(2^k\theta)$ via direct library calls and (b) using the recursion for $j = 1{:}2^k-1$.

Algorithm 1.4.5 (Logarithmic Recursion) If $L = 2^q$ and $L_* = L/2$, then the following algorithm computes the vector $w = w_{L_*} = [1, \omega_L, \ldots, \omega_L^{L_*-1}]^T$:

$$\theta \leftarrow 2\pi/L$$
$$w(0) \leftarrow 1; w(1) \leftarrow \cos(\theta) - i\sin(\theta)$$
$$\textbf{for } k = 1{:}q-1$$
$$\qquad p \leftarrow 2^{k-1}$$
$$\qquad w(p) \leftarrow \cos(p\theta) - i\sin(p\theta)$$
$$\qquad \tau \leftarrow 2w(p)$$
$$\qquad \textbf{for } j = 1{:}p-1$$
$$\qquad\qquad w^R(p+j) \leftarrow \tau^R w^R(j) - w^R(p-j)$$
$$\qquad\qquad w^I(p+j) \leftarrow \tau^I w^R(j) - w^I(p-j)$$
$$\qquad \textbf{end}$$
$$\textbf{end}$$

This algorithm requires $2L$ flops. A somewhat involved error analysis shows that $O(\mathbf{u}(|\cos(\theta)| + \sqrt{|\cos(\theta)|^2 + 1})^{\log j})$ error can be expected to contaminate $w_{L_*}(j)$.

Our final method is based upon the following rearrangement of (1.4.2):

$$
\begin{aligned}
\cos(A) &= \frac{1}{2\cos(B)}\left(\cos(A-B) + \cos(A+B)\right), \\[2mm]
\sin(A) &= \frac{1}{2\cos(B)}\left(\sin(A-B) + \sin(A+B)\right).
\end{aligned}
\tag{1.4.3}
$$

These can be thought of as interpolation formulae, since A is "in between" $A - B$ and $A + B$. To derive the method, it is convenient to define $c_k = \cos(2\pi k/L)$ and $s_k = \sin(2\pi k/L)$ for $k = 0{:}L_* - 1$. It follows from (1.4.3) that

$$
\begin{aligned}
c_j &= \frac{1}{2c_p}\left(c_{j-p} + c_{j+p}\right), \\[2mm]
s_j &= \frac{1}{2c_p}\left(s_{j-p} + s_{j+p}\right)
\end{aligned}
\tag{1.4.4}
$$

for integers p and j. Suppose $L = 64$ and that for $p = 0$, 1, 2, 4, 8, 16, and 32 we have computed (c_p, s_p). If we apply (1.4.4) with $(j, p) = (24, 8)$, then we can compute (c_{24}, s_{24}):

$$
\begin{aligned}
c_{24} &= \frac{1}{2c_8}\left(c_{16} + c_{32}\right), \\[2mm]
s_{24} &= \frac{1}{2c_8}\left(s_{16} + s_{32}\right).
\end{aligned}
$$

With (c_{24}, s_{24}) available, we are able to compute

$$
\begin{aligned}
c_{28} &= \frac{1}{2c_4}\left(c_{24} + c_{32}\right), \\[2mm]
s_{28} &= \frac{1}{2c_4}\left(s_{24} + s_{32}\right).
\end{aligned}
$$

In general, the weight vector $w_{32}(0{:}31)$ is filled in through a sequence of steps which we depict in Fig. 1.4.1. The numbers indicate the indices of the cosine/sine pairs that

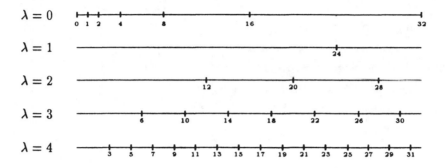

FIG. 1.4.1. *The recursive bisection method* $(n = 64)$.

are produced during steps $\lambda = 1, 2, 3$, and 4. The key to the algorithm is that when (c_j, s_j) is to be computed, (c_{j-p}, s_{j-p}) and (c_{j+p}, s_{j+p}) are available.

Algorithm 1.4.6 (Recursive Bisection) If $L = 2^q$ and $L_* = L/2$, then the following algorithm computes the vector $w = w_{L_*} = [1, \omega_L, \ldots, \omega_L^{L_*-1}]^T$:

$$\theta \leftarrow 2\pi/L;\ c_0 \leftarrow 1;\ s_0 \leftarrow 0$$
$$\text{for } k = 0{:}q-1$$
$$\quad p \leftarrow 2^k;\ c_p \leftarrow \cos(p\theta);\ s_p \leftarrow -\sin(p\theta)$$
$$\text{end}$$
$$\text{for } \lambda = 1{:}q-2$$
$$\quad p \leftarrow 2^{q-\lambda-2}$$
$$\quad h \leftarrow 1/(2c_p)$$
$$\quad \text{for } k = 0{:}2^\lambda - 2$$
$$\quad\quad j \leftarrow (3 + 2k)p$$
$$\quad\quad c_j \leftarrow h(c_{j-p} + c_{j+p})$$
$$\quad\quad s_j \leftarrow h(s_{j-p} + s_{j+p})$$
$$\quad \text{end}$$
$$\text{end}$$
$$w(0{:}L_* - 1) \leftarrow c(0{:}L_* - 1) + is(0{:}L_* - 1)$$

This algorithm requires $2L$ flops and a careful analysis shows that the error in the computed $w_{L_*}(j)$ has order $\mathbf{u} \log j$. See Buneman (1987b).

1.4.3 Summary

The essential roundoff properties of the six methods are summarized in Table 1.4.1. See Chu (1988) for details and a comprehensive error analysis of the overall FFT process.

Whether or not the roundoff behavior of a method is acceptable depends upon the accuracy requirements of the underlying application. However, one thing is clear: for

TABLE 1.4.1
Summary of roundoff error behavior $(c_1 = \cos(2\pi/L))$.

Method	Roundoff in ω_L^j
Direct Call (Algorithm 1.4.1)	$O(\mathbf{u})$
Repeated Multiplication (Algorithm 1.4.2)	$O(\mathbf{u}j)$
Subvector Scaling (Algorithm 1.4.3)	$O(\mathbf{u}\log j)$
Forward Recursion (Algorithm 1.4.4)	$O(\mathbf{u}(|c_1| + \sqrt{|c_1|^2 + 1})^j)$
Logarithmic Recursion (Algorithm 1.4.5)	$O(\mathbf{u}(|c_1| + \sqrt{|c_1|^2 + 1})^{\log j})$
Recursive Bisection (Algorithm 1.4.6)	$O(\mathbf{u}\log j)$

large j, we can expect trouble with repeated scaling and forward recursion. For this reason we regard these methods as *unstable*.

1.4.4   Further Symmetries in the Weight Vector

By carefully considering the real and imaginary parts of the weight vector w_{L_*}, it is possible to reduce by a factor of four the amount of arithmetic in Algorithms 1.4.1–1.4.6. Assume that $L = 2^q = 8m$ and that we have computed $w_{L_*}(0{:}m)$. For clarity, identify the real and imaginary portions of this vector by $u(0{:}m)$ and $v(0{:}m)$, i.e., $u_k = \cos(k\theta)$ and $v_k = -\sin(k\theta)$ where $\theta = 2\pi/L$. Using elementary trigonometric identities, it is easy to show that

$$
w_{L_*} = \left[\begin{array}{ccc} u(0{:}m-1) & + & iv(0{:}m-1) \\ -v(m{:}-1{:}1) & - & iu(m{:}-1{:}1) \\ v(0{:}m-1) & - & iu(0{:}m-1) \\ -u(m{:}-1{:}1) & + & v(m{:}-1{:}1) \end{array} \right].
\tag{1.4.5}
$$

Hence, once we compute $w_{L_*}(0{:}(L/8))$, the rest of w_{L_*} can be determined without additional floating point arithmetic.

1.4.5   Butterflies

Consider the matrix-vector product $y = B_L z$, where $z \in \mathbb{C}^L$. If $L_* = L/2$ and we designate the top and bottom halves of y and z by y_T, z_T, y_B, and z_B, then

$$
\left[\begin{array}{c} y_T \\ y_B \end{array} \right] = \left[\begin{array}{cc} I_{L_*} & \Omega_{L_*} \\ I_{L_*} & -\Omega_{L_*} \end{array} \right] \left[\begin{array}{c} z_T \\ z_B \end{array} \right] = \left[\begin{array}{c} z_T + \Omega_{L_*} z_B \\ z_T - \Omega_{L_*} z_B \end{array} \right]
$$

and we obtain

$$
\begin{aligned}
&L_* \leftarrow L/2 \\
&\textbf{for } j = 0{:}L_* - 1 \\
&\quad \tau \leftarrow w_{L_*}(j) \cdot z(j + L_*) \\
&\quad y(j) \leftarrow z(j) + \tau \\
&\quad y(j + L_*) \leftarrow z(j) - \tau \\
&\textbf{end}
\end{aligned}
$$

Identifying y with z does *not* result in the overwriting of z with $B_L z$, because the update of $y(j + L_*)$ requires the old version of $z(j)$. However, if we compute $y(j + L_*)$ before $y(j)$, then overwriting is possible.

Algorithm 1.4.7 If $z \in \mathbb{C}^L$, $L = 2L_*$, and $w_{L_*}(0{:}L_* - 1)$ is available, then the following algorithm overwrites z with $B_L z$:

$$L_* \leftarrow L/2$$
$$\text{for } j = 0{:}L_* - 1$$
$$\qquad \tau \leftarrow w_{L_*}(j)\cdot z(j + L_*)$$
$$\qquad z(j + L_*) \leftarrow z(j) - \tau$$
$$\qquad z(j) \leftarrow z(j) + \tau$$
$$\text{end}$$

This algorithm requires $5L = 10L_*$ flops. The update of $z(j)$ and $z(j + L_*)$ can be expressed as a two-dimensional matrix-vector product:

$$\begin{bmatrix} z(j) \\ z(j + L_*) \end{bmatrix} \leftarrow \begin{bmatrix} 1 & \omega^j \\ 1 & -\omega^j \end{bmatrix} \begin{bmatrix} z(j) \\ z(j + L_*) \end{bmatrix}.$$

Because of its central importance in radix-2 FFT work, we refer to a multiplication of this form as a *Cooley–Tukey butterfly*. See Fig. 1.9.1 for a graphical representation of this operation that explains why the term "butterfly" is used.

1.4.6 The Update $x \leftarrow A_q x$

Now consider the application of $(I_r \otimes B_L)$ to $x \in \mathbb{C}^n$, where $n = rL$. By Kron5 this matrix-vector product is equivalent to the matrix-matrix product $B_L x_{L \times r}$. As with any such product, we have the option of computing the result by column or by row. Although identical mathematically, these options can lead to significantly different levels of performance. Consider the column-by-column approach first.

Algorithm 1.4.8 (*kj Butterfly Updates*) Suppose $x \in \mathbb{C}^n$ with $n = 2^t$. If q satisfies $1 \le q \le t$ and the weight vector w_{L_*} is available with $L_* = 2^{q-1}$, then the following algorithm overwrites x with $A_q x$:

$$L \leftarrow 2^q$$
$$r \leftarrow n/L$$
$$L_* \leftarrow L/2$$
$$\text{for } k = 0{:}r - 1$$
$$\qquad \{\text{Apply } B_L \text{ to } k\text{th column of } x_{L \times r}.\}$$
$$\qquad \text{for } j = 0{:}L_* - 1$$
$$\qquad\qquad \{\text{Apply } j\text{th butterfly.}\}$$
$$\qquad\qquad \tau \leftarrow w_{L_*}(j)\cdot x(kL + j + L_*)$$
$$\qquad\qquad x(kL + j + L_*) \leftarrow x(kL + j) - \tau$$
$$\qquad\qquad x(kL + j) \leftarrow x(kL + j) + \tau$$
$$\qquad \text{end}$$
$$\text{end}$$

This algorithm requires $5n$ flops. During the jth pass through the inner loop, the butterfly

$$\begin{bmatrix} x(kL + j) \\ x(kL + j + L_*) \end{bmatrix} \leftarrow \begin{bmatrix} 1 & \omega_L^j \\ 1 & -\omega_L^j \end{bmatrix} \begin{bmatrix} x(kL + j) \\ x(kL + j + L_*) \end{bmatrix}$$

is computed.

If we reverse the order of the two loops in Algorithm 1.4.8, then we obtain a procedure that computes $B_L x_{L \times r}$ by row.

Algorithm 1.4.9 (*jk* **Butterfly Updates**) Suppose $x \in \mathbb{C}^n$ with $n = 2^t$. If q satisfies $1 \le q \le t$ and the weight vector w_{L_*} is available with $L_* = 2^{q-1}$, then the following algorithm overwrites x with $A_q x$:

$$L \leftarrow 2^q$$
$$r \leftarrow n/L$$
$$L_* \leftarrow L/2$$

    for $j = 0{:}L_* - 1$
        {Apply the jth butterfly to rows j and $j + L_*$ of $x_{L \times r}$.}
        for $k = 0{:}r - 1$
            {Apply jth butterfly to elements j and $j + L_*$ of
                subvector $x(kL{:}(k+1)L - 1).$}
            $\tau \leftarrow w_{L_*}(j) \cdot x(kL + j + L_*)$
            $x(kL + j + L_*) \leftarrow x(kL + j) - \tau$
            $x(kL + j) \leftarrow x(kL + j) + \tau$
        end
    end

The algorithm requires $5n$ flops.

Although both of our butterfly frameworks involve the same amount of arithmetic, they differ in other respects, as we now discuss.

1.4.7   On-Line Versus Off-Line Weight Computation

For simplicity, Algorithms 1.4.8 and 1.4.9 assume that the weights $1, \omega_L, \ldots, \omega_L^{L_* - 1}$ are precomputed and available through the vector w_{L_*}. This is the *off-line paradigm*: the weights are computed once and for all and are retained in a vector workspace. The *on-line paradigm* assumes that the weights are generated as the butterfly progresses and that (at most) a very limited workspace is used. For example, if in either Algorithm 1.4.8 or 1.4.9 we replace the statement

$$\tau \leftarrow w_{L_*}(j) \cdot x(kL + j + L_*)$$

with

$$\tau \leftarrow (\cos(2\pi j/L) - i\sin(2\pi j/L)) \cdot x(kL + j + L_*),$$

then an on-line approach is adopted that is based upon the direct-call method of weight computation (Algorithm 1.4.1).

On-line butterflies based on repeated multiplication (Algorithm 1.4.2) and forward recursion (Algorithm 1.4.4) are also possible. However, these techniques are generally unstable and should be avoided. On-line butterflies based upon subvector scaling (Algorithm 1.4.3) and logarithmic recursion (Algorithm 1.4.5) are not possible, as they require a workspace for implementation. (In these methods certain "old" weights must be kept around.) An on-line implementation of recursive bisection that requires a small workspace is discussed in Buneman (1987).

On-line versions of Algorithms 1.4.8 and 1.4.9 bring up a new and interesting computational dilemma. Assume on-line weight computation via the method of direct call, i.e., Algorithm 1.4.1. In the case of Algorithm 1.4.8 we have

$$L \leftarrow 2^q$$
$$r \leftarrow n/L$$
$$L_* \leftarrow L/2$$
$$\text{for } k = 0{:}r - 1$$
$$\quad \text{for } j = 0{:}L_* - 1 \qquad\qquad (1.4.6)$$
$$\quad\quad \tau \leftarrow (\cos(2\pi j/L) - i\sin(2\pi j/L))\cdot x(kL + j + L_*)$$
$$\quad\quad x(kL + j + L_*) \leftarrow x(kL + j) - \tau$$
$$\quad\quad x(kL + j) \leftarrow x(kL + j) + \tau$$
$$\quad \text{end}$$
$$\text{end}$$

Note that since each weight is computed r times, there is an unfortunate level of redundancy. This is not true when an on-line version of Algorithm 1.4.9 is correctly organized:

$$L \leftarrow 2^q$$
$$r \leftarrow n/L$$
$$L_* \leftarrow L/2$$
$$\text{for } j = 0{:}L_* - 1$$
$$\quad \omega \leftarrow \cos(2\pi j/L) - i\sin(2\pi j/L)$$
$$\quad \text{for } k = 0{:}L_* - 1 \qquad\qquad (1.4.7)$$
$$\quad\quad \tau \leftarrow \omega \cdot x(kL + j + L_*)$$
$$\quad\quad x(kL + j + L_*) \leftarrow x(kL + j) - \tau$$
$$\quad\quad x(kL + j) \leftarrow x(kL + j) + \tau$$
$$\quad \text{end}$$
$$\text{end}$$

It follows that the jk organization of $A_q x$ is more efficient than the kj version when on-line weight generation is used. However, as we show in the next section, Algorithm 1.4.8 accesses the x-data in a manner that is much more attractive on machines that "like" to access subvectors whose entries are logically contiguous in memory.

1.4.8 The Stride Issue

The speed with which a computer can access the components of a vector is sometimes a function of *stride*. Stride refers to the "spacing" of the components that are named in a vector reference. For example, in the vector update

$$x(0{:}7) \leftarrow y(0{:}2{:}15) + \alpha z(1{:}3{:}22)$$

x has unit stride, y has stride two, and z has stride three.

In many advanced computer architectures, large power-of-two strides can severely degrade performance. Machines with interleaved memories serve as a nice case study. An interleaved memory is arranged in *banks* into which the components of the stored vector are "dealt." For example, the 4-bank storage of a length-25 vector would be arranged as shown in Fig. 1.4.2.

The figure shows that component x_j is stored in bank(j mod 4). In an interleaved memory system, the retrieval of a vector would proceed as follows. When component x_j is retrieved, bank(j mod 4) is "tied up" for four machine cycles because the path between the bank and the CPU is active and cannot be disturbed. If a vector load is initiated, then the components are retrieved sequentially, with the retrieval of each

bank(0)	bank(1)	bank(2)	bank(3)
x_0	x_1	x_2	x_3
x_4	x_5	x_6	x_7
x_8	x_9	x_{10}	x_{11}
x_{12}	x_{13}	x_{14}	x_{15}
x_{16}	x_{17}	x_{18}	x_{19}
x_{20}	x_{21}	x_{22}	x_{23}
x_{24}			

FIG. 1.4.2. *Vector storage in a four-bank interleaved memory.*

component beginning at the earliest possible cycle. Thus, in the loading of the unit stride vector $x(0{:}20)$, components would be retrieved at a rate of one per cycle, because the request for $x(j)$ is initiated just as the 4-cycle sending of $x(j-4)$ is completed. This is an example of *pipelining*, a term that is used to describe an assembly line style of processing. In our case, the assembly line has four "stations," each of which must be "visited" by the retrieved x-value. Once the steady-state streaming of data is achieved, the pipeline is full with four components at different stages of retrieval.

On the other hand, a stride-4 access in our four-bank system would forbid the rapid streaming of data out of memory. Indeed, there would be no pipelining and the requested components (all from the same bank) would emerge from memory once every four cycles. This is an example of *memory bank conflict*, a phenomenon that can greatly diminish performance. Interleaved memory systems invariably have a power-of-two number of banks and so power-of-two strides can be particularly lethal. Unfortunately, power-of-two strides are typical in the radix-2 setting. For example, the jk butterfly (1.4.7) has stride $L = 2^q$. On the other hand, (1.4.6) has unit stride. This sets up a typical high performance computing dilemma: one procedure has attractive stride properties but an excess of arithmetic, while the alternative is arithmetically efficient with nonunit stride. The resolution of this particular tension is discussed in later sections.

1.4.9   Real Implementation of Complex Butterflies

In order to get highly optimized FFT procedures, it is sometimes necessary to work with real data types and to perform all complex arithmetic by "hand." This is because in some programming languages like Fortran, the real and imaginary parts of a complex vector are stored in stride-2 fashion. For example, a complex n-vector $u + iv$ is stored in a length-$2n$ real array as follows:

$$[u_0,\ v_0,\ u_1,\ v_1, \ldots,\ u_{n-1},\ v_{n-1}].$$

The extraction of either the real or the imaginary parts involves stride-2 access, making this an unattractive complex vector representation.

In light of this, it is instructive to see what is precisely involved in a real formulation of a complex butterfly, beginning with the following operation:

$$\begin{bmatrix} a \\ b \end{bmatrix} \leftarrow \begin{bmatrix} 1 & \omega \\ 1 & -\omega \end{bmatrix} \begin{bmatrix} a \\ b \end{bmatrix}.$$

If $\tau = \omega b$, then this has the real implementation

$$
\begin{aligned}
\tau^R &= \omega^R b^R - \omega^I b^I, \\
\tau^I &= \omega^R b^I + \omega^I b^R, \\
b^R &= a^R - \tau^R, \\
b^I &= a^I - \tau^I, \\
a^R &= a^R + \tau^R, \\
a^I &= a^I + \tau^I.
\end{aligned}
$$

Building on this, we are able to derive a real specification of Algorithm 1.4.8:

$$
\begin{aligned}
&L \leftarrow 2^q; \ r \leftarrow n/L; \ L_* \leftarrow L/2 \\
&\{x \leftarrow (I_r \otimes B_L)x\} \\
&\text{for } k = 0{:}r-1 \\
&\quad \text{for } j = 0{:}L_* - 1 \\
&\quad\quad \tau^R \leftarrow w^R(j)x^R(kL+j+L_*) - w^I(j)x^I(kL+j+L_*) \\
&\quad\quad \tau^I \leftarrow w^R(j)x^I(kL+j+L_*) + w^I(j)x^R(kL+j+L_*) \\
&\quad\quad x^R(kL+j+L_*) \leftarrow x^R(kL+j) - \tau^R \\
&\quad\quad x^I(kL+j+L_*) \leftarrow x^I(kL+j) - \tau^I \\
&\quad\quad x^R(kL+j) \leftarrow x^R(kL+j) + \tau^R \\
&\quad\quad x^I(kL+j) \leftarrow x^I(kL+j) + \tau^I \\
&\quad \text{end} \\
&\text{end}
\end{aligned}
\tag{1.4.8}
$$

Note how the explicit reference to real and imaginary parts clutters the presentation. Because of this and because we are interested in computational frameworks and not specific implementations, we make it a habit *not* to express complex arithmetic in real terms. In subsequent sections, exceptions will be made only if the complex specification hides some key algorithmic point.

1.4.10 Vector versus Scalar Performance

At the end of §1.1 we mentioned the importance of being able to express scalar algorithms in vector notation whenever possible. We continue this discussion by using (1.4.8) to illustrate how vector performance depends upon the length of the vector arguments. Assume that a vector computer has vector registers of length ℓ and that all vector operations take place in these registers. The time required to execute a *real* vector operation of length m is typically modeled by an expression of the form

$$
T(m) = \alpha + \beta m, \qquad m \leq \ell.
\tag{1.4.9}
$$

Here, α represents the start-up overhead (in seconds) and β the time required to produce a component of the result once the pipeline is full. This model of vector operations is discussed in Golub and Van Loan (1989, p. 36–37). See also Hockney and Jesshope (1981). We suppress the fact that the precise values for α and β may depend upon the underlying vector operation.

If m is larger than ℓ, then the vector operation is partitioned into ceil(m/ℓ) parts, each of which "fits" into the registers. To illustrate this, consider a length-2^s vector operation on a machine with $\ell = 2^d$. If $s \geq d$, then the time required is approximately given by

$$
T(m) = 2^{s-d}(\alpha + 2^d \beta) = \frac{m}{\ell}\alpha + \beta m.
$$

Let us apply this model to (1.4.8). However, before we do this we clarify the exact nature of the underlying vector operations that are carried out by the inner loop by rewriting the algorithm as follows:

$$
\begin{aligned}
&L \leftarrow 2^q; \ r \leftarrow n/L; \ L_* \leftarrow L/2 \\
&\text{for } k = 0{:}r-1 \\
&\qquad top \leftarrow kL{:}kL + L_* - 1 \\
&\qquad bot \leftarrow kL + L_*{:}(k+1)L - 1 \\
&\qquad a \leftarrow w^R \,.* \, x^R(bot) \\
&\qquad b \leftarrow w^I \,.* \, x^I(bot) \\
&\qquad c \leftarrow w^R \,.* \, x^I(bot) \\
&\qquad d \leftarrow w^I \,.* \, x^R(bot) \\
&\qquad e \leftarrow a - b \\
&\qquad f \leftarrow c + d \\
&\qquad x^R(bot) \leftarrow x^R(top) - e \\
&\qquad x^I(bot) \leftarrow x^I(top) - f \\
&\qquad x^R(top) \leftarrow x^R(top) + e \\
&\qquad x^I(top) \leftarrow x^I(top) + f \\
&\text{end}
\end{aligned}
$$

Notice that there are ten length-L_* vector operations to perform each pass through the loop. It follows that the whole process requires time

$$
T_{1.4.8} = \begin{cases} 5n\alpha/L_* + 5n\beta & \text{if } L_* \le \ell, \\[2mm] 5n\alpha/\ell + 5n\beta & \text{if } L_* > \ell \end{cases} \tag{1.4.10}
$$

for completion. Notice that the start-up factor α has a greater bearing upon performance when L_* is small.

1.4.11   The Long Weight Vector

When we consider the overall Cooley–Tukey procedure, we see that the weights associated with A_q are a subset of the weights associated with A_{q+1}. In particular, since $\omega_{2L}^{2j} = \omega_L^j$ we have

$$
w_{L_*} = w_L(0{:}2{:}L-1) .
$$

Thus, in preparation for all the weights that arise during the algorithm, it seems reasonable to compute $w_{n/2}$, the weight vector for A_t. Unfortunately, this results in a power-of-two stride access into $w_{n/2}$. This is because the scaling operation

$$
\tau \leftarrow w_{L_*}(j){\cdot}x(kL + j + L_*) ,
$$

which arises in either Algorithm 1.4.8 or 1.4.9, transforms to

$$
\tau \leftarrow w_{n/2}(jr){\cdot}x(kL + j + L_*),
$$

where $j = n/L$.

A way around this difficulty suggested by Bailey (1987) is to precompute the *long weight vector* $w_n^{(long)}$ defined by

$$
w_n^{(long)} = \begin{bmatrix} w_1 \\ w_2 \\ \vdots \\ w_{n/2} \end{bmatrix} . \tag{1.4.11}
$$

This $(n-1)$-vector is just a stacking of the weight vectors w_{L_*}. In particular, if $L = 2^q$ and $L_* = 2^{q-1}$, then $w_{L_*} = w_n^{(long)}(L_* - 1{:}L - 1)$

With $w_n^{(long)}$ available, the above τ computation becomes.

$$\tau \leftarrow w_n^{(long)}(L_* - 1 + j) \cdot x(kL + j + L_*)$$

and unit stride access is achieved. It is clear that $w_n^{(long)}$ can be constructed in $O(n)$ flops using any of Algorithms 1.4.1–1.4.6.

Problems

P1.4.1 Using the identities

$$\begin{aligned}
\cos(a+b) &= \cos(a)\cos(b) - \sin(a)\sin(b), \\
\sin(a+b) &= \sin(a)\cos(b) + \cos(a)\sin(b)
\end{aligned}$$

prove (1.4.2) and (1.4.5).

P1.4.2 Show that if $j = (b_{t-1} \cdots b_1 b_0)_2$, then $w_{L_*}(j)$ is the consequence of $b_{t-1} + \cdots + b_1 + b_0$ complex multiplications in Algorithm 1.4.3.

P1.4.3 Develop a complete algorithm for $w_n^{(long)}$ that uses Algorithm 1.4.3 to compute the individual weight vectors. How many flops are required?

P1.4.4 Using the concepts of §1.4.10, analyze the performance of Algorithm 1.4.3.

Notes and References for Section

Interleaved memory systems, vectorization models, and various pipelining issues are discussed in

J.J. Dongarra, I.S. Duff, D.C. Sorensen, and H.A. van der Vorst (1991). *Solving Linear Systems on Vector and Shared Memory Computers*, Society for Industrial and Applied Mathematics, Philadelphia, PA.

J.L. Hennessy and D.A. Patterson (1990). *Computer Architecture: A Quantitative Approach*, Morgan Kaufmann Publishers, San Mateo, CA.

R.W. Hockney and C.R. Jesshope (1981). *Parallel Computers*, Adam Hilger Ltd., Bristol, England.

For a discussion of stride and memory organization, see

P. Budnik and D.J. Kuck (1971). "The Organization and Use of Parallel Memories," *IEEE Trans. Comput. C-20*, 1566–1569.

D.H. Lawrie (1975). "Access and Alignment of Data in an Array Processor," *IEEE Trans. Comput. 24*, 99–109.

D.H. Lawrie and C.R. Vora (1982). "The Prime Memory System for Array Access," *IEEE Trans. Comput. C-31*, 1435–1442.

Various approaches to the weight-generation problem are covered in Chapter 8 of

R.N. Bracewell (1986). *The Hartley Transform*, Oxford University Press, New York.

A standard discussion of roundoff error may be found in

G.H. Golub and C. Van Loan (1989). *Matrix Computations, 2nd Ed.*, Johns Hopkins University Press, Baltimore, MD.

The numerical properties of the fast Fourier transform have attracted a lot of attention over the years, as shown in the following excellent references:

O. Buneman (1987b). "Stable On-Line Creation of Sines and Cosines of Successive Angles," *Proc. IEEE 75*, 1434–1435.

C. Chu (1988). *The Fast Fourier Transform on Hypercube Parallel Computers*, Ph.D. Thesis, Center for Applied Mathematics, Cornell University, Ithaca, NY.

J. Oliver (1975). "Stable Methods for Evaluating the Points $\cos(i\pi/n)$," *J. Inst. Maths. Applic. 16*, 247–257.

Once the properties of the computed weights are known, then it is possible to address the accuracy of the FFT itself. The following papers take a statistical approach to the problem:

R. Alt (1978). "Error Propagation in Fourier Transforms," *Math. Comp. Simul.* 20, 37–43.

P. Bois and J. Vignes (1980). "Software for Evaluating Local Accuracy in the Fourier Transform," *Math. Comput. Simul.* 22, 141–150.

C.J. Weinstein, "Roundoff Noise in Floating Point Fast Fourier Transform Computation," *IEEE Trans. Audio and Electroacoustics AU-17*, 209–215.

Other papers include

F. Abramovici (1975). "The Accuracy of Finite Fourier Transforms," *J. Comput. Phys.* 17, 446–449.

M. Arioli, H. Munthe-Kaas, and L. Valdettaro (1991). "Componentwise Error Analysis for FFT's with Applications to Fast Helmoltz Solvers," CERFACS Report TR/IT/PA/91/55, Toulouse, France.

T. Kaneko and B. Liu (1970). "Accumulation of Roundoff Error in Fast Fourier Transforms," *J. Assocs. Comput. Mach.* 17, 637–654.

G.U. Ramos (1971). "Roundoff Error Analysis of the Fast Fourier Transform," *Math. Comp.* 25, 757–768.

D.R. Reddy and V.V. Rao (1982). "Error Analysis of FFT of a Sparse Sequence," *J. Electr. Electron. Eng. Aust.* 2, 169–175.

R.C. Singleton (1968a). "On Computing the Fast Fourier Transform," *Comm. ACM 10*, 647–654.

G.C. Temes (1977). "Worst Case Error Analysis for the Fast Fourier Transform," *IEEE J. Electron. Circuits Systems 1*, 110–115.

T. Thong and B. Liu (1977). "Accumulation of Roundoff Errors in Floating Point FFT," *IEEE Trans. Circuits and Systems CAS-24*, 132–143.

In many VLSI settings it is necessary to work in fixed-point arithmetic. The analysis of error in this context is discussed in

W.R. Knight and R. Kaiser (1979). "A Simple Fixed Point Error Bound for the Fast Fourier Transform," *IEEE Trans. Acoust. Speech Signal Proc.* ASSP-27, 615–620.

A. Oppenheim and C. Weinstein (1972). "Effects of Finite Register Length in Digital Filtering and the Fast Fourier Transform," *Proc. IEEE 60*, 957–976.

The idea of computing the long weight vector is proposed in

D.H. Bailey (1987). "A High-Performance Fast Fourier Transform Algorithm for the Cray-2," *J. Supercomputing 1*, 43–60.

1.5   Bit Reversal and Transposition

We continue to assume that $n = 2^t$ and recall that the Cooley–Tukey framework requires manipulation with the bit-reversal permutation P_n. Two characterizations of P_n are given in §1.3. We reproduce them here for convenience:

$$P_n = \Pi_n(I_2 \otimes P_m), \qquad n = 2m, \tag{1.5.1}$$

$$P_n = R_t \cdots R_1, \qquad R_q = I_{n/2^q} \otimes \Pi_{2^q}. \tag{1.5.2}$$

We start this section by explaining what we mean by "bit reversal." Practical bit-reversal procedures are specified, and we develop a facility with the even-odd sort and its inverse.

1.5.1   Bit Reversal

In §1.3.3 we showed that

$$P_{16}^T x = [\, x_0 \; x_8 \; x_4 \; x_{12} \; x_2 \; x_{10} \; x_6 \; x_{14} \; x_1 \; x_9 \; x_5 \; x_{13} \; x_3 \; x_{11} \; x_7 \; x_{15}\,]^T \; .$$

Let $r_n(k)$ be the function on the set $\{\, 0, 1, \ldots, n-1 \,\}$, which is defined as follows:

$$\left[P_n^T x \right]_k = x_{r_n(k)} . \tag{1.5.3}$$

TABLE 1.5.1

Bit reversal $(n = 16)$.

k	$r_{16}(k)$
0000	0000
0001	1000
0010	0100
0011	1100
0100	0010
0101	1010
0110	0110
0111	1110
1000	0001
1001	1001
1010	0101
1011	1101
1100	0011
1101	1011
1110	0111
1111	1111

A table of values for $r_{16}(k)$ expressed in binary notation is given in Table 1.5.1. It appears from the table that $r_{16}(k)$ is obtained by reversing the order of the four bits in the binary expansion of k. Let us prove this conjecture about $r_n(\cdot)$.

Theorem 1.5.1 *If* $x \in \mathbb{C}^n$ *with* $n = 2^t$ *and* $r_n(k)$ *is defined by* (1.5.3), *then*

$$r_n((b_{t-1} \cdots b_1 b_0)_2) = (b_0 b_1 \cdots b_{t-1})_2 .$$

Proof. The result clearly holds for $t = 1$, since $P_2 = I_2$. Pursuing an induction argument, assume that if $m = 2^{t-1}$ and $w \in \mathbb{C}^m$, then

$$\left[P_m^T w\right]_k = w_{r_m(k)}, \qquad k = 0{:}m - 1.$$

Now using the recursive definition (1.5.1) of P_n, the definition (1.2.2) of Π_n^T, and Kron2 we have

$$y = P_n^T x = (I_2 \otimes P_m^T)\Pi_n^T x = \left[\begin{array}{c} P_m^T z_T \\ P_m^T z_B \end{array} \right] ,$$

where $z_T = x(0{:}2{:}n-1)$ and $z_B = x(1{:}2{:}n-1)$. Suppose $k = b_0 + b_1 \cdot 2 + \cdots + b_{t-1} \cdot 2^{t-1}$. We must show that

$$y(b_{t-1} + b_{t-2} \cdot 2 + \cdots + b_1 \cdot 2^{t-2} + b_0 \cdot 2^{t-1}) = x(k) .$$

If k is even, then

$$z_T(b_1 + b_2 \cdot 2 + \cdots + b_{t-1} \cdot 2^{t-2}) = x(k) .$$

Thus, if P_m^T is applied to z_T, then $x(k)$ is sent to position

$$j = b_{t-1} + \cdots + b_2 \cdot 2^{t-3} + b_1 \cdot 2^{t-2} .$$

But since k is even, $b_0 = 0$ and so $x(k)$ becomes

$$y(j) = y(b_{t-1} + \cdots + b_2 \cdot 2^{t-3} + b_1 \cdot 2^{t-2} + b_0 \cdot 2^{t-1}) = y(r_n(k)).$$

If k is odd, then similarly

$$z_B(b_1 + b_2 \cdot 2 + \cdots + b_{t-1} \cdot 2^{t-2}) = x(k).$$

Thus, when P_m^T is applied to z_B, $x(k)$ is sent to position

$$j = b_{t-1} + \cdots + b_2 \cdot 2^{t-3} + b_1 \cdot 2^{t-2}.$$

But since k is odd, $b_0 = 1$ and so $x(k)$ is sent to

$$y(j + n/2) = y(b_{t-1} + \cdots + b_2 \cdot 2^{t-3} + b_1 \cdot 2^{t-2} + b_0 \cdot 2^{t-1}) = y(r_n(k)).$$

Thus, $x(k) = y(r_n(k))$ for all k that satisfy $0 \le k \le n - 1$.   □

By way of illustration, $r_8(5) = 5$, $r_{16}(5) = 10$, and $r_{1024}(5) = 640$. With Theorem 1.5.1 it is easy to show that P_n is symmetric.

Theorem 1.5.2 *P_n is symmetric.*

Proof. If an index is bit reversed twice, then we end up with the original index. Thus, $P_n^T(P_n^T x) = x$ for all $x \in \mathbb{C}^n$. It follows that $P_n P_n = I$. But since P_n is orthogonal, we also have $P_n^T P_n = I$. Thus $(P_n^T - P_n)P_n = 0$, i.e., $P_n^T = P_n$.   □

1.5.2   Evaluating $r_n(k)$

Suppose $x \in \mathbb{C}^n$, with $n = 2^t$, and consider the computation of $P_n x$. An obvious approach is to develop an effective means of evaluating

$$r_n(k) = b_{t-1} + \cdots + b_1 \cdot 2^{t-2} + b_0 \cdot 2^{t-1}$$

given

$$k = b_0 + b_1 \cdot 2 + \cdots + b_{t-1} \cdot 2^{t-1}.$$

Note that $r_n(k)$ is a $t - 1$ degree polynomial in 2 with coefficients $b_{t-1}, \ldots, b_0$. It follows that $r_n(k)$ can be efficiently evaluated using a "Horner"-type expansion, e.g.,

$$r_8(k) = ((2b_0 + b_1)2 + b_2)2 + b_3.$$

Thus, one way to compute $j = r_n(k)$ is as follows:

```
j ← 0
for q = 0:t − 1
      Determine b_q.
      j ← 2j + b_q
end
```

Each bit b_q can be found by simple shifting and subtracting. For example, if

$$k = (\,0\,1\,0\,1\,)_2\;,$$

then

$$s = k/2 = (\,0\,0\,1\,0\,)_2$$

and so

$$k - 2s = (\,0\,0\,0\,1\,)_2$$

indicating that the low order bit b_0 is one. If we assign s to k and repeat the process, then we can discover b_1. Continuing in this way we obtain the following algorithm.

Algorithm 1.5.1 (Bit Reversing an Index) If $t \geq 1$ and k satisfies $0 \leq k < 2^t = n$, then the following algorithm computes $j = r_n(k)$.

$$
\begin{aligned}
&j \leftarrow 0;\; m \leftarrow k \\
&\textbf{for } q = 0{:}t - 1 \\
&\qquad s \leftarrow \textbf{floor}(m/2) \\
&\qquad \{b_q = m - 2s\} \\
&\qquad j \leftarrow 2j + (m - 2s) \\
&\qquad m \leftarrow s \\
&\textbf{end}
\end{aligned}
$$

Observe that a single evaluation of $r_n(\cdot)$ involves $O(\log_2 n)$ integer operations. If we use this procedure repeatedly, we then obtain the following index-reversal procedure:

Algorithm 1.5.2 ($P_n x$ via Bit Reversal) If $x \in \mathbb{C}^n$ and $n = 2^t$, then the following algorithm overwrites x with $P_n x$:

$$
\begin{aligned}
&\textbf{for } k = 0{:}n - 1 \\
&\qquad j \leftarrow r_n(k) \qquad \text{(Algorithm 1.5.1)} \\
&\qquad \textbf{if } j > k \\
&\qquad\qquad x(j) \leftrightarrow x(k) \\
&\qquad \textbf{end} \\
&\textbf{end}
\end{aligned}
$$

Here, "$\leftrightarrow$" denotes swapping. See Burrus and Parks (1985) for a Fortran implementation of this approach.

Note that Algorithm 1.5.1 requires $O(n \log_2 n)$ integer arithmetic operations to complete but no vector workspace. Thus, the amount of integer arithmetic involved in Algorithm 1.5.2 has the same order of magnitude as the amount of floating point arithmetic in the butterfly $A_q x$. The overhead associated with bit reversal is nontrivial, sometimes accounting for 10–30 percent of the overall computation time.

1.5.3 P_n and the Permutations Π^T and Π

We next consider alternative approaches to bit reversal that have appeal in vector computer environments. (See Korn and Lambiotte (1979) for further discussion.)

Using the product $P_n = R_t \cdots R_1$ given in (1.5.2) and noting that $R_1 = I_n$, we can compute $P_n x$ as follows:

> **for** $q = 2:t$
> $\quad L \leftarrow 2^q;\ r \leftarrow n/L$
> $\quad x \leftarrow R_q x = (I_r \otimes \Pi_L)x$
> **end**

Using Kron5, this may be expressed as follows:

> **for** $q = 2:t$
> $\quad L \leftarrow 2^q;\ r \leftarrow n/L$ (1.5.4)
> $\quad x_{L \times r} \leftarrow \Pi_L x_{L \times r}$
> **end**

The permutation Π_L is called the *perfect shuffle*, and we shall discuss what it does shortly.

Since P_n is symmetric, it follows from (1.5.2) that $P_n = R_1^T \cdots R_t^T$. This enables us to compute $P_n x$ as follows:

> **for** $q = t:-1:2$
> $\quad L \leftarrow 2^q;\ r \leftarrow n/L$
> $\quad x \leftarrow R_q^T x = (I_r \otimes \Pi_L^T)x$
> **end**

Analogous to (1.5.4) we have

> **for** $q = t:-1:2$
> $\quad L \leftarrow 2^q;\ r \leftarrow n/L$ (1.5.5)
> $\quad x_{L \times r} \leftarrow \Pi_L^T x_{L \times r}$
> **end**

In this formulation, the even-odd sort permutation has center stage.

Before we can detail (1.5.4) and (1.5.5), we need a firmer understanding of Π^T and its inverse, Π.

1.5.4   Even-Odd Sorts and the Perfect Shuffle

The even-odd sort permutation groups the even-indexed and odd-indexed components together. Thus, if $w \in \mathbb{C}^L$, then an operation of the form $z = \Pi_L^T w$ can be handled as follows:

> $L_* \leftarrow L/2$
> **for** $j = 0:L_* - 1$
> $\quad z(j) \leftarrow w(2j)$ (1.5.6)
> $\quad z(j + L_*) \leftarrow w(2j + 1)$
> **end**

In array terms, this action can be defined as a matrix transposition:

$$z = \Pi_L^T w \quad \Leftrightarrow \quad z_{L_* \times 2} = w_{2 \times L_*}^T .$$ (1.5.7)

For example, if $z = \Pi_8^T w$, then

$$\begin{bmatrix} z_0 & z_4 \\ z_1 & z_5 \\ z_2 & z_6 \\ z_3 & z_7 \end{bmatrix} = \begin{bmatrix} w_0 & w_2 & w_4 & w_6 \\ w_1 & w_3 & w_5 & w_7 \end{bmatrix}^T .$$

Thus, $z(0:3) = w(0:2:7)$ and $z(4:7) = w(1:2:7)$. In general, (1.5.7) says $z(0:(L/2)-1) = w(0:2:L-1)$ and $z((L/2):L-1) = w(1:2:L-1)$ in agreement with how we defined Π^T in §1.2.2.

Now if $\Pi_L^T w$ transposes w regarded as a 2-by-L_* matrix, then the inverse operation must transpose w regarded as an L_*-by-2 matrix. Thus, we have the following array interpretation of Π_L:

$$z = \Pi_L w \quad \Leftrightarrow \quad z_{2 \times L_*} = w_{L_* \times 2}^T . \tag{1.5.8}$$

For example, if $z = \Pi_8 w$, then

$$\left[\begin{array}{cccc} z_0 & z_2 & z_4 & z_6 \\ z_1 & z_3 & z_5 & z_7 \end{array} \right] = \left[\begin{array}{cc} w_0 & w_4 \\ w_1 & w_5 \\ w_2 & w_6 \\ w_3 & w_7 \end{array} \right]^T .$$

The term "perfect shuffle" is now seen to be appropriate, since the vector z in (1.5.8) is obtained by splitting w in half and then "shuffling" the top and bottom halves of the "deck":

$$\Pi_8 w = \left[\begin{array}{cccccccc} w_0 & w_4 & w_1 & w_5 & w_2 & w_6 & w_3 & w_7 \end{array} \right]^T .$$

These observations about the perfect shuffle having been made, here is how to carry out the operation $z \leftarrow \Pi_L w$:

$$
\begin{aligned}
& L_* \leftarrow L/2 \\
& \textbf{for } j = 0{:}L_* - 1 \\
& \qquad z(2j) \leftarrow w(j) \\
& \qquad z(2j+1) \leftarrow w(L_* + j) \\
& \textbf{end}
\end{aligned}
\tag{1.5.9}
$$

1.5.5 $P_n x$ Using Even-Odd Sorts and Perfect Shuffles

We now proceed to complete the development of the bit-reversal procedures (1.5.4) and (1.5.5). In the former case we must apply a perfect shuffle to each column of $x_{L \times r}$. Guided by (1.5.9), we obtain the following algorithm.

Algorithm 1.5.3 If $x \in \mathbb{C}^n$ with $n = 2^t$, then the following algorithm overwrites x with $P_n x$ and requires an n-vector workspace:

$$
\begin{aligned}
& \textbf{for } q = 2{:}t \\
& \qquad \{ x \leftarrow (I_r \otimes \Pi_{2,L})x \} \\
& \qquad L \leftarrow 2^q; \; r \leftarrow n/L; \; L_* \leftarrow L/2 \\
& \qquad y \leftarrow x \\
& \qquad \textbf{for } k = 0{:}r - 1 \\
& \qquad\qquad \textbf{for } j = 0{:}L_* - 1 \\
& \qquad\qquad\qquad x(kL + 2j) \leftarrow y(kL + j) \\
& \qquad\qquad\qquad x(kL + 2j + 1) \leftarrow y(kL + L_* + j) \\
& \qquad\qquad \textbf{end} \\
& \qquad \textbf{end} \\
& \textbf{end}
\end{aligned}
$$

Likewise, using (1.5.6) to expand the even-odd sorts of the columns of $x_{L \times r}$, we may derive the following algorithm from (1.5.5).

Algorithm 1.5.4 If $x \in \mathbb{C}^n$ with $n = 2^t$, then the following algorithm overwrites x with $P_n x$ and requires an n-vector workspace:

$$
\begin{aligned}
&\textbf{for } q = t: -1:2 \\
&\qquad \{ x \leftarrow (I_r \otimes \Pi_{2,L}^T) x \} \\
&\qquad L \leftarrow 2^q; \ r \leftarrow n/L; \ L_* \leftarrow L/2 \\
&\qquad y \leftarrow x \\
&\qquad \textbf{for } k = 0{:}r-1 \\
&\qquad\qquad \textbf{for } j = 0{:}L_* - 1 \\
&\qquad\qquad\qquad x(kL + j) \leftarrow y(kL + 2j) \\
&\qquad\qquad\qquad x(kL + L_* + j) \leftarrow y(kL + 2j + 1) \\
&\qquad\qquad \textbf{end} \\
&\qquad \textbf{end} \\
&\textbf{end}
\end{aligned}
$$

Note that Algorithms 1.5.3 and 1.5.4 both have stride-2 access.

1.5.6   Memory References

Traditional measures of "work" in scientific computation quantify the amount of floating point arithmetic. Data permutations typified by Algorithms 1.5.3 and 1.5.4 do not involve any floating point arithmetic. Thus, we need a different way of measuring work for such procedures. We could tabulate the amount of integer subscripting required, but it turns out that counting memory references is more relevant. The statement

$$ x(kL + j) = y(kL + 2j) $$

involves two memory references. We read from y (one reference) and we write to x (another reference). If we scrutinize Algorithms 1.5.3 and 1.5.4, we find that there are a total of $2n(\log_2 n - 1)$ memory references, which indicates that they are $O(n \log n)$ procedures just like Algorithm 1.5.2.

1.5.7   An Array Interpretation of P_n

Another way to connect P_n with the bit reversal of indices is to exploit the characterization of Π_L as a transposing operator. In the qth step of Algorithm 1.5.3, x is overwritten with $y = (I_r \otimes \Pi_L) x$, where $L = 2^q$ and $r = n/L$. If $L_* = L/2$ and we identify x and y with the three-dimensional arrays $X(0{:}L_* - 1, 0{:}1, 0{:}r - 1)$ and $Y(0{:}1, 0{:}L_* - 1, 0{:}r - 1)$, then from the equation

$$ y_{L \times r} = \Pi_L x_{L \times r} $$

we see that step q in Algorithm 1.5.3 realizes a transposition in the first two coordinates:

$$ Y(\alpha, \beta, \gamma) \leftarrow X(\beta, \alpha, \gamma). \qquad (1.5.10) $$

Here, $(\beta, \alpha, \gamma) \in \{0, \ldots, L_* - 1\} \times \{0, 1\} \times \{0, \ldots, r - 1\}$.

To show that a sequence of these maneuvers results in the bit-reversal permutation, regard x and y as t-dimensional arrays:

$$x((b_{t-1}\cdots b_1 b_0)_2) \quad \Leftrightarrow \quad X(b_0,\ldots,b_{t-1}),$$
$$y((b_{t-1}\cdots b_1 b_0)_2) \quad \Leftrightarrow \quad Y(b_0,\ldots,b_{t-1}).$$

The assignment (1.5.10) can therefore be expressed as follows:

$$Y(b_q, b_0, b_1, \ldots, b_{q-1}, b_{q+1}, \ldots, b_{t-1}) \leftarrow X(b_0,\ldots,b_{t-1})\,.$$

It is clear that after steps $q = 2{:}t$ we have replaced $X(b_0,\ldots,b_{t-1})$ with $X(b_{t-1},\ldots,b_0)$. For example, in the $t = 5$ case, the data in the original $X(b_0,b_1,b_2,b_3,b_4)$ moves as follows during the execution of Algorithm 1.5.3:

$$X(b_0, b_1, b_2, b_3, b_4)$$
$$\downarrow$$
$$X(b_1, b_0, b_2, b_3, b_4)$$
$$\downarrow$$
$$X(b_2, b_1, b_0, b_3, b_4)$$
$$\downarrow$$
$$X(b_3, b_2, b_1, b_0, b_4)$$
$$\downarrow$$
$$X(b_4, b_3, b_2, b_1, b_0).$$

The "multidimensional" point of view of bit reversal is used by many authors.

Problems

P1.5.1 Show how to implement Algorithms 1.5.3 and 1.5.4 with only an $n/2$ workspace. Hint: set $y = x(m{:}n - 1)$ where $m = n/2$.

P1.5.2 How many times is the $j > k$ conditional true in Algorithm 1.5.2?

P1.5.3 This problem is about a linear time bit-reversal scheme proposed by Elster (1989). It is a nice illustration of the time-space trade-off. Assume that $n = 2^t$ and define the vector $c(1{:}n/2 - 1)$ by

$$r_n(k) = c_k 2^{t-q},$$

where $1 \le q \le t$, and $2^{q-1} \le k < 2^q$. (a) Show that c_k is an odd integer. (b) Show that if $L_* = 2^{q-1} \le k < 2^q = L$, then $c_{2k} = c_k$ and $c_{2k+1} = c_k + L$. (c) Write an efficient algorithm for computing $c(0{:}(n/2) - 1)$ and explain why it involves $O(n)$ operations.

Notes and References for Section 1.5

General references for computing $P_n x$ include

E.O. Brigham (1974). *The Fast Fourier Transform*, Prentice-Hall, Englewood Cliffs, NJ.
C.S. Burrus and T.W. Parks (1985). *DFT/FFT and Convolution Algorithms*, John Wiley & Sons, New York.

Connections between Π_n and bit reversal are exploited in

D.G. Korn and J.J. Lambiotte (1979). "Computing the Fast Fourier Transform on a Vector Computer," *Math. Comp. 33*, 977–992.
H. Stone (1971). "Parallel Processing with the Perfect Shuffle," *IEEE Trans. Comput. C-20*, 153–161.

Twelve different bit-reversal algorithms are compared in

P. Rosel (1989). "Timing of Some Bit Reversal Algorithms," *Signal Processing 18*, 425–433.

Some fast methods include

A.C. Elster (1989). "Fast Bit-Reversal Algorithms," *ICASSP '89 Proceedings*, 1099–1102.
D.M.W. Evans (1987). "An Improved Digit-Reversal Permutation Algorithm for the Fast Fourier and Hartley Transforms," *IEEE Trans. Acoust. Speech Signal Process.* ASSP-35, 1120–1125.
R.J. Polge, B.K. Bhagavan, and J.M. Carswell (1974). "Fast Algorithms for Bit-Reversal," *IEEE Trans. Comput.* C-23, 1–9,

but they require auxiliary storage. Finally we mention

P. Duhamel (1990). "A Connection Between Bit Reversal and Matrix Transposition: Hardware and Software Consequences," *IEEE Trans. on Acoust. Speech Signal Process.* ASSP-38, 1893–1896,

which has interesting ramifications in the two-dimensional DFT setting. See §3.4.

1.6   The Cooley–Tukey Framework

We concluded §1.3 with the following high-level version of the Cooley–Tukey radix-2 algorithm for $n = 2^t$:

$$
\begin{aligned}
&x \leftarrow P_n x \\
&\textbf{for } q = 1{:}t \\
&\qquad x \leftarrow A_q x \\
&\textbf{end}
\end{aligned}
\tag{1.6.1}
$$

From what we learned in §§1.4 and 1.5, a detailed implementation of this procedure requires the selection of a bit-reversal permutation algorithm for $x \leftarrow P_n x$, a decision with respect to weight (pre-)computation, and a choice of loop orderings for the butterfly update $x \leftarrow A_q x$. We examine two of the several possibilities in this section. One requires minimal storage but has a stride problem, and the other has unit stride but requires extra storage. We complete the analysis of the Cooley–Tukey framework with a mathematical description of the underlying process.

1.6.1   An In-Place Formulation

Many FFT procedures require storage beyond what is required for the x-vector. A notable exception to this is the following version of the Cooley–Tukey algorithm.

Algorithm 1.6.1   If $x \in \mathbb{C}^n$ and $n = 2^t$, then the following algorithm overwrites x with $F_n x$:

$$
\begin{aligned}
&x \leftarrow P_n x \qquad \text{(Algorithm 1.5.2)} \\
&\textbf{for } q = 1{:}t \\
&\qquad L \leftarrow 2^q; \; r \leftarrow n/L; \; L_* \leftarrow L/2 \\
&\qquad \textbf{for } j = 0{:}L_* - 1 \\
&\qquad\qquad \omega \leftarrow \cos(2\pi j/L) - i\sin(2\pi j/L) \\
&\qquad\qquad \textbf{for } k = 0{:}r - 1 \\
&\qquad\qquad\qquad \tau \leftarrow \omega \cdot x(kL + j + L_*) \\
&\qquad\qquad\qquad x(kL + j + L_*) \leftarrow x(kL + j) - \tau \\
&\qquad\qquad\qquad x(kL + j) \leftarrow x(kL + j) + \tau \\
&\qquad\qquad \textbf{end} \\
&\qquad \textbf{end} \\
&\textbf{end}
\end{aligned}
$$

We use Algorithm 1.5.2 for the bit reversal of x because, unlike some of the other methods in §1.5, it does not require a vector workspace for execution. For the butterfly calculation $x \leftarrow A_q x$, we use the nonunit stride jk update (Algorithm 1.4.9) to obviate the need for a weight vector workspace. The weights are computed on-line using the method of direct call (Algorithm 1.4.1). These strategies are of interest in limited storage situations. An FFT algorithm that does not require a vector workspace is called an *in-place* FFT.

1.6.2   A Unit Stride Formulation

A unit stride version of (1.6.1) can be obtained if we implement the kj version of $A_q x$ (Algorithm 1.4.2) with weight precomputation.

Algorithm 1.6.2   If $x \in \mathbb{C}^n$ and $n = 2^t$, then the following algorithm overwrites x with $F_n x$:

$$x \leftarrow P_n x$$
$$w \leftarrow w_n^{(long)} \qquad \text{(See §1.4.11.)}$$
$$\text{for } q = 1{:}t$$
$$\qquad L \leftarrow 2^q; \; r \leftarrow n/L; \; L_* \leftarrow L/2$$
$$\qquad \text{for } k = 0{:}r - 1$$
$$\qquad\qquad \text{for } j = 0{:}L_* - 1$$
$$\qquad\qquad\qquad \tau \leftarrow w(L_* - 1 + j){\cdot}x(kL + j + L_*)$$
$$\qquad\qquad\qquad x(kL + j + L_*) \leftarrow x(kL + j) - \tau$$
$$\qquad\qquad\qquad x(kL + j) \leftarrow x(kL + j) + \tau$$
$$\qquad\qquad \text{end}$$
$$\qquad \text{end}$$
$$\text{end}$$

The fact that this algorithm requires a workspace devalues its importance, for as we said above, a key attribute of the Cooley–Tukey framework is that it permits the in-place computation of $F_n x$. Indeed, if an additional workspace is tolerable, then one of the autosort frameworks which we describe in §1.7 is preferable, because it avoids bit reversal altogether and can be arranged in unit stride fashion. Algorithm 1.6.2 is given merely to highlight the stride/workspace trade-off.

1.6.3   An Assessment of Work

With either of the above algorithms, there are $n/2$ butterflies per pass through the q-loop. Each butterfly requires 10 flops, so together both procedures involve $5n \log_2 n$ "butterfly" flops. The weight calculations, being $O(n)$, do not figure in the overall flop counting.

   The overall efficiency of an FFT implementation is a complicated function of flops, subscripting, memory traffic patterns, and countless other details. It is not appropriate for us to make a blanket statement such as "Algorithm 1.6.2 is faster than Algorithm 1.6.1," because the former has unit stride while the latter does not. Indeed, for very large n the extra workspace required by Algorithm 1.6.2 may imply frequent access to a secondary storage device, thereby negating the advantage of unit stride. The point to stress is that what we call "algorithms" in this book are just computational frameworks. The frameworks are detailed enough to help us anticipate performance,

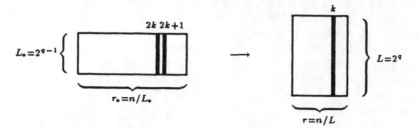

FIG. 1.6.1. *Cooley–Tukey step: array interpretation.*

but they are a long way from the finished code, whose benchmarks are of ultimate interest. Before the stopwatch can be applied to a full implementation of Algorithms 1.6.1 and 1.6.2, they would have to be expressed in some programming language and "cleaned up." Among other things, the complex arithmetic would probably have to be carried out with real data types (see §1.4.9) and the subscripting could be more efficiently organized. Some of these refinements would no doubt be under the control of the underlying compiler.

1.6.4   An Array Interpretation

Recall from §1.2.4 that after q steps in the radix-2 FFT process we have intermediate DFTs $F_L x(k{:}r{:}n-1)$, where $L = 2^q$, $r = n/L$, and $k = 0{:}r-1$. In the Cooley–Tukey framework, these intermediate DFTs are assembled in the x-vector. As the DFTs double in length, the "shape" of x as an array of intermediate DFTs changes shape.

To be specific, since $A_q = I_r \otimes B_L$, we can use Kron5 to relate the matrix-vector product $A_q x$ to the matrix-matrix product $B_L x_{L \times r}$. This leads to an "array version" of (1.6.1):

$$\begin{aligned}
&x \leftarrow P_n x \\
&\textbf{for } q = 1{:}t \\
&\qquad L \leftarrow 2^q; \; r \leftarrow n/L \\
&\qquad x_{L \times r} \leftarrow B_L x_{L \times r} \\
&\textbf{end}
\end{aligned} \qquad (1.6.2)$$

Here,

$$B_L \;=\; \begin{bmatrix} I_{L_*} & \Omega_{L_*} \\ I_{L_*} & -\Omega_{L_*} \end{bmatrix}, \qquad\qquad L = 2^q, \; r = n/L, \; L_* = L/2$$

and

$$\Omega_{L_*} \;=\; \text{diag}(1, \omega_L, \ldots, \omega_L^{L_*-1})\,.$$

A schematic that depicts the change in shape of the intermediate DFT array is offered in Fig. 1.6.1.

Thus, in step q the x-vector is transformed from an $(L/2)$-by-$(2r)$ array to an array of size L-by-r. These arrays are arrays of *intermediate DFTs*. Let $x^{(q)}$ denote the contents of the x-vector after q steps in (1.6.2). The following is a trace of how the intermediate DFT changes shape during execution of the $n = 16$ case:

$$x^{(1)}_{2 \times 8} \;=\; F_2 \begin{bmatrix} x_0 & x_4 & x_2 & x_6 & x_1 & x_5 & x_3 & x_7 \\ x_8 & x_{12} & x_{10} & x_{14} & x_9 & x_{13} & x_{11} & x_{15} \end{bmatrix},$$

$$x_{4\times4}^{(2)} = F_4 \begin{bmatrix} x_0 & x_2 & x_1 & x_3 \\ x_4 & x_6 & x_5 & x_7 \\ x_8 & x_{10} & x_9 & x_{11} \\ x_{12} & x_{14} & x_{13} & x_{15} \end{bmatrix},$$

$$x_{8\times2}^{(3)} = F_8 \begin{bmatrix} x_0 & x_1 \\ x_2 & x_3 \\ x_4 & x_5 \\ x_6 & x_7 \\ x_8 & x_9 \\ x_{10} & x_{11} \\ x_{12} & x_{13} \\ x_{14} & x_{15} \end{bmatrix},$$

$$x_{16\times1}^{(4)} = F_{16}x.$$

With this array interpretation of the x-vector, we can rewrite Algorithm 1.6.1 as follows:

$$
\begin{aligned}
&x \leftarrow P_n x \\
&\textbf{for } q = 1{:}t \\
&\qquad L \leftarrow 2^q; \; r \leftarrow n/L; \; L_* \leftarrow L/2; \; r_* \leftarrow 2r; \; y \leftarrow x \\
&\qquad \{Y(0{:}L_* - 1, 0{:}r_* - 1) \equiv y_{L_* \times r_*}\} \\
&\qquad \{X(0{:}L - 1, 0{:}r - 1) \equiv x_{L \times r}\} \\
&\qquad \textbf{for } j = 0{:}L_* - 1 \\
&\qquad\qquad \textbf{for } k = 0{:}r - 1 \\
&\qquad\qquad\qquad \tau \leftarrow \omega_L^j \cdot Y(j, 2k + 1) \\
&\qquad\qquad\qquad X(j + L_*, k) \leftarrow Y(j, 2k) - \tau \\
&\qquad\qquad\qquad X(j, k) \leftarrow Y(j, 2k) + \tau \\
&\qquad\qquad \textbf{end} \\
&\qquad \textbf{end} \\
&\textbf{end}
\end{aligned}
\qquad (1.6.3)
$$

We have introduced a work vector y for clarity.

Let us prove a theorem that rigorously characterizes *in array terms* the qth update of the x-vector as produced by the Cooley–Tukey process.

Theorem 1.6.1 *Suppose* $x \in \mathbb{C}^n$ *with* $n = 2^t$. *For* $q = 0{:}t$, *define* $x^{(q)}$ *by*

$$x^{(q)} = A_q \cdots A_1(P_n x),$$

i.e., the x-*vector in Algorithm 1.6.1 after* q *steps. If* $L = 2^q$ *and* $r = n/L$, *then*

$$x_{L\times r}^{(q)} = \left[F_L x_{r\times L}^T \right] P_r.$$

Proof. The result is obviously true if $q = 0$, since $x_{1\times n}^{(0)} = x_{1\times n}P_n$. Now assume that

$$x_{L_* \times r_*}^{(q-1)} = \left[F_{L_*} x_{r_* \times L_*}^T \right] P_{r_*},$$

where $L_* = L/2$ and $r_* = 2r$. Define

$$
\begin{aligned}
X_0 &= \left[x(0{:}r_*{:}n - 1) \mid \cdots \mid x(r - 1{:}r_*{:}n - 1) \right] \in \mathbb{C}^{L_* \times r}, \\
X_1 &= \left[x(r{:}r_*{:}n - 1) \mid \cdots \mid x(r_* - 1{:}r_*{:}n - 1) \right] \in \mathbb{C}^{L_* \times r}
\end{aligned}
$$

and note that $x_{r_\bullet \times L_\bullet}^T = [\, X_0 \mid X_1 \,]$. Using Lemma 1.3.1, we obtain

$$\Pi_{r_\bullet}(I_2 \otimes P_r) \; = \; P_{r_\bullet} \; = \; P_{r_\bullet}^T \; = \; (I_2 \otimes P_r)\Pi_{r_\bullet}^T$$

and so by induction

$$x_{L_\bullet \times r_\bullet}^{(q-1)} \; = \; F_{L_\bullet} x_{r_\bullet \times L_\bullet}^T (I_2 \otimes P_r)\Pi_{r_\bullet}^T \; = \; [\, F_{L_\bullet} X_0 P_r \mid F_{L_\bullet} X_1 P_r \,]\Pi_{r_\bullet}^T \, .$$

This says that $x^{(q-1)}$ as an $L_\bullet$-by-$r_\bullet$ matrix is obtained by perfect shuffling the columns of $[\, F_{L_\bullet} X_0 P_r \mid F_{L_\bullet} X_1 P_r \,]$. Regarding the result of this operation as an L-by-r matrix gives

$$x_{L \times r}^{(q-1)} \; = \; \left[\begin{array}{c} F_{L_\bullet} X_0 P_r \\ F_{L_\bullet} X_1 P_r \end{array}\right] \; = \; \left[\begin{array}{c} F_{L_\bullet} X_0 \\ F_{L_\bullet} X_1 \end{array}\right] P_r \, .$$

Now (1.3.1) says that for $k = 0{:}r-1$,

$$F_L x(k{:}r{:}n-1) \; = \; B_L \left[\begin{array}{c} F_{L_\bullet} x(k{:}r_\bullet{:}n-1) \\ F_{L_\bullet} x(k + r{:}r_\bullet{:}n-1) \end{array}\right],$$

or, in matrix terms,

$$F_L x_{r \times L}^T \; = \; B_L \left[\begin{array}{c} F_{L_\bullet} X_0 \\ F_{L_\bullet} X_1 \end{array}\right].$$

Thus,

$$x_{L \times r}^{(q)} \; = \; B_L x_{L \times r}^{(q-1)} \; = \; B_L \left[\begin{array}{c} F_{L_\bullet} X_0 \\ F_{L_\bullet} X_1 \end{array}\right] P_r \; = \; F_L x_{r \times L}^T P_r,$$

thereby completing the proof of the theorem. $\square$

The theorem says that in the Cooley–Tukey framework, the intermediate DFTs are "stacked" in the x-array in bit-reversed order. There are other ways to organize the storage of the intermediate DFTs, and these lead to alternative frameworks, as we shall see in the next two sections.

Problems

P1.6.1 Organize Algorithm 1.6.1 so that the integer arithmetic associated with the subscripting is minimized.

P1.6.2 Assume that a sine or cosine evaluation costs μ flops. Count flops in Algorithm 1.6.1, keeping track of both the $O(n \log_2 n)$ and $O(n)$ terms.

Notes and References for Section 1.6

The Cooley–Tukey framework is presented in the classic paper

J.W. Cooley and J.W. Tukey (1965). "An Algorithm for the Machine Calculation of Complex Fourier Series," *Math. Comp. 19*, 297–301.

Very readable accounts of the overall process may be found in

E.O. Brigham (1974). *The Fast Fourier Transform*, Prentice-Hall, Englewood Cliffs, NJ.
C.S. Burrus and T. Parks (1985). *DFT/FFT and Convolution Algorithms*, John Wiley & Sons, New York.

The latter volume includes Fortran listings.

1.7 The Stockham Autosort Frameworks

In this section we derive a pair of FFT frameworks in which the bit-reversing computations required by the Cooley–Tukey process are avoided at the expense of a workspace. The idea behind these *autosort* frameworks is to intermingle certain data movements with the butterfly operations. For example, instead of the Cooley–Tukey factorization

$$F_n P_n = A_t \cdots A_1, \qquad n = 2^t,$$

we seek permutations $\Gamma_0, \ldots, \Gamma_{t-1}$ such that

$$F_n = A_t \Gamma_{t-1} \cdots A_2 \Gamma_1 A_1 \Gamma_0. \tag{1.7.1}$$

An FFT framework based upon this factorization would proceed as follows:

$$
\begin{aligned}
&\textbf{for } q = 1{:}t \\
&\qquad x \leftarrow A_q(\Gamma_{q-1}x) \\
&\textbf{end}
\end{aligned}
\tag{1.7.2}
$$

Observe that the butterfly operator A_q is applied to a permuted version of the current x-array. It turns out that the Γ_q permutations are easy to implement and the overall framework is attractive in vector processing environments where bit reversal represents a substantial overhead.

The first autosort algorithm that we develop is called the transposed Stockham algorithm, and it is derived by reorganizing the Cooley–Tukey procedure so that the intermediate DFTs are stored by column in *natural order*. If the intermediate DFTs are stored by row in natural order, then the Stockham algorithm results. After working out the factorizations and the algorithms, we examine the vectorization properties of the autosort approaches.

1.7.1 Storing the Intermediate DFTs

Recall from Theorem 1.6.1 that after q steps in the Cooley–Tukey algorithm, the x-array is overwritten by $x^{(q)}$, where

$$x^{(q)}_{L \times r} = F_L x^T_{r \times L} P_r, \tag{1.7.3}$$

$L = 2^q$ and $r = n/L$. In other words, the intermediate DFTs are "stacked" in bit-reversed order. In our first autosort framework, the intermediate DFTs appear in *natural* order, i.e.,

$$x^{(q)}_{L \times r} = F_L x^T_{r \times L}. \tag{1.7.4}$$

For example, if $n = 32$ and $q = 2$, then the distinction between natural and permuted storage of the intermediate DFTs is as follows:

$$
x^{(q)}_{natural} =
\begin{bmatrix}
F_4 x(0{:}8{:}31) \\
F_4 x(1{:}8{:}31) \\
F_4 x(2{:}8{:}31) \\
F_4 x(3{:}8{:}31) \\
F_4 x(4{:}8{:}31) \\
F_4 x(5{:}8{:}31) \\
F_4 x(6{:}8{:}31) \\
F_4 x(7{:}8{:}31)
\end{bmatrix},
\qquad
x^{(q)}_{permuted} =
\begin{bmatrix}
F_4 x(0{:}8{:}31) \\
F_4 x(4{:}8{:}31) \\
F_4 x(2{:}8{:}31) \\
F_4 x(6{:}8{:}31) \\
F_4 x(1{:}8{:}31) \\
F_4 x(5{:}8{:}31) \\
F_4 x(3{:}8{:}31) \\
F_4 x(7{:}8{:}31)
\end{bmatrix}.
$$

1.7.2   The Transposed Stockham Factorization

By carefully looking at the transition

$$x_{L_{\bullet} \times r_{\bullet}}^{(q-1)} \longrightarrow x_{L \times r}^{(q)}, \qquad L = 2^q, \; r = n/L, \; L_{\bullet} = L/2, \; r_{\bullet} = 2r,$$

we can derive the factorization (1.7.1) along with a complete specification of the permutations $\Gamma_0, \ldots, \Gamma_{t-1}$.

Theorem 1.7.1 (Transposed Stockham Radix-2 Factorization) *If $n = 2^t$, then*

$$F_n = S_t \cdots S_2 S_1,$$

where for $q = 1{:}t$ the factor $S_q = A_q \Gamma_{q-1}$ is defined by

$$A_q = I_r \otimes B_L, \qquad\qquad L = 2^q, \; r = n/L,$$

$$\Gamma_{q-1} = \Pi_{r_{\bullet}} \otimes I_{L_{\bullet}}, \qquad\qquad L_{\bullet} = L/2, \; r_{\bullet} = 2r,$$

$$B_L = \begin{bmatrix} I_{L_{\bullet}} & \Omega_{L_{\bullet}} \\ I_{L_{\bullet}} & -\Omega_{L_{\bullet}} \end{bmatrix},$$

$$\Omega_{L_{\bullet}} = \mathrm{diag}(1, \omega_L, \ldots, \omega_L^{L_{\bullet}-1}).$$

Proof. Since $x(k{:}r_{\bullet}{:}n - 1)$ and $x(k + r{:}r_{\bullet}{:}n - 1)$ are the even and odd portions of $x(k{:}r{:}n - 1)$, it follows from Corollary 1.2.2 that for $k = 0{:}r - 1$

$$F_L x(k{:}r{:}n - 1) = B_L \begin{bmatrix} F_{L_{\bullet}} x(k{:}r_{\bullet}{:}n - 1) \\ F_{L_{\bullet}} x(k + r{:}r_{\bullet}{:}n - 1) \end{bmatrix}.$$

If we define $y \in \mathbb{C}^n$ by

$$y_{L \times r} = \begin{bmatrix} F_{L_{\bullet}} x(0{:}r_{\bullet}{:}n - 1) & \cdots & F_{L_{\bullet}} x(r - 1{:}r_{\bullet}{:}n - 1) \\ F_{L_{\bullet}} x(r{:}r_{\bullet}{:}n - 1) & \cdots & F_{L_{\bullet}} x(r_{\bullet} - 1{:}r_{\bullet}{:}n - 1) \end{bmatrix},$$

then

$$x_{L \times r}^{(q)} = F_L x_{r \times L}^T = F_L \left[x(0{:}r{:}n - 1) \mid \cdots \mid x(r - 1{:}r{:}n - 1) \right] = B_L y_{L \times r}.$$

In other words,

$$x^{(q)} = (I_r \otimes B_L) y = A_q y. \tag{1.7.5}$$

Now the DFTs that make up y are precisely the DFTs that make up $x^{(q-1)}$, since

$$x_{L_{\bullet} \times r_{\bullet}}^{(q-1)} = \left[F_{L_{\bullet}} x(0{:}r_{\bullet}{:}n - 1) \mid \cdots \mid F_{L_{\bullet}} x(r_{\bullet} - 1{:}r_{\bullet}{:}n - 1) \right].$$

In particular, to obtain $y_{L_{\bullet} \times r_{\bullet}}$, we perfect shuffle the columns of $x_{L_{\bullet} \times r_{\bullet}}^{(q-1)}$:

$$y_{L_{\bullet} \times r_{\bullet}} = x_{L_{\bullet} \times r_{\bullet}}^{(q-1)} \Pi_{r_{\bullet}}^T.$$

It follows from Kron6 that $y = (\Pi_{r_{\bullet}} \otimes I_{L_{\bullet}}) x^{(q-1)} = \Gamma_{q-1} x^{(q-1)}$ and so upon combination with (1.7.5) we obtain

$$x^{(q)} = A_q y = A_q \left(\Gamma_{q-1} x^{(q-1)} \right) = S_q x^{(q-1)}.$$

A simple induction shows that $x^{(t)} = S_t \cdots S_1$. But from (1.7.4),

$$x^{(t)} = x_{n \times 1}^{(t)} = F_n x_{n \times 1} = F_n x,$$

and so $F_n x = S_t \cdots S_1 x$. Since this holds for all $x \in \mathbb{C}^n$, we have $F_n = S_t \cdots S_1$. $\square$

With this factorization loop (1.7.2) expands to

$$
\begin{aligned}
&\textbf{for } q = 1{:}t \\
&\qquad L \leftarrow 2^q; \ r \leftarrow n/L; \ L_* \leftarrow L/2; \ r_* \leftarrow 2r \\
&\qquad y \leftarrow (\Pi_{r_*} \otimes I_{L_*})x \\
&\qquad x \leftarrow (I_r \otimes B_L)y \\
&\textbf{end}
\end{aligned}
\qquad (1.7.6)
$$

The butterfly operation $(I_r \otimes B_L)x$ has been detailed in §1.4 and requires no further attention. However, the perfect shuffle computation $y \leftarrow (\Pi_{r_*} \otimes I_{L_*})x$ needs to be discussed before we can present a more finished version of (1.7.6).

1.7.3 Some Perfect Shuffle Manipulations

The operation $y \leftarrow (\Pi_{r_*} \otimes I_{L_*})x$ amounts to a perfect shuffle of x as a block vector. For example,

$$
(\Pi_4 \otimes I_2)
\begin{bmatrix}
x_0 \\ x_1 \\ \hline
x_2 \\ x_3 \\ \hline
x_4 \\ x_5 \\ \hline
x_6 \\ x_7
\end{bmatrix}
=
\begin{bmatrix}
x_0 \\ x_1 \\ \hline
x_4 \\ x_5 \\ \hline
x_2 \\ x_3 \\ \hline
x_6 \\ x_7
\end{bmatrix}
$$

shuffles $x \in \mathbb{C}^8$ regarded as a 4-vector.

In general, since $y \leftarrow (\Pi_{r_*} \otimes I_{L_*})x$ is equivalent to $y_{L_* \times r_*} = x_{L_* \times r_*} \Pi_{r_*}^T$, we see that $y_{L_* \times r_*}$ is obtained by carrying out a perfect shuffle of the columns of $x_{L_* \times r_*}$. It follows from the discussion of this permutation in §1.5.4 that if $x_{L_* \times r_*} = [x_0 \mid \cdots \mid x_{r_*-1}]$ and $y_{L_* \times r_*} = [y_0 \mid \cdots \mid y_{r_*-1}]$ are column partitionings, then

$$
\begin{aligned}
&\textbf{for } k = 0{:}r-1 \\
&\qquad y_{2k} \leftarrow x_k \\
&\qquad y_{2k+1} \leftarrow x_{k+r} \\
&\textbf{end}
\end{aligned}
$$

Since $x_k = x(kL_*{:}(k+1)L_* - 1)$ and $y_k = y(kL_*{:}(k+1)L_* - 1)$, this becomes

$$
\begin{aligned}
&\textbf{for } k = 0{:}r-1 \\
&\qquad y(kL{:}kL + L_* - 1) \leftarrow x(kL_*{:}(k+1)L_* - 1) \\
&\qquad y(kL + L_*{:}(k+1)L - 1) \leftarrow x((k+r)L_*{:}(k+r+1)L_* - 1) \\
&\textbf{end}
\end{aligned}
$$

or, in double loop notation:

$$\begin{aligned}
&\textbf{for } k = 0{:}r - 1 \\
&\qquad \textbf{for } j = 0{:}L_* - 1 \\
&\qquad\qquad y(kL + j) \leftarrow x(kL_* + j) \\
&\qquad\qquad y(kL + L_* + j) \leftarrow x((k + r)L_* + j) \\
&\qquad \textbf{end} \\
&\textbf{end}
\end{aligned} \qquad (1.7.7)$$

Note that this is a unit stride computation.

1.7.4   The Transposed Stockham Algorithm

There is corresponding to (1.7.7) a similar kj implementation for the computation $x \leftarrow (I_r \otimes B_L)y$:

$$\begin{aligned}
&\textbf{for } k = 0{:}r - 1 \\
&\qquad \textbf{for } j = 0{:}L_* - 1 \\
&\qquad\qquad \tau \leftarrow \omega_L^j \cdot y(kL + L_* + j) \\
&\qquad\qquad x(kL + j) \leftarrow y(kL + j) + \tau \\
&\qquad\qquad x(kL + L_* + j) \leftarrow y(kL + j) - \tau \\
&\qquad \textbf{end} \\
&\textbf{end}
\end{aligned} \qquad (1.7.8)$$

By merging this double loop with (1.7.7) we obtain the following expansion of (1.7.6) for the update $x \leftarrow S_q x$:

$$\begin{aligned}
&L \leftarrow 2^q; \ r \leftarrow n/L; \ L_* \leftarrow L/2 \\
&y \leftarrow x \\
&\textbf{for } k = 0{:}r - 1 \\
&\qquad \textbf{for } j = 0{:}L_* - 1 \\
&\qquad\qquad \tau \leftarrow \omega_L^j \cdot y((k + r)L_* + j) \\
&\qquad\qquad x(kL + j) \leftarrow y(kL_* + j) + \tau \\
&\qquad\qquad x(kL + L_* + j) \leftarrow y(kL_* + j) - \tau \\
&\qquad \textbf{end} \\
&\textbf{end}
\end{aligned}$$

Repetition of this process for $q = 1{:}t$ renders the *transposed Stockham FFT framework*.

Algorithm 1.7.1   If $x \in \mathbb{C}^n$ with $n = 2^t$, then the following algorithm overwrites x with $F_n x$. A workspace of length n is required.

$$\begin{aligned}
&w \leftarrow w_n^{(long)}. \qquad \text{(See §1.4.11.)} \\
&\textbf{for } q = 1{:}t \\
&\qquad L \leftarrow 2^q; \ r \leftarrow n/L; \ L_* \leftarrow L/2 \\
&\qquad y \leftarrow x \\
&\qquad \textbf{for } k = 0{:}r - 1 \\
&\qquad\qquad \textbf{for } j = 0{:}L_* - 1 \\
&\qquad\qquad\qquad \tau \leftarrow w(L_* - 1 + j) \cdot y((k + r)L_* + j) \\
&\qquad\qquad\qquad x(kL + j) \leftarrow y(kL_* + j) + \tau \\
&\qquad\qquad\qquad x(kL + L_* + j) \leftarrow y(kL_* + j) - \tau \\
&\qquad\qquad \textbf{end} \\
&\qquad \textbf{end} \\
&\textbf{end}
\end{aligned}$$

This algorithm requires $5n \log_2 n$ flops and is an example of an *in-order* FFT, meaning that no scrambling of input or output is required. Note, however, that a workspace y is used to facilitate the butterfly computations. This is because when two half-length DFTs are synthesized, the result does *not* occupy the same location in the x-array. (However, with some cleverness it is possible to develop an in-place, in-order radix-2 procedure. See Johnson and Burrus (1984) and Temperton (1991).)

1.7.5 An Array Interpretation

As with the Cooley-Tukey framework, it is useful to interpret the Stockham process in array terms. Using Kron5 and Kron6 we can transform the matrix-vector products in (1.7.6) to matrix-matrix products and so obtain

$$
\begin{aligned}
&\textbf{for } q = 1{:}t \\
&\qquad L \leftarrow 2^q;\ r \leftarrow n/L;\ L_* \leftarrow L/2;\ r_* \leftarrow 2r \\
&\qquad y_{L_* \times r_*} \leftarrow x_{L_* \times r_*} \Pi_{r_*} \\
&\qquad x_{L \times r} \leftarrow B_L y_{L \times r} \\
&\textbf{end}
\end{aligned}
\qquad (1.7.9)
$$

Thus, during the qth stage the kth column of the intermediate DFT array

is computed by applying B_L to columns k and $k + r$ of the "previous" intermediate DFT array

If $n = 8$, then this array of intermediate DFTs changes shape as follows:

$$
\begin{bmatrix} \times & \times & \times & \times & \times & \times & \times & \times \end{bmatrix}
\;\rightarrow\;
\begin{bmatrix} \times & \times & \times & \times \\ \times & \times & \times & \times \end{bmatrix}
\;\rightarrow\;
\begin{bmatrix} \times & \times \\ \times & \times \\ \times & \times \\ \times & \times \end{bmatrix}
\;\rightarrow\;
\begin{bmatrix} \times \\ \times \\ \times \\ \times \\ \times \\ \times \\ \times \\ \times \end{bmatrix}.
$$

This array point of view prompts us to consider a new FFT framework.

1.7.6 The Stockham Framework

Let us reorganize the transposed Stockham process so that the intermediate DFTs are stored by *row* instead of by column. In the $n = 8$ setting this means that the intermediate DFT array undergoes the following dimension changes:

$$
\begin{bmatrix} \times \\ \times \\ \times \\ \times \\ \times \\ \times \\ \times \\ \times \end{bmatrix}
\rightarrow
\begin{bmatrix} \times\,\times \\ \times\,\times \\ \times\,\times \\ \times\,\times \end{bmatrix}
\rightarrow
\begin{bmatrix} \times\,\times\,\times\,\times \\ \times\,\times\,\times\,\times \end{bmatrix}
\rightarrow
\begin{bmatrix} \times\,\times\,\times\,\times\,\times\,\times\,\times\,\times \end{bmatrix}.
$$

Now the central maneuver in the qth step is to compute the kth row of $x_{r \times L}$ from rows k and $k + r$ of $y_{r_\bullet \times L_\bullet}$. In particular, we start with a row-oriented intermediate DFT array

$$
x_{r_\bullet \times L_\bullet}^{(q-1)} = x_{r_\bullet \times L_\bullet} F_{L_\bullet} =
$$

(array with rows labeled k and $k+r$, $r_\bullet = n/L_\bullet$, width $L_\bullet = 2^{q-1}$)

and proceed to a new intermediate DFT array that is twice as wide and half as high:

$$
x_{r \times L}^{(q)} = x_{r \times L} F_L =
$$

(array with row labeled k, $r = n/L$, width $L = 2^q$)

To express this transition in Kronecker form, we note that if $A_0, A_1 \in \mathbb{C}^{r \times L_\bullet}$ and

$$
x_{r_\bullet \times L_\bullet} F_{L_\bullet} \;=\; x_{r_\bullet \times L_\bullet}^{(q-1)} \;=\; \begin{bmatrix} A_0 \\ A_1 \end{bmatrix},
$$

then

$$
x_{r \times L} F_L \;=\; x_{r \times L}^{(q)} \;=\; \begin{bmatrix} A_0 \mid A_1 \end{bmatrix} B_L^T,
$$

because the kth row of $x_{r \times L}^{(q)}$ is synthesized from the DFTs that occupy the kth rows of A_0 and A_1. Now the even and odd columns of $x_{r \times L}^{(q-1)}$ make up A_0 and A_1, respectively, so

$$
\begin{bmatrix} A_0 \mid A_1 \end{bmatrix} \;=\; x_{r \times L}^{(q-1)} \Pi_L \,.
$$

With the transition from $x_{r \times L}^{(q-1)}$ to $x_{r \times L}^{(q)}$ determined by

$$
x_{r \times L}^{(q)} \;=\; x_{r \times L}^{(q-1)} \Pi_L B_L^T \tag{1.7.10}
$$

we obtain a high-level description of the Stockham process,

$$
\begin{aligned}
&\textbf{for } q = 1{:}t\\
&\qquad L \leftarrow 2^q;\ r \leftarrow n/L;\ L_* \leftarrow L/2;\ r_* \leftarrow n/L_*\\
&\qquad y_{r\times L} \leftarrow x_{r\times L}\Pi_L\\
&\qquad x_{r\times L} \leftarrow y_{r\times L}B_L^T\\
&\textbf{end}
\end{aligned}
$$

and a corresponding factorization, which is given in the following theorem.

Theorem 1.7.2 (Stockham Factorization) *If $n = 2^t$, then*

$$
F_n \;=\; G_t \cdots G_2 G_1,
$$

where for $q = 1{:}t$:

$$
G_q \;=\; (B_L \otimes I_r)(\Pi_L^T \otimes I_r), \qquad L = 2^q,\ r = n/L,
$$

$$
B_L \;=\; \begin{bmatrix} I_{L_*} & \Omega_{L_*} \\ I_{L_*} & -\Omega_{L_*} \end{bmatrix}, \qquad\qquad L_* = L/2
$$

$$
\Omega_{L_*} \;=\; \mathrm{diag}(1,\, \omega_L, \ldots, \omega_L^{L_*-1})\, .
$$

Proof. Using Kron1 and Kron6, we can express (1.7.10) in matrix-vector form:

$$
x^{(q)} \;=\; (B_L\Pi_L^T \otimes I_r)x^{(q-1)} \;=\; (B_L \otimes I_r)(\Pi_L^T \otimes I_r)x^{(q-1)} \;=\; G_q x^{(q-1)}\, .
$$

A simple induction shows that

$$
x^{(t)} = G_t \cdots G_1 x\, .
$$

Since $x^{(t)}_{1\times n} = x_{1\times n}F_n$, it follows that $F_n x = G_t \cdots G_1 x$. The theorem is established, since x is arbitrary. $\square$

Note that (a) $G_q = \left(B_L\,\Pi_L^T \right) \otimes I_r$ and (b) $B_L\Pi_L^T$ amounts to a perfect shuffle of the columns of the butterfly matrix B_L. For example,

$$
B_8\Pi_8^T \;=\; \begin{bmatrix}
1 & 1 & 0 & 0 & 0 & 0 & 0 & 0 \\
0 & 0 & 1 & \omega_8 & 0 & 0 & 0 & 0 \\
0 & 0 & 0 & 0 & 1 & \omega_8^2 & 0 & 0 \\
0 & 0 & 0 & 0 & 0 & 0 & 1 & \omega_8^3 \\
1 & -1 & 0 & 0 & 0 & 0 & 0 & 0 \\
0 & 0 & 1 & -\omega_8 & 0 & 0 & 0 & 0 \\
0 & 0 & 0 & 0 & 1 & -\omega_8^2 & 0 & 0 \\
0 & 0 & 0 & 0 & 0 & 0 & 1 & -\omega_8^3
\end{bmatrix}.
$$

This form is discussed by Glassman (1970). We could derive the Stockham algorithm through exploitation of this structure. However, an alternative development is offered in the next subsection.

1.7.7   The Stockham Algorithm

We start by expressing the transposed Stockham process in double subscript array terms. In particular, we rewrite Algorithm 1.7.1 as follows:

$$
\begin{aligned}
&\textbf{for } q = 1{:}t \\
&\quad L \leftarrow 2^q; \; r \leftarrow n/L; \; L_* \leftarrow L/2 \\
&\quad y \leftarrow x \\
&\quad \{X(0{:}L-1, 0{:}r-1) \equiv x_{L \times r}\} \\
&\quad \{Y(0{:}L_*-1, 0{:}r_*-1) \equiv y_{L_* \times r_*}\} \\
&\quad \textbf{for } j = L_* - 1 \\
&\qquad \textbf{for } k = 0{:}r-1 \\
&\qquad\quad \tau \leftarrow \omega_L^j \cdot Y(j, k+r) \\
&\qquad\quad X(j, k) \leftarrow Y(j, k) + \tau \\
&\qquad\quad X(j+L_*, k) \leftarrow Y(j, k) - \tau \\
&\qquad \textbf{end} \\
&\quad \textbf{end} \\
&\textbf{end}
\end{aligned}
$$

In order to adapt this so that intermediate DFTs are stored by row, we merely interchange the subscript order:

$$
\begin{aligned}
&\textbf{for } q = 1{:}t \\
&\quad L \leftarrow 2^q; \; r \leftarrow n/L; \; L_* \leftarrow L/2 \\
&\quad y \leftarrow x \\
&\quad \{X(0{:}r-1, 0{:}L-1) \equiv \; ; x_{r \times L}\} \\
&\quad \{Y(0{:}r_*-1, 0{:}L_*-1) \equiv y_{r_* \times L_*}\} \\
&\quad \textbf{for } j = L_* - 1 \\
&\qquad \textbf{for } k = 0{:}r-1 \\
&\qquad\quad \tau \leftarrow \omega_L^j \cdot Y(k+r, j) \\
&\qquad\quad X(k, j) \leftarrow Y(k, j) + \tau \\
&\qquad\quad X(k, j+L_*) \leftarrow Y(k, j) - \tau \\
&\qquad \textbf{end} \\
&\quad \textbf{end} \\
&\textbf{end}
\end{aligned}
\qquad (1.7.11)
$$

It is important to stress that X and Y have size r-by-L and r_*-by-L_*, respectively. With these dimensions we have the following identifications:

$$Y(k+r, j) \equiv y(jr_* + k + r),$$

$$Y(k, j) \equiv y(jr_* + k),$$

$$X(k, j) \equiv x(jr + k),$$

$$X(k, j+L_*) \equiv x((j+L_*)r + k).$$

If we substitute these conversions into (1.7.11), we obtain a one-dimensional array formulation. Making this change and computing weights off-line gives the following specification of the Stockham process.

Algorithm 1.7.2   If $x \in \mathbb{C}^n$ and $n = 2^t$, then the following algorithm overwrites x with $F_n x$. A workspace $y \in \mathbb{C}^n$ is required.

$$\text{for } q = 1{:}t$$
$$\quad L \leftarrow 2^q; \ r \leftarrow n/L$$
$$\quad L_* \leftarrow L/2; \ r_* \leftarrow n/L_*$$
$$\quad y \leftarrow x$$
$$\quad \text{for } j = 0{:}L_* - 1$$
$$\quad\quad \omega \leftarrow \cos(2\pi j/L) - i\sin(2\pi j/L)$$
$$\quad\quad \text{for } k = 0{:}r - 1$$
$$\quad\quad\quad \tau \leftarrow \omega \cdot y(jr_* + k + r)$$
$$\quad\quad\quad x(jr + k) \leftarrow y(jr_* + k) + \tau$$
$$\quad\quad\quad x((j + L_*)r + k) \leftarrow y(jr_* + k) - \tau$$
$$\quad\quad \text{end}$$
$$\quad \text{end}$$
$$\text{end}$$

It is easy to show that $5n \log n$ flops are required.

1.7.8 Some Vector Length Considerations

Algorithms 1.7.1 and 1.7.2 have unit stride. If we reverse the order of the inner two loops in either of these algorithms, then power-of-two strides are encountered. Such a modification also affects the dynamics of innermost loop length. The possibilities are summarized in Table 1.7.1. Consider the effect of inner loop length on the performance

TABLE 1.7.1
Stride and vector length attributes.

FFT Framework	Loop Order	Inner Loop Stride during Step q	Inner Loop Length during Step q
Transposed Stockham	kj	1	2^{q-1}
Transposed Stockham	jk	2^{q-1}	2^{t-q}
Stockham	kj	2^{t-q}	2^{q-1}
Stockham	jk	1	2^{t-q}

of the kj transposed Stockham framework (Algorithm 1.7.1), which we write as follows to stress vector-level operations:

$$\text{for } q = 1{:}t$$
$$\quad L \leftarrow 2^q; \ r \leftarrow n/L$$
$$\quad L_* \leftarrow L/2$$
$$\quad y \leftarrow x$$
$$\quad \text{for } k = 0{:}r - 1$$
$$\quad\quad u \leftarrow w_n^{(long)}(L_* - 1{:}L - 2).*\, y((k + r)L_*{:}(k + r + 1)L_* - 1)$$
$$\quad\quad x(kL{:}kL + L_* - 1) \leftarrow y(kL_*{:}(k + 1)L_* - 1) + u \qquad (1.7.12)$$
$$\quad\quad x(kL + L_*{:}(k + 1)L - 1) \leftarrow y(kL_*{:}(k + 1)L_* - 1) - u$$
$$\quad \text{end}$$
$$\text{end}$$

Following the model of vector processing presented in §1.4.10, we assume that a real vector operation of length m executes in time

$$
T(m) = \begin{cases} \alpha + \beta m, & m \le \ell, \\[2mm] \dfrac{m}{\ell}(\alpha + \beta\ell), & m > \ell. \end{cases}
$$

For simplicity, we assume here that $\ell = 2^d$ divides m. Since the j loop in Algorithm 1.7.1 oversees ten length-L_* vector operations, it follows that approximately

$$
T_{1.7.1} = 10 \sum_{q=1}^{t} 2^{t-q} \tau_q
$$

seconds are devoted to floating point vector manipulations, where

$$
\tau_q = \begin{cases} \alpha + 2^{q-1}\beta, & q - 1 \le d, \\[2mm] 2^{q-1-d}(\alpha + 2^d\beta), & q - 1 > d. \end{cases}
$$

It follows that

$$
T_{1.7.1} \approx 10\alpha n \left(1 + \frac{t-d}{2\ell}\right) + 5nt\beta . \tag{1.7.13}
$$

Observe that the length of the inner loop doubles with each pass through the outermost loop; as a result, the algorithm begins with some short vector computations. The opposite is true of the jk version. Since long vector computation reduces vector start-up overhead, this suggests that we begin with the jk variant and then switch over to the kj version once the vectors get long enough. This idea is called *loop inversion* and is discussed in Swarztrauber (1982). If we switch from the jk to the kj variant when $q = d + 1$, then $T_{1.7.1}$ is reduced to

$$
\tilde{T}_{1.7.1} = \frac{5nt}{\ell}\alpha + 5nt\beta . \tag{1.7.14}
$$

Since $T_{1.7.1} - \tilde{T}_{1.7.1} \approx 10\alpha n(1 - (d/2\ell))$, we see that this technique can enhance performance whenever α is large. However, the jk version of Algorithm 1.7.1 has power-of-two stride, and so the gain in vector length during the first $d + 1$ steps can be nullified.

A way around this difficulty might be to switch loop orderings *and* algorithms at the inversion point. We observe from Table 1.7.1 that the jk version of Algorithm 1.7.2 has desirable stride and vector length properties for small q. Thus, we could run kj Stockham for small q and then switch to jk transposed Stockham. The problem with this idea is that the intermediate DFT array would have to be transposed at the crossover point. Unfortunately, the transposition itself involves nonunit stride manipulations (see §3.2), making it difficult to predict the performance level of this hybrid approach.

Problems

P1.7.1 Show how both Algorithms 1.7.1 and 1.7.2 can be implemented with y having size $n/2$.

P1.7.2 Show how to reduce the amount of memory traffic in either Algorithm 1.7.1 or 1.7.2 by flip-floppping the role of y and x after each pass through the outer loop.

P1.7.3 Rewrite Algorithms 1.7.1 and 1.7.2 so that the weights are generated on-line using the method of direct call.

P1.7.4 Prove (1.7.13) and (1.7.14).

Notes and References for Section 1.7

Autosort ideas attributed to T.G. Stockham are first referenced in

W.T. Cochrane, J.W. Cooley, J.W. Favin, D.L. Helms, R.A. Kaenel, W.W. Lang, G.C. Maling, D.E. Nelson, C.M. Rader, and P.D. Welch (1967). "What Is the Fast Fourier Transform?," *IEEE Trans. Audio and Electroacoustics AU-15*, 45–55.

Good algorithmic descriptions of the autosort frameworks and their vectorization properties may be found in

D.H. Bailey (1987). "A High-Performance Fast Fourier Transform Algorithm for the Cray-2," *J. Supercomputing 1*, 43–62.

D.H. Bailey (1988). "A High-Performance FFT Algorithm for Vector Supercomputers," *International J. Supercomputer Applications 2*, 82–87.

D.G. Korn and J.J. Lambiotte (1979). "Computing the Fast Fourier Transform on a Vector Computer," *Math. Comp. 33*, 977–992.

P.N. Swarztrauber (1982). "Vectorizing the FFTs," in *Parallel Computations*, G. Rodrigue (ed.), Academic Press, New York, 490–501.

P.N. Swarztrauber (1984b). "FFT Algorithms for Vector Computers," *Parallel Comput. 1*, 45–63.

C. Temperton (1983b). "Self-Sorting Mixed Radix Fast Fourier Transforms," *J. Comput. Phys. 52*, 1–23.

C. Temperton (1983). "Fast Mixed Radix Real Fourier Transforms," *J. Comput. Phys. 52*, 340–50.

The Stockham algorithm is a special case of the Glassman algorithm. See

M. Drubin (1971). "Kronecker Product Factorization of the FFT Matrix," *IEEE Trans. Comput. C-20*, 590–593.

W.E. Ferguson Jr. (1982). "A Simple Derivation of the Glassman General-N Fast Fourier Transform," *Comput. Math. Appl. 8*, 401–411.

B. Fornberg (1981). "A Vector Implementation of the Fast Fourier Transform," *Math. Comp. 36*, 189–191.

J.A. Glassman (1970). "A Generalization of the Fast Fourier Transform," *IEEE Trans. Comput. C-19*, 105–116.

The in-order/workspace trade-off is not inevitable. The following papers discuss how the autosort framework can be implemented without a workspace requirement:

H.W. Johnson and C.S. Burrus (1984). "An In-Place, In-Order Radix-2 FFT," *Proc. IEEE ICASSP*, San Diego, CA, 28A.2.

C. Temperton (1991). "Self-Sorting In-Place Fast Fourier Transforms," *SIAM J. Sci. Stat. Comput. 12*, 808–823.

For a Kronecker-based discussion of the autosort algorithms, see

M.J. Corinthios (1971). "The Design of a Class of Fast Fourier Transform Computers," *IEEE Trans. Comput. C-20*, 617–623.

H. Sloate (1974). "Matrix Representations for Sorting and the Fast Fourier Transform," *IEEE Trans. Circuits and Systems CAS-21*, 109–116.

R. Tolimieri, M. An, and C. Lu (1989). *Algorithms for Discrete Fourier Transform and Convolution*, Springer-Verlag, New York.

1.8   The Pease Framework

Just as we transposed the intermediate DFT array in one autosort algorithm to obtain another in §1.7, so can we transpose the Cooley–Tukey algorithm to obtain yet another framework. The resulting FFT has the curious feature that the two inner loops collapse into a single loop of length $n/2$.

1.8.1   Transposing the Cooley–Tukey Algorithm

In the radix-2 Cooley–Tukey algorithm, the intermediate DFTs are stored by column, i.e., $x_{L \times r}^{(q)} = F_L x_{r \times L}^T P_r$. An interesting new FFT framework results by rearranging the computation so that the intermediate DFTs are stored by row in the same permuted order. To derive this algorithm, we reproduce our array formulation (1.6.3) of the Cooley–Tukey procedure:

$$
\begin{aligned}
&x \leftarrow P_n x \\
&\textbf{for } q = 1{:}t \\
&\qquad L \leftarrow 2^q;\ r \leftarrow n/L;\ L_* \leftarrow L/2;\ r_* \leftarrow n/L_* \\
&\qquad y \leftarrow x \\
&\qquad \{Y(0{:}L_* - 1, 0{:}r_* - 1) \equiv y_{L_* \times r_*}\} \\
&\qquad \{X(0{:}L - 1, 0{:}r - 1) \equiv x_{L \times r}\} \\
&\qquad \textbf{for } j = 0{:}L_* - 1 \\
&\qquad\qquad \textbf{for } k = 0{:}r - 1 \\
&\qquad\qquad\qquad \tau \leftarrow \omega_L^j \cdot Y(j, 2k+1) \\
&\qquad\qquad\qquad X(j, k) \leftarrow Y(j, 2k) + \tau \\
&\qquad\qquad\qquad X(L_* + j, k) \leftarrow Y(j, 2k) - \tau \\
&\qquad\qquad \textbf{end} \\
&\qquad \textbf{end} \\
&\textbf{end}
\end{aligned}
$$

Following our derivation of the Stockham algorithm in §1.7.7, let us reverse the double subscripts. Rewriting the inner loops with this change gives

$$
\begin{aligned}
&\textbf{for } j = 0{:}L_* - 1 \\
&\qquad \textbf{for } k = 0{:}r - 1 \\
&\qquad\qquad \tau \leftarrow \omega_L^j \cdot Y(2k+1, j) \\
&\qquad\qquad X(k, j) \leftarrow Y(2k, j) + \tau \\
&\qquad\qquad X(k, L_* + j) \leftarrow Y(2k, j) - \tau \\
&\qquad \textbf{end} \\
&\textbf{end}
\end{aligned}
\qquad (1.8.1)
$$

Note that we now regard Y and X as arrays of size r_*-by-L_* and r-by-L, respectively. With these dimensions, array elements $X(\alpha, \beta)$ and $Y(\alpha, \beta)$ correspond to vector elements $x(\beta r + \alpha)$ and $y(\beta r_* + \alpha)$ and so we have

$$
\begin{aligned}
&\textbf{for } j = 0{:}L_* - 1 \\
&\qquad \textbf{for } k = 0{:}r - 1 \\
&\qquad\qquad \tau \leftarrow \omega_L^j \cdot y(jr_* + 2k + 1) \\
&\qquad\qquad x(jr + k) \leftarrow y(jr_* + 2k) + \tau \\
&\qquad\qquad x((L_* + j)r + k) \leftarrow y(jr_* + 2k) - \tau \\
&\qquad \textbf{end} \\
&\textbf{end}
\end{aligned}
\qquad (1.8.2)
$$

Noting that $L_*r = n/2$ and $r_* = 2r$, we obtain a simplified subscripting by introducing the index $\mu = jr + k$:

$$
\begin{aligned}
&\textbf{for } j = 0{:}L_* - 1 \\
&\quad \textbf{for } k = 0{:}r - 1 \\
&\qquad \mu \leftarrow jr + k \\
&\qquad \tau \leftarrow \omega_L^j \cdot y(2\mu + 1) \\
&\qquad x(\mu) \leftarrow y(2\mu) + \tau \\
&\qquad x(\mu + n/2) \leftarrow y(2\mu) - \tau \\
&\quad \textbf{end} \\
&\textbf{end}
\end{aligned}
\qquad (1.8.3)
$$

Notice that as the j-loop and k-loop run their course, μ ranges from 0 to $n/2-1$. The two loops can thus be replaced by a single μ-loop once we figure out how to express the assignment

$$
\tau \leftarrow \omega_L^j \cdot y(2\mu + 1)
$$

without reference to the index j. This can be done by setting up an array of weights $W_n^{(P)}(0{:}n/2 - 1, 1{:}t)$ with the property that the qth column of $W_n^{(P)}$ houses the vector of weights required by the qth pass of the algorithm so that (1.8.3) becomes

$$
\begin{aligned}
&\textbf{for } j = 0{:}L_* - 1 \\
&\quad \textbf{for } k = 0{:}r - 1 \\
&\qquad \mu \leftarrow jr + k \\
&\qquad \tau \leftarrow W_n^{(P)}(\mu, q) \cdot y(2\mu + 1) \\
&\qquad x(\mu) \leftarrow y(2\mu) + \tau \\
&\qquad x(\mu + n/2) \leftarrow y(2\mu) - \tau \\
&\quad \textbf{end} \\
&\textbf{end}
\end{aligned}
$$

It is not hard to show from (1.8.3) that $W_n^{(P)}$ is specified by

$$
\begin{aligned}
&\textbf{for } q = 1{:}t \\
&\quad L \leftarrow 2^q; \ r \leftarrow n/L; \ L_* \leftarrow L/2 \\
&\quad \textbf{for } j = 0{:}L_* - 1 \\
&\qquad \omega \leftarrow \cos(2\pi j/L) - i\sin(2\pi j/L) \\
&\qquad \textbf{for } k = 0{:}r - 1 \\
&\qquad\quad \mu \leftarrow jr + k \\
&\qquad\quad W_n^{(P)}(\mu, q) \leftarrow \omega \\
&\qquad \textbf{end} \\
&\quad \textbf{end} \\
&\textbf{end}
\end{aligned}
\qquad (1.8.4)
$$

Note that the columns of $W_n^{(P)}$ are indexed from one, not zero. Here is an example:

$$
W_{16}^{(P)} = \begin{bmatrix}
1 & 1 & 1 & 1 \\
1 & 1 & 1 & \omega_{16} \\
1 & 1 & \omega_8 & \omega_{16}^2 \\
1 & 1 & \omega_8 & \omega_{16}^3 \\
1 & \omega_4 & \omega_8^2 & \omega_{16}^4 \\
1 & \omega_4 & \omega_8^2 & \omega_{16}^5 \\
1 & \omega_4 & \omega_8^3 & \omega_{16}^6 \\
1 & \omega_4 & \omega_8^3 & \omega_{16}^7
\end{bmatrix}.
$$

Computational details associated with the Pease weight array may be found in Swarztrauber (1984b).

Returning to our development of the transposed Cooley–Tukey algorithm, we obtain the following algorithm due to Pease (1968).

Algorithm 1.8.1 If $x \in \mathbb{C}^n$, $n = 2^t$, and $W_n^{(P)}(0{:}n/2-1, 1{:}t)$ is initialized according
to (1.8.4), then the following algorithm overwrites x with $F_n x$:

$$
\begin{aligned}
&x \leftarrow P_n x \\
&m \leftarrow n/2 \\
&\text{for } q = 1{:}t \\
&\qquad y \leftarrow x \\
&\qquad u \leftarrow W_n^{(P)}(0{:}m-1, q) \,.{*}\, y(1{:}2{:}n-1) \\
&\qquad x(0{:}m-1) \leftarrow y(0{:}2{:}n-1) + u \\
&\qquad x(m{:}n-1) \leftarrow y(0{:}2{:}n-1) - u \\
&\text{end}
\end{aligned}
$$

The algorithm requires $5n \log_2 n$ flops. Note that y is accessed in stride-2 fashion and
that the u-vector is not necessary. If we apply the vector length analysis techniques
of §1.7.8, then we find that approximately

$$
T_{1.8.1} = \frac{5nt}{\ell}\alpha \,+\, 5nt\beta
$$

seconds are required for floating point vector operations, precisely what we determined
for the loop inversion method of §1.7.8. This assumes that $n \geq 2\ell$.

1.8.2   The Pease Factorization

As with the Cooley–Tukey and Stockham procedures, the Pease algorithm is based
upon a sparse factorization of the DFT matrix. We derive the factorization by making
some observations about the algorithm and $W_n^{(P)}$.

Lemma 1.8.1 *If $n = 2^t$ and $W_n^{(P)}(0{:}n/2-1, 1{:}t)$ is defined by (1.8.4), then for $q = 1{:}t$
we have*

$$
W_n^{(P)}(:, q) \,=\, \mathrm{diag}(D_q),
$$

where

$$
D_q = \Omega_{L_*} \otimes I_r, \qquad L_* = 2^{q-1}, \qquad r = 2^{t-q},
$$

with $\Omega_{L_*} = \mathrm{diag}(1, \omega_L, \ldots, \omega_L^{L_*-1})$ and $L = 2^q$.

Proof. Suppose $\mu = jr + k$, where $(j, k) \in \{0, \ldots, L_* - 1\} \times \{0, \ldots, r - 1\}$. It
follows from (1.8.4), that $W_n^{(P)}(\mu, q) = \omega_L^j$. But a brief calculation also shows that
$[\,\Omega_{L_*} \otimes I_r\,]_{\mu,\mu} = \omega_L^j$. $\square$

Theorem 1.8.2 (The Pease Factorization) *If $n = 2^t$, then*

$$
F_n P_n \,=\, H_t \cdots H_1,
$$

where

$$
H_q \,=\, (F_2 \otimes I_{n/2})\mathrm{diag}(I_{n/2}, \Omega_{L_*} \otimes I_r)\Pi_n^T,
$$

with $L = 2^q$, $r = n/L$, $L_* = L/2$, and $\Omega_{L_*} = \mathrm{diag}(1, \omega_L, \ldots, \omega_L^{L_*-1})$.

Proof. Recall that if $y \in \mathbb{C}^n$, then

$$\Pi_n^T y = \begin{bmatrix} y(0{:}2{:}n-1) \\ y(1{:}2{:}n-1) \end{bmatrix}.$$

It follows that in the qth step of Algorithm 1.8.1 we perform the computation

$$x \leftarrow \begin{bmatrix} I_{n/2} & D_q \\ I_{n/2} & -D_q \end{bmatrix} \begin{bmatrix} y(0{:}2{:}n-1) \\ y(1{:}2{:}n-1) \end{bmatrix} = (F_2 \otimes I_{n/2})\text{diag}(I_{n/2}, D_q)\Pi_n^T y,$$

where D_q is defined in Lemma 1.8.1. In other words, $x = H_q y$. Thus, Algorithm 1.8.1 has the form

$$x \leftarrow P_n x$$
$$\text{for } q = 1{:}t$$
$$\quad y \leftarrow x$$
$$\quad x \leftarrow H_q y$$
$$\text{end}$$

from which it follows that $F_n P_n = H_t \cdots H_1$. $\quad\square$

Problems

P1.8.1 Give an efficient algorithm for setting up the Pease weight matrix $W_n^{(P)}$. Pattern your solution after the techniques of §1.4.

P1.8.2 Give a double loop formulation of Algorithm 1.8.1.

Notes and References for Section 1.8

The original reference for the algorithm discussed in this section is

M.C. Pease (1968). "An Adaptation of the Fast Fourier Transform for Parallel Processing," *J. Assoc. Comput. Mach. 15*, 252–264.

Other matrix-based derivations of the Pease approach may be found in

D.J. Rose (1980). "Matrix Identities of the Fast Fourier Transform," *Linear Algebra Appl. 29*, 423–443.
H. Sloate (1974). "Matrix Representations for Sorting and the Fast Fourier Transform," *IEEE Trans. Circuits and Systems CAS-21*, 109–116.
C. Temperton (1983a). "Self-Sorting Mixed Radix Fast Fourier Transforms," *J. Comput. Phys. 52*, 1–23.
R. Tolimieri, M. An, and C. Lu (1989). *Algorithms for Discrete Fourier Transform and Convolution*, Springer-Verlag, NY.

The following papers provide additional insight into the vector properties of the algorithm:

B. Fornberg (1981). "A Vector Implementation of the Fast Fourier Transform," *Math. Comp. 36*, 189–191.
D.G. Korn and J.J. Lambiotte (1979). "Computing the Fast Fourier Transform on a Vector Computer," *Math. Comp. 33*, 977–992.
P.N. Swarztrauber (1982). "Vectorizing the FFTs," in *Parallel Computations*, G. Rodrigue (ed.), Academic Press, New York, 490–501.
P.N. Swarztrauber (1984b). "FFT Algorithms for Vector Computers," *Parallel Comput. 1*, 45–63.
C. Temperton (1984). "Fast Fourier Transforms on the Cyber 205," in *High Speed Computation*, J. Kowalik (ed.), Springer-Verlag, Berlin.

1.9   Decimation in Frequency and Inverse FFTs

In this section we obtain "dual" versions of the Cooley–Tukey, Pease, transposed Stockham, and Stockham procedures. This is accomplished by taking transposes of the corresponding factorizations and using the fact that F_n is symmetric. Thus, in the Cooley–Tukey case we obtain the new factorization $F_n = P_n A_1^T \cdots A_t^T$ by transposing $F_n = A_t \cdots A_1 P_n$. This maneuver gives rise to the algorithm of Gentleman and Sande (1966) and is an example of a decimation-in-frequency (DIF) FFT. The DIF versions of the Stockham, transposed Stockham, and Pease approaches bring the total number of basic radix-2 frameworks to eight. Of course, within each framework there are a host of implementation questions, such as how to order the inner loops, how to carry out (if at all) the bit-reversal permutation, and how we proceed (if at all) with weight precomputation. It should be clear that the designer of a production radix-2 FFT code is faced with a large number of possibilities. (The range options are even greater when we proceed to mixed-radix frameworks in the next chapter.)

Inverse FFT frameworks can also be derived through the manipulation of our DFT matrix factorizations. Since $F_n^{-1} = \bar{F}_n/n$, we can derive an inverse FFT by conjugating and scaling any of our DFT matrix factorizations. For example, in the Cooley–Tukey case,

$$F_n^{-1} = (1/n)\bar{F}_n = (1/n)\bar{A}_t \cdots \bar{A}_1 P_n.$$

At the code level, we merely replace each reference to ω_n with a reference to $\bar{\omega}_n$. A final scaling by $1/n$ produces the desired result.

In reading this section, take care to distinguish between the two different notions of transposition. The Pease framework is the transpose of the Cooley–Tukey framework in that the intermediate DFTs are stored by row, whereas the intermediate DFTs are stored by column in the Cooley–Tukey framework. On the other hand, the Gentleman–Sande framework is derived by taking the transpose of the Cooley–Tukey factorization.

1.9.1   Summary of the Four Factorizations

We start by summarizing the current situation. So far we have derived four different sparse factorizations of the DFT matrix when $n = 2^t$:

$$
\begin{aligned}
\text{Cooley–Tukey:} \qquad\qquad & F_n = A_t \cdots A_1 P_n, \\[2mm]
\text{Pease:} \qquad\qquad & F_n = H_t \cdots H_1 P_n, \\[2mm]
\text{Transposed Stockham :} \quad & F_n = S_t \cdots S_1, \\[2mm]
\text{Stockham:} \qquad\qquad & F_n = G_t \cdots G_1.
\end{aligned}
\qquad (1.9.1)
$$

Here P_n is the bit-reversal permutation and the factors are defined by

$$A_q = I_r \otimes B_L, \qquad\qquad\qquad L = 2^q, \ r = n/L,$$

$$H_q = \begin{bmatrix} I_{n/2} & (\Omega_{L_*} \otimes I_r) \\ I_{n/2} & -(\Omega_{L_*} \otimes I_r) \end{bmatrix} \Pi_n^T, \qquad L_* = L/2,$$

$$S_q = (I_r \otimes B_L)(\Pi_{r_*} \otimes I_{L_*}), \qquad\qquad r_* = 2r,$$

$$G_q = (B_L \otimes I_r)(\Pi_L^T \otimes I_r),$$

where the permutation Π is defined in §1.2 and

$$B_L \;=\; \begin{bmatrix} I_{L_*} & \Omega_{L_*} \\ I_{L_*} & -\Omega_{L_*} \end{bmatrix},$$

$$\Omega_{L_*} \;=\; \mathrm{diag}(1, \omega_L, \ldots, \omega_L^{L_*-1}),$$

$$\omega_L \;=\; \exp(-2\pi i/L).$$

Each of these factorizations gives rise to an algorithm in which the x-array houses the intermediate DFTs, either by row or by column and in either bit-reversed or natural order. Letting $x^{(q)}$ denote the status of the x-array after q steps, we have

$$
\begin{aligned}
\text{Cooley–Tukey:} && x^{(q)}_{L \times r} &= F_L x^T_{r \times L} P_r, \\[2mm]
\text{Pease:} && x^{(q)}_{r \times L} &= P_r x_{r \times L} F_L, \\[2mm]
\text{Transposed Stockham :} && x^{(q)}_{L \times r} &= F_L x^T_{r \times L}, \\[2mm]
\text{Stockham:} && x^{(q)}_{r \times L} &= x_{r \times L} F_L.
\end{aligned}
\tag{1.9.2}
$$

1.9.2 The Gentleman–Sande Idea

By taking the transpose of the Cooley–Tukey factorization $F_n = A_t \cdots A_1 P_n$, we obtain another sparse factorization of the DFT matrix:

$$F_n \;=\; P_n A_1^T \cdots A_t^T.$$

This is the foundation of an algorithm due to Gentleman and Sande (1966):

$$
\begin{aligned}
&\textbf{for } q = t: -1{:}1 \\
&\qquad x \leftarrow A_q^T x \\
&\textbf{end} \\
&x \leftarrow P_n x
\end{aligned}
\tag{1.9.3}
$$

Note the duality between this and Cooley–Tukey:

$$
\begin{aligned}
&x \leftarrow P_n x \\
&\textbf{for } q = 1{:}t \\
&\qquad x \leftarrow A_q x \\
&\textbf{end}
\end{aligned}
$$

Cooley–Tukey begins with bit reversal, whereas bit reversal comes after the butterfly computations in the Gentleman–Sande algorithm. In many important appplications such as convolution and the solution of the discrete Poisson equation, the exploitation of this duality permits the design of in-place FFT solutions that avoid bit reversal altogether. See §§4.1 and 4.5.

1.9.3   Gentleman–Sande Butterflies

Our next task is to work out the details of the Gentleman–Sande algorithm (1.9.3).
Consider the matrix-vector product $y = B_L^T z$, where $z \in \mathbb{C}^L$ and

$$B_L^T = \left[\begin{array}{cc} I_{L_*} & I_{L_*} \\ \Omega_{L_*} & -\Omega_{L_*} \end{array} \right]$$

is the transpose of the usual butterfly matrix. This operation is central to the computation

$$x \leftarrow A_q^T x = (I_r \otimes B_L^T)x$$

in (1.9.3). We take a moment to see how it can be implemented.

Designate the top and bottom halves of $y \in \mathbb{C}^L$ and $z \in \mathbb{C}^L$ by y_T, y_B, z_T, and
z_B, respectively. If $y = B_L^T z$, then

$$\left[\begin{array}{c} y_T \\ y_B \end{array} \right] = \left[\begin{array}{cc} I_{L_*} & I_{L_*} \\ \Omega_{L_*} & -\Omega_{L_*} \end{array} \right] \left[\begin{array}{c} z_T \\ z_B \end{array} \right] = \left[\begin{array}{c} z_T + z_B \\ \Omega_{L_*}(z_T - z_B) \end{array} \right],$$

where $L_* = L/2$. If a single loop is used to perform the top and bottom updates, then
we obtain

> **for** $j = 0:L_* - 1$
> $y(j) \leftarrow z(j) + z(j + L_*)$
> $y(j + L_*) \leftarrow \omega_L^j \cdot (z(j) - z(j + L_*))$
> **end**

If $y(j)$ and $y(j + L_*)$ are computed in reverse order, then it is possible to overwrite
the z vector with its butterfly update.

Algorithm 1.9.1   If $z \in \mathbb{C}^L$, $L = 2L_*$, and $w_{L_*} = [\,1, \omega_L, \dots, \omega_L^{L_*-1}\,]^T$, then the
following algorithm overwrites z with $B_L^T z$:

> **for** $j = 0:L_* - 1$
> $\tau \leftarrow z(j + L_*)$
> $z(j + L_*) \leftarrow w_{L_*}(j) \cdot (z(j) - \tau)$
> $z(j) \leftarrow z(j) + \tau$
> **end**

This algorithm requires $5L$ flops, exactly the same as Algorithm 1.4.7, the Cooley–
Tukey analog.

The update of $z(j)$ and $z(j + L_*)$ can be expressed in the form of a 2-by-2 matrix-
vector product:

$$\left[\begin{array}{c} z(j) \\ z(j + L_*) \end{array} \right] \longleftarrow \left[\begin{array}{cc} 1 & 1 \\ \omega_L^j & -\omega_L^j \end{array} \right] \left[\begin{array}{c} z(j) \\ z(j + L_*) \end{array} \right].$$

We refer to this as a *Gentleman–Sande butterfly*.

1.9.4 The Gentleman–Sande Algorithm

We now expand the computation (1.9.3), the high-level specification of the Gentleman–Sande procedure. Building upon Algorithm 1.9.1 and the direct call method of on-line weight computation, we obtain the following procedure.

Algorithm 1.9.2 If $x \in \mathbb{C}^n$ and $n = 2^t$, then the following algorithm overwrites x with $F_n x$:

$$
\begin{aligned}
&\textbf{for} \quad q = t: -1 : 1 \\
&\qquad L \leftarrow 2^q; \ r \leftarrow n/L; \ L_* \leftarrow L/2 \\
&\qquad \textbf{for} \ j = 0 : L_* - 1 \\
&\qquad\qquad \omega \leftarrow \cos(2\pi j/L) - i\sin(2\pi j/L) \\
&\qquad\qquad \textbf{for} \ k = 0 : r - 1 \\
&\qquad\qquad\qquad \tau \leftarrow x(kL + L_* + j) \\
&\qquad\qquad\qquad x(kL + j + L_*) \leftarrow \omega \cdot (x(kL + j) - \tau) \\
&\qquad\qquad\qquad x(kL + j) \leftarrow x(kL + j) + \tau \\
&\qquad\qquad \textbf{end} \\
&\qquad \textbf{end} \\
&\textbf{end} \\
&x \leftarrow P_n x \qquad \text{(Algorithm 1.5.2)}
\end{aligned}
$$

We have organized the computations so that an in-place procedure results. As with the Cooley–Tukey algorithm, $5n \log n$ flops are required. Unlike the Cooley–Tukey algorithm, we do not have an array of intermediate DFTs at the end of each pass through the outer loop. For example, if $n = 8$, then after one step we have computed the matrix-vector product

$$
\begin{bmatrix} 1 & 1 \\ \omega_8 & -\omega_8 \end{bmatrix} \begin{bmatrix} x_1 \\ x_5 \end{bmatrix},
$$

but this is not a 2-point DFT.

1.9.5 Decimation in Time and Frequency

The Cooley–Tukey and Gentleman–Sande algorithms are based upon two different splitting ideas which are important to identify.

The Cooley–Tukey, Pease, transposed Stockham, and Stockham algorithms that we developed in §§1.6–1.8 are examples of *decimation-in-time* FFTs. The terminology has a signal processing interpretation. If $n = 2m = 2^t$ and $y = F_n x$, then for $k = 0:n-1$ we have

$$
y_k = \sum_{j=0}^{n-1} \omega_n^{jk} x_j .
$$

A decimation-in-time FFT is derived by decimating (breaking apart) the time-dependent input vector x:

$$
\begin{aligned}
y_k &= \sum_{j=0}^{m-1} \omega_n^{2jk} x_{2j} + \sum_{j=0}^{m-1} \omega_n^{(2j+1)k} x_{2j+1} \\
&= \sum_{j=0}^{m-1} \omega_m^{jk} x_{2j} + \omega_n^k \sum_{j=0}^{m-1} \omega_m^{jk} x_{2j+1} .
\end{aligned}
$$

This is just a scalar statement of our familiar radix-2 splitting. The subvectors $x(0{:}2{:}n-1)$ and $x(1{:}2{:}n-1)$ correspond to reduced sampling rates of the underlying signal.

The Gentleman–Sande algorithm is an example of a *decimation-in-frequency* (DIF) FFT. Here the decimation is of the frequency-dependent vector y, again into even- and odd-indexed components:

$$
\begin{aligned}
y_{2k} &= \sum_{j=0}^{n-1} \omega_n^{j(2k)} x_j \;=\; \sum_{j=0}^{n-1} \omega_m^{jk} x_j \\
&= \sum_{j=0}^{m-1} (\omega_m^{jk} x_j + \omega_m^{(m+j)k} x_{m+j}) \;=\; \sum_{j=0}^{m-1} \omega_m^{jk}(x_j + x_{m+j}),
\end{aligned}
$$

$$
\begin{aligned}
y_{2k+1} &= \sum_{j=0}^{n-1} \omega_n^{j(2k+1)} x_j \;=\; \sum_{j=0}^{n-1} \omega_m^{jk} \omega_n^{j} x_j \\
&= \sum_{j=0}^{m-1} (\omega_m^{jk} \omega_n^{j} x_j + \omega_m^{(m+j)k} \omega_n^{m+j} x_{m+j}) \;=\; \sum_{j=0}^{m-1} \omega_m^{jk} \omega_n^{j}(x_j - x_{m+j}) \,.
\end{aligned}
$$

For further discussion of the "decimination" terminology, we refer the reader to Cochrane *et al.* (1967).

1.9.6   The Decimation-in-Frequency Frameworks

By transposing the four decimation-in-time (DIT) factorizations (1.9.1), we obtain the following four decimation-in-frequency (DIF) factorizations:

$$
\begin{aligned}
\text{(DIF)-Cooley–Tukey:} && F_n &= P_n A_1^T \cdots A_t^T, \\[4pt]
\text{(DIF)-Pease:} && F_n &= P_n H_1^T \cdots H_t^T, \\[4pt]
\text{(DIF)-Transposed Stockham:}\quad && F_n &= S_1^T \cdots S_t^T, \\[4pt]
\text{(DIF)-Stockham:} && F_n &= G_1^T \cdots G_t^T.
\end{aligned}
$$

Corresponding to each of these sparse factorizations is an FFT framework. We have already pursued this in the (DIF)-Cooley–Tukey case. We leave it to the reader to fill in the details for the (DIF)-Pease,

$$
\begin{aligned}
&\textbf{for } q = t:-1{:}1 \\
&\qquad L \leftarrow 2^q;\; r \leftarrow n/L;\; L_* \leftarrow L/2 \\[6pt]
&\qquad x \leftarrow \Pi_n
\begin{bmatrix}
I_{n/2} & I_{n/2} \\[8pt]
(\Omega_{L_*} \otimes I_r) & -(\Omega_{L_*} \otimes I_r)
\end{bmatrix} x \\
&\textbf{end} \\
&x \leftarrow P_n x
\end{aligned}
\tag{1.9.4}
$$

the (DIF)-transposed Stockham,

$$\textbf{for } q = t: -1:1$$
$$L \leftarrow 2^q; \; r \leftarrow n/L; \; L_* \leftarrow L/2; \; r_* \leftarrow 2r$$
$$x \leftarrow (\Pi^T_{r_*} \otimes I_{L_*})(I_r \otimes B^T_L)x \qquad (1.9.5)$$
$$\textbf{end}$$

and the (DIF)-Stockham,

$$\textbf{for } q = t: -1:1$$
$$L \leftarrow 2^q; \; r \leftarrow n/L; \; L_* \leftarrow L/2$$
$$x \leftarrow (\Pi^T_L \otimes I_r)(B^T_L \otimes I_r)x \qquad (1.9.6)$$
$$\textbf{end}$$

frameworks. Clearly, the refinement of these high-level specifications requires the incorporation of familiar perfect-shuffle operations and Gentleman–Sande butterfly manipulations à la Algorithm 1.9.1.

1.9.7 Inverse Transforms

From Theorem 1.1.2 we know that the transformation

$$x \longrightarrow \frac{1}{n}\bar{F}_n x$$

is the inverse of the map $x \longrightarrow F_n x$, and thus it is referred to as the *inverse discrete Fourier transform* (IDFT). IDFTs can also be computed with $O(n \log_2 n)$ work. Consider the Cooley–Tukey case where we have the sparse factorization

$$F_n P_n = A_t \cdots A_1.$$

Taking complex conjugates, it follows that $\bar{F}_n P_n = \bar{A}_t \cdots \bar{A}_1$ and so

$$F_n^{-1} = (1/n)\bar{A}_t \cdots \bar{A}_1 P_n.$$

Thus, we can overwrite x with its IDFT as follows:

$$x \leftarrow P_n x$$
$$\textbf{for } q = 1:t$$
$$x \leftarrow \bar{A}_q x$$
$$\textbf{end}$$
$$x \leftarrow x/n$$

Let us look carefully at the operation $x \leftarrow \bar{A}_q x$. From the definition of A_q we see that

$$\bar{A}_q = I_r \otimes \bar{B}_L,$$

where

$$\bar{B}_L = \begin{bmatrix} I_{L_*} & \bar{\Omega}_{L_*} \\ I_{L_*} & -\bar{\Omega}_{L_*} \end{bmatrix}$$

and

$$\bar{\Omega}_{L_*} = \text{diag}(1, \bar{\omega}_L, \ldots, \bar{\omega}_L^{L_*-1}).$$

Thus, corresponding to each FFT there is an inverse FFT obtained by replacing each reference to $\omega_L = \exp(-2\pi i/L)$ with a reference to $\bar{\omega}_L = \exp(2\pi i/L)$. It is therefore easy to design a general procedure that handles either forward or inverse DFTs.

Algorithm 1.9.3 If $x \in \mathbb{C}^n$ with $n = 2^t$ and *flag* $= -1$ or 1, then the following algorithm overwrites x with $F_n x$ if *flag* $= 1$ and with $\overline{F}_n^{-1} x/n$ if *flag* $= -1$.

$$x \leftarrow P_n x$$
$$\textbf{for } q = 1{:}t$$
$$\qquad L \leftarrow 2^q; \ r \leftarrow n/L; \ L_* \leftarrow L/2$$
$$\qquad \textbf{for } j = 0{:}L_* - 1$$
$$\qquad\qquad \omega \leftarrow \cos(2\pi j/L) - i \cdot \textit{flag} \cdot \sin(2\pi j/L)$$
$$\qquad\qquad \textbf{for } k = 0{:}r - 1$$
$$\qquad\qquad\qquad \tau \leftarrow \omega \cdot x(kL + j + L_*)$$
$$\qquad\qquad\qquad x(kL + j + L_*) \leftarrow x(kL + j) - \tau$$
$$\qquad\qquad\qquad x(kL + j) \leftarrow x(kL + j) + \tau$$
$$\qquad\qquad \textbf{end}$$
$$\qquad \textbf{end}$$
$$\textbf{end}$$
$$\textbf{if } \textit{flag} = \text{-1}$$
$$\qquad x \leftarrow x/n$$
$$\textbf{end}$$

1.9.8   Signal Flow Graphs

The DIT and DIF FFTs rely on different butterflies. In the DIT case we have

$$\begin{bmatrix} a \\ b \end{bmatrix} \leftarrow \begin{bmatrix} 1 & \omega \\ 1 & -\omega \end{bmatrix} \begin{bmatrix} a \\ b \end{bmatrix},$$

which may be depicted as follows:

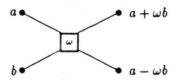

FIG. 1.9.1. *The Cooley-Tukey butterfly.*

Readers with imagination may now see the origin of the term "butterfly"!
    In the DIF case the butterflies have the form

$$\begin{bmatrix} a \\ b \end{bmatrix} \leftarrow \begin{bmatrix} 1 & 1 \\ \omega & -\omega \end{bmatrix} \begin{bmatrix} a \\ b \end{bmatrix}$$

and the corresponding schematic:

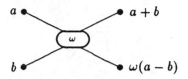

FIG. 1.9.2. *The Gentleman–Sande butterfly.*

Using these schematics, we can obtain a good picture of data flow during execution of either a DIT or DIF algorithm. Consider the $n = 8$ execution of the Cooley–Tukey procedure. Assume that x has been overwritten by $P_8 x$. Using the butterfly schemata of Fig. 1.9.1 we depict as follows the four 2-point DFTs that initiate the computation:

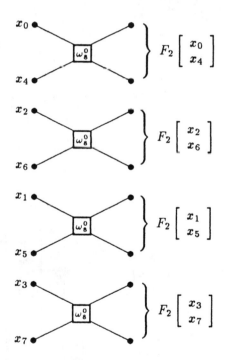

FIG. 1.9.3. *Cooley–Tukey framework: (stage 1, $n = 8$).*

At the next stage ($q = 2$), there are two 4-point DFTs to generate. The x-array is again updated with four butterflies, two for each DFT, as depicted in Fig. 1.9.4. The final 8-point DFT can then be found as shown in Fig. 1.9.5. Again, four overwriting butterflies are required.

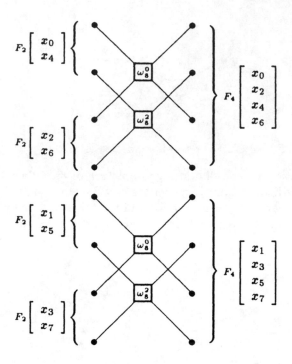

FIG. 1.9.4. *Cooley–Tukey framework*: (*stage 2, n = 8*).

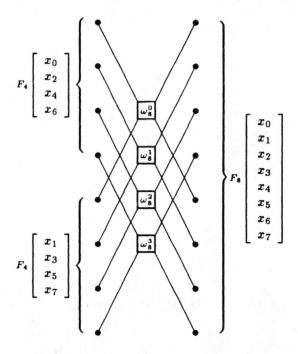

FIG. 1.9.5.   *Cooley–Tukey framework*: (*stage 3, n = 8*).

To acquire a perspective of the overall flow of data, we conjoin the graphs associated with the three stages, streamline the notation, and obtain the complete *signal flow graph* as depicted in Fig. 1.9.6. The corresponding $n = 8$ signal flow graph for the Gentleman–Sande algorithm is given in Fig. 1.9.7. Notice that its shape is a reflection of the Cooley–Tukey signal flow graph.

The signal flow graph method of visualizing the intermingling of the data during the butterfly computations is used by many authors, e.g., Brigham (1974).

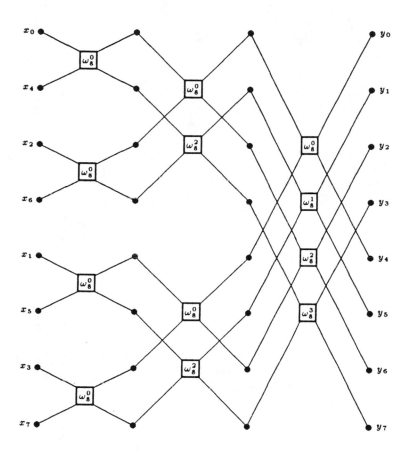

FIG. 1.9.6. *Cooley–Tukey signal flow graph: ($n = 8$).*

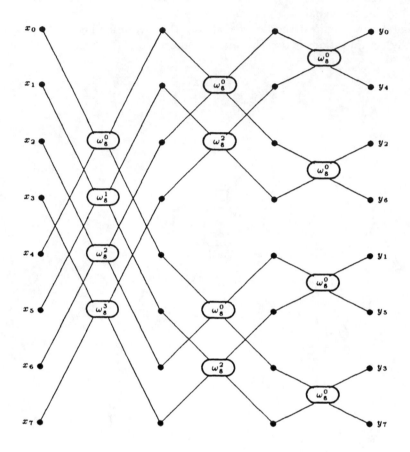

FIG. 1.9.7. *The Gentleman–Sande signal flow graph:* $(n = 8)$.

Problems

P1.9.1 Develop a unit stride (DIF)-transposed Stockham procedure.

P1.9.2 Develop a unit stride (DIF)-Stockham procedure.

P1.9.3 Develop a unit stride (DIF)-Pease procedure.

Notes and References for Section 1.9

The original formulation of the decimation-in-frequency framework is given in

W.M. Gentleman and G. Sande (1966). "Fast Fourier Transforms for Fun and Profit," *Proc. 1966 Fall Joint Computer Conference AFIPS 29*, 563–578.

Interconnections between the various frameworks are usefully discussed in

P.N. Swarztrauber (1984b). "FFT Algorithms for Vector Computers," *Parallel Comput. 1*, 45–63.

C. Temperton (1983a). "Self-Sorting Mixed Radix Fast Fourier Transforms," *J. Comput. Phys. 52*, 1–23.

The derivation of the DIF algorithms via the transposition of factorizations appears in

H. Sloate (1974). "Matrix Representations for Sorting and the Fast Fourier Transform," *IEEE Trans. Circuits and Systems CAS-21*, 109–116.

Other derivation strategies appear in

S. Bertram (1970). "On the Derivation of the Fast Fourier Transform," *IEEE Trans. Audio and Electroacoustics AU-18*, 55–58.

P.N. Swarztrauber (1982). "Vectorizing the FFTs," in *Parallel Computations*, G. Rodrigue (ed.), Academic Press, New York, 490–501.

For a complete roundoff analysis of both DIT or DIF radix-2 FFTs see

C. Chu (1988). *The Fast Fourier Transform on Hypercube Parallel Computers*, Ph.D. Thesis, Center for Applied Mathematics, Cornell University, Ithaca, NY.

The idea of decimation-in-frequency from the signal processing point of view is given in

W.T. Cochrane, J.W. Cooley, J.W. Favin, D.L. Helms, R.A. Kaenel, W.W. Lang, G.C. Maling, D.E. Nelson, C.M. Rader, and P.D. Welch (1967). "What Is the Fast Fourier Transform?," *IEEE Trans. Audio Electroacoustics AU-15*, 45–55.

The art of choosing the proper framework is discussed in Swarztrauber (1982) and

C.S. Burrus (1983). "Comments on Selection Criteria for Efficient Implementation of FFT Algorithms," *IEEE Trans. Acoust. Speech Signal Process. ASSP-31*, 206.

H.F. Silverman (1978). "How to Select an Algorithm for the Calculation of the Discrete Fourier Transform," *Proc. 1978 IEEE Int. Symp. Circuits Systems*, 1083–1084.

A discussion of the two different decimation strategies may be found in either of the following two classic signal processing textbooks:

L.R. Rabiner and B. Gold (1975). *Theory and Application of Digital Signal Processing*, Prentice-Hall, Englewood Cliffs, NJ.

A.V. Oppenheimer and R.W. Schafer (1975). *Digital Signal Processing*, Prentice–Hall, Englewood Cliffs, NJ.

Chapter 2

General Radix Frameworks

The frameworks of Chapter 1 revolve around the efficient synthesis of an even-order DFT from two half-length DFTs. However, if n is not a power of two, then the radix-2 divide-and-conquer process breaks down. The mission of this section is to show that it is possible to formulate FFT frameworks for general n, as long as n is highly composite. In some important cases, the resulting algorithms involve fewer flops and better memory traffic patterns than their radix-2 counterparts.

The first three sections cover the underlying mathematics and generalize the factorization notions developed in Chapter 1. As a case study, we detail the central calculations associated with radix-4 and radix-8 frameworks in §2.4. We conclude in §2.5 with a discussion of the split-radix algorithm, an interesting reduced-arithmetic rearrangement of the radix-2 Cooley–Tukey algorithm.

2.1   General Radix Ideas

Suppose $n = pm$ with $1 < p < n$. The primary purpose of this section is to express F_n as a function of the two smaller DFT matrices F_p and F_m. The key result is the *radix-p splitting*:

$$F_n \Pi_{p,n} = (F_p \otimes I_m)\mathrm{diag}(I_m, \Omega_{p,m}, \ldots, \Omega_{p,m}^{p-1})(I_p \otimes F_m) .$$

Here, $\Pi_{p,n}$ is a generalization of the perfect shuffle permutation Π_n and

$$\Omega_{p,m} = \mathrm{diag}(1, \omega_n, \ldots, \omega_n^{m-1}) .$$

If $p = 2$, then $\Omega_{p,m} = \Omega_m = \mathrm{diag}(1, \omega_n, \ldots, \omega_n^{(n/2)-1})$, the radix-2 scaling matrix of Chapter 1.

The radix-p splitting can be anticipated at the scalar level by relating the roots of unity that define F_n, F_p, and F_m, i.e., ω_n, $\omega_p = \omega_n^m$, and $\omega_m = \omega_n^p$. Since the (k, j) entry of F_n is given by ω_n^{kj}, we see that if

$$
\begin{aligned}
k &= \alpha_1 m + \alpha_2, & 0 \le \alpha_1 < p, \quad 0 \le \alpha_2 < m, \\
j &= \beta_1 p + \beta_2, & 0 \le \beta_1 < m, \quad 0 \le \beta_2 < p,
\end{aligned}
$$

then

$$
\omega_n^{kj} = \omega_n^{(\alpha_1 m + \alpha_2)(\beta_1 p + \beta_2)} = \omega_p^{\alpha_1 \beta_2} \omega_n^{\alpha_2 \beta_2} \omega_m^{\alpha_2 \beta_1} .
$$

This says that $[F_n]_{kj}$ is a product of $[F_p]_{\alpha_1 \beta_2}$, some entry in the diagonal matrix $\mathrm{diag}(I_m, \Omega_{p,m}, \ldots, \Omega_{p,m}^{p-1})$, and $[F_m]_{\alpha_2 \beta_1}$. This three-factor scalar product corresponds to the three-factor matrix product that defines the radix-p splitting of F_n.

In this opening section of the chapter we define the permutation $\Pi_{p,n}$, examine its properties, and proceed to prove the radix-p splitting. A general FFT framework based on this splitting is informally derived and expressed in recursive form.

2.1.1 The Mod p Sort Permutation

In order to establish the radix-p splitting, we need a generalization of the even-odd sort mapping $x \to \Pi_n^T x$ of Chapter 1. If $n = pm$ and $x \in \mathbb{C}^n$, then we define the *mod p sort permutation* $\Pi_{p,n}^T$ as follows:

$$
\Pi_{p,n}^T x = \begin{bmatrix} x(0{:}p{:}n-1) \\ x(1{:}p{:}n-1) \\ \vdots \\ x(p-1{:}p{:}n-1) \end{bmatrix} . \tag{2.1.1}
$$

Here is an example with $n = 15 = 3 \cdot 5 \equiv p \cdot m$:

$$
\Pi_{3,15}^T x = \begin{bmatrix} x_0 \ x_3 \ x_6 \ x_9 \ x_{12} \mid x_1 \ x_4 \ x_7 \ x_{10} \ x_{13} \mid x_2 \ x_5 \ x_8 \ x_{11} \ x_{14} \end{bmatrix}^T .
$$

It is clear that $\Pi_{p,n}^T$ sorts the components of x according to the mod p value of the indices. Thus, all of the components with indices equal to 0 mod p come first, followed by all of the components with indices equal to 1 mod p, etc. A more concise way to describe the action of $\Pi_{p,n}^T$ is in terms of arrays.

Lemma 2.1.1 *Suppose $n = pm$ and that $x, y \in \mathbb{C}^n$. If $y = \Pi_{p,n}^T x$, then*

$$
y_{m \times p} = x_{p \times m}^T . \tag{2.1.2}
$$

In other words, $y_{\beta m + \alpha} = x_{\alpha p + \beta}$ for all $0 \le \alpha < m$ and $0 \le \beta < p$. Thus, if we make the identifications $x_{p \times m} \equiv X(0{:}p-1, 0{:}m-1)$ and $y_{m \times p} \equiv Y(0{:}m-1, 0{:}p-1)$, then $X(\beta, \alpha) = Y(\alpha, \beta)$.

Proof. If $y = \Pi_{p,n}^T x$, then from definition (2.1.1) we have

$$
y_{m \times p} = \begin{bmatrix} x(0{:}p{:}n-1) \mid x(1{:}p{:}n-1) \mid \cdots \mid x(p-1{:}p{:}n-1) \end{bmatrix} = x_{p \times m}^T .
$$

Since $y_{\beta m + \alpha} = [y_{m \times p}]_{\alpha, \beta} = [x_{p \times m}]_{\beta, \alpha} = x_{\beta + \alpha p}$, we see that the remaining portion of the lemma is established. $\square$

Here is an illustration of the lemma:

$$[\Pi_{3,15}^T x]_{5\times 3} = \begin{bmatrix} x_0 & x_1 & x_2 \\ x_3 & x_4 & x_5 \\ x_6 & x_7 & x_8 \\ x_9 & x_{10} & x_{11} \\ x_{12} & x_{13} & x_{14} \end{bmatrix} = x_{3\times 5}^T .$$

Observe that if $n = 2m$, then $\Pi_{2,n} = \Pi_n$, the even-odd sort permutation that figures so heavily in the first chapter.

2.1.2   The Mod p Perfect Shuffle

The inverse of the mod p sort permutation is the *mod p perfect shuffle* $\Pi_{p,n}$. Since $\Pi_{p,n}^T x$ transposes x as a p-by-m array, $\Pi_{p,m} x$ must transpose x as an m-by-p array.

Lemma 2.1.2 *Suppose $n = pm$ and that $x, y \in \mathbb{C}^n$. If $y = \Pi_{p,n} x$, then*

$$y_{p\times m} = x_{m\times p}^T . \tag{2.1.3}$$

In other words $y_{\beta p + \alpha} = x_{\alpha m + \beta}$ for all $0 \le \alpha < p$ and $0 \le \beta < m$. Thus, if we make the identifications $x_{m\times p} \equiv X(0{:}m-1, 0{:}p-1)$ and $y_{p\times m} \equiv Y(0{:}p-1, 0{:}m-1)$, then $X(\beta, \alpha) = Y(\alpha, \beta)$.

Proof. The proof is very similar to the proof of Lemma 2.1.1 and is left as an exercise for the reader.

In block-vector notation it is easy to show that

$$\Pi_{p,n} x = \begin{bmatrix} x(0{:}m{:}n-1) \\ x(1{:}m{:}n-1) \\ \vdots \\ x(m-1{:}m{:}n-1) \end{bmatrix} . \tag{2.1.4}$$

In the $n = 15 = 3 \cdot 5 \equiv p \cdot m$ case we have

$$\Pi_{3,15} x = [\, x_0\ x_5\ x_{10} \mid x_1\ x_6\ x_{11} \mid x_2\ x_7\ x_{12} \mid x_3\ x_8\ x_{13} \mid x_4\ x_9\ x_{14} \,]^T$$

and conclude that $\Pi_{p,n}$ "works" by dividing x into p parts and then shuffling the components. For example,

$$[\Pi_{3,15} x]_{3\times 5} = \begin{bmatrix} x_0 & x_1 & x_2 & x_3 & x_4 \\ x_5 & x_6 & x_7 & x_8 & x_9 \\ x_{10} & x_{11} & x_{12} & x_{13} & x_{14} \end{bmatrix} = x_{5\times 3}^T .$$

2.1.3   The Radix-p Splitting

We are now set to establish the important radix-p splitting.

Theorem 2.1.3 *If $n = pm$, then*

$$F_n \Pi_{p,n} = (F_p \otimes I_m)\mathrm{diag}(I_m, \Omega_{p,m}, \ldots, \Omega_{p,m}^{p-1})(I_p \otimes F_m), \tag{2.1.5}$$

where

$$\Omega_{p,m} = \mathrm{diag}(1, \omega_n, \ldots, \omega_n^{m-1}),$$

with $\omega_n = \exp(-2\pi i/n)$.

Proof. Since postmultiplication by $\Pi_{p,n}$ sorts columns mod p, we have

$$F_n\Pi_{p,n} = [\, F_n(:,0{:}p{:}n-1)\,|\,F_n(:,1{:}p{:}n-1)\,|\,\cdots\,|\,F_n(:,p-1{:}p{:}n-1)\,]\,.$$

Regard $F_n\Pi_{p,n}$ as a p-by-p block matrix with m-by-m blocks:

$$F_n\Pi_{p,n} = (G_{qr}), \qquad G_{qr}\in\mathbb{C}^{m\times m},\ 0\le q,r<p\,.$$

It follows that $G_{qr} = F_n(qm{:}(q+1)m-1, r{:}p{:}n-1)$ and thus,

$$[G_{qr}]_{kj} = \omega_n^{(qm+k)(r+jp)} = \omega_p^{qr}\omega_n^{kr}\omega_m^{kj}\,.$$

Here we have used the identities $\omega_n^{mqr}=\omega_p^{qr}$, $\omega_n^{pkj}=\omega_m^{kj}$, and $\omega_n^{qmjp}=(\omega_n^n)^{qj}=1$. Looking at the corresponding block structure on the right-hand side of (2.1.5) leads us to the conclusion that if

$$(F_p\otimes I_m)\mathrm{diag}(I_m,\Omega_{p,m},\ldots,\Omega_{p,m}^{p-1})(I_p\otimes F_m) = (H_{qr}), \qquad H_{qr}\in\mathbb{C}^{m\times m},$$

then $H_{qr}=\omega_p^{qr}\Omega_{p,m}^r F_m$. Since

$$[H_{qr}]_{kj} = \omega_p^{qr}\,[\Omega_{p,m}^r]_{kk}\,[F_m]_{kj} = \omega_p^{qr}\omega_n^{kr}\omega_m^{kj} = [G_{qr}]_{kj}$$

holds for all k and j, the theorem follows. $\square$

The radix-p splitting is a generalization of Theorem 1.2.1, the radix-2 splitting. Indeed, if we set $p=2$ in Theorem 2.1.3, then

$$F_n\Pi_n = (F_2\otimes I_{n/2})\mathrm{diag}(I_{n/2},\Omega_{n/2})(I_2\otimes F_{n/2})\,.$$

The matrix

$$(F_2\otimes I_{n/2})\mathrm{diag}(I_{n/2},\Omega_{n/2}) = \begin{bmatrix} I_{n/2} & \Omega_{n/2} \\ I_{n/2} & -\Omega_{n/2} \end{bmatrix}$$

is just a Kronecker description of the radix-2 butterfly. In Chapter 1, we proceeded quite nicely without this Kronecker characterization, but the added complexity of the *radix-p butterfly*

$$B_{p,n} = (F_p\otimes I_m)\mathrm{diag}(I_m,\Omega_{p,m},\ldots,\Omega_{p,m}^{p-1}) \qquad (2.1.6)$$

requires the added power of the notation.

The radix-p splitting can be used to obtain an n-point DFT by gluing together p DFTs of length $m=n/p$.

Corollary 2.1.4 *If $n=pm$ and $x\in\mathbb{C}^n$, then*

$$F_nx = B_{p,n}\begin{bmatrix} F_mx(0{:}p{:}n-1) \\ F_mx(1{:}p{:}n-1) \\ \vdots \\ F_mx(p-1{:}p{:}n-1) \end{bmatrix}. \qquad (2.1.7)$$

Proof. Apply both sides of (2.1.5) to $\Pi_{p,n}^T x$ and use the definition of $B_{p,n}$. $\square$

The Cooley-Tukey, transposed Stockham, Pease, and Stockham frameworks manipulate arrays of intermediate DFTs. To simplify the derivation of the underlying factorizations in §2.3, it is handy to have the following "array version" of Corollary 2.1.4.

Corollary 2.1.5 *Suppose* $n = L_* pr$ *and that* $x \in \mathbb{C}^n$. *If*

$$F_{L_*} x_{r_* \times L_*}^T = \left[\ C_0 \ | \ \cdots \ | \ C_{p-1} \ \right],$$

$C_j \in \mathbb{C}^{L_* \times r_*}$, *and* $L = pL_*$, *then*

$$F_L x_{r \times L}^T = B_{p,L} \begin{bmatrix} C_0 \\ \vdots \\ C_{p-1} \end{bmatrix}. \qquad (2.1.8)$$

Proof. By using the radix-p splitting we find that the kth column on the left-hand side of (2.1.8) is given by

$$F_L x(k{:}r{:}n-1) = B_{p,L}(I_p \otimes F_{L_*})\Pi_{p,L}^T x(k{:}r{:}n-1)$$

$$= B_{p,L} \begin{bmatrix} F_{L_*} x(k{:}r_*{:}n-1) \\ F_{L_*} x(k+r{:}r_*{:}n-1) \\ \vdots \\ F_{L_*} x(k+(p-1)r{:}r_*{:}n-1) \end{bmatrix}.$$

But since

$$F_{L_*} x(k+jr{:}r_*{:}n-1) = C_j(:,k),$$

it follows that

$$F_L x(k{:}r{:}n-1) = B_{p,L} \begin{bmatrix} C_0(:,k) \\ C_1(:,k) \\ \vdots \\ C_{p-1}(:,k) \end{bmatrix}.$$

Since this result holds for $k = 0{:}r-1$, equation (2.1.8) follows. $\square$

2.1.4 General Radix Framework

The repeated application of the radix-p splitting is the basis of the general radix framework. Consider the case $n = 96$. Using (2.1.7), $F_{96}x$ can be expressed in terms of $p = 2, 3, 4, 6, 8, 12, 16, 24, 32,$ or 48 smaller DFTs. If we set $p = 4$, then the top level synthesis has the form

$$F_{96}x \longleftarrow \begin{cases} F_{24}x(0{:}4{:}95) \\ F_{24}x(1{:}4{:}95) \\ F_{24}x(2{:}4{:}95) \\ F_{24}x(3{:}4{:}95) \end{cases}.$$

Each of the 24-point DFTs can be split in several ways, e.g., 2×12, 3×8, 4×6, 6×4, 8×3, or 12×2. We could, for example, build $F_{96}x$ as follows:

$$
F_{96}x \longleftarrow \left\{
\begin{array}{l}
F_{24}x(0\!:\!4\!:\!95) \longleftarrow \left\{
\begin{array}{l}
F_{12}x(0\!:\!8\!:\!95) \\
F_{12}x(4\!:\!8\!:\!95)
\end{array}
\right. \\[2ex]
F_{24}x(1\!:\!4\!:\!95) \longleftarrow \left\{
\begin{array}{l}
F_{8}x(1\!:\!12\!:\!95) \\
F_{8}x(5\!:\!12\!:\!95) \\
F_{8}x(9\!:\!12\!:\!95)
\end{array}
\right. \\[3ex]
F_{24}x(2\!:\!4\!:\!95) \longleftarrow \left\{
\begin{array}{l}
F_{6}x(2\!:\!16\!:\!95) \\
F_{6}x(6\!:\!16\!:\!95) \\
F_{6}x(10\!:\!16\!:\!95) \\
F_{6}x(14\!:\!16\!:\!95)
\end{array}
\right. \\[4ex]
F_{24}x(3\!:\!4\!:\!95) \longleftarrow \left\{
\begin{array}{l}
F_{4}x(3\!:\!24\!:\!95) \\
F_{4}x(7\!:\!24\!:\!95) \\
F_{4}x(11\!:\!24\!:\!95) \\
F_{4}x(15\!:\!24\!:\!95) \\
F_{4}x(19\!:\!24\!:\!95) \\
F_{4}x(23\!:\!24\!:\!95)
\end{array}
\right.
\end{array}
\right.
$$

Of course, the DFTs of length 12, 8, 6, and 4 can be further split. However, the essentials of the divide-and-conquer process have been demonstrated and we are sufficiently prepared to give the following recursive specification of the general radix framework:

> **function** $y =\mathbf{genfft}(x, n)$
> $\omega \leftarrow \exp(-2\pi i/n)$
>   **if** n is prime
> $y \leftarrow F_n x$.
>   **else**
>   Pick a nontrivial divisor p of n.
> $m \leftarrow n/p$
> $\Omega \leftarrow \mathrm{diag}(1, \omega, \omega^2, \ldots, \omega^{m-1})$
> $\{z \leftarrow \mathrm{diag}(I_m, \Omega, \ldots, \Omega^{p-1})(I_p \otimes F_m)\Pi_{p,n}^T x\}$
>   **for** $j = 0\!:\!p-1$
> $z(jm\!:\!(j+1)m-1) \leftarrow \Omega^j\, \mathbf{genfft}(x(j\!:\!p\!:\!n-1), m)$
>   **end**
> $\{y \leftarrow (F_p \otimes I_m)z \Leftrightarrow y_{m \times p} \leftarrow z_{m \times p}F_p\}$
>   **for** $j = 0\!:\!m-1$
> $y(j\!:\!m\!:\!n-1) \leftarrow \mathbf{genfft}(z(j\!:\!m\!:\!n-1), p)$
>   **end**
>   **end**
> **end**

The second j loop in **genfft** oversees the *multiple DFT* problem $y_{m \times p} \leftarrow z_{m \times p}F_p$. In multiple DFT problems we are called upon to compute the DFT of several vectors at once, a topic of considerable importance that is covered in §3.1.

There is an important ambiguity in **genfft**; it concerns the factorization of the "current" n. For highly composite n there are clearly many ways that this can be done. The split-radix framework of §2.5 is an example where different splitting rules are applied across each level in the computation tree.

If the same splitting rules are used at each level in **genfft**, then a *mixed-radix* framework results. That is, if the "current n" in **genfft** is factored the same way across any level of the associated computation tree, then a mixed-radix FFT results. An example is given in Fig. 2.1.1. In that schematic we have indicated the lengths of

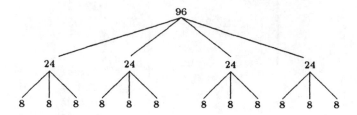

FIG. 2.1.1. *A mixed-radix framework* $(p_1, p_2, p_3) = (8, 3, 4)$.

the DFTs at each node. The computation begins with twelve 8-point DFTs. These DFTs are grouped in threes and combined via Corollary 2.1.4 to give four 24-point DFTs. These are in turn synthesized to produce the required 96-point DFT. Mixed-radix frameworks are pursued in §§2.3 and 2.4. A mixed-radix framework in which $p_1 = \cdots = p_t = p$ is referred to as a *radix-p* framework.

2.1.5   An Array Interpretation

It is instructive to characterize the action of the radix-p butterfly in array terms.

Theorem 2.1.6 *If $n = pm$ and $x \in \mathbb{C}^n$, then*

$$[F_n x]_{m \times p} = \left[F_n(0{:}m - 1, 0{:}p - 1) \,.* (F_m x_{p \times m}^T) \right] F_p . \qquad (2.1.9)$$

Proof. From Theorem 2.1.3 and Kron6 we have

$$
\begin{aligned}
[F_n x]_{m \times p} &= \left[(F_p \otimes I_m) \mathrm{diag}(I_m, \Omega_{p,m}, \ldots, \Omega_{p,m}^{p-1})(I_p \otimes F_m) \Pi_{p,n}^T x \right]_{m \times p} \\
&= \left[\mathrm{diag}(I_m, \Omega_{p,m}, \ldots, \Omega_{p,m}^{p-1})(I_p \otimes F_m) \Pi_{p,n}^T x \right]_{m \times p} F_p .
\end{aligned}
$$

It is easy to show that the diagonal of $\Omega_{p,m}^k$ is the kth column of $F_n(0{:}m - 1, 0{:}p - 1)$, so for any $z \in \mathbb{C}^n$ we have

$$
\begin{aligned}
&\left[\mathrm{diag}(I_m, \Omega_{p,m}, \ldots, \Omega_{p,m}^{p-1}) z \right]_{m \times p} \\
&= \left[z(0{:}m - 1) \mid \Omega_{p,m} z(m{:}2m - 1) \mid \cdots \mid \Omega_{p,m}^{p-1} z(n - m{:}n - 1) \right] \\
&= F_n(0{:}m - 1, 0{:}p - 1) \,.* z_{m \times p} .
\end{aligned}
$$

(Pointwise multiplication is reviewed in §1.1.9.) Thus,

$$[F_n x]_{m \times p} = \left\{ F_n(0{:}m - 1, 0{:}p - 1) \,.* \left[(I_p \otimes F_m) \Pi_{p,n}^T x \right]_{m \times p} \right\} F_p .$$

But from Kron5 and Lemma 2.1.1 we conclude that

$$
\begin{aligned}
[F_n x]_{m \times p} &= \left\{ F_n(0{:}m - 1, 0{:}p - 1) \,.* \left[F_m [\Pi_{p,n}^T x]_{m \times p} \right] \right\} F_p \\
&= \left\{ F_n(0{:}m - 1, 0{:}p - 1) \,.* \left[F_m x_{p \times m}^T \right] \right\} F_p ,
\end{aligned}
$$

thereby proving the theorem.   □

As a preview of some interesting FFT frameworks that revolve around (2.1.9), suppose that $(n, p, m) = (1024, 16, 64)$. It follows that

$$[F_{1024}x]_{64 \times 16} = \left[F_{1024}(0:63, 0:15). * (F_{64}x_{16 \times 64})^T \right] F_{16} . \qquad (2.1.10)$$

Any of our radix-2 procedures could be used for the 16-point and 64-point multiple DFTs. See §§3.1 and 3.3 for more details.

Problems

P2.1.1 Prove Lemma 2.1.2.

P2.1.2 How many flops are required to evaluate (2.1.10), assuming that the designated DFTs are obtained via the Stockham radix-2 procedure and that the vector of weights $w = \left[\; 1, \; \omega, \dots, \omega^{511} \; \right]$ is precomputed where $\omega = \omega_{1024}$?

P2.1.3 Assume that for composite n in **genfft** that p is chosen to be the largest divisor of n less than or equal to $\sqrt{n}$. Using a tree notation, indicate the size of each splitting that arises during execution in the $n = 96$ case.

P2.1.4 Write a detailed algorithm for the computation $y \leftarrow \Pi_{p,n}^T x$.

P2.1.5 Write a detailed algorithm for the computation $y \leftarrow \Pi_{p,n} x$.

Notes and References for Section 2.1

Gauss (1805) was aware of the radix-p splitting idea. For appropriate pointers to the Latin notebooks of the great mathematician, we refer the reader to

M.T. Heideman, D.H. Johnson, and C.S. Burrus (1985). "Gauss and the History of the Fast Fourier Transform," *Arch. Hist. Exact Sciences 34*, 265–277.

Further references to the radix-p splitting with a particularly strong matrix flavor include

M.J. Corinthios (1971). "The Design of a Class of Fast Fourier Transform Computers," *IEEE Trans. Comput. C-20*, 617–623.

D.J. Rose (1980). "Matrix Identities of the Fast Fourier Transform," *Linear Algebra Appl. 29*, 423–443.

H. Sloate (1974). "Matrix Representations for Sorting and the Fast Fourier Transform," *IEEE Trans. Circuits and Systems CAS-21*, 109–116.

C. Temperton (1983a). "Self-Sorting Mixed Radix Fast Fourier Transforms," *J. Comput. Phys. 52*, 1–23.

R. Tolimieri, M. An, and C. Lu (1989). *Algorithms for Discrete Fourier Transform and Convolution*, Springer-Verlag, NY.

A scalar description of the radix-p splitting appears in

J.W. Cooley and J.W. Tukey (1965). "An Algorithm for the Machine Calculation of Complex Fourier Series," *Math. Comp. 19*, 297–301.

2.2   Index Reversal and Transposition

In §2.3 we develop a number of important factorizations based upon the radix-p splitting. The derivations require fairly detailed algebraic manipulation. To make the exposition smoother, we use this section to establish a collection of useful properties that relate the Kronecker product, the permutation $\Pi_{p,n}$, and various transposition operations. A generalization of the bit-reversal permutation that plays a role in the general radix Cooley–Tukey framework is also derived.

2.2.1   Some Kronecker Product Properties

Our first Kronecker property shows that the matrix $A^T \otimes I$ is similar to $I \otimes A$ and that the mod p sort permutation is the required similarity transformation.

$\boxed{\text{Kron8}}$

If $n = \mu\lambda$ and $A \in \mathbb{C}^{\lambda \times \lambda}$, then $\Pi_{\lambda,n}^T (I_\mu \otimes A) = (A \otimes I_\mu)\Pi_{\lambda,n}^T$.

Proof. If $x \in \mathbb{C}^n$, then from Lemma 2.1.1 and Kron5 we have

$$\left[\Pi_{\lambda,n}^T (I_\mu \otimes A)x\right]_{\mu \times \lambda} = \left[(I_\mu \otimes A)x\right]_{\lambda \times \mu}^T = \left[Ax_{\lambda \times \mu}\right]^T = x_{\lambda \times \mu}^T A^T.$$

On the other hand, from Kron6 and Lemma 2.1.1 we have

$$\left[(A \otimes I_\mu)\Pi_{\lambda,n}^T x\right]_{\mu \times \lambda} = \left[\Pi_{\lambda,n}^T x\right]_{\mu \times \lambda} A^T = x_{\lambda \times \mu}^T A^T.$$

Since these results hold for all x, the property is established.   □

The next four Kronecker facts show that various block shuffles of an x-vector correspond to certain transpositions of x regarded as a three-dimensional array.

$\boxed{\text{Kron9}}$

Suppose $d = abc$ and $x \in \mathbb{C}^d$. If $y = (I_c \otimes \Pi_{a,ab}^T)x$, and we make the identifications

$$
\begin{aligned}
x &\equiv X(0{:}a-1, 0{:}b-1, 0{:}c-1), \\
y &\equiv Y(0{:}b-1, 0{:}a-1, 0{:}c-1),
\end{aligned}
$$

then $Y(\beta, \alpha, \gamma) = X(\alpha, \beta, \gamma)$ for all $\alpha \in \{0, \ldots, a-1\}$, $\beta \in \{0, \ldots, b-1\}$, and $\gamma \in \{0, \ldots, c-1\}$. In block matrix terms this result says that if we write

$$x_{a \times bc} = \left[\; X_0 \mid X_1 \mid \cdots \mid X_{c-1} \;\right], \qquad X_j \in \mathbb{C}^{a \times b},$$

then

$$y_{b \times ac} = \left[\; X_0^T \mid X_1^T \mid \cdots \mid X_{c-1}^T \;\right].$$

Proof. From Kron5 it follows that

$$y_{ab \times c} = \Pi_{a,ab}^T x_{ab \times c}. \tag{2.2.1}$$

Applying $\Pi_{a,ab}^T$ to each column of $x_{ab \times c}$ means that each column of that array is transposed as an a-by-b array. A component of column γ in $x_{ab \times c}$ has the form $x(\alpha + \beta a + \gamma ab)$, where $0 \le \alpha \le a-1$ and $0 \le \beta \le b-1$. It follows from Lemma 2.1.1

that $x(\alpha+\beta a+\gamma ab)$ maps to $y(\beta+\alpha b+\gamma ab)$. But in the language of three-dimensional arrays, these two components are named by $X(\alpha,\beta,\gamma)$ and $Y(\beta,\alpha,\gamma)$.

The block description follows because X_j is obtained by taking the jth column of $x_{ab \times c}$ and writing it as an a-by-b array. From (2.2.1), each of these arrays is transposed. $\square$

As an illustration of the result, suppose that $(a,b,c) = (2,3,5)$. If we regard x as the following partitioned 2-by-15 array,

$$x_{2 \times 15} = \left[\begin{array}{ccc|ccc|ccc|ccc|ccc} x_0 & x_2 & x_4 & x_6 & x_8 & x_{10} & x_{12} & x_{14} & x_{16} & x_{18} & x_{20} & x_{22} & x_{24} & x_{26} & x_{28} \\ x_1 & x_3 & x_5 & x_7 & x_9 & x_{11} & x_{13} & x_{15} & x_{17} & x_{19} & x_{21} & x_{23} & x_{25} & x_{27} & x_{29} \end{array} \right],$$

and we compute $y = (I_5 \otimes \Pi_{2,6})x$, then

$$y_{3 \times 10} = \left[\begin{array}{cc|cc|cc|cc|cc} x_0 & x_1 & x_6 & x_3 & x_{12} & x_{13} & x_{19} & x_{21} & x_{24} & x_{25} \\ x_2 & x_3 & x_8 & x_9 & x_{14} & x_{15} & x_{20} & x_{21} & x_{26} & x_{27} \\ x_4 & x_5 & x_{10} & x_{11} & x_{16} & x_{17} & x_{22} & x_{23} & x_{28} & x_{29} \end{array} \right].$$

Kron10

Suppose $d = abc$ and $x \in \mathbb{C}^d$. If $y = (I_c \otimes \Pi_{a,ab})x$ and we make the identifications

$$x \equiv X(0{:}b-1, 0{:}a-1, 0{:}c-1),$$
$$y \equiv Y(0{:}a-1, 0{:}b-1, 0{:}c-1),$$

then $X(\beta,\alpha,\gamma) = Y(\alpha,\beta,\gamma)$ for all $\alpha \in \{0,\ldots,a-1\}$, $\beta \in \{0,\ldots,b-1\}$, and $\gamma \in \{0,\ldots,c-1\}$. In block matrix terms this result says that if we write

$$x_{b \times ac} = \left[\begin{array}{c|c|c|c} X_0 & X_1 & \cdots & X_{c-1} \end{array} \right], \qquad X_j \in \mathbb{C}^{b \times a},$$

then

$$y_{a \times bc} = \left[\begin{array}{c|c|c|c} X_0^T & X_1^T & \cdots & X_{c-1}^T \end{array} \right].$$

Proof. We know from Kron2 that $I_c \otimes \Pi_{a,ab}$ is the inverse of $I_c \otimes \Pi_{a,ab}^T$. Therefore, it must undo the transposition described in Kron9. $\square$

While Kron8 and Kron9 involve transposition in the first and second dimensions, Kron10 and Kron11 show how to carry out a transposition in the second and third dimensions.

Kron11

Suppose $d = abc$ and $x \in \mathbb{C}^d$. If $y = (\Pi_{b,bc}^T \otimes I_a)x$, and we make the identifications

$$x \equiv X(0{:}a-1, 0{:}b-1, 0{:}c-1),$$
$$y \equiv Y(0{:}a-1, 0{:}c-1, 0{:}b-1),$$

then $Y(\alpha,\gamma,\beta) = X(\alpha,\beta,\gamma)$ for all $\alpha \in \{0,\ldots,a-1\}$, $\beta \in \{0,\ldots,b-1\}$, and $\gamma \in \{0,\ldots,c-1\}$. In block matrix terms this result says that if we write

$$x_{ab \times c} = \left[\begin{array}{c} X_0 \\ X_1 \\ \vdots \\ X_{b-1} \end{array} \right], \qquad X_j \in \mathbb{C}^{a \times c},$$

then

$$y_{a \times bc} = \left[\; X_0 \mid X_1 \mid \cdots \mid X_{b-1} \;\right].$$

Proof. From Kron6

$$y_{a \times bc} = x_{a \times bc} \Pi_{b,bc} \qquad\qquad (2.2.2)$$

and so from Lemma 2.1.1, a mod p sort is performed on each row of $x_{a \times bc}$. An entry in row α of that array can be expressed in the form $x(\alpha + a(\beta + \gamma b))$, where $0 \le \beta \le b-1$ and $0 \le \gamma \le c-1$. This component is mapped to $y(\alpha + a(\gamma + \beta c))$, according to Lemma 2.1.1. But $x(\alpha + \beta a + \gamma ab) \equiv X(\alpha, \beta, \gamma)$ and $y(\alpha + \gamma a + \beta ac) \equiv Y(\alpha, \gamma, \beta)$, which demonstrates the required transposition.

To establish the block matrix interpretation result, note that $x_{a \times bc} \Pi_{b,bc}$ is obtained by grouping columns of $x_{a \times bc}$ according to the mod b values of their index, i.e., $y_{a \times bc}(:, jc{:}(j+1)c - 1) = x_{a \times bc}(:, j{:}b{:}bc - 1) = X_j$ for $j = 0{:}b - 1$.   □

As an example, suppose that $(a, b, c) = (2, 5, 3)$. If we regard x as the following partitioned 10-by-3 array,

$$x_{10 \times 3} = \begin{bmatrix} x_0 & x_{10} & x_{20} \\ x_1 & x_{11} & x_{21} \\ \hline x_2 & x_{12} & x_{22} \\ x_3 & x_{13} & x_{23} \\ \hline x_4 & x_{14} & x_{24} \\ x_5 & x_{15} & x_{25} \\ \hline x_6 & x_{16} & x_{26} \\ x_7 & x_{17} & x_{27} \\ \hline x_8 & x_{18} & x_{28} \\ x_9 & x_{19} & x_{29} \end{bmatrix}$$

and compute $y = (\Pi_{5,15}^T \otimes I_2)x$, then

$$y_{2 \times 15} = \left[\begin{array}{ccc|ccc|ccc|ccc|ccc} x_0 & x_{10} & x_{20} & x_2 & x_{12} & x_{22} & x_4 & x_{14} & x_{24} & x_6 & x_{16} & x_{26} & x_8 & x_{18} & x_{28} \\ x_1 & x_{11} & x_{21} & x_3 & x_{13} & x_{23} & x_5 & x_{15} & x_{25} & x_7 & x_{17} & x_{27} & x_9 & x_{19} & x_{29} \end{array}\right].$$

$\boxed{\textbf{Kron12}}$

Suppose $d = abc$ and $x \in \mathbb{C}^d$. If $y = (\Pi_{b,bc} \otimes I_a)x$, and we make the identifications

$$\begin{aligned} x &\equiv X(0{:}a - 1, 0{:}c - 1, 0{:}b - 1), \\ y &\equiv Y(0{:}a - 1, 0{:}b - 1, 0{:}c - 1), \end{aligned}$$

then $X(\alpha, \gamma, \beta) = Y(\alpha, \beta, \gamma)$ for all $\alpha \in \{0, \ldots, a - 1\}$, $\beta \in \{0, \ldots, b - 1\}$, and $\gamma \in \{0, \ldots, c - 1\}$. In block matrix terms this result says that if we write

$$x_{a \times bc} = \left[\; X_0 \mid X_1 \mid \cdots \mid X_{b-1} \;\right], \qquad X_j \in \mathbb{C}^{a \times c},$$

then

$$y_{ab \times c} = \begin{bmatrix} X_0 \\ X_1 \\ \vdots \\ X_{b-1} \end{bmatrix}.$$

Proof. Just observe that $\Pi_{b,bc} \otimes I_a$ is the inverse of $\Pi_{b,bc}^T \otimes I_a^T$. It must therefore undo the transposition described in Kron11.   □

2.2.2   Index Reversal

Recall from (1.9.2) that in the radix-2 Cooley–Tukey and Pease frameworks, the intermediate DFTs are stored in bit-reversed order. In the mixed-radix versions of these procedures, the scrambling is according to an index permutation, which we now study. Assume that $n = p_1 \cdots p_t$ and set

$$\rho = [\, p_1, \ldots, p_t \,].$$

If $m = p_1 \cdots p_{t-1}$, then the *index-reversal permutation* $P_n(\rho)$ is defined as follows:

$$P_n(\rho) = \begin{cases} I_n & (t = 1), \\[2mm] \Pi_{p_t,n}(I_{p_t} \otimes P_m(\rho(1{:}t-1))) & (t > 1). \end{cases} \tag{2.2.3}$$

Using this recursive definition, we can write $P_n(\rho)$ as a product of block perfect shuffle operations.

Lemma 2.2.1 *If $\rho = [\, p_1, \ldots, p_t \,]$ and $n = p_1 \cdots p_t$, then*

$$P_n(\rho) = R_t \cdots R_1, \tag{2.2.4}$$

where

$$R_q = I_{r_q} \otimes \Pi_{p_q, L_q}, \qquad q = 1{:}t, \tag{2.2.5}$$

with $L_q = p_1 \cdots p_q$ and $r_q = n/L_q$. Note that $R_1 = I_n$.

Proof. The proof is by induction on the value of t. If $t = 1$, then both $P_n(\rho)$ and $R_1 = \Pi_{p_1,p_1}$ are the identity, thereby establishing the base case.

Now suppose $m = p_1 \cdots p_{t-1}$ and by induction assume

$$P_m(\rho(1{:}t-1)) = \Gamma_{t-1} \cdots \Gamma_1,$$

where $\Gamma_q = I_{r_q/p_t} \otimes \Pi_{p_q, L_q}$ for $q = 1{:}t-1$. Note from (2.2.5) that $R_t = \Pi_{p_t,n}$ and so from definition (2.2.3) and Kron1 we have

$$\begin{aligned} P_n(\rho) &= \Pi_{p_t,n}(I_{p_t} \otimes P_m(\rho(1{:}t-1))) \\ &= R_t(I_{p_t} \otimes \Gamma_{t-1} \cdots \Gamma_1) \\ &= R_t(I_{p_t} \otimes \Gamma_{t-1}) \cdots (I_{p_t} \otimes \Gamma_1) \,. \end{aligned}$$

The lemma follows by invoking Kron7 to show that

$$I_{p_t} \otimes \Gamma_q = I_{p_t} \otimes (I_{r_q/p_t} \otimes \Pi_{p_q, L_q}) = I_{r_q} \otimes \Pi_{p_q, L_q} = R_q$$

for $q = 1{:}t-1$.   □

From the lemma, we obtain the following framework for computing $P_n(\rho)u$, where $u \in \mathbb{C}^n$:

$$
\begin{aligned}
&\textbf{for} \quad q = 2{:}t \\
&\qquad L_q \leftarrow p_1 \cdots p_q \\
&\qquad r_q \leftarrow p_{q+1} \cdots p_t \\
&\qquad u \leftarrow R_q u \; = \; (I_{r_q} \otimes \Pi_{p_q, L_q}) u \\
&\textbf{end}
\end{aligned}
\qquad (2.2.6)
$$

To acquire an intuition about this operation, we examine the action of the R_q permutations.

Lemma 2.2.2 *Suppose $u, v \in \mathbb{C}^n$ with $n = L_{q-1} p_q r_q$. If*

$$
v = R_q u = (I_{r_q} \otimes \Pi_{p_q, L_q}) u
$$

and we identify $u, v \in \mathbb{C}^n$ with the arrays

$$
\begin{aligned}
u &\equiv U(0{:}L_{q-1} - 1, 0{:}p_q - 1, 0{:}r_q - 1), \\
v &\equiv V(0{:}p_q - 1, 0{:}L_{q-1} - 1, 0{:}r_q - 1),
\end{aligned}
$$

then $U(\beta, \alpha, \gamma) = V(\alpha, \beta, \gamma)$ for all $\beta \in \{0, \ldots, L_{q-1} - 1\}$, $\alpha \in \{0, \ldots, p_q - 1\}$, and $\gamma \in \{0, \ldots, r_q - 1\}$.

Proof. Just apply Kron10 with $(b, a, c) = (L_{q-1}, p_q, r_q)$ and $(x, y) = (u, v)$. $\square$

The lemma permits the following revision of (2.2.6):

$$
\begin{aligned}
&\textbf{for} \quad q = 2{:}t \\
&\qquad L_{q-1} \leftarrow p_1 \cdots p_{q-1} \\
&\qquad r_q \leftarrow p_{q+1} \cdots p_t \\
&\qquad \{u \equiv U(0{:}L_{q-1} - 1, 0{:}p_q - 1, 0{:}r_q - 1)\} \\
&\qquad \{v \equiv V(0{:}p_q - 1, 0{:}L_{q-1} - 1, 0{:}r_q - 1)\} \\
&\qquad \textbf{for} \; \beta = 0{:}L_{q-1} - 1 \\
&\qquad\qquad \textbf{for} \; \alpha = 0{:}p_q - 1 \\
&\qquad\qquad\qquad V(\alpha, \beta, 0{:}r_q - 1) \leftarrow U(\beta, \alpha, 0{:}r_q - 1) \\
&\qquad\qquad \textbf{end} \\
&\qquad \textbf{end} \\
&\qquad u \leftarrow v \\
&\textbf{end}
\end{aligned}
\qquad (2.2.7)
$$

Thus, the vector u undergoes a sequence of transpositions. The qth transposition swaps the first and second components of $U(0{:}L_{q-1} - 1, 0{:}p_q - 1, 0{:}r_q - 1)$. Note that the third component is empty when $q = t$.

A very neat characterization of the whole process unfolds if we identify u with a t-dimensional array at each step. Suppppose $t = 5$. We initially make the identification

$$
u \equiv U(0{:}p_1 - 1, \; 0{:}p_2 - 1, \; 0{:}p_3 - 1, \; 0{:}p_4 - 1, \; 0{:}p_5 - 1).
$$

If we trace the path of $U(\alpha_1, \alpha_2, \alpha_3, \alpha_4, \alpha_5)$ during the execution of (2.2.7) and keep track of the dimension changes, we obtain

$$
\begin{array}{cc}
U(\alpha_1, \alpha_2, \alpha_3, \alpha_4, \alpha_5) & p_1 \times p_2 \times p_3 \times p_4 \times p_5 \\
\downarrow & \downarrow \\
U(\alpha_2, \alpha_1, \alpha_3, \alpha_4, \alpha_5) & p_2 \times p_1 \times p_3 \times p_4 \times p_5 \\
\downarrow & \downarrow \\
U(\alpha_3, \alpha_2, \alpha_1, \alpha_4, \alpha_5) & p_3 \times p_2 \times p_1 \times p_4 \times p_5 \\
\downarrow & \downarrow \\
U(\alpha_4, \alpha_3, \alpha_2, \alpha_1, \alpha_5) & p_4 \times p_3 \times p_2 \times p_1 \times p_5 \\
\downarrow & \downarrow \\
U(\alpha_5, \alpha_4, \alpha_3, \alpha_2, \alpha_1) & p_5 \times p_4 \times p_3 \times p_2 \times p_1 \,.
\end{array}
$$

Thus, component $(\alpha_1, \alpha_2, \alpha_3, \alpha_4, \alpha_5)$ of u regarded as a $p_1 \times p_2 \times p_3 \times p_4 \times p_5$ array maps to component $(\alpha_5, \alpha_4, \alpha_3, \alpha_2, \alpha_1)$ of u regarded as a $p_5 \times p_4 \times p_3 \times p_2 \times p_1$ array. In one-dimensional array notation:

$$ u(\alpha_1 + \alpha_2 p_1 + \alpha_3 p_1 p_2 + \alpha_4 p_1 p_2 p_3 + \alpha_5 p_1 p_2 p_3 p_4) $$
$$ \downarrow $$
$$ u(\alpha_5 + \alpha_4 p_5 + \alpha_3 p_5 p_4 + \alpha_2 p_5 p_4 p_3 + \alpha_1 p_5 p_4 p_3 p_2) \,. $$

The reason for referring to $P_n(\rho)$ as the "index-reversal" permutation should now be obvious. The general result follows.

Theorem 2.2.3 *Suppose* $\rho = [\, p_1, \ldots, p_t \,]$ *and set* $n = p_1 \cdots p_t$. *Identify* $u, v \in \mathbb{C}^n$ *with the arrays*

$$
\begin{aligned}
u &\equiv U(0{:}p_1 - 1, 0{:}p_2 - 1, \ldots, 0{:}p_t - 1), \\
v &\equiv V(0{:}p_t - 1, 0{:}p_{t-1} - 1, \ldots, 0{:}p_1 - 1).
\end{aligned}
$$

If $v = P_n(\rho)u$, *then*

$$ U(\alpha_1, \ldots, \alpha_t) = V(\alpha_t, \ldots, \alpha_1), $$

where $\alpha_q \in \{0, 1, \ldots, p_q - 1\}$ *for* $q = 1{:}t$.

Proof. Suppose $w = R_q \cdots R_1 u$ and that we identify

$$ w \equiv W(0{:}p_q - 1, 0{:}p_{q-1} - 1, \ldots, 0{:}p_1 - 1, 0{:}p_{q+1} - 1, \ldots, 0{:}p_t - 1) \,. $$

We proceed by induction. Assume that

$$ W(\alpha_q, \alpha_{q-1}, \ldots, \alpha_1, \alpha_{q+1}, \ldots, \alpha_t) = U(\alpha_1, \ldots, \alpha_t) \,. \tag{2.2.8} $$

This is certainly true if $q = 1$. Now let $z = R_{q+1} w$ and identify

$$ z \equiv Z(0{:}p_{q+1} - 1, 0{:}p_q - 1, 0{:}p_{q-1} - 1, \ldots, 0{:}p_1 - 1, 0{:}p_{q+2} - 1, \ldots, 0{:}p_t - 1). $$

Lemma 2.2.2 describes how z is obtained from w in the language of triply subscripted arrays. In particular, we think of w as a $(p_1 \cdots p_q)$-by-p_{q+1}-by-$(p_{q+2} \cdots p_t)$ array and obtain z by transposing the first two components. Thus,

$$ Z(\alpha_{q+1}, \alpha_q, \ldots, \alpha_1, \alpha_{q+2}, \ldots, \alpha_t) = W(\alpha_q, \alpha_{q-1}, \ldots, \alpha_1, \alpha_{q+1}, \ldots, \alpha_t) $$

and so by (2.2.8)

$$ Z(\alpha_{q+1}, \alpha_q, \ldots, \alpha_1, \alpha_{q+2}, \ldots, \alpha_t) = U(\alpha_1, \ldots, \alpha_t) $$

completing the inductive step.   □

In general, $P_n(\rho)$ is not symmetric. However, its transpose is easily characterized.

Theorem 2.2.4 *If* $\rho = [\, p_1, \ldots, p_t \,]$ *and* $n = p_1 \cdots p_t$, *then*

$$P_n(\rho)^T = P_n(\rho(t:-1:1)).\tag{2.2.9}$$

Proof. For $u, v \in \mathbb{C}^n$ we make the identifications

$$
\begin{aligned}
u &\equiv U(0{:}p_1 - 1, \ldots, 0{:}p_t - 1), \\
v &\equiv V(0{:}p_t - 1, \ldots, 0{:}p_1 - 1).
\end{aligned}
$$

Since $P_n(\rho)$ sends $U(\alpha_1, \ldots, \alpha_t)$ to $V(\alpha_t, \ldots, \alpha_1)$ and $P_n(\rho(t{:}-1{:}1))$ sends $V(\alpha_t, \ldots, \alpha_1)$ back to $U(\alpha_1, \ldots, \alpha_t)$, it follows that $P_n(\rho(t:-1:1)) = P_n(\rho)^{-1} = P_n(\rho)^T$. $\quad\square$

One more result about index reversal is useful. It relates $P_n(\rho)$ to the index-reversal permutation of the last $t - 1$ factors.

Theorem 2.2.5 *If* $m = p_2 \cdots p_t$ *and* $n = p_1 m$, *then*

$$P_n(\rho) = (I_{p_1} \otimes P_m(\rho(2{:}t)))\Pi_{p_1,n}^T.\tag{2.2.10}$$

Proof. To prove (2.2.10), we use (2.2.9) and definition (2.2.3):

$$P_n(\rho)^T = P_n(\rho(t:-1:1)) = \Pi_{p_1,n}(I_{p_1} \otimes P_m(\rho(t:-1:2))).$$

By taking transposes and invoking (2.2.9) we obtain

$$P_n(\rho) = (I_{p_1} \otimes P_m(\rho(t:-1:2))^T)\Pi_{p_1,n}^T = (I_{p_1} \otimes P_m(\rho(2{:}t)))\Pi_{p_1,n}^T$$

and thereby prove the theorem. $\quad\square$

2.2.3   The Function $r_{n,\rho}(k)$

Suppose $n = p_1 \cdots p_t$. The mixed-radix Cooley–Tukey framework that is developed in the next section requires the following scrambling of the input data:

$$x \leftarrow P_n(\rho)^T x,$$

where $\rho = [\, p_1, \ldots, p_t \,]$. For that reason it is important for us to understand the function $r_{n,\rho}(k)$ defined by

$$y = P_n(\rho)^T x \quad\Leftrightarrow\quad y_{r_{n,\rho}(k)} = x_k, \; k = 0{:}n - 1.$$

Using Theorem 2.2.3, we make the identifications

$$
\begin{aligned}
x &\equiv X(0{:}p_t - 1, \ldots, 0{:}p_1 - 1), \\
y &\equiv Y(0{:}p_1 - 1, \ldots, 0{:}p_t - 1)
\end{aligned}
$$

and note that if $k = \alpha_t + p_t \alpha_{t-1} + p_t p_{t-1} \alpha_{t-2} + \cdots + p_t \cdots p_2 \alpha_1$, then

$$r_{n,\rho}(k) = \alpha_1 + \alpha_2 p_1 + \alpha_3 p_1 p_2 + \cdots + \alpha_t p_1 \cdots p_{t-1}.\tag{2.2.11}$$

As an illustration of the index-reversal process, here is a tabulation of the function $r_{24,\rho}(k)$ for case $\rho = [\, 4, 3, 2 \,]$:

$$
\begin{aligned}
0 &= \underline{0}+\underline{0}\cdot 2+\underline{0}\cdot 6 \;\rightarrow\; \underline{0}+\underline{0}\cdot 4+\underline{0}\cdot 12 = \;\;0\\
1 &= \underline{1}+\underline{0}\cdot 2+\underline{0}\cdot 6 \;\rightarrow\; \underline{0}+\underline{0}\cdot 4+\underline{1}\cdot 12 = 12\\
2 &= \underline{0}+\underline{1}\cdot 2+\underline{0}\cdot 6 \;\rightarrow\; \underline{0}+\underline{1}\cdot 4+\underline{0}\cdot 12 = \;\;4\\
3 &= \underline{1}+\underline{1}\cdot 2+\underline{0}\cdot 6 \;\rightarrow\; \underline{0}+\underline{1}\cdot 4+\underline{1}\cdot 12 = 16\\
4 &= \underline{0}+\underline{2}\cdot 2+\underline{0}\cdot 6 \;\rightarrow\; \underline{0}+\underline{2}\cdot 4+\underline{0}\cdot 12 = \;\;8\\
5 &= \underline{1}+\underline{2}\cdot 2+\underline{0}\cdot 6 \;\rightarrow\; \underline{0}+\underline{2}\cdot 4+\underline{1}\cdot 12 = 20\\
6 &= \underline{0}+\underline{0}\cdot 2+\underline{1}\cdot 6 \;\rightarrow\; \underline{1}+\underline{0}\cdot 4+\underline{0}\cdot 12 = \;\;1\\
7 &= \underline{1}+\underline{0}\cdot 2+\underline{1}\cdot 6 \;\rightarrow\; \underline{1}+\underline{0}\cdot 4+\underline{1}\cdot 12 = 13\\
8 &= \underline{0}+\underline{1}\cdot 2+\underline{1}\cdot 6 \;\rightarrow\; \underline{1}+\underline{1}\cdot 4+\underline{0}\cdot 12 = \;\;5\\
9 &= \underline{1}+\underline{1}\cdot 2+\underline{1}\cdot 6 \;\rightarrow\; \underline{1}+\underline{1}\cdot 4+\underline{1}\cdot 12 = 17\\
10 &= \underline{0}+\underline{2}\cdot 2+\underline{1}\cdot 6 \;\rightarrow\; \underline{1}+\underline{2}\cdot 4+\underline{0}\cdot 12 = \;\;9\\
11 &= \underline{1}+\underline{2}\cdot 2+\underline{1}\cdot 6 \;\rightarrow\; \underline{1}+\underline{2}\cdot 4+\underline{1}\cdot 12 = 21\\
12 &= \underline{0}+\underline{0}\cdot 2+\underline{2}\cdot 6 \;\rightarrow\; \underline{2}+\underline{0}\cdot 4+\underline{0}\cdot 12 = \;\;2\\
13 &= \underline{1}+\underline{0}\cdot 2+\underline{2}\cdot 6 \;\rightarrow\; \underline{2}+\underline{0}\cdot 4+\underline{1}\cdot 12 = 14\\
14 &= \underline{0}+\underline{1}\cdot 2+\underline{2}\cdot 6 \;\rightarrow\; \underline{2}+\underline{1}\cdot 4+\underline{0}\cdot 12 = \;\;6\\
15 &= \underline{1}+\underline{1}\cdot 2+\underline{2}\cdot 6 \;\rightarrow\; \underline{2}+\underline{1}\cdot 4+\underline{1}\cdot 12 = 18\\
16 &= \underline{0}+\underline{2}\cdot 2+\underline{2}\cdot 6 \;\rightarrow\; \underline{2}+\underline{2}\cdot 4+\underline{0}\cdot 12 = 10\\
17 &= \underline{1}+\underline{2}\cdot 2+\underline{2}\cdot 6 \;\rightarrow\; \underline{2}+\underline{2}\cdot 4+\underline{1}\cdot 12 = 22\\
18 &= \underline{0}+\underline{0}\cdot 2+\underline{3}\cdot 6 \;\rightarrow\; \underline{3}+\underline{0}\cdot 4+\underline{0}\cdot 12 = \;\;3\\
19 &= \underline{1}+\underline{0}\cdot 2+\underline{3}\cdot 6 \;\rightarrow\; \underline{3}+\underline{0}\cdot 4+\underline{1}\cdot 12 = 15\\
20 &= \underline{0}+\underline{1}\cdot 2+\underline{3}\cdot 6 \;\rightarrow\; \underline{3}+\underline{1}\cdot 4+\underline{0}\cdot 12 = \;\;7\\
21 &= \underline{1}+\underline{1}\cdot 2+\underline{3}\cdot 6 \;\rightarrow\; \underline{3}+\underline{1}\cdot 4+\underline{1}\cdot 12 = 19\\
22 &= \underline{0}+\underline{2}\cdot 2+\underline{3}\cdot 6 \;\rightarrow\; \underline{3}+\underline{2}\cdot 4+\underline{0}\cdot 12 = 11\\
23 &= \underline{1}+\underline{2}\cdot 2+\underline{3}\cdot 6 \;\rightarrow\; \underline{3}+\underline{2}\cdot 4+\underline{1}\cdot 12 = 23
\end{aligned}
$$

From the standpoint of computation, notice that $r_{n,\rho}(k)$ has a Horner expansion, e.g.,

$$
r_{4,\rho}(k) = ((\alpha_4 p_3 + \alpha_3)p_2 + \alpha_2)p_1 + \alpha_1.
$$

Thus, if $\alpha_t, \alpha_{t-1}, \ldots, \alpha_1$ are known, then

```
j ← 0
for q = t: − 1:1
    j ← p_q j + α_q
end
```

terminates with $j = r_{n,\rho}(k)$. Each α_q can be found via a divide/subtract. For example, if $s = \mathbf{floor}(k/p_t)$, then $\alpha_t = k - sp_t$. We then repeat the process with t replaced by $t - 1$ and k replaced by s. This reveals α_{t-1}, etc.

Algorithm 2.2.1 If $n = p_1 \cdots p_t$ and $\rho = [\,p_1, \ldots, p_t\,]$, then the following algorithm computes $j = r_{n,\rho}(k)$:

```
j ← 0; m ← k
for q = t: − 1:1
    s ← floor(m/p_q)
    α_q ← m − sp_q
    j ← p_q j + α_q
    m ← s
end
```

2.2.4   Practical Index Reversal

We conclude this section with a discussion about the computation of $x \leftarrow P_n(\rho)^T x$. It follows from (2.2.8) that $P_n(\rho)$ is symmetric if and only if $p_k = p_{t-k+1}$. In this case if x_k maps to x_j, then x_j maps to x_k. This permits the following analog of Algorithm 1.5.2.

Algorithm 2.2.2 (Symmetric ρ Index Reversal) Suppose $n = p_1 \cdots p_t$ and that $p_k = p_{t-k+1}$ for $k = 1{:}t$. If $x \in \mathbb{C}^n$, then the following algorithm overwrites x with $P_n(\rho)^T x$.

> **for** $k = 0{:}n-1$
> > $j \leftarrow r_{n,\rho}(k)$ (Algorithm 2.2.1)
> > **if** $j > k$
> > > $x(j) \leftrightarrow x(k)$
> > **end**
> **end**

The radix-p framework ($n = p^t$) is an obvious case when this algorithm is applicable. If the size of the splitting factors varies, then sometimes it is possible to order the p_q so that a symmetric $P_n(\rho)$ results. For example, if $n = 2^4 \cdot 3^2 \cdot 5^3$, then

$$\rho = [\, 2,\, 2,\, 3,\, 5,\, 5,\, 5,\, 3,\, 2,\, 2 \,]$$

leads to a symmetric $P_n(\rho)$ but

$$\rho = [\, 2,\, 2,\, 2,\, 2,\, 3,\, 3,\, 5,\, 5,\, 5 \,]$$

does not.

The unsymmetric $P_n(\rho)$ case is discussed by Lafkin and Brebner (1970), Polge and Bhagavan (1976), and Singleton (1969). The central challenge is to organize the permutation so that a minimum workspace is required. This can be done through the use of cycles and by exploiting some alternative factorizations of $P_n(\rho)$. We conclude this section with a brief discussion of these topics.

2.2.5   Permuting by Cycle

Suppose g is a 1:1 function from $\{0, 1, \ldots, n-1\}$ onto itself and that Q is an n-by-n permutation defined by

$$[\, Qx \,]_k = x_{g(k)}, \qquad k = 0{:}n-1 \,.$$

For example, if $n = 32$ and

$$g(k) = \begin{cases} 2k, & k < 16, \\ 2(k-16)+1, & k \geq 16, \end{cases}$$

then $Q = \Pi_{2,32}^T$. To motivate the idea of cycles, suppose we store x_3 in τ and then perform the following transfers:

$$\begin{array}{llll}
x_3 & \leftarrow x_6 & \text{because} & g(3) = 6, \\
x_6 & \leftarrow x_{12} & \text{because} & g(6) = 12, \\
x_{12} & \leftarrow x_{24} & \text{because} & g(12) = 24, \\
x_{24} & \leftarrow x_{17} & \text{because} & g(24) = 17, \\
x_{17} & \leftarrow \tau & \text{because} & g(17) = 3.
\end{array}$$

We say that $(3, 6, 12, 24, 17)$ is a *cycle* for the permutation $\Pi_{2,32}^T$. Other cycles for this permutation are (0), $(1, 2, 4, 8, 16)$, $(5, 10, 20, 9, 18)$, $(7, 14, 28, 25, 19)$, $(11, 22, 13, 26, 21)$, $(15, 30, 29, 27, 23)$, and (31). We could complete the computation of $x \leftarrow \Pi_{2,32}^T x$ by performing similar shifts on these cycles.

In the general case, a bit vector can be used to keep track of which entries have been swapped as the permutation is processed. This leads to an algorithm of the form given below.

Algorithm 2.2.3 Suppose Q is an n-by-n permutation defined by $[\, Qx\,]_k = x_{g(k)}$, where $x \in \mathbb{C}^n$ and g is a 1-to-1 mapping on $\{0, 1, \ldots, n-1\}$. The following algorithm requires a bit vector $\beta(0{:}n-1)$ and overwrites x with Qx.

$$
\begin{aligned}
&\beta(0{:}n-1) \leftarrow 0 \\
&\textbf{for } k = 0{:}n-1 \\
&\qquad \textbf{if } \beta_k = 0 \\
&\qquad\qquad j \leftarrow k; \ \tau \leftarrow x_k; \ next \leftarrow g(k) \\
&\qquad\qquad \textbf{while } next \neq k \\
&\qquad\qquad\qquad x_j \leftarrow x_{next}; \ \beta_j \leftarrow 1 \\
&\qquad\qquad\qquad j \leftarrow next \\
&\qquad\qquad\qquad next \leftarrow g(j) \\
&\qquad\qquad \textbf{end} \\
&\qquad\qquad x_j \leftarrow \tau; \ \beta_j \leftarrow 1 \\
&\qquad \textbf{end} \\
&\textbf{end}
\end{aligned}
$$

Note that each entry in x is read exactly once.

2.2.6 The Unsymmetric $P_n(\rho)$ Case

One way to compute $x \leftarrow P_n(\rho)^T x$ is to use Algorithm 2.2.3 with $g(k) = r_{n,\rho}(k)$. Strictly speaking, the algorithm is not in-place, but the length n bit vector occupies less than one percent of the space required by x if 64-bit floating point words are assumed.

Nevertheless, some authors have shown how to reduce this requirement through the judicious choice of ρ and a careful factoring of $P_n(\rho)$. To illustrate the ideas along this line, assume that $n = 2^2 \cdot 3^2 \cdot 5^2 \cdot 7 \cdot 11$. Note that by setting

$$\rho = [\, 2, 3, 5, 7, 11, 5, 3, 2\,]$$

we have symmetry except in the middle portion. In array language, we start with a permutation that performs the following map:

$$
\begin{array}{cc}
X(\alpha_1, \alpha_2, \alpha_3, \alpha_4, \alpha_5, \alpha_6, \alpha_7, \alpha_8) & 2 \times 3 \times 5 \times 7 \times 11 \times 5 \times 3 \times 2 \\
\downarrow & \downarrow \\
X(\alpha_8, \alpha_7, \alpha_6, \alpha_4, \alpha_5, \alpha_3, \alpha_2, \alpha_1) & 2 \times 3 \times 5 \times 7 \times 11 \times 5 \times 3 \times 2
\end{array}
$$

The permutation, call it Λ_1, which oversees this transition is symmetric. It follows that $x \leftarrow \Lambda_1 x$ can be performed in-place.

To complete the index reversal, we must transpose the middle two components:

$$
\begin{array}{cc}
X(\alpha_8, \alpha_7, \alpha_6, \alpha_4, \alpha_5, \alpha_3, \alpha_2, \alpha_1) & 2 \times 3 \times 5 \times 7 \times 11 \times 5 \times 3 \times 2 \\
\downarrow & \downarrow \\
X(\alpha_8, \alpha_7, \alpha_6, \alpha_5, \alpha_4, \alpha_3, \alpha_2, \alpha_1) & 2 \times 3 \times 5 \times 11 \times 7 \times 5 \times 3 \times 2
\end{array}
$$

If we call this permutation Λ_2, then it follows that $P_n(\rho)^T = \Lambda_2 \Lambda_1$. It is not hard to show that Λ_2 can be implemented with a short bit vector having length 77.

Problems

P2.2.1 Show that if $n = pm$ then

$$\text{(a)} \qquad F_n = \Pi_{p,n}(I_p \otimes F_m)\text{diag}(I_m, \Omega_{p,m}, \ldots, \Omega_{p,m}^{p-1})(F_p \otimes I_m),$$

$$\text{(b)} \qquad F_n = (F_p \otimes I_m)\text{diag}(I_m, \Omega_{p,m}, \ldots, \Omega_{p,m}^{p-1})\Pi_{p,n}^T(F_m \otimes I_p),$$

$$\text{(c)} \qquad F_n = (F_m \otimes I_p)\Pi_{p,n}\text{diag}(I_m, \Omega_{p,m}, \ldots, \Omega_{p,m}^{p-1})(F_p \otimes I_m),$$

where $\Omega_{p,m} = \text{diag}(1, \omega_n, \ldots, \omega_n^{m-1})$ and $\omega_n = \exp(-2\pi i/n)$.

P2.2.2 Suppose $d = abc$ and that $x \in \mathbb{C}^d$. Write detailed algorithms for computing

$$\text{(a)} \quad y \quad = \quad (I_c \otimes \Pi_{a,ab}^T)x,$$
$$\text{(b)} \quad y \quad = \quad (I_c \otimes \Pi_{a,ab})x,$$
$$\text{(c)} \quad y \quad = \quad (\Pi_{b,bc}^T \otimes I_a)x,$$
$$\text{(d)} \quad y \quad = \quad (\Pi_{b,bc} \otimes I_a)x.$$

Indicate the amount of auxiliary storage that is required in each case.

P2.2.3 Obtain in-place algorithms for each of the four permutations in P2.2.2. Use Algorithm 2.2.3. How long must the bit vector be?

P2.2.4 Suppose $n = p_1 \cdots p_t$. Show that if $0 \le k < n$, then there exist unique integers $\alpha_1, \ldots, \alpha_t$ with $0 \le \alpha_q < p_q$ such that

$$k = \sum_{q=1}^{t} \alpha_q \cdot (p_1 \cdots p_{q-1}).$$

P2.2.5 Give a detailed algorithm for the computations $x \leftarrow \Lambda_1 x$ and $x \leftarrow \Lambda_2 x$ discussed in §2.2.6.

Notes and References for Section 2.2

Various practical issues associated with index reversal are covered in

C.S. Burrus (1988). "Unscrambling for Fast DFT Algorithms," *IEEE Trans. Acoust. Speech Signal Process. 36*, 1086–1087.

The Kronecker/index-reversal connection is discussed in

M. Davio (1981). "Kronecker Products and Shuffle Algebra," *IEEE Trans. Comput. C-30*, 116–125.

The implementation of index-reversal permutation is discussed in

S. Lafkin and M.A. Brebner (1970). "In-situ Transposition of a Rectangular Matrix," *Comm. ACM 13*, 324–326.

R.J. Polge and B.K. Bhagavan (1976). "Efficient Fast Fourier Transform Programs for Arbitrary Factors with One Step Loop Unscrambling," *IEEE Trans. Comput. C-25*, 534–539.

R.C. Singleton (1969). "An Algorithm for Computing the Mixed Radix Fast Fourier Transform," *IEEE Trans. Audio and Electroacoustics AU-17*, 93–103.

A connection between index reversal and matrix transposition that is useful in large, secondary storage problems is explored in

P. Duhamel (1990). "A Connection between Bit Reversal and Matrix Transposition: Hardware and Software Consequences," *IEEE Trans. Acoust. Speech Signal Process. ASSP-38*, 1893–1896.

D. Fraser (1976). "Array Permutation by Index-Digit Permutation," *J. Assoc. Comput. Mach. 23*, 298–309.

2.3   Mixed-Radix Factorizations

Recall that an FFT procedure with identical splittings at each level in the computation tree is called a *mixed-radix FFT*. Associated with each mixed-radix FFT is a
factorization of n:

$$n = p_1 \cdots p_t .$$

The integers p_q are the *splitting factors*, and they determine the "size" of the synthesis
at each stage. We shall develop mixed-radix generalizations of the radix-2 Cooley–
Tukey, transposed Stockham, Pease, and Stockham frameworks. At the top level,
these frameworks have a common organization:

> **for** $q = 1{:}t$
> $\qquad L_q = p_1 \cdots p_q$
> $\qquad r_q = n/L_q$
> $\qquad L_{q-1} = L_q/p_q$
> $\qquad r_{q-1} = n/L_{q-1}$
> $\qquad$ Compute $F_{L_q} x^T_{r_q \times L_q}$ from $F_{L_{q-1}} x^T_{r_{q-1} \times L_{q-1}}$
> **end**

These definitions of $L_0, \ldots, L_t$ and $r_0, \ldots, r_t$ remain in force throughout this section.
The four major frameworks differ in how the intermediate DFTs are stored. See
Table 2.3.1. In this section mixed-radix factorizations and precise specifications of the

TABLE 2.3.1
Intermediate DFT storage schemes.

FFT Framework	Intermediate DFT Array Orientation	Intermediate DFT Array Order
Cooley–Tukey	column	scrambled
Transposed Stockham	column	natural
Pease	row	scrambled
Stockham	row	natural

intermediate DFT arrays are given in each case. The corresponding decimation-in-
frequency and inverse frameworks are also discussed.

In order to make the material more accessible, we summarize the major results in
§2.3.1. The proofs follow in §§2.3.2–2.3.5.

2.3.1   The Main Results

Assume that $n = p_1 \cdots p_t$ and set $\rho = [p_1, \ldots, p_t]$. All of the factorizations derived
in this section make use of the butterfly matrices

$$B_{p_q, L_q} = (F_{p_q} \otimes I_{L_{q-1}}) \operatorname{diag}(I_{L_{q-1}}, \Omega_{p_q, L_{q-1}}, \ldots, \Omega^{p_q-1}_{p_q, L_{q-1}}),$$

where

$$\Omega_{p_q, L_{q-1}} = \operatorname{diag}(1, \omega_{L_q}, \ldots, \omega^{(L_{q-1})-1}_{L_q})$$

and $\omega_{L_q} = \exp(-2\pi i/L_q)$. Throughout the section, $P_n(\rho)$ denotes the index-reversal permutation defined by (2.2.3). If

$$A_q \;=\; I_{r_q} \otimes B_{p_q, L_q} \,, \tag{2.3.1}$$

$$S_q \;=\; (I_{r_q} \otimes B_{p_q, L_q})(\Pi_{p_q, r_{q-1}} \otimes I_{L_{q-1}}) \,, \tag{2.3.2}$$

$$H_q \;=\; (B_{p_q, L_q} \otimes I_{r_q})\Pi_{p_q, n}^T \,, \tag{2.3.3}$$

$$G_q \;=\; (B_{p_q, L_q} \otimes I_{r_q})(\Pi_{p_q, L_q}^T \otimes I_{r_q}) \,, \tag{2.3.4}$$

then we have the following factorizations:

$$\text{Cooley–Tukey:} \qquad F_n = A_t \cdots A_1 P_n(\rho)^T \,, \tag{2.3.5}$$

$$\text{Transposed Stockham:} \qquad F_n = S_t \cdots S_1 \,, \tag{2.3.6}$$

$$\text{Pease:} \qquad F_n = H_t \cdots H_1 P_n(\rho)^T \,, \tag{2.3.7}$$

$$\text{Stockham:} \qquad F_n = G_t \cdots G_1 \,. \tag{2.3.8}$$

These factorizations are established in subsequent subsections along with the following characterizations of the intermediate DFT arrays:

$$\left[A_q \cdots A_1 P_n(\rho)^T x\right]_{L_q \times r_q} \;=\; F_{L_q} x_{r_q \times L_q}^T P_{r_q}(\rho(q+1{:}t)) \,, \tag{2.3.9}$$

$$\left[S_q \cdots S_1 x\right]_{L_q \times r_q} \;=\; F_{L_q} x_{r_q \times L_q}^T \,, \tag{2.3.10}$$

$$\left[H_q \cdots H_1 P_n(\rho)^T x\right]_{r_q \times L_q} \;=\; P_{r_q}(\rho(q+1{:}t))^T x_{r_q \times L_q} F_{L_q} \,, \tag{2.3.11}$$

$$\left[G_q \cdots G_1 x\right]_{r_q \times L_q} \;=\; x_{r_q \times L_q} F_{L_q} \,. \tag{2.3.12}$$

The corresponding decimation-in-frequency factorizations follow by transposing the factorizations (2.3.5)–(2.3.8):

$$\text{(DIF)-Cooley–Tukey:} \qquad F_n = P_n(\rho) A_1^T \cdots A_t^T \,,$$

$$\text{(DIF)-Transposed Stockham:} \qquad F_n = S_1^T \cdots S_t^T \,,$$

$$\text{(DIF)-Pease:} \qquad F_n = P_n(\rho) H_1^T \cdots H_t^T \,,$$

$$\text{(DIF)-Stockham:} \qquad F_n = G_1^T \cdots G_t^T \,.$$

Similarly, factorizations of the inverse require conjugation and scaling:

$$\text{Inverse Cooley–Tukey:} \qquad F_n^{-1} = \bar{A}_t \cdots \bar{A}_1 P_n(\rho)^T / n \,,$$

$$\text{Inverse Transposed Stockham:} \qquad F_n^{-1} = \bar{S}_t \cdots \bar{S}_1 / n \,,$$

$$\text{Inverse Pease:} \qquad F_n^{-1} = \bar{H}_t \cdots \bar{H}_1 P_n(\rho)^T / n \,,$$

$$\text{Inverse Stockham:} \qquad F_n^{-1} = \bar{G}_t \cdots \bar{G}_1 / n \,.$$

The remainder of this section is devoted to the derivation of (2.3.5)–(2.3.12). The proofs involve Kronecker technicalities and may be skipped at first reading.

2.3.2 The Cooley–Tukey Mixed-Radix Factorization

We establish (2.3.5) by induction on t. The $t = 1$ case holds because $A_1 = B_{p_1,p_1} = F_{p_1} = F_n$. Now suppose (2.3.5) holds, with t replaced by $t - 1$, and set

$$
\begin{aligned}
m &= p_1 \cdots p_{t-1}, \\
p &= p_t.
\end{aligned}
$$

By induction we have $F_m P_m(\rho(1{:}t-1)) = C_{t-1} \cdots C_1$, where

$$
C_q = I_{m/L_q} \otimes B_{p_q,L_q}, \qquad q = 1{:}t-1 .
$$

Using the definition (2.2.3) of $P_n(\rho)$, the radix-p splitting (Theorem 2.1.3), and the identity $A_t = B_{p_t,n}$, we have

$$
\begin{aligned}
F_n P_n(\rho) &= F_n \Pi_{p_t,n}(I_{p_t} \otimes P_m(\rho(1{:}t-1))) \\
&= B_{p_t,n}(I_{p_t} \otimes F_m)(I_{p_t} \otimes P_m(\rho(1{:}t-1))) \\
&= A_t(I_{p_t} \otimes F_m P_m(\rho(1{:}t-1))) \\
&= A_t(I_{p_t} \otimes C_{t-1} \cdots C_1) \\
&= A_t(I_{p_t} \otimes C_{t-1}) \cdots (I_{p_t} \otimes C_1) .
\end{aligned}
$$

Using Kron7 and the definition (2.3.1) of A_q, we have

$$
I_{p_t} \otimes C_q = I_{p_t} \otimes (I_{m/L_q} \otimes B_{p_q,L_q}) = I_{r_q} \otimes B_{p_q,L_q} = A_q,
$$

thereby establishing the Cooley–Tukey factorization (2.3.5). It follows that

$$
\begin{aligned}
&x^{(0)} \leftarrow P_n(\rho)^T x \\
&\textbf{for } q = 1{:}t \\
&\qquad x^{(q)} \leftarrow A_q x^{(q-1)} \\
&\textbf{end}
\end{aligned} \tag{2.3.13}
$$

terminates with $x^{(t)} = F_n x$.

We next use induction to verify (2.3.9), the array characterization of $x^{(q)}$. The result clearly holds in the $q = 0$ case, since

$$
x^{(0)}_{1 \times n} = F_1 x^T_{n \times 1} P_n(\rho) = x^T P_n(\rho) .
$$

For convenience, set $L = L_q$, $r = r_q$, $L_* = L_{q-1}$, $r_* = r_{q-1}$, and $p = p_q$. Assume by induction that

$$
x^{(q-1)}_{L_* \times r_*} = F_{L_*} x^T_{r_* \times L_*} P_{r_*}(\rho(q{:}t)) . \tag{2.3.14}
$$

If we partition

$$
F_{L_*} x^T_{r_* \times L_*} = \begin{bmatrix} C_0 \mid \cdots \mid C_{p-1} \end{bmatrix},
$$

with $C_j \in \mathbb{C}^{L_* \times r}$, then by using (2.2.10) and (2.3.14) we obtain

$$
\begin{aligned}
x^{(q-1)}_{L_* \times r_*} &= F_{L_*} x^T_{r_* \times L_*} P_{r_*}(\rho(q{:}t)) \\
&= F_{L_*} x^T_{r_* \times L_*}(I_p \otimes P_r)\Pi^T_{p,r_*} \\
&= \begin{bmatrix} C_0 P_r \mid \cdots \mid C_{p-1} P_r \end{bmatrix} \Pi^T_{p,r_*} .
\end{aligned}
$$

where we have set $P_r = P_r(\rho(q+1{:}t))$. Using Kron12 with $(a,b,c) = (L_*, p, r)$ it follows that

$$x_{L \times r}^{(q-1)} = \begin{bmatrix} C_0 P_r \\ \vdots \\ C_{p-1} P_r \end{bmatrix} = \begin{bmatrix} C_0 \\ \vdots \\ C_{p-1} \end{bmatrix} P_r$$

and so by using Corollary 2.1.5

$$B_{p,L} x_{L \times r}^{(q-1)} = B_{p,L} \begin{bmatrix} C_0 \\ \vdots \\ C_{p-1} \end{bmatrix} P_r = F_L x_{r \times L}^T P_r .$$

The characterization (2.3.3) now follows, because $x^{(q)} = A_q x^{(q-1)} = (I_r \otimes B_{p,L}) x^{(q-1)}$ implies $x_{L \times r}^{(q)} = B_{p,L} x_{L \times r}^{(q-1)}$.

2.3.3   The Transposed Stockham Factorization

The Cooley–Tukey mixed-radix algorithm stores the intermediate DFTs by column and in index-reversed fashion. The mixed-radix transposed Stockham algorithm arises if we store the intermediate DFTs by column in *natural* order. To verify (2.3.6) and (2.3.10) we must show that if S_q is defined by (2.3.4) and

$$x^{(0)} \leftarrow x$$
$$\text{for } q = 1{:}t$$
$$\qquad x^{(q)} \leftarrow S_q x^{(q-1)}$$
$$\textbf{end}$$

then $x_{L \times r}^{(q)} = F_{L_q} x_{r_q \times L_q}^T$ for $q = 1{:}t$.

We may assume by induction that

$$x_{L_* \times r_*}^{(q-1)} = F_{L_*} x_{r_* \times L_*}^T,$$

where $r_* = r_{q-1}$ and $L_* = L_{q-1}$. Let us examine the array structure of

$$x^{(q)} = S_q x^{(q-1)} = (I_r \otimes B_{p,L})(\Pi_{p,r_*} \otimes I_{L_*}) x^{(q-1)}, \qquad (2.3.15)$$

where $r = r_q$, $L = L_q$, and $p = p_q$. If

$$x_{L_* \times r_*}^{(q-1)} = [C_0 \mid \cdots \mid C_{p-1}], \qquad C_j \in \mathbb{C}^{L_* \times r},$$

then by applying Kron12 with $(a,b,c) = (L_*, p, r)$ we obtain

$$\left[(\Pi_{p,r_*} \otimes I_{L_*}) x^{(q-1)} \right]_{L \times r} = \begin{bmatrix} C_0 \\ \vdots \\ C_{p-1} \end{bmatrix}.$$

It follows from Corollary 2.1.5 and (2.3.15) that

$$x_{L \times r}^{(q)} = \left[(I_r \otimes B_{p,L})(\Pi_{p,r_*} \otimes I_{L_*}) x^{(q-1)} \right]_{L \times r} = B_{p,L} \begin{bmatrix} C_0 \\ \vdots \\ C_{p-1} \end{bmatrix} = F_L x_{r \times L}^T,$$

completing the verification of (2.3.6) and (2.3.10).

2.3.4   The Mixed-Radix Pease Factorization

The mixed-radix Pease algorithm is the transpose of the mixed-radix Cooley–Tukey procedure, meaning that the intermediate DFTs are stored by *rows* in index-reversed order. The transposition of the intermediate DFT array $x_{L \times r}^{(q)}$ can be expressed as follows:

$$y^{(q)} = \Pi_{L_q, n}^T x^{(q)} .$$

By substituting $x^{(q)} = \Pi_{L, n} y^{(q)}$ into the Cooley–Tukey procedure (2.3.13), we obtain

$$y^{(0)} \leftarrow P_n(\rho)^T x$$
$$\text{for} \quad q = 1{:}t$$
$$\qquad y^{(q)} \leftarrow \left(\Pi_{L_q, n}^T A_q \Pi_{L_{q-1}, n} \right) y^{(q-1)} \qquad\qquad (2.3.16)$$
$$\text{end}$$

This procedure stores the intermediate DFTs by row:

$$y_{r_q \times L_q}^{(q)} = P_{r_q}(\rho(q+1{:}t))^T x_{r_q \times L_q} F_{L_q} .$$

From the definition of A_q and Kron8 we have

$$\Pi_{L, n}^T A_q \Pi_{L_*, n} = \Pi_{L, n}^T (I_r \otimes B_{p,L}) \Pi_{L_*, n} = (B_{p,L} \otimes I_r) \Pi_{L, n}^T \Pi_{L_*, n} , \qquad (2.3.17)$$

where we have set $L = L_q$, $r = r_q$, $L_* = L_{q-1}$, $r_* = r_{q-1}$, and $p = p_q$. Consider the action of $\Pi_{L, n}^T \Pi_{L_*, n}$ on an n-vector w. Set $v = \Pi_{L_*, n} w$ and $z = \Pi_{L, n}^T v$ and make the identifications

$$w \equiv W(0{:}p-1, 0{:}r-1, 0{:}L_*-1),$$
$$v \equiv V(0{:}L_*-1, 0{:}p-1, 0{:}r-1),$$
$$z \equiv Z(0{:}r-1, 0{:}L_*-1, p-1).$$

Let us see what happens to $W(\alpha, \beta, \gamma)$ under these permutations. Since $\Pi_{L_*, n} w$ transposes w as an r_*-by-L_* array, we see that

$$W(\alpha, \beta, \gamma) = V(\gamma, \alpha, \beta) .$$

Since $\Pi_{L, n}^T v$ transposes v as an L-by-r array, it follows that

$$V(\gamma, \alpha, \beta) = Z(\beta, \gamma, \alpha) .$$

Thus, $W(\alpha, \beta, \gamma)$ is mapped to $Z(\beta, \gamma, \alpha)$. It follows that z is obtained by transposing w regarded as a p-by-(n/p) array, i.e.,

$$z = \Pi_{p, n}^T w .$$

We have shown that $\Pi_{L, n}^T \Pi_{L_*, n} = \Pi_{p, n}^T$. From (2.3.3) and (2.3.17) it follows that

$$\Pi_{L_q, n}^T A_q \Pi_{L_{q-1}, n} = (B_{p,L} \otimes I_r) \Pi_{p, n}^T = H_q,$$

completing the verification of (2.3.7) and (2.3.11).

Recall from our discussion of the radix-2 Pease factorization in §1.8 that we found

$$H_q = (F_2 \otimes I_{n/2}) \text{diag}(I_{n/2}, \Omega_{L_*} \otimes I_r) \Pi_{2, n}^T,$$

which does not appear to be a special case of (2.3.3). However, if we substitute the
definition

$$B_{p,L} = (F_p \otimes I_{L_*})\text{diag}(I_{L_*}, \Omega_{L_*}, \ldots, \Omega_{L_*}^{p-1})$$

and use Kron1 and Kron7, then we obtain the "long vector" version of the Pease factor
H_q:

$$
\begin{aligned}
H_q &= \left([(F_p \otimes I_{L_*})\text{diag}(I_{L_*}, \Omega_{L_*}, \ldots, \Omega_{L_*}^{p-1})] \otimes I_r\right) \Pi_{p,n}^T \\
&= \left([(F_p \otimes I_{L_*}) \otimes I_r] \left[\text{diag}(I_{L_*}, \Omega_{L_*}, \ldots, \Omega_{L_*}^{p-1}) \otimes I_r\right]\right) \Pi_{p,n}^T \quad (2.3.18) \\
&= (F_p \otimes I_{n/p})\text{diag}(I_{n/p}, \Omega_{L_*} \otimes I_r, \ldots, \Omega_{L_*}^{p-1} \otimes I_r)\Pi_{p,n}^T .
\end{aligned}
$$

2.3.5   The Stockham Factorization

In a process analogous to that of the Pease development, we can derive a factorization
that corresponds to the Stockham algorithm. Starting with the transposed Stockham
factorization

$$F_n = S_t \cdots S_1$$

we define

$$G_q = \Pi_{L_q,n}^T S_q \Pi_{L_{q-1},n} \qquad (2.3.19)$$

and observe that

$$F_n = G_t \cdots G_1$$

because $\Pi_{n,n}^T = \Pi_{1,n} = I_n$. Set $L = L_q$, $L_* = L_{q-1}$, $r = r_q$, and $r_* = r_{q-1}$. Since
$G_q \cdots G_1 x = \Pi_{L,n}^T S_q \cdots S_1 x$, it follows from (2.3.2) that

$$[G_q \cdots G_1 x]_{r \times L} = \Pi_{L,n}^T [S_q \cdots S_1 x]_{L \times r} = \Pi_{L,n}^T [F_L x_{r \times L}^T]_{L \times r} = [x_{r \times L} F_L].$$

The verification of (2.3.8) and (2.3.12) is complete once we show that $\Pi_{L,n}^T S_q \Pi_{L_*,n} = (B_{p,L} \otimes I_r)(\Pi_{p,L}^T \otimes I_r)$.

Using the definition of S_q in (2.3.2) and Kron8, we obtain

$$
\begin{aligned}
\Pi_{L,n}^T S_q \Pi_{L_*,n} &= \Pi_{L,n}^T (I_r \otimes B_L)(\Pi_{p,r_*} \otimes I_{L_*})\Pi_{L_*,n} \\
&= (B_L \otimes I_r)\Pi_{L,n}^T (\Pi_{p,r_*} \otimes I_{L_*})\Pi_{L_*,n} .
\end{aligned}
$$

Thus, we need to examine the permutation $\Pi_{L,n}^T(\Pi_{p,r_*} \otimes I_{L_*})\Pi_{L_*,n}$. To that end define

$$
\begin{aligned}
v &= \Pi_{L_*,n}w, \\
z &= (\Pi_{p,r_*} \otimes I_{L_*})v, \\
u &= \Pi_{L,n}^T z,
\end{aligned}
$$

and make the identifications

$$
\begin{aligned}
w &\equiv W(0{:}r-1, 0{:}p-1, 0{:}L_*-1), \\
v &\equiv V(0{:}L_*-1, 0{:}r-1, 0{:}p-1), \\
z &\equiv Z(0{:}L_*-1, 0{:}p-1, 0{:}r-1), \\
u &\equiv U(0{:}r-1, 0{:}L_*-1, 0{:}p-1).
\end{aligned}
$$

Let us see what happens to $W(\alpha, \beta, \gamma)$ as it is subjected to this sequence of transformations. Since $\Pi_{L_*,n}w$ transposes w as an r_*-by-L_* matrix, it follows that $W(\alpha, \beta, \gamma) =$

$V(\gamma, \alpha, \beta)$. Note that $(\Pi_{p,r_*} \otimes I_{L_*})v$ postmultiplies each row of $v_{L_* \times r_*}$ by Π_{p,r_*}^T. It follows that each of those rows is transposed as an r-by-p matrix and so $V(\gamma, \alpha, \beta) = Z(\gamma, \beta, \alpha)$. Finally, $\Pi_{L,n}^T z$ transposes z as an L-by-r array, so $Z(\gamma, \beta, \alpha) = U(\alpha, \gamma, \beta)$. We see that the overall transition $W(\alpha, \beta, \gamma) \rightarrow U(\alpha, \gamma, \beta)$ involves a permutation of the rows of w regarded as an r-by-L array. Indeed, each of those rows is transposed as a p-by-L array and so by Kron11 $u = (\Pi_{p,L}^T \otimes I_r)w$. Thus, the qth Stockham factor is given by $G_q = (B_L \otimes I_r)(\Pi_{p,L}^T \otimes I_r)$.

Problems

P2.3.1 Prove the Stockham factorization without reference to the transposed Stockham factorization.

Notes and References for Section 2.3

As we mentioned in the Preface, the correspondence between factorizations of the DFT matrix and FFT algorithms has been known for a long time. See

M.J. Corinthios (1971). "The Design of a Class of Fast Fourier Transform Computers," *IEEE Trans. Comput. C-20*, 617–623.

J. Johnson, R.W. Johnson, D. Rodriguez, and R. Tolimieri (1990). "A Methodology for Designing, Modifying, and Implementing Fourier Transform Algorithms on Various Architectures," *Circuits Systems Signal Process. 9*, 449–500.

M.C. Pease (1968). "An Adaptation of the Fast Fourier Transform for Parallel Processing," *J. Assoc. Comput. Mach. 15*, 252–264.

D. Rodriguez (1987). *On Tensor Product Formulations of Additive Fast Fourier Transform Algorithms and Their Implementations*, Ph.D. Thesis, Department of Electrical Engineering, The City College of New York, CUNY.

D.J. Rose (1980). "Matrix Identities of the Fast Fourier Transform," *Linear Algebra Appl. 29*, 423–443.

H. Sloate (1974). "Matrix Representations for Sorting and the Fast Fourier Transform," *IEEE Trans. Circuits and Systems CAS-21*, 109–116.

C. Temperton (1983). "Self-Sorting Mixed Radix Fast Fourier Transforms," *J. Comput. Phys. 52*, 1–23.

R. Tolimieri, M. An, and C. Lu (1989). *Algorithms for Discrete Fourier Transform and Convolution*, Springer-Verlag, New York.

2.4   Radix-4 and Radix-8 Frameworks

As an application of the mixed-radix developments just presented, we detail the organization the Cooley–Tukey and Stockham radix-4 procedures. Properly arranged, these algorithms involve fewer flops and better memory traffic patterns than their radix-2 counterparts. The benefits of a higher radix algorithm are further illustrated through a discussion of the radix-8 butterfly. Other themes in the section include the in-line and off-line generation of weights and the art of exploiting structure.

2.4.1   The Cooley–Tukey Radix-4 Framework

The Cooley–Tukey radix-4 approach assumes that $n = 4^t$ and is based upon the Cooley–Tukey factorization (2.3.5). If

$$\rho = [\underbrace{4, \ldots, 4}_{t}]$$

in that equation, then we obtain

$$F_n P_n(\rho) = A_t \cdots A_1,$$

where $P_n(\rho)$ is the (symmetric) radix-4 index-reversal permutation, and

$$A_q = I_r \otimes B_{4,L}, \qquad\qquad\qquad\qquad L = 4^q, \; r = n/L,$$

$$B_{4,L} = (F_4 \otimes I_{L_*}) \mathrm{diag}(I_{L_*}, \Omega_{4,L_*}, \Omega_{4,L_*}^2, \Omega_{4,L_*}^3), \qquad L_* = L/4,$$

$$\Omega_{4,L_*} = \mathrm{diag}(1, \omega_L, \ldots, \omega_L^{L_*-1}), \qquad\qquad \omega_L = \exp(-2\pi i/L) \, .$$

Since the update $x \leftarrow A_q x$ is equivalent to $x_{L \times r} \leftarrow B_{4,L} x_{L \times r}$, we have the following high-level framework:

$$
\begin{aligned}
&x \leftarrow P_n(\rho)x \\
&\textbf{for } q = 1{:}t \\
&\qquad L \leftarrow 4^q; \; r \leftarrow n/L; \; L_* \leftarrow L/4 \\
&\qquad x_{L \times r} \leftarrow B_{4,L} x_{L \times r} \\
&\textbf{end}
\end{aligned}
\tag{2.4.1}
$$

Our goal is to develop an in-place implementation of this procedure. The index-reversal poses no problem in this regard because Algorithm 2.2.2 is applicable. Thus, the primary task is to produce an in-place implementation of the butterfly update.

2.4.2 The Radix-4 Butterfly

A method for computing $B_{4,L} x_{L \times r}$ can be developed by considering separately the diagonal scaling

$$x_{L \times r} \leftarrow \mathrm{diag}(I_{L_*}, \Omega_{4,L_*}, \Omega_{4,L_*}^2, \Omega_{4,L_*}^3) x_{L \times r} \tag{2.4.2}$$

and the multiple 4-point DFT computation

$$x_{L \times r} \leftarrow (F_4 \otimes I_{L_*}) x_{L \times r} \, . \tag{2.4.3}$$

If we update by row in (2.4.2), then we obtain

$$
\begin{aligned}
&\textbf{for } j = 0{:}L_* - 1 \\
&\qquad \omega \leftarrow \cos(2\pi j/L) - i\sin(2\pi j/L) \\
&\qquad \tilde{\omega} \leftarrow \omega\omega \\
&\qquad \hat{\omega} \leftarrow \omega\tilde{\omega} \\
&\qquad \textbf{for } k = 0{:}r - 1 \\
&\qquad\qquad x(kL + L_* + j) \;\; \leftarrow \omega \cdot x(kL + L_* + j) \\
&\qquad\qquad x(kL + 2L_* + j) \leftarrow \tilde{\omega} \cdot x(kL + 2L_* + j) \\
&\qquad\qquad x(kL + 3L_* + j) \leftarrow \hat{\omega} \cdot x(kL + 3L_* + j) \\
&\qquad \textbf{end} \\
&\textbf{end}
\end{aligned}
\tag{2.4.4}
$$

Notice that weights $\{1, \omega_L, \ldots, \omega_L^{L_*-1}\}$ are required along with their squares and cubes. Keeping in mind the remarks made in §1.4.3 about the accuracy of computed weights, we could adopt a slightly more accurate in-line strategy of computing

$$
\begin{aligned}
\tilde{\omega} &= \cos(4\pi j/L) - i\sin(4\pi j/L), \\
\hat{\omega} &= \cos(6\pi j/L) - i\sin(6\pi j/L)
\end{aligned}
$$

by direct call. However, we have chosen to specify these factors through multiplication in (2.4.4) because the resulting roundoff is of little consequence.

The "other half" of the radix-4 butterfly involves the computation of multiple 4-point DFTs. From (2.4.3) we see that the central calculation to understand is the matrix-vector product

$$v = (F_4 \otimes I_{L_*}) \begin{bmatrix} a \\ b \\ c \\ d \end{bmatrix},$$

where $L_* = L/4$ and $a, b, c, d \in \mathbb{C}^{L_*}$. In array terms,

$$v_{L_* \times 4} \leftarrow \begin{bmatrix} a \mid b \mid c \mid d \end{bmatrix} F_4$$

and so we need a loop to oversee the production of L_* DFTs of length 4. Recalling the definition of F_4, we see that

$$v = \begin{bmatrix} I & I & I & I \\ I & -iI & -I & iI \\ I & -I & I & -I \\ I & iI & -I & -iI \end{bmatrix} \begin{bmatrix} a \\ b \\ c \\ d \end{bmatrix} = \begin{bmatrix} (a+c) + (b+d) \\ (a-c) - i(b-d) \\ (a+c) - (b+d) \\ (a-c) + i(b-d) \end{bmatrix},\qquad (2.4.5)$$

where each identity is L_*-by-L_*. If we compute the common subexpressions $a \pm c$ and $b \pm d$, then only $16L_* = 4L$ flops are required:

for $j = 0:L_* - 1$
$\quad \tau_0 \leftarrow a(j) + c(j)$
$\quad \tau_1 \leftarrow a(j) - c(j)$
$\quad \tau_2 \leftarrow b(j) + d(j)$
$\quad \tau_3 \leftarrow b(j) - d(j)$
$\quad v(j) \leftarrow \tau_0 + \tau_2$
$\quad v(L_* + j) \leftarrow \tau_1 - i\tau_3$
$\quad v(2L_* + j) \leftarrow \tau_0 - \tau_2$
$\quad v(3L_* + j) \leftarrow \tau_1 + i\tau_3$
end
$\qquad\qquad (2.4.6)$

Returning to the development of an algorithm for (2.4.3), a computation of the form (2.4.6) is required in each column and so we obtain

for $k = 0:r - 1$
$\quad$ for $j = 0:L_* - 1$
$\quad\quad \tau_0 \leftarrow x(kL + j) + x(kL + 2L_* + j)$
$\quad\quad \tau_1 \leftarrow x(kL + j) - x(kL + 2L_* + j)$
$\quad\quad \tau_2 \leftarrow x(kL + L_* + j) + x(kL + 3L_* + j)$
$\quad\quad \tau_3 \leftarrow x(kL + L_* + j) - x(kL + 3L_* + j)$
$\quad\quad x(kL + j) \leftarrow \tau_0 + \tau_2$
$\quad\quad x(kL + L_* + j) \leftarrow \tau_1 - i\tau_3$
$\quad\quad x(kL + 2L_* + j) \leftarrow \tau_0 - \tau_2$
$\quad\quad x(kL + 3L_* + j) \leftarrow \tau_1 + i\tau_3$
$\quad$ end
end
$\qquad\qquad (2.4.7)$

This can be derived by making the identifications

$$
\begin{aligned}
a &\equiv x(kL{:}kL + L_* - 1), \\
b &\equiv x(kL + L_*{:}kL + 2L_* - 1), \\
c &\equiv x(kL + 2L_*{:}kL + 3L_* - 1), \\
d &\equiv x(kL + 3L_*{:}(k + 1)L - 1)
\end{aligned}
$$

and applying (2.4.6) for $k = 0{:}r - 1$. The body of the inner loop in (2.4.7) is executed $rL_* = n/4$ times and each execution involves 16 flops.

2.4.3 The Cooley–Tukey Radix-4 Algorithm

An in-place algorithm for the butterfly update $x_{Lxr} \leftarrow B_L x_{Lxr}$ can be obtained by carefully merging (2.4.4) and a jk version of (2.4.7). Repetition of the process for $q = 1{:}t$ leads to the following Cooley–Tukey radix-4 framework.

Algorithm 2.4.1 If $x \in \mathbb{C}^n$ with $n = 4^t$, then the following algorithm overwrites x with $F_n x$:

$$
\begin{aligned}
&x \leftarrow P_n([4, \ldots, 4])x \qquad \text{(Algorithm 2.2.2)} \\
&\textbf{for } q = 1{:}t \\
&\qquad L \leftarrow 4^q; \ r = n/L; \ L_* \leftarrow L/4 \\
&\qquad \textbf{for } j = 0{:}L_* - 1 \\
&\qquad\qquad \omega \leftarrow \cos(2\pi j/L) - i\sin(2\pi j/L) \\
&\qquad\qquad \tilde{\omega} \leftarrow \omega\omega \\
&\qquad\qquad \hat{\omega} \leftarrow \omega\tilde{\omega} \\
&\qquad\qquad \textbf{for } k = 0{:}r - 1 \\
&\qquad\qquad\qquad \alpha \leftarrow x(kL + j) \\
&\qquad\qquad\qquad \beta \leftarrow \omega \cdot x(kL + L_* + j) \\
&\qquad\qquad\qquad \gamma \leftarrow \tilde{\omega} \cdot x(kL + 2L_* + j) \\
&\qquad\qquad\qquad \delta \leftarrow \hat{\omega} \cdot x(kL + 3L_* + j) \\
&\qquad\qquad\qquad \tau_0 \leftarrow \alpha + \gamma \\
&\qquad\qquad\qquad \tau_1 \leftarrow \alpha - \gamma \\
&\qquad\qquad\qquad \tau_2 \leftarrow \beta + \delta \\
&\qquad\qquad\qquad \tau_3 \leftarrow \beta - \delta \\
&\qquad\qquad\qquad x(kL + j) \leftarrow \tau_0 + \tau_2 \\
&\qquad\qquad\qquad x(kL + L_* + j) \leftarrow \tau_1 - i\tau_3 \\
&\qquad\qquad\qquad x(kL + 2L_* + j) \leftarrow \tau_0 - \tau_2 \\
&\qquad\qquad\qquad x(kL + 3L_* + j) \leftarrow \tau_1 + i\tau_3 \\
&\qquad\qquad \textbf{end} \\
&\qquad \textbf{end} \\
&\textbf{end}
\end{aligned}
$$

Each pass through the k-loop involves 34 flops, as there are three complex multiplications and eight complex additions. The total number of flops is therefore given by

$$
\sum_{q=1}^{t} \sum_{j=0}^{4^{q-1}-1} \sum_{k=0}^{4^{t-q}-1} 34 \ = \ 34\frac{n}{4}t \ = \ 8.5n \log_4 n \ = \ 4.25n \log_2 n \ .
$$

Recall that a radix-2 Cooley–Tukey FFT requires $5n \log_2 n$ flops; there is thus a 15 percent reduction in the amount of arithmetic.

2.4.4   The Radix-4 Stockham Framework

Algorithm 2.4.1 has power-of-two stride. As an example of a unit stride algorithm with off-line weight generation, we develop a radix-4 procedure based upon the Stockham factorization (2.3.8). Starting with this factorization, we obtain the following high-level specification:

$$
\begin{aligned}
&\textbf{for } q = 1{:}t \\
&\qquad L \leftarrow 4^q; \ r \leftarrow n/L; \ L_* \leftarrow L/4 \\
&\qquad y \leftarrow x \\
&\qquad x \leftarrow (B_L \otimes I_r)(\Pi_{4,L}^T \otimes I_r)y \\
&\textbf{end}
\end{aligned}
\qquad (2.4.8)
$$

In array language the computation of x from y has the form

$$
x_{r \times L} \leftarrow y_{r \times L} \Pi_{4,L} B_{4,L}^T. \qquad (2.4.9)
$$

Set $r_* = 4r$ and $L_* = L/4$. If we partition $y_{r_* \times L_*}$ as

$$
y_{r_* \times L_*} \ = \ \begin{bmatrix} C_0 \\ C_1 \\ C_2 \\ C_3 \end{bmatrix}, \qquad C_j \in \mathbb{C}^{r \times L_*}, \ j = 0{:}3, \qquad (2.4.10)
$$

and set $z = (\Pi_{4,L}^T \otimes I_r)y$, then by applying Kron11 with $(a,b,c) = (r,4,L_*)$ we may conclude that

$$
z_{r \times L} \ = \ \begin{bmatrix} C_0 \,|\, C_1 \,|\, C_2 \,|\, C_3 \end{bmatrix}.
$$

Applying this to (2.4.9) gives

$$
x_{r \times L} \leftarrow \begin{bmatrix} C_0 \,|\, C_1 \,|\, C_2 \,|\, C_3 \end{bmatrix} B_{4,L}^T \ = \ \begin{bmatrix} C_0 \,|\, C_1 \Omega_{4,L_*} \,|\, C_2 \Omega_{4,L_*}^2 \,|\, C_3 \Omega_{4,L_*}^3 \end{bmatrix} (F_4 \otimes I_{L_*}).
$$

Note that if $0 \le j < L_* - 1$, then

$$
x_{r \times L}(:, j{:}L_*{:}L - 1) \leftarrow \begin{bmatrix} C_0(:,j) \,|\, C_1(:,j)\omega_L^j \,|\, C_2(:,j)\omega_L^{2j} \,|\, C_3(:,j)\omega_L^{3j} \end{bmatrix} F_4. \qquad (2.4.11)
$$

From (2.4.10)

$$
\begin{aligned}
C_0(:,j) &= y(jr_*{:}jr_* + r - 1), \\
C_1(:,j) &= y(jr_* + r{:}jr_* + 2r - 1), \\
C_2(:,j) &= y(jr_* + 2r{:}jr_* + 3r - 1), \\
C_3(:,j) &= y(jr_* + 3r{:}(j-1)r_* - 1),
\end{aligned}
$$

so through substitution and transposition of (2.4.11), we obtain

$$
\begin{aligned}
&\textbf{for } j = 0{:}L_* - 1 \\
&\qquad \textbf{for } k = 0{:}r - 1 \\
&\qquad\qquad \begin{bmatrix} x(jr + k) \\ x((j + L_*)r + k) \\ x((j + 2L_*)r + k) \\ x((j + 3L_*)r + k) \end{bmatrix} \leftarrow F_4 \begin{bmatrix} y(jr_* + k) \\ y(jr_* + r + k)\omega_L^j \\ y(jr_* + 2r + k)\omega_L^{2j} \\ y(jr_* + 3r + k)\omega_L^{3j} \end{bmatrix} \\
&\qquad \textbf{end} \\
&\textbf{end}
\end{aligned}
$$

The 4-point butterfly operation submits to the same economies that we discussed in §2.4.2. Suppressing the issue of weights enables us to specify the overall process.

Algorithm 2.4.2 If $x \in \mathbb{C}^n$ with $n = 4^t$, then the following algorithm overwrites x with $F_n x$:

$$
\begin{aligned}
&\textbf{for } q = 1{:}t \\
&\qquad L \leftarrow 4^q; \; r \leftarrow n/L; \; L_* \leftarrow L/4; \; r_* \leftarrow 4r \\
&\qquad y \leftarrow x \\
&\qquad \textbf{for } j = 0{:}L_* - 1 \\
&\qquad\qquad \textbf{for } k = 0{:}r - 1 \\
&\qquad\qquad\qquad \alpha \leftarrow y(jr_* + k) \\
&\qquad\qquad\qquad \beta \leftarrow \omega_L^j \cdot y(jr_* + r + k) \\
&\qquad\qquad\qquad \gamma \leftarrow \omega_L^{2j} \cdot y(jr_* + 2r + k) \\
&\qquad\qquad\qquad \delta \leftarrow \omega_L^{3j} \cdot y(jr_* + 3r + k) \\
&\qquad\qquad\qquad \tau_0 \leftarrow \alpha + \gamma \\
&\qquad\qquad\qquad \tau_1 \leftarrow \alpha - \gamma \\
&\qquad\qquad\qquad \tau_2 \leftarrow \beta + \delta \\
&\qquad\qquad\qquad \tau_3 \leftarrow \beta - \delta \\
&\qquad\qquad\qquad x(jr + k) \leftarrow \tau_0 + \tau_2 \\
&\qquad\qquad\qquad x((j + L_*)r + k) \leftarrow \tau_1 - i\tau_3 \\
&\qquad\qquad\qquad x((j + 2L_*)r + k) \leftarrow \tau_0 - \tau_2 \\
&\qquad\qquad\qquad x((j + 3L_*)r + k) \leftarrow \tau_1 + i\tau_3 \\
&\qquad\qquad \textbf{end} \\
&\qquad \textbf{end} \\
&\textbf{end}
\end{aligned}
$$

2.4.5 Weight Precomputation

During the qth pass in Algorithm 2.4.2, the weights $\{1, \omega_L, \omega_L^2, \ldots, \omega_L^{L_*-1}\}$ together with their squares and cubes are required. These scaling factors are precisely the entries in the matrix W_{L_*}, which we define as follows:

$$ W_{L_*} = F_L(0{:}L_* - 1, 1{:}3). $$

If this array is available, then the formulae for β, γ, and δ in Algorithm 2.4.2 transform to

$$
\begin{aligned}
\beta &\leftarrow W_{L_*}(j, 1) \cdot y(jr_* + r + k) \\
\gamma &\leftarrow W_{L_*}(j, 2) \cdot y(jr_* + 2r + k) \\
\delta &\leftarrow W_{L_*}(j, 3) \cdot y(jr_* + 3r + k).
\end{aligned}
$$

Note that if $m = n/4$, then

$$ W_{L_*} = W_m(0{:}r{:}m - 1, 1{:}3). $$

If we precompute W_m and proceed with the q-loop, then the scalings involve power-of-two stride access:

$$
\begin{aligned}
\beta &\leftarrow W_m(jr, 1) \cdot y(jr_* + r + k) \\
\gamma &\leftarrow W_m(jr, 2) \cdot y(jr_* + 2r + k) \\
\delta &\leftarrow W_m(jr, 3) \cdot y(jr_* + 3r + k).
\end{aligned}
$$

This suggests that we apply the $w^{(long)}$ philosophy of §1.4.11 and precompute the array $W_n^{(long)}$ defined by

$$
W_n^{(long)} = \begin{bmatrix} W_1 \\ W_4 \\ W_{16} \\ \vdots \\ W_{n/4} \end{bmatrix}. \tag{2.4.12}
$$

This array has $(n-1)/3$ rows and three columns. Since $W_{L_*}(j,s)$ is situated in $W_n^{long}(\nu+j,s)$, where $\nu = 1 + 4 + \cdots 4^{q-2} = (4^{q-1}-1)/3$, we obtain

$$
\begin{aligned}
\nu &\leftarrow (4^{q-1}-1)/3 \\
\beta &\leftarrow W_n^{(long)}(\nu+j,1) \cdot y(jr_* + r + k) \\
\gamma &\leftarrow W_n^{(long)}(\nu+j,2) \cdot y(jr_* + 2r + k) \\
\delta &\leftarrow W_n^{(long)}(\nu+j,3) \cdot y(jr_* + 3r + k).
\end{aligned}
$$

The generation of $W_n^{(long)}$ requires an algorithm for generating each W_{L_*}. Here is one possibility that builds upon the subvector scaling method of §1.4.2.

Algorithm 2.4.3 If $L = 4^q$ and $L_* = L/4$, then the following algorithm computes the matrix $W = F_L(0{:}L_* - 1, 1{:}3) = W_{L_*}$.

$$
\begin{aligned}
&W(0,1) \leftarrow 1 \\
&\textbf{for } j = 1{:}2(q-1) \\
&\qquad \omega_L \leftarrow \exp(-2^j \pi i/L) \\
&\qquad W(2^{j-1}{:}2^j - 1, 1) \leftarrow \omega_L \cdot W(0{:}2^{j-1} - 1, 1) \\
&\textbf{end} \\
&W(0{:}L_* - 1, 2) \leftarrow W(0{:}L_* - 1, 1).*W(0{:}L_* - 1, 1) \\
&W(0{:}L_* - 1, 3) \leftarrow W(0{:}L_* - 1, 1).*W(0{:}L_* - 1, 2)
\end{aligned}
$$

2.4.6 The Radix-8 Butterfly

The exploitation of structure led to the reduced arithmetic requirements of the radix-4 butterfly. Let us repeat the exercise by developing an efficient implementation of the radix-8 butterfly. An 8-point DFT $x = F_8 z$ has the form

$$
\begin{bmatrix} x_0 \\ x_1 \\ x_2 \\ x_3 \\ x_4 \\ x_5 \\ x_6 \\ x_7 \end{bmatrix} = \begin{bmatrix} 1 & 1 & 1 & 1 & 1 & 1 & 1 & 1 \\ 1 & a & -i & b & -1 & -a & i & -b \\ 1 & -i & -1 & i & 1 & -i & -1 & i \\ 1 & b & i & a & -1 & -b & -i & -a \\ 1 & -1 & 1 & -1 & 1 & -1 & 1 & -1 \\ 1 & -a & -i & -b & -1 & a & i & b \\ 1 & i & -1 & -i & 1 & i & -1 & -i \\ 1 & -b & i & -a & -1 & b & -i & a \end{bmatrix} \begin{bmatrix} z_0 \\ z_1 \\ z_2 \\ z_3 \\ z_4 \\ z_5 \\ z_6 \\ z_7 \end{bmatrix},
$$

where $a = (1-i)/\sqrt{2}$ and $b = -1(1+i)/\sqrt{2} = -ia$. Observe that

$$
\begin{aligned}
x_0 &= (z_0 + z_4) &+& (z_2 + z_6) &+& (z_1 + z_5) &+& (z_3 + z_7),\\
x_4 &= (z_0 + z_4) &+& (z_2 + z_6) &-& (z_1 + z_5) &-& (z_3 + z_7),\\
x_2 &= (z_0 + z_4) &-& (z_2 + z_6) &-& i(z_1 + z_5) &+& i(z_3 + z_7),\\
x_6 &= (z_0 + z_4) &-& (z_2 + z_6) &+& i(z_1 + z_5) &-& i(z_3 + z_7),\\
x_1 &= (z_0 - z_4) &-& i(z_2 - z_6) &+& a(z_1 - z_5) &+& b(z_3 - z_7),\\
x_5 &= (z_0 - z_4) &-& i(z_2 - z_6) &-& a(z_1 - z_5) &-& b(z_3 - z_7),\\
x_3 &= (z_0 - z_4) &+& i(z_2 - z_6) &+& b(z_1 - z_5) &+& a(z_3 - z_7),\\
x_7 &= (z_0 - z_4) &+& i(z_2 - z_6) &-& b(z_1 - z_5) &-& a(z_3 - z_7),
\end{aligned}
$$

and so we begin by computing the real and imaginary parts of the vectors $z_0 \pm z_4$, $z_2 \pm z_6$, $z_1 \pm z_5$, and $z_3 \pm z_7$. For $(j,k) = (0,4),(2,6),(1,5),(3,7)$ we define

$$
\begin{aligned}
u_{jk}^+ &= \mathrm{Re}(z_j) + \mathrm{Re}(z_k), & v_{jk}^+ &= \mathrm{Im}(z_j) + \mathrm{Im}(z_k),\\
u_{jk}^- &= \mathrm{Re}(z_j) - \mathrm{Re}(z_k), & v_{jk}^- &= \mathrm{Im}(z_j) - \mathrm{Im}(z_k),
\end{aligned}
$$

and so

$$
\mathrm{Re}\left\{\begin{bmatrix} x_0\\x_4\\x_2\\x_6\\x_1\\x_5\\x_3\\x_7 \end{bmatrix}\right\} =
\begin{bmatrix}
(u_{04}^+ + u_{26}^+) + (u_{15}^+ + u_{37}^+)\\
(u_{04}^+ + u_{26}^+) - (u_{15}^+ + u_{37}^+)\\
(u_{04}^+ - u_{26}^+) + (v_{15}^+ - v_{37}^+)\\
(u_{04}^+ - u_{26}^+) - (v_{15}^+ - v_{37}^+)\\
(u_{04}^- + v_{26}^-) + \dfrac{(v_{37}^- + u_{15}^-) + (v_{15}^- - u_{37}^-)}{\sqrt{2}}\\
(u_{04}^- + v_{26}^-) - \dfrac{(v_{37}^- + u_{15}^-) + (v_{15}^- - u_{37}^-)}{\sqrt{2}}\\
(u_{04}^- - v_{26}^-) + \dfrac{(v_{37}^- - u_{15}^-) + (v_{15}^- + u_{37}^-)}{\sqrt{2}}\\
(u_{04}^- - v_{26}^-) - \dfrac{(v_{37}^- - u_{15}^-) + (v_{15}^- + u_{37}^-)}{\sqrt{2}}
\end{bmatrix}
$$

and

$$
\mathrm{Im}\left\{\begin{bmatrix} x_0\\x_4\\x_2\\x_6\\x_1\\x_5\\x_3\\x_7 \end{bmatrix}\right\} =
\begin{bmatrix}
(v_{04}^+ + v_{26}^+) + (v_{15}^+ + v_{37}^+)\\
(v_{04}^+ + v_{26}^+) - (v_{15}^+ + v_{37}^+)\\
(v_{04}^+ - v_{26}^+) - (u_{15}^+ - u_{37}^+)\\
(v_{04}^+ - v_{26}^+) + (u_{15}^+ - u_{37}^+)\\
(v_{04}^- - u_{26}^-) + \dfrac{-(v_{37}^- + u_{15}^-) + (v_{15}^- - u_{37}^-)}{\sqrt{2}}\\
(v_{04}^- - u_{26}^-) - \dfrac{-(v_{37}^- + u_{15}^-) + (v_{15}^- - u_{37}^-)}{\sqrt{2}}\\
(v_{04}^- + u_{26}^-) + \dfrac{(v_{37}^- - u_{15}^-) - (v_{15}^- + u_{37}^-)}{\sqrt{2}}\\
(v_{04}^- + u_{26}^-) - \dfrac{(v_{37}^- - u_{15}^-) - (v_{15}^- + u_{37}^-)}{\sqrt{2}}
\end{bmatrix}.
$$

With these specifications of the real and imaginary parts, and taking care to identify common subexpressions, we obtain the following algorithm for $x = F_8 z$:

for $(j, k) = (0, 4), (2, 6), (1, 5), (3, 7)$
$\quad u_{jk}^+ \leftarrow \text{Re}(z_j) + \text{Re}(z_k); \quad v_{jk}^+ \leftarrow \text{Im}(z_j) + \text{Im}(z_k)$
$\quad u_{jk}^- \leftarrow \text{Re}(z_j) - \text{Re}(z_k); \quad v_{jk}^- \leftarrow \text{Im}(z_j) - \text{Im}(z_k)$
end
$a^+ \leftarrow u_{04}^+ + u_{26}^+; \quad a^- \leftarrow u_{04}^+ - u_{26}^+$
$b^+ \leftarrow u_{15}^+ + u_{37}^+; \quad b^- \leftarrow u_{15}^+ - u_{37}^+$
$c^+ \leftarrow v_{04}^+ + v_{26}^+; \quad c^- \leftarrow v_{04}^+ - v_{26}^+$
$d^+ \leftarrow v_{15}^+ + v_{37}^+; \quad d^- \leftarrow v_{15}^+ - v_{37}^+$

$\text{Re}(x_0) \leftarrow a^+ + b^+; \quad \text{Im}(x_0) \leftarrow c^+ + d^+$
$\text{Re}(x_4) \leftarrow a^+ - b^+; \quad \text{Im}(x_4) \leftarrow c^+ - d^+$
$\text{Re}(x_2) \leftarrow a^- + d^-; \quad \text{Im}(x_2) \leftarrow c^- - b^-$
$\text{Re}(x_6) \leftarrow a^- - d^-; \quad \text{Im}(x_6) \leftarrow c^- + b^-$

$e^+ \leftarrow u_{04}^- + v_{26}^-; \qquad e^- \leftarrow u_{04}^- - v_{26}^-$
$f^+ \leftarrow v_{04}^- + u_{26}^-; \qquad f^- \leftarrow v_{04}^- - u_{26}^-$
$g^+ \leftarrow v_{37}^- + u_{15}^-; \qquad g^- \leftarrow v_{37}^- - u_{15}^-$
$h^+ \leftarrow v_{15}^- + u_{37}^-; \qquad h^- \leftarrow v_{15}^- - u_{37}^-$
$r^+ \leftarrow (g^+ + h^-)/\sqrt{2}; \quad r^- \leftarrow (-g^+ + h^-)/\sqrt{2}$
$t^+ \leftarrow (g^- + h^+)/\sqrt{2}; \quad t^- \leftarrow (g^- - h^+)/\sqrt{2}$

$\text{Re}(x_1) \leftarrow e^+ + r^+; \quad \text{Im}(x_1) \leftarrow f^- + r^-$
$\text{Re}(x_5) \leftarrow e^+ - r^+; \quad \text{Im}(x_5) \leftarrow f^- - r^-$
$\text{Re}(x_3) \leftarrow e^- + t^+; \quad \text{Im}(x_3) \leftarrow f^+ + t^-$
$\text{Re}(x_7) \leftarrow e^- - t^+; \quad \text{Im}(x_7) \leftarrow f^+ - t^-$

This algorithm involves 56 flops. The vector version for

$$x \leftarrow (F_8 \otimes I_{L_*})z, \qquad L = 8L_*, \ z \in \mathbb{C}^L$$

requires $56L_* = 7L$ flops. The radix-8 scaling

$$z \leftarrow \text{diag}(I_{L_*}, \Omega_{8,L_*}, \dots \Omega_{8,L_*}^7)z$$

involves 7 complex vector products of length L_*, i.e., $7 \cdot 6 \cdot L_* = 5.25L$ flops. Thus, premultiplication by B_{8,L_*} requires $12.25L$ flops. Summing the flops in a radix-8 Cooley–Tukey (or Stockham) framework, we find

$$\sum_{q=1}^{t} \sum_{k=0}^{8^{t-q}-1} (12.25)8^q = 12.25n \log_8 n \approx 4.08n \log_2 n \ .$$

This amounts to a 20 percent reduction in flops compared to the radix-2 version.

2.4.7 Data Re-Use and Radix

The radix-2, 4, and 8 frameworks involve $5n \log_2 n$, $4.25n \log_2 n$, and $4.08n \log_2 n$ flops, respectively, and so from that perspective, the radix-4 and 8 frameworks have added appeal. However, another advantage of these higher radix frameworks concerns the re-use of data. We discuss this important concept in the context of butterfly execution in a vector processor whose essential organization we depict as follows:

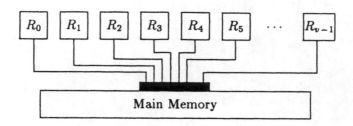

FIG. 2.4.1. *Registers and memory.*

Assume that the R_i are vector registers capable of *real* vector operations such as vector addition, vector multiply, vector load, and vector store. The act of performing an operation of the form $z \leftarrow B_{p,L_*} z$, where $L = pL_*$ and $z \in \mathbb{C}^L$ involves (a) loading z and the weights into the registers, (b) performing the actual vector adds and multiplies, and (c) writing the updated z to memory. In a paradigm where loads and stores are costly overheads, it pays to engage in a lot of arithmetic once data is loaded into the registers. From Table 2.4.1 we see that the amount of arithmetic associated with a length-L butterfly increases with radix. Looked at another way, if $n = 8^t$, then $3t$,

TABLE 2.4.1
Flops per butterfly.

p	$B_{p,L}$ Flops
2	$5L$
4	$8.5L$
8	$12.25L$

$2t$, and t passes through the data are required by the radix-2, 4, and 8 frameworks, respectively. The reduced memory traffic requirements of the higher radix frameworks makes them attractive in many environments. See Bailey (1987).

Problems

P2.4.1 Develop a handcrafted butterfly $z \leftarrow (F_6 \otimes I_m)z$. How many real operations are there?

P2.4.2 Develop a transposed Stockham radix-4 procedure with weight precomputation.

P2.4.3 Develop a radix-4 Pease algorithm with weight precomputation.

P2.4.4 How would you define W_n^{long} for the radix-p case?

P2.4.5 Develop a complete radix-8 Stockham procedure.

P2.4.6 Modify Algorithms 2.4.1 and 2.4.2 to handle the case $n = 4^{t-1} \cdot 2$. Be sure to detail the index-reversal computations in conjunction with the Cooley–Tukey framework.

Notes and References for Section 2.4

The organization of various radix-p algorithms have been well studied. See

G.D. Bergland (1968b). "A Fast Fourier Transform Algorithm Using Base 8 Iterations," *Math. Comp.* 22, 275–279.

E.O. Brigham (1988). *The Fast Fourier Transform and Its Applications*, Prentice-Hall, Englewood Cliffs, NJ.

E. Dubois and A. Venetsanopoulos (1978a). "A New Algorithm for the Radix-3 FFT," *IEEE Trans. Acoust. Speech Signal Process.* ASSP-26, 222–225.

S. Prakash and V.V. Rao (1981). "A New Radix-6 FFT Algorithm," *IEEE Trans. Acoust. Speech Signal Process.* ASSP-29, 939–941.

Y. Suzuki, T. Sone, and K. Kido (1986). "A New FFT Algorithm of Radix 3, 6, and 12," *IEEE Trans. Acoust. Speech Signal Process.* 34, 380–383.

A discussion of the radix-4 framework in the context of vector computing can be found in

D.H. Bailey (1987). "A High-Performance Fast Fourier Transform Algorithm for the Cray-2," *J. Supercomputing 1*, 43–62.

Practical aspects of the mixed-radix framework are covered in

E. Garcia-Torano (1983). "FASTF: Fast Fourier Transform with Arbitrary Factors," *Comput. Phys. Comm.* 30, 397–403.

R.J. Polge and B.K. Bhagavan (1976). "Efficient Fast Fourier Transform Programs for Arbitrary Factors with One Step Loop Unscrambling," *IEEE Trans. Comput.* C-25, 534–539.

R.C. Singleton (1968a). "An Algol Procedure for the Fast Fourier Transform with Arbitrary Factors– Algorithm 339," *Comm. ACM 11*, 776–779.

R.C. Singleton (1969). "An Algorithm for Computing the Mixed Radix Fast Fourier Transform," *IEEE Trans. Audio and Electroacoustics AU-17*, 93–103.

C. Temperton (1983a). "Self-Sorting Mixed-Radix Fast Fourier Transforms," *J. Comput. Phys. 52*, 1–23.

C. Temperton (1983b). "Fast Mixed-Radix Real Fourier Transforms," *J. Comput. Phys. 52*, 340–350.

2.5 The Split-Radix Framework

Standard radix-2 procedures are based upon the fast synthesis of two half-length DFTs. The *split-radix* algorithm is based upon a clever synthesis of one half-length DFT together with two quarter-length DFTs, i.e.,

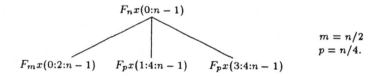

$$m = n/2$$
$$p = n/4.$$

It turns out that the resulting procedure involves less arithmetic than any of the standard radix-2, radix-4, or radix-8 procedures. The split-radix idea is due to Duhamel and Hollmann (1984). Our presentation is slightly different and more matrix-based.

2.5.1 The Split-Radix Splitting

We begin with the radix-2 splitting. If $n = 2m$, $\Omega_m = \text{diag}(1, \omega_n, \ldots, \omega_n^{m-1})$, and $x \in \mathbb{C}^n$, then

$$F_n x = \begin{bmatrix} I_m & \Omega_m \\ I_m & -\Omega_m \end{bmatrix} \begin{bmatrix} F_m x(0{:}2{:}n-1) \\ F_m x(1{:}2{:}n-1) \end{bmatrix}. \qquad (2.5.1)$$

The derivation of the split-radix algorithm is based upon a 4-by-4 blocking of this matrix-vector product. To that end, we assume that $m = 2p$ and examine Ω_m as a 2-by-2 block matrix with p-by-p blocks. Since $\omega_n^p = \omega_n^{n/4} = -i$, we have

$$\text{diag}(\omega_n^p, \ldots, \omega_n^{m-1}) = -i \cdot \text{diag}(1, \omega_n, \ldots, \omega_n^{p-1})$$

and so if

$$\Delta_p = \mathrm{diag}(1,\omega_n,\ldots,\omega_n^{p-1}),$$

then

$$\Omega_m = \left[\begin{array}{cc} \Delta_p & 0 \\ 0 & -i\Delta_p \end{array}\right].$$

If $y_T, y_B, z_T, z_B \in \mathbb{C}^m$ are defined by

$$F_m x(0{:}2{:}n-1) = \left[\begin{array}{c} y_T \\ y_B \end{array}\right]$$

and

$$F_m x(1{:}2{:}n-1) = \left[\begin{array}{c} z_T \\ z_B \end{array}\right],$$

then (2.5.1) can be written as

$$F_n x = \left[\begin{array}{cc|cc} I_p & 0 & \Delta_p & 0 \\ 0 & I_p & 0 & -i\Delta_p \\ \hline I_p & 0 & -\Delta_p & 0 \\ 0 & I_p & 0 & i\Delta_p \end{array}\right] \left[\begin{array}{c} y_T \\ y_B \\ \hline z_T \\ z_B \end{array}\right]. \tag{2.5.2}$$

Again making use of the radix-2 splitting we have

$$\left[\begin{array}{c} z_T \\ z_B \end{array}\right] = F_m x(1{:}2{:}n-1) = \left[\begin{array}{cc} I_p & \Omega_p \\ I_p & -\Omega_p \end{array}\right] \left[\begin{array}{c} F_p x(1{:}4{:}n-1) \\ F_p x(3{:}4{:}n-1) \end{array}\right].$$

Define the vectors

$$w_T = F_p x(1{:}4{:}n-1)$$

and

$$w_B = F_p x(3{:}4{:}n-1)$$

and observe that

$$\Omega_p = \mathrm{diag}(1,\omega_m,\ldots,\omega_m^{p-1}) = \left[\mathrm{diag}(1,\omega_n,\ldots,\omega_n^{p-1})\right]^2 = \Delta_p^2.$$

It follows that

$$\left[\begin{array}{c} z_T \\ z_B \end{array}\right] = \left[\begin{array}{cc} I_p & \Delta_p^2 \\ I_p & -\Delta_p^2 \end{array}\right] \left[\begin{array}{c} w_T \\ w_B \end{array}\right]. \tag{2.5.3}$$

By substituting (2.5.3) into (2.5.2) we obtain

$$F_n x = \left[\begin{array}{cc|cc} I_p & 0 & \Delta_p & 0 \\ 0 & I_p & 0 & -i\Delta_p \\ \hline I_p & 0 & -\Delta_p & 0 \\ 0 & I_p & 0 & i\Delta_p \end{array}\right] \left[\begin{array}{cc|cc} I_p & 0 & 0 & 0 \\ 0 & I_p & 0 & 0 \\ \hline 0 & 0 & I_p & \Delta_p^2 \\ 0 & 0 & I_p & -\Delta_p^2 \end{array}\right] \left[\begin{array}{c} y_T \\ y_B \\ \hline w_T \\ w_B \end{array}\right]$$

$$= \left[\begin{array}{cc|cc} I_p & 0 & I_p & I_p \\ 0 & I_p & -iI_p & iI_p \\ \hline I_p & 0 & -I_p & -I_p \\ 0 & I_p & iI_p & -iI_p \end{array}\right] \left[\begin{array}{cc|cc} I_p & 0 & 0 & 0 \\ 0 & I_p & 0 & 0 \\ \hline 0 & 0 & \Delta_p & 0 \\ 0 & 0 & 0 & \Delta_p^3 \end{array}\right] \left[\begin{array}{c} y_T \\ y_B \\ \hline w_T \\ w_B \end{array}\right].$$

Observe that if we compute

$$u = \Delta_p w_T + \Delta_p^3 w_B,$$
$$v = \Delta_p w_T - \Delta_p^3 w_B,$$

then

$$F_n x = \begin{bmatrix} y_T + u \\ y_B - iv \\ y_T - u \\ y_B + iv \end{bmatrix}.$$

Thus, a split-radix synthesis of length n involves a pair of length $n/4$ scalings ($\Delta_p w_T$ and $\Delta_p^3 w_B$) and six vector additions of length $n/4$.

2.5.2 The Split-Radix Butterfly

The computations just described are worth encapsulating because they turn out to be central to the overall split-radix process. To that end, we define the n-by-n *split-radix butterfly matrix* by

$$\Sigma_n = \left[\begin{array}{cc|cc} I_p & 0 & I_p & I_p \\ 0 & I_p & -iI_p & iI_p \\ \hline I_p & 0 & -I_p & -I_p \\ 0 & I_p & iI_p & -iI_p \end{array}\right] \left[\begin{array}{cc|cc} I_p & 0 & 0 & 0 \\ 0 & I_p & 0 & 0 \\ \hline 0 & 0 & \Delta_p & 0 \\ 0 & 0 & 0 & \Delta_p^3 \end{array}\right], \qquad (2.5.4)$$

where $n = 2m = 4p$ and $\Delta_p = \text{diag}(1, \omega_n, \ldots, \omega_n^{p-1})$. Note that an update of the form $z \leftarrow \Sigma_n z$, where $z \in \mathbb{C}^n$, can be managed without a vector workspace:

$$
\begin{aligned}
&m \leftarrow n/2 \\
&p \leftarrow n/4 \\
&\textbf{for } j = 0{:}p - 1 \\
&\qquad \omega \leftarrow \exp(-2\pi i j/n) \\
&\qquad \hat{\omega} \leftarrow \omega^3 \\
&\qquad \tau_1 \leftarrow \omega \cdot z(m + j) \\
&\qquad \tau_2 \leftarrow \hat{\omega} \cdot z(m + p + j) \\
&\qquad \alpha \leftarrow \tau_1 + \tau_2 \\
&\qquad \gamma \leftarrow \tau_1 - \tau_2 \\
&\qquad z(m + p + j) \leftarrow z(p + j) + i\gamma \\
&\qquad z(m + j) \leftarrow z(j) - \alpha \\
&\qquad z(p + j) \leftarrow z(p + j) - i\gamma \\
&\qquad z(j) \leftarrow z(j) + \alpha \\
&\textbf{end}
\end{aligned}
\qquad (2.5.5)
$$

If we ignore the weight computations, then it is easy to verify that this operation requires $6n$ flops.

2.5.3 The Algorithm in Recursive Form

The splitting that we just detailed can be applied repeatedly. We illustrate this for the case $n = 32$. Starting at the top, we have

$$F_{32} x = \Sigma_{32} \begin{bmatrix} F_{16} x(0{:}2{:}31) \\ F_8 x(1{:}4{:}31) \\ F_8 x(3{:}4{:}31) \end{bmatrix}.$$

The three DFTs on the right-hand side of this equation also have split-radix formulations:

$$F_{16}x(0{:}2{:}31) \;=\; \Sigma_{16} \left[\begin{array}{c} F_8x(0{:}4{:}31) \\ F_4x(2{:}8{:}31) \\ F_4x(6{:}8{:}31) \end{array} \right],$$

$$F_8x(1{:}4{:}31) \;=\; \Sigma_8 \left[\begin{array}{c} F_4x(1{:}8{:}31) \\ F_2x(5{:}16{:}31) \\ F_2x(13{:}16{:}31) \end{array} \right],$$

$$F_8x(3{:}4{:}31) \;=\; \Sigma_8 \left[\begin{array}{c} F_4x(3{:}8{:}31) \\ F_2x(7{:}16{:}31) \\ F_2x(15{:}16{:}31) \end{array} \right].$$

The remaining 8-point and 4-point DFTs submit to a split-radix synthesis as well. However, the 2-point DFTs do not, and so we compute them "conventionally," e.g.,

$$F_2x(13{:}16{:}31) = \left[\begin{array}{c} x_{13} + x_{29} \\ x_{13} - x_{29} \end{array} \right].$$

Fig. 2.5.1 depicts the overall splitting strategy in the $n = 32$ case. The numbers at

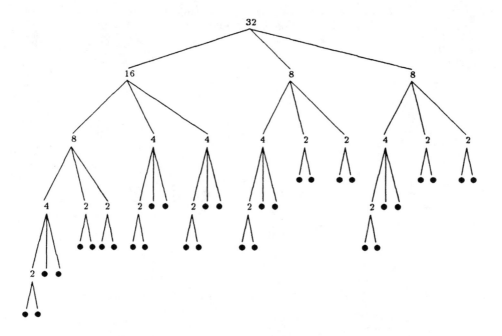

FIG. 2.5.1. *The split-radix computation tree ($n = 32$).*

each node in the tree indicate the length of the DFT formed. The black dots indicate 1-point DFTs, i.e., original x components. Notice that the computation tree is not balanced and that the algorithm does not produce all of the intermediate DFTs that arise in conventional radix-2 procedures. For example, only five of the eight 4-point

DFTs are computed that arise in the Cooley–Tukey process. Nevertheless, we are able to give a rigorous specification of the overall computation in the form of a recursive procedure.

Algorithm 2.5.1 If $x \in \mathbb{C}^n$ and $n = 2^t$, then the following algorithm computes $y = F_n x$:

> **function** $y = \text{split}(x, n)$
>   **if** $n = 1$
> $y \leftarrow x$
>   **elseif** $n = 2$
> $y \leftarrow F_2 x$
>   **else**
> $$y \leftarrow \Sigma_n \begin{bmatrix} \text{split}(x(0{:}2{:}n-1), n/2) \\ \text{split}(x(1{:}4{:}n-1), n/4) \\ \text{split}(x(3{:}4{:}n-1), n/4) \end{bmatrix}$$
>   **end**
> **end**

2.5.4 Derivation of a Sequential Version

The imbalance of the computation tree in Fig. 2.5.1 makes the derivation of a split-radix factorization of the DFT matrix more difficult than in the mixed-radix case. In the latter setting we have uniform computations across each level of the tree and this enables us to express the transition from level to level very succinctly, e.g., $x \leftarrow A_q x = (I_r \otimes B_L)x$.

However, we can regard the split-radix procedure as a Cooley–Tukey radix-2 algorithm in which we (a) "skip over" the unnecessary intermediate DFTs and (b) synthesize via Σ_L instead of the conventional radix-2 butterfly matrix B_L. Fig. 2.5.2 clarifies when and where the split-radix butterfly is applied. For each q, the as-

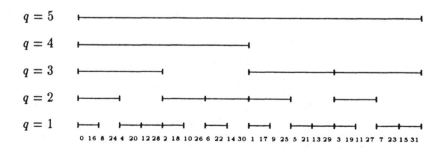

FIG. 2.5.2. *The selective application of* Σ_{2^q} $(q = 5)$.

sociated line segments indicate which L-point DFTs are computed where $L = 2^q$.

Thus, at step $q = 2$, five 4-point DFTs are computed. The indices along the bottom of the figure indicate which of these intermediate DFTs are found: $F_4 x(0{:}8{:}31)$, $F_4 x(2{:}8{:}31)$, $F_4 x(6{:}8{:}31)$, $F_4 x(1{:}8{:}31)$, and $F_4 x(3{:}8{:}31)$. Notice that intermediate DFTs $F_4 x(4{:}8{:}31)$, $F_4 x(5{:}8{:}31)$, and $F_4 x(7{:}8{:}31)$ are *not* found.

By defining the mission of the qth step in the split-radix algorithm to be the application of the required Σ_L butterflies, we obtain the following high-level organization:

$$
\begin{aligned}
&x \leftarrow P_n x \\
&\textbf{for } q = 1{:}t \\
&\qquad L \leftarrow 2^q \\
&\qquad \text{Perform all of the } \Sigma_L \text{ updates.} \\
&\textbf{end}
\end{aligned}
\qquad (2.5.6)
$$

Here, and throughout the remainder of this section, we define $\Sigma_2 = F_2$ for notational convenience.

To specify where intermediate DFTs of length $L = 2^q$ are found in the x-array after step q, we define a bit vector $\beta_r(0{:}r-1)$. Here, $r = n/L$ and for $k = 0{:}r-1$ we set

$$
\beta_r(k) = \begin{cases} 1 & \text{if } x(kL{:}(k+1)L-1) \text{ houses a length-}L \text{ DFT after step } q, \\ 0 & \text{if } x(kL{:}(k+1)L-1) \text{ does not house a length-}L \text{ DFT after step } q. \end{cases}
$$

These bit vectors permit the following expansion of (2.5.6):

$$
\begin{aligned}
&x \leftarrow P_n x \\
&\textbf{for } q = 1{:}t \\
&\qquad L \leftarrow 2^q; \ r \leftarrow n/L \\
&\qquad \textbf{for } k = 0{:}r-1 \\
&\qquad\qquad \textbf{if } \beta_r(k) = 1 \\
&\qquad\qquad\qquad x(kL{:}(k+1)L-1) \leftarrow \Sigma_L x(kL{:}(k+1)L-1) \\
&\qquad\qquad \textbf{end} \\
&\qquad \textbf{end} \\
&\textbf{end}
\end{aligned}
\qquad (2.5.7)
$$

It follows that if we define

$$
\Lambda_q = \text{diag}(\Lambda_q^{(0)}, \Lambda_q^{(1)}, \ldots, \Lambda_q^{(r-1)}), \qquad \Lambda_q^{(k)} = \begin{cases} I_L & \text{if } \beta_r(k) = 0, \\ \Sigma_L & \text{if } \beta_r(k) = 1, \end{cases}
$$

then the mission of the qth step in (2.5.7) is to carry out the update $x \leftarrow \Lambda_q x$. This establishes the following *split-radix factorization*:

$$
F_n P_n = \Lambda_t \cdots \Lambda_1 . \qquad (2.5.8)
$$

In the $n = 32$ case the following bit vectors arise:

$$
\begin{aligned}
\beta_{16} &= [\,1\,0\,1\,1\,1\,0\,1\,0\,1\,0\,1\,1\,1\,0\,1\,1\,], \\
\beta_8 &= [\,1\,0\,1\,1\,1\,0\,1\,0\,], \\
\beta_4 &= [\,1\,0\,1\,1\,], \\
\beta_2 &= [\,1\,0\,], \\
\beta_1 &= [\,1\,].
\end{aligned}
$$

It follows that

$$
\begin{aligned}
\Lambda_1 &= \mathrm{diag}(\Sigma_2, I_2, \Sigma_2, \Sigma_2, \Sigma_2, I_2, \Sigma_2, I_2, \Sigma_2, I_2, \Sigma_2, \Sigma_2, \Sigma_2, I_2, \Sigma_2, \Sigma_2), \\
\Lambda_2 &= \mathrm{diag}(\Sigma_4, I_4, \Sigma_4, \Sigma_4, \Sigma_4, I_4, \Sigma_4, I_4), \\
\Lambda_3 &= \mathrm{diag}(\Sigma_8, I_8, \Sigma_8, \Sigma_8), \\
\Lambda_4 &= \mathrm{diag}(\Sigma_{16}, I_{16}), \\
\Lambda_5 &= \mathrm{diag}(\Sigma_{32}).
\end{aligned}
$$

2.5.5   The β-Vectors

To complete the algorithmic development, we need a method for generating the β-vectors. We begin with a lemma that shows how to obtain β_{2r} from β_r.

Lemma 2.5.1 *If* $\beta_r(k) = 1$, *then* $\beta_{2r}(2k) = 1$ *and* $\beta_{2r}(2k+1) = 0$. *If* $\beta_r(k) = 0$, *then* $\beta_{2r}(2k) = 1$ *and* $\beta_{2r}(2k+1) = 1$.

Proof. Suppose upon completion of step q in (2.5.7) that $x(kL{:}(k+1)L - 1)$ houses a length-L DFT. It follows that upon completion of step $q - 1$, $x(2kL_*{:}(2k+1)L_* - 1)$ houses a length $L_* = L/2$ DFT but $x((2k+1)L_*{:}(2k+2)L_* - 1)$ does not. Thus, $\beta_r(k) = 1$ implies $\beta_{2r}(2k) = 1$ and $\beta_{2r}(2k+1) = 0$.

Likewise, if $x(kL{:}(k+1)L - 1)$ does not house a length-L DFT upon completion of step q, then upon completion of step $q - 1$, subvectors $x(2kL_*{:}(2k+1)L_* - 1)$ and $x((2k+1)L_*{:}(2k+2)L_* - 1)$ each house DFTs of length L_*. Thus, $\beta_r(k) = 0$ implies $\beta_{2r}(2k) = 1$ and $\beta_{2r}(2k+1) = 1$. $\square$

Using this result, it is possible to establish a more useful specification of the β-vectors.

Theorem 2.5.2 *If* $n = 2^t$, *then* $\beta_1 = [\,1\,]$ *and*

$$
\beta_{2r} = [\ \beta_r \mid \tilde{\beta}_r \ ]
$$

for $r = 1, 2, 4, \ldots, n/4$. *Here,* $\tilde{\beta}_r$ *equals* β_r *with a reversal in the last bit position. Moreover,* $\beta_r = \beta_{n/2}(0{:}r - 1)$.

Proof. The theorem follows by induction, Lemma 2.5.1, and the observation that $\beta_{2r} = [\beta_{r/2} \mid \tilde{\beta}_{r/2} \mid \beta_{r/2} \mid \beta_{r/2}\,]$. Details are left to the reader. $\square$

From the theorem we see how to build up $\beta_{n/2}$ through repeated concatenation.

Algorithm 2.5.2 If $n = 2^t$, then the following algorithm computes $\beta = \beta_{n/2}$.

```
β ← [ 1 ]
for q = 1:t − 1
        β ← [ β | β ]
        s ← 2^q − 1
        if β(s) = 0
                β(s) ← 1
        else
                β(s) ← 0
        end
end
```

Once $\beta_{n/2}$ is available, the extraction of β_r is a simple matter, for according to Theorem 2.5.2, $\beta_r = \beta_{n/2}(0{:}r-1)$. This leads to the following refinement of (2.5.7):

$$x \leftarrow P_n x$$
$$\beta \leftarrow \beta_{n/2} \qquad \text{(Algorithm 2.5.2)}$$
$$\textbf{for } q = 1{:}t$$
$$\qquad L \leftarrow 2^q; \ r \leftarrow n/L$$
$$\qquad \textbf{for } k = 0{:}r-1$$
$$\qquad\qquad \textbf{if } \beta(k) = 1$$
$$\qquad\qquad\qquad x(kL{:}(k+1)L-1) \leftarrow \Sigma_L x(kL{:}(k+1)L-1)$$
$$\qquad\qquad \textbf{end}$$
$$\qquad \textbf{end}$$
$$\textbf{end}$$

2.5.6   The Complete Algorithm

If we identify n with L and z with $x(kL{:}(k+1)L-1)$, then (2.5.5) shows how to carry out the Σ_L update. The redundant weight computation can be removed by reversing the k and j loops.

Algorithm 2.5.3 If $n = 2^t$ and $x \in \mathbb{C}^n$, then the following algorithm overwrites x with $F_n x$.

$$x \leftarrow P_n x \qquad \text{(Algorithm 1.5.2)}$$
$$\beta \leftarrow \beta_{n/2} \qquad \text{(Algorithm 2.5.1)}$$
$$\{\text{Compute the necessary 2-point DFTs.}\}$$
$$\textbf{for } k = 0{:}(n/2)-1$$
$$\qquad \textbf{if } \beta(k) = 1$$
$$\qquad\qquad \tau \leftarrow x(2k+1); \ x(2k+1) \leftarrow x(2k) - \tau; \ x(2k) \leftarrow x(2k) + \tau;$$
$$\qquad \textbf{end}$$
$$\textbf{end}$$
$$\textbf{for } q = 2{:}t$$
$$\qquad L \leftarrow 2^q; \ r \leftarrow n/L; \ m \leftarrow L/2; \ p \leftarrow L/4$$
$$\qquad \textbf{for } j = 0{:}p-1$$
$$\qquad\qquad \omega \leftarrow \exp(-2\pi i j/L)$$
$$\qquad\qquad \hat{\omega} \leftarrow \omega^3$$
$$\qquad\qquad \textbf{for } k = 0{:}r-1$$
$$\qquad\qquad\qquad \textbf{if } \beta(k) = 1$$
$$\qquad\qquad\qquad\qquad \tau_1 \leftarrow \omega \cdot x(kL + m + j)$$
$$\qquad\qquad\qquad\qquad \tau_2 \leftarrow \hat{\omega} \cdot x(kL + m + p + j)$$
$$\qquad\qquad\qquad\qquad \alpha \leftarrow \tau_1 + \tau_2$$
$$\qquad\qquad\qquad\qquad \gamma \leftarrow \tau_1 - \tau_2$$
$$\qquad\qquad\qquad\qquad x(kL + m + p + j) \leftarrow x(kL + p + j) + i\gamma$$
$$\qquad\qquad\qquad\qquad x(kL + m + j) \leftarrow x(kL + j) - \alpha$$
$$\qquad\qquad\qquad\qquad x(kL + p + j) \leftarrow x(kL + p + j) - i\gamma$$
$$\qquad\qquad\qquad\qquad x(kL + j) \leftarrow x(kL + j) + \alpha$$
$$\qquad\qquad\qquad \textbf{end}$$
$$\qquad\qquad \textbf{end}$$
$$\qquad \textbf{end}$$
$$\textbf{end}$$

We mention that it is possible to organize the computation without space allocated for the length-$n/2$ bit vector $\beta_{n/2}$. See Burrus and Parks (1985); Sorensen, Heideman, and Burrus (1986); or Duhamel (1986). However, it should be noted that if 64-bit words are used to house real floating point numbers, then $\beta_{n/2}$ represents a memory allocation overhead of less than a half of a percent.

It is important to work out the flop count for Algorithm 2.5.3, since it is more favorable than the flop counts for the standard radix-2, 4, and 8 algorithms. Let $g(L)$ be the number of flops required to execute the product $\Sigma_L v$, where $v \in \mathbb{C}^L$. We know from the discussion of (2.5.5) that

$$
g(L) \;=\; \begin{cases} 4 & \text{if } L = 2, \\[2mm] 6L & \text{if } L \geq 4. \end{cases}
$$

It is clear that the number of flops required by Algorithm 2.5.3 is given by

$$
\mu \;=\; \sum_{q=1}^{t} \sum_{k=0}^{(n/2^q)-1} \beta(k) g(2^q) \;=\; \sum_{q=1}^{t} g(2^q) \left(\sum_{k=0}^{2^{t-q}-1} \beta(k) \right),
$$

where it should be noted from Theorem 2.5.2 that

$$
\nu_q \;=\; \sum_{k=0}^{2^{t-q}-1} \beta(k)
$$

is the number of 1's in the bit vector β_r. Again referring to Theorem 2.5.2, it is not hard to show that the ν_q satisfy the following recurrence:

$$
\nu_q \;=\; \begin{cases} 2\nu_{q+1} + (-1)^{t-q} & (q < t), \\[2mm] 1 & (q = t). \end{cases}
$$

Using elementary difference equation theory we have

$$
\nu_q \;=\; \frac{2}{3} 2^{t-q} + \frac{1}{3}(-1)^{t-q} . \tag{2.5.9}
$$

Making approximations for large n we find

$$
\mu \;=\; 4\nu_1 + 6 \sum_{q=2}^{t} 2^q \nu_q \;\approx\; 4n \log_2 n .
$$

Compared to the radix-2 ($5n \log_2 n$ flops), radix-4 ($4.25n \log_2 n$ flops), and radix-8 ($4.08n \log_2 n$ flops) frameworks, we see that the split-radix approach is very attractive from the standpoint of the number of flops.

Problems

P2.5.1 Prove Theorem 2.5.2.

P2.5.2 Develop a decimation-in-frequency version of Algorithm 2.5.3.

P2.5.3 Develop a qkj version of Algorithm 2.5.3 with weight precomputation.

P2.5.4 Prove (2.5.9).

P2.5.5 Show that if $n = 2^t$, then $\beta = \beta_{n/2}$ can be computed as follows:

$\beta(0{:}(n/2) - 1) \leftarrow 0$
for $q = 0{:}\mathbf{floor}((t - 1)/2)$
        $m \leftarrow 4^q$
        for $k = m - 1{:}2m{:}n - 1$
                $\beta(k) \leftarrow 1$
        end
end

Use this result to obtain a version of Algorithm 2.5.3 that does not explicitly require a β-vector.

P2.5.6 Show that for $k \geq 4$,

$$\beta_k = [\,\beta_{k/2} \mid \beta_{k/4} \mid \beta_{k/4}\,]\,.$$

P2.5.7 Develop a split-radix algorithm based on the synthesis of one half-length, one quarter-length, and two eighth-length DFTs. Use the recursion of P2.5.6 to develop a recipe for the β-vector.

Notes and References for Section 2.5

The split-radix approach was first proposed in

P. Duhamel and H. Hollmann (1984). "Split Radix FFT Algorithms," *Electron. Lett. 20*, 14–16.

Implementation details are discussed in

C.S. Burrus and T. Parks (1985). *DFT/FFT and Convolution*, John Wiley, New York.
P. Duhamel (1986). "Implementation of the Split-Radix FFT Algorithms for Complex, Real, and Real-Symmetric Data," *IEEE Trans. Acoust. Speech Signal Process. ASSP-34*, 285–295.
H.V. Sorensen, M.T. Heideman, and C.S. Burrus (1986). "On Calculating the Split-Radix FFT," *IEEE Trans. Acoust. Speech Signal Process. ASSP-34*, 152–156.

The split-radix idea can be extended to other radix pairs, e.g., 3 and 9. See

M. Vetterli and P. Duhamel (1989). "Split-Radix Algorithms for Length p^m DFTs," *IEEE Trans. Acoust. Speech Signal Process. ASSP-34*, 57–64.

Chapter 3

High-Performance Frameworks

Suppose $X \in \mathbb{C}^{n_1 \times n_2}$. The computations $X \leftarrow F_{n_1} X$ and $X \leftarrow X F_{n_2}$ are referred to as multiple DFT problems. Applying an FFT algorithm to the columns or rows of a matrix is an important problem in many applications. However, there is more to the problem than just the repeated application of a single-vector technique, as we show in §3.1.

Single-vector DFT problems can be converted into a pair of multiple DFT problems with a scaling in between by exploiting the radix-p splitting. For example, setting $m = n_1$ and $p = n_2$ in (2.1.9) gives

$$[F_n x]_{n_1 \times n_2} = [F_n(0{:}n_1 - 1, 0{:}n_2 - 1).* (F_{n_1} x_{n_2 \times n_1}^T)] F_{n_2} .$$

This amounts to a "blocking" of the single-vector FFT problem and is very effective in many high-performance environments. The transpositions that are required by this framework are detailed in §3.2, and this is followed by a discussion of large single-vector FFTs in §3.3.

The multidimensional DFT problem is discussed in §3.4. Successful approaches in this area involve interesting combinations of matrix transposition and multiple DFT computation.

We conclude with two sections on parallel FFTs. Our aim is to highlight how one reasons about parallel computation in both distributed-memory and shared-memory environments.

3.1   The Multiple DFT Problem

Suppose $X \in \mathbb{C}^{n_1 \times n_2}$. The computations

$$X \leftarrow F_{n_1} X, \tag{3.1.1}$$
$$X \leftarrow X F_{n_2} \tag{3.1.2}$$

are examples of the *multiple DFT problem*. In a sense, these problems pose no new computational challenge. The *multicolumn DFT problem* (3.1.1) requires the DFT of each X-column, whereas the *multirow DFT problem* (3.1.2) requires the DFT of each X-row. However, if memory traffic and vectorization issues are considered, then these calculations have some interesting aspects that are not present in the single-vector DFT problem.

3.1.1   Stockham-Based Multiple DFT Algorithms

If we approach the multicolumn DFT problem (3.1.1) on a column-by-column basis, then we are led to a procedure of the following form:

> **for** $col = 0{:}n_2 - 1$
> $\quad X(0{:}n_1 - 1, col) \leftarrow F_{n_1} X(0{:}n_1 - 1, col)$
> **end**

The selection of an appropriate single-vector FFT is central. For example, if $n_1 = 2^{t_1}$ and we apply the qjk radix-2 Stockham framework (Algorithm 1.7.2), then we obtain

> **for** $col = 0{:}n_2 - 1$
> $\quad$ **for** $q = 1{:}t_1$
> $\qquad L \leftarrow 2^q;\ r \leftarrow n_1/L;\ L_* \leftarrow L/2;\ r_* \leftarrow 2r$
> $\qquad y \leftarrow X(0{:}n_1 - 1, col)$
> $\qquad$ **for** $j = 0{:}L_* - 1$
> $\qquad\quad$ **for** $k = 0{:}r - 1$
> $\qquad\qquad \tau \leftarrow \omega_L^j y(jr_* + r + k)$
> $\qquad\qquad X(jr + k, col) \leftarrow y(jr_* + k) + \tau$ $\qquad$ (3.1.3)
> $\qquad\qquad X((j + L_*)r + k, col) \leftarrow y(jr_* + k) - \tau$
> $\qquad\quad$ **end**
> $\qquad$ **end**
> $\quad$ **end**
> **end**

We assume that the weights are obtained by an appropriate access to the long weight vector $w_n^{(long)}$ that is defined in §1.4.11. Note that only one vector workspace for the Stockham y-vector is required in the above "$(col)qjk$" version.

If vector length is an issue, then we might gravitate towards a $qjk(col)$ implementation of (3.1.3) because the col-loop has length n_1 which would probably dominate vector register length in applications of interest. This modification is not particularly attractive, because it involves nonunit stride access and requires an n_1-by-n_2 workspace array.

A Stockham-based method for the multirow DFT problem (3.1.2) can be similarly arranged. Assuming that $n_2 = 2^{t_2}$, we have

for $row = 0{:}n_1 - 1$
    for $q = 1{:}t_2$
        $L \leftarrow 2^q; \; r \leftarrow n_2/L; \; L_* \leftarrow L/2; \; r_* \leftarrow 2r$
        $y \leftarrow X(row, 0{:}n_2 - 1)$
        for $j = 0{:}L_* - 1$
            for $k = 0{:}r - 1$
                $\tau \leftarrow \omega_L^j y(jr_* + r + k)$ (3.1.4)
                $X(row, jr + k) \leftarrow y(jr_* + k) + \tau$
                $X(row, (j + L_*)r + k) \leftarrow y(jr_* + k) - \tau$
            end
        end
    end
end

This is *not* a unit-stride procedure. However, we can correct this by making the inner-most loop the *row*-loop. This means that all n_1 row DFTs are processed concurrently, an approach that requires an n_1-by-n_2 work array. However, there is no loss in performance if we process the row DFTs in groups of size ℓ, where ℓ is the vector register length. With this approach, a Y-array of size $\ell \times n_2$ is required. In particular, if we assume for clarity that $n_1 = \nu\ell$, then

for $b = 0{:}\nu - 1$
    for $q = 1{:}t_2$
        $L \leftarrow 2^q; \; r \leftarrow n_2/L; \; L_* \leftarrow L/2; \; r_* \leftarrow 2r$
        $Y(0{:}\ell - 1, 0{:}n_2 - 1) \leftarrow X(b\ell{:}(b + 1)\ell - 1, 0{:}n_2 - 1)$
        for $j = 0{:}L_* - 1$
            for $k = 0{:}r - 1$
                for $s = 0{:}\ell - 1$
                    $row \leftarrow b\ell + s$
                    $\tau \leftarrow \omega_L^j Y(s, jr_* + r + k)$ (3.1.5)
                    $X(row, jr + k) \leftarrow Y(s, jr_* + k) + \tau$
                    $X(row, (j + L_*)r + k) \leftarrow Y(s, jr_* + k) - \tau$
                end
            end
        end
    end
end

overwrites X with XF_{n_2}. Overall, we conclude that if we can afford an $\ell \times n_2$ workspace, then it is easier to reconcile stride and vector length in the multirow DFT problem than in the multicolumn DFT problem.

3.1.2 Cooley–Tukey-Based Multiple DFTs

The Cooley–Tukey framework can also be applied to multiple DFT problems. We consider the multirow DFT problem first. Assume that $n_2 = 2^{t_2}$. The Cooley–Tukey process begins with the bit-reversal permutation of each row in X. This could be achieved by applying Algorithm 1.5.2 to each row. However, to avoid the redundant evaluation of the bit-reversal function $r_{n_2}(j)$, it is better to process the columns concurrently and thereby obtain the following vectorized version of the procedure:

$$\textbf{for } k = 0{:}n_2 - 1$$
$$\quad j \leftarrow r_{n_2}(k) \qquad \text{(Algorithm 1.5.1)}$$
$$\quad \textbf{if } j > k \qquad\qquad\qquad\qquad\qquad\qquad (3.1.6)$$
$$\qquad X(0{:}n_1 - 1, k) \leftrightarrow X(0{:}n_1 - 1, j)$$
$$\quad \textbf{end}$$
$$\textbf{end}$$

Notice that the interchanges involve swapping unit stride column vectors.

After the bit-reversal permutation has been applied to each row in X, we may proceed with the butterfly operations. There are two major possibilities, the first being the row-by-row resolution of XF_{n_2}:

$$\textbf{for } row = 0{:}n_1 - 1$$
$$\quad \textbf{for } q = 1{:}t_2$$
$$\qquad X(row, 0{:}n_2 - 1) \leftarrow X(row, 0{:}n_2 - 1)A_q^T$$
$$\quad \textbf{end}$$
$$\textbf{end}$$

Here, $F_{n_2}P_{n_2} = A_{t_2} \cdots A_1$ is the Cooley–Tukey factorization described in §1.3.4. This approach has poor stride properties because X is accessed by row. Alternatively, if we are to compute $XF_{n_2} = XP_{n_2}A_1^T \cdots A_{t_2}^T$, then we can apply each A_q across the entire X array as follows:

$$\textbf{for } q = 1{:}t_2$$
$$\quad \textbf{for } row = 0{:}n_1 - 1$$
$$\qquad X(row, 0{:}n_2 - 1) \leftarrow X(row, 0{:}n_2 - 1)A_q^T$$
$$\quad \textbf{end}$$
$$\textbf{end}$$

Unlike the Stockham case (3.1.5), this process does *not* require an array workspace. Using direct call for the on-line generation of weights we obtain

$$X \leftarrow XP_{n_2} \qquad \text{(Use (3.1.6))}$$
$$\textbf{for } q = 1{:}t_2$$
$$\quad L \leftarrow 2^q; \; r \leftarrow n_2/L; \; L_* \leftarrow L/2$$
$$\quad \textbf{for } j = 0{:}L_* - 1$$
$$\qquad \omega \leftarrow \cos(2\pi j/L) - i\sin(2\pi j/L)$$
$$\qquad \textbf{for } k = 0{:}r - 1$$
$$\qquad\quad \textbf{for } row = 0{:}n_1 - 1$$
$$\qquad\qquad \tau \leftarrow \omega \cdot X(row, kL + L_* + j) \qquad\qquad (3.1.7)$$
$$\qquad\qquad X(row, kL + L_* + j) \leftarrow X(row, kL + j) - \tau$$
$$\qquad\qquad X(row, kL + j) \leftarrow X(row, kL + j) + \tau$$
$$\qquad\quad \textbf{end}$$
$$\qquad \textbf{end}$$
$$\quad \textbf{end}$$
$$\textbf{end}$$

Thus, the combination of (3.1.6) and (3.1.7) is attractive in terms of stride, vector length, and work array requirements.

Unfortunately, the same cannot be said of the Cooley–Tukey approach to the $X \leftarrow F_{n_1}X$ calculation. If we insist on unit stride, then the bit reversal must proceed column by column and a $(col)qkj$ loop ordering must be followed during the butter-fly computations. Recall from §1.6.2 that qkj orderings imply weight computation redundancy. However, this can be resolved with weight precomputation, because the required $n/2$ workspace is not significant given the size of the X-array itself.

3.1.3 The Truncated Stockham Framework

Recall that the Stockham frameworks produce intermediate DFT arrays in natural order. This fact can be harnessed to solve multirow DFT problems.

Suppose we wish to compute $X(0{:}n_1-1, 0{:}n_2-1)F_{n_2}$, where $n_1 = 2^{t_1}$ and $n_2 = 2^{t_2}$. Set $n = n_1 n_2$ and $t = t_1 + t_2$, and identify $x \in \mathbb{C}^n$ with X:

$$x_{n_1 \times n_2} \equiv X.$$

Suppose we apply t_2 steps of Algorithm 1.7.2, the jk version of the radix-2 Stockham procedure. From the intermediate DFT array characterization (1.9.2) we know that after t_2 steps the vector x is overwritten with $x_{n_1 \times n_2} F_{n_2} = X F_{n_2}$. Thus, by halting the algorithm at the proper point, the required multirow DFT is obtained. This is called the *truncated Stockham algorithm*. Recall that Algorithm 1.7.2 has unit stride and inner loop length 2^{t-q}. Thus, the truncated Stockham framework manipulates vectors that are longer than $n_1 = 2^{t-t_2}$. See Korn and Lambiotte (1979) for details.

Problems

P3.1.1 Modify (3.1.5) so that it can handle the case when n_2 is not a multiple of ℓ.

P3.1.2 Formulate a truncated autosort approach to the multicolumn DFT problem.

Notes and References for Section 3.1

Practical aspects of the multiple DFT problem are discussed in

B. Fornberg (1981). "A Vector Implementation of the Fast Fourier Transform," *Math. Comp. 36*, 189–191.

D.G. Korn and J.J. Lambiotte (1979). "Computing the Fast Fourier Transform on a Vector Computer," *Math. Comp. 33*, 977–992.

P.N. Swarztrauber (1984b). "FFT Algorithms for Vector Computers," *Parallel Comput. 1*, 45–63.

3.2 Matrix Transposition

In this section we consider the matrix transpose problem

$$Z \leftarrow X^T, \qquad X \in \mathbb{C}^{n_1 \times n_2}. \tag{3.2.1}$$

Efficient algorithms for this operation are particularly important in the context of large single-vector DFTs and multidimensional DFTs. Our development focuses on the attributes of stride and the re-use of data. Good general references include Bailey (1990) and Eklundh (1981).

Before we begin, we mention that in practice the complex X-array is actually a pair of real arrays. This merely requires a twofold application of whatever transpose technique is invoked. However, for simplicity we suppress this detail and act as if the real and imaginary parts of X are transposed "at the same time."

3.2.1   Scalar-Level Transposition

The simplest algorithm for the transposition problem is the following double-loop scheme:

Algorithm 3.2.1 Given $X \in \mathbb{C}^{n_1 \times n_2}$, the following algorithm computes $Z = X^T$:

> **for** $col = 0{:}n_2 - 1$
> > **for** $row = 0{:}n_1 - 1$
> > > $Z(col, row) \leftarrow X(row, col)$
> >
> > **end**
>
> **end**

A problem with Algorithm 3.2.1 is the nonunit stride access into Z. If we reverse the loop order, then the same problem surfaces with X. Thus, this conventional transpose algorithm has stride problems that can be acute if n_1 and n_2 are powers of two, as is frequently the case in FFT applications.

3.2.2   Transposition by Diagonal

One way to address the stride issue in matrix transposition is to transpose by diagonal. For any matrix $A = (a_{kj})$, we say that a_{kj} is on the dth *diagonal* of A if $j = k + d$. Thus the main diagonal is the zeroth diagonal. The positive (negative) diagonals are in the strictly upper (lower) triangular portion of A. The entries that make up the diagonals of $X = x_{n_1 \times n_2}$ have stride $n_1 + 1$. For example, if $d > 0$, then the dth diagonal is situated in $x(n_1 d{:}n_1 + 1{:}n_1 n_2 - d - 1)$. Transposition by diagonal amounts to mapping the dth diagonal of X onto the $-d$th diagonal of Z.

Algorithm 3.2.2 Given $X \in \mathbb{C}^{n_1 \times n_2}$, the following algorithm computes $Z = X^T$:

> **for** $d = -n_1 + 1{:}n_2 - 1$
> > Compute $\mu_d = $ length of the dth diagonal.
> > **if** $d \leq 0$
> > > **for** $k = 0{:}\mu_d - 1$
> > > > $Z(k, k - d) \leftarrow X(k - d, k)$
> > >
> > > **end**
> >
> > **else**
> > > **for** $k = 0{:}\mu_d - 1$
> > > > $Z(k + d, k) \leftarrow X(k, k + d)$
> > >
> > > **end**
> >
> > **end**
>
> **end**

Consider the execution of this procedure on a machine whose memory is partitioned into 2^7 banks. Assume that $n_1 = 2^{t_1}$. Using the fact that 2^7 and $2^{t_1} + 1$ are relatively prime (meaning that their greatest common divisor is 1), it is possible to show that diagonal access can proceed without bank conflict. (See §1.4.8 for a discussion of the memory bank conflict problem.)

3.2.3   In-Place Transposition via Permutation Cycles

If $n_1 = n_2$, then it is easy to modify Algorithms 3.2.1 and 3.2.2 so that $X = x_{n_1 \times n_2}$ is overwritten by X^T. If $n_1 \neq n_2$, then the in-place transposition problem

$$x_{n_2 \times n_1} \leftarrow x_{n_1 \times n_2}^T$$

is a little more difficult.

We start by recalling that if $n = n_1 n_2$ and $y = \Pi_{n_1,n}^T x$, then $y_{n_2 \times n_1} = x_{n_1 \times n_2}^T$. Given n_1 and n_2, define the index function f by

$$y = \Pi_{n_1,n}^T x = \begin{bmatrix} x_{f(0)} \\ x_{f(1)} \\ \vdots \\ x_{f(n-1)} \end{bmatrix}.$$

Observe that if $0 \leq k < n - 1$ and we compute

$$\begin{aligned} \beta &\leftarrow \mathbf{floor}(k/n_1) \\ \alpha &\leftarrow k - \beta n_1 \\ j &\leftarrow \alpha n_2 + \beta, \end{aligned}$$

then $j = f(k)$. The required transposition can therefore be obtained by executing Algorithm 2.2.3 with $g = f$.

3.2.4   Matrix Transposition in a Memory Hierarchy

We now develop some transposition algorithms that are attractive when the underlying computer system has a memory hierarchy as depicted in Fig. 3.2.1. In this schematic,

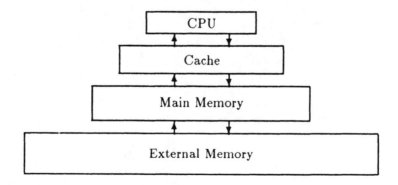

FIG. 3.2.1. *A hierarchical memory system.*

the *cache* is a small but fast memory whose purpose is to hold currently "active" data, thereby reducing the number of reads and writes to main memory. A sample external memory device might be a disk or some other cheap-per-byte device. In this model we assume that

- Data transfers between the memory levels are expensive and care should be exercised so as to minimize their frequency. Thus, data in cache can be retrieved much more quickly by the CPU than data in main memory, which in turn can be retrieved much more quickly than data in external memory.

- Cache is much smaller than main memory, which in turn is much smaller than external memory.

In the most general situation, the matrix to be transposed resides in external memory. "Chunks" of the matrix migrate to the top of the memory hierarchy, where they are rearranged and subsequently restored to the lower levels of the hierarchy in some systematic fashion. To acquire an intuition about transposition in a memory hierarchy, we detail a pair of specific subproblems:

- The X-matrix resides in main memory and we focus on the cache/main memory interface.

- The X-matrix resides in external memory and we focus on the data flow between the external and main memories.

We remind the reader that, in practice, the techniques we are about to detail would be applied separately to the arrays that house the real and imaginary portions of the matrix to be transposed.

3.2.5 Transposition with a Cache

As we mentioned, a *cache* is a small but fast memory whose purpose is to hold currently "active" data and thereby reduce access to main memory. The rules by which data move into and out of cache vary from machine to machine. An excellent discussion about the various protocols may be found in §8.3 of Hennessy and Patterson (1990). We consider just enough detail to convey the spirit of "cache thinking."

Common to all caches is the notion of a *cache line*. If we think of the cache as an array, then it is convenient to regard the cache lines as its columns. Fig. 3.2.2 depicts a cache with n_c lines, each of length ℓ_c. During the transposition $Z \leftarrow X^T$,

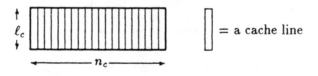

FIG. 3.2.2. *A cache.*

array elements flow between the cache and main memory in accordance with various read and write protocols. To facilitate the description of these rules, we work with the blockings

$$
X = \begin{bmatrix} X_{00} & \cdots & X_{0,n_2-1} \\ \vdots & & \vdots \\ X_{s-1,0} & \cdots & X_{s-1,n_2-1} \end{bmatrix}, \quad
Z = \begin{bmatrix} Z_{00} & \cdots & Z_{0,n_1-1} \\ \vdots & & \vdots \\ Z_{r-1,0} & \cdots & Z_{r-1,n_1-1} \end{bmatrix},
$$

where $X_{kj} \in \mathbb{C}^{\ell_c \times 1}$ and $Z_{kj} \in \mathbb{C}^{\ell_c \times 1}$. For the sake of clarity, we have assumed that $n_1 = s\ell_c$ and $n_2 = r\ell_c$. A snapshot of the cache during execution would reveal Z_{kj}'s and X_{kj}'s occupying the cache lines. It is instructive to describe qualitatively the flow of these subcolumns as they are ushered into and out of the cache during the execution of Algorithm 3.2.1.

If the CPU requests a component of X_{kj} and if this subcolumn is in cache, then a *cache hit* occurs and the requested component is retrieved without a reference to main memory. Otherwise, a *cache miss* results and X_{kj} is copied from main memory into a cache line, "bumping" the previous contents of that line. To minimize the chance of removing "currently active" data, the protocol of bumping least recently used cache lines is often adopted.

The copying of cache entries into main memory also proceeds according to a fixed protocol. For example, if the CPU wishes to store a component of Z_{kj}, then with the *write-back protocol*

- Z_{kj} is brought into cache if it is not already there,

- the cache line associated with Z_{kj} is updated, and

- subcolumn Z_{kj} in main memory is updated only when the cache line associated with Z_{kj} is bumped.

Now consider execution of Algorithm 3.2.1 in a cache environment with the assumption that n_1 and n_2 are each much larger than both ℓ_c and n_c. Assume that the X and Z arrays are situated in main memory. With the *col-row* loop ordering in Algorithm 3.2.1, X is accessed by column. This is good, because when subcolumn X_{kj} is brought into cache, it stays there until all of its components have found their way into Z. However, the situation is not so attractive for Z. The entries in each column of X get "mapped" into n_1 different Z-blocks. If $n_1 > n_c$, then every reference to a Z-entry in Algorithm 3.2.1 will require the loading of the corresponding Z_{kj} into cache. For example, the assignment $z_{00} \leftarrow x_{00}$ prompts the loading of Z_{00}. However, this loaded subvector is not required again until the assignment $z_{10} \leftarrow x_{01}$. Unfortunately, in between the z_{00} and z_{10} updates are $n_1 - 1$ other references to Z:

$$z_{01} \leftarrow x_{10}$$
$$\vdots$$
$$z_{0,n_1-1} \leftarrow x_{n_1-1,0}$$

Each of these assignments requires the loading of the corresponding Z-block into cache, which means that Z_{00} will have been bumped long before the algorithm carries out $z_{10} \leftarrow x_{01}$. It follows that each Z-block is read into cache ℓ_c times during the execution of Algorithm 3.2.1. Nothing is solved by inverting the loops, because the inversion of the loops causes the problems to shift to the X array.

From this discussion we see that the standard double-loop transposition algorithm is poorly designed for efficient cache utilization. A better approach is to transpose X *by block*. Assume that $n_1 = \alpha_1 N_1$ and $n_2 = \alpha_2 N_2$ and partition the X and Z arrays as follows:

$$X = \begin{bmatrix} X_{00} & \cdots & X_{0,N_2-1} \\ \vdots & & \vdots \\ X_{N_1-1,0} & \cdots & X_{N_1-1,N_2-1} \end{bmatrix}, \qquad X_{kj} \in \mathbb{C}^{\alpha_1 \times \alpha_2},$$

$$Z = \begin{bmatrix} Z_{00} & \cdots & Z_{0,N_1-1} \\ \vdots & & \vdots \\ Z_{N_2-1,0} & \cdots & Z_{N_2-1,N_1-1} \end{bmatrix}, \qquad Z_{kj} \in \mathbb{C}^{\alpha_2 \times \alpha_1}.$$

Here is an algorithm that transposes X in block-by-block fashion, i.e., $Z_{kj} \leftarrow X_{jk}^T$.

Algorithm 3.2.3 Given $X \in \mathbb{C}^{n_1 \times n_2}$, the following algorithm computes $Z = X^T$ with the assumption that $n_1 = \alpha_1 N_1$ and $n_2 = \alpha_2 N_2$:

> **for** $k = 0{:}N_1 - 1$
> > $rows \leftarrow \alpha_1 k{:}\alpha_1(k+1) - 1$
> > **for** $j = 0{:}N_2 - 1$
> > > $cols \leftarrow \alpha_2 j{:}\alpha_2(j+1) - 1$
> > > $Z(cols, rows) \leftarrow X(rows, cols)^T$
> > **end**
> **end**

Suppose the block dimensions α_1 and α_2 are multiples of ℓ_c and that $2\alpha_1\alpha_2 \leq n_c\ell_c$. This implies that an X-block and a Z-block can simultaneously fit into cache. With this arrangement, it is not hard to see that each entry in X and Z is loaded into cache exactly once and that each component of Z is written to main memory exactly once. Stated another way, when a cache line is updated, every component in the line is used.

3.2.6   External Memory Matrix Transpose

We now consider the transposition of an array $X \in \mathbb{C}^{n_1 \times n_2}$, stored in column-major order in an external memory array x that has length $n = n_1 n_2$, i.e., $x_{n_1 \times n_2} = X$. We work with the following constraints:

- The matrix X is so large that it cannot be entirely housed in main memory.

- A pair of main memory workspaces are available. We denote these buffers by u and v and assume that they have length B.

- Array entries move between memory levels in length-b blocks.

Our goal is to minimize the data motion across the external/main memory interface. We first consider a pair of in-place algorithms that do *not* require an external memory workspace but do require relatively large main memory buffers. A schematic that depicts the situation is given in Fig. 3.2.3.

3.2.7   The Large Buffer Case for Square Matrices

Suppose that $n_1 = n_2 = Nb$. We assume that the main memory buffer length B satisfies

$$b^2 \leq B \tag{3.2.2}$$

so that the u and v workspaces can each house a block in the following partition:

$$X = \begin{bmatrix} X_{00} & \cdots & X_{0,N-1} \\ \vdots & & \vdots \\ X_{N-1,0} & \cdots & X_{N-1,N-1} \end{bmatrix}, \qquad X_{kj} \in \mathbb{C}^{b \times b}. \tag{3.2.3}$$

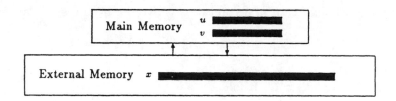

FIG. 3.2.3. *In-place external memory transposition.*

This suggests the following block transposition algorithm.

Algorithm 3.2.4 Suppose $X \in \mathbb{C}^{n_1 \times n_2}$ resides in external memory and that $n_1 = n_2 = Nb$. For $0 \le k, j \le N$ define $X_{kj} = X(kb:(k+1)b-1, jb:(j+1)b-1)$. If main memory buffers u and v have length b^2, then the following algorithm overwrites X with X^T:

> **for** $k = 0:N-1$
> > $u_{b \times b} \leftarrow X_{kk};\ u_{b \times b} \leftarrow u_{b \times b}^T;\ X_{kk} \leftarrow u_{b \times b}$
> > **for** $j = k+1:N-1$
> > > $u_{b \times b} \leftarrow X_{kj};\ v_{b \times b} \leftarrow X_{jk}$
> > > $u_{b \times b} \leftarrow u_{b \times b}^T;\ v_{b \times b} \leftarrow v_{b \times b}^T$
> > > $X_{kj} \leftarrow v_{b \times b};\ X_{jk} \leftarrow u_{b \times b}$
> > **end**
> **end**

To appreciate the execution of this procedure in the context of Fig. 3.2.3, we make two observations. First, the assignments to u and v require a read from external memory, whereas copying u and v into an X-block involves a write to external memory. Second, reading from, or writing to, a main-memory buffer requires a loop of length b. For example, the external-memory read operation $u_{b \times b} \leftarrow X_{kj}$ would be carried out as follows:

> **for** $\tau = 0:b-1$
> > $u(\tau b:(\tau+1)b-1) \leftarrow x((jb+\tau)n_1 + kb:(jb+\tau)n_1 + (k+1)b - 1)$
> **end**

Algorithm 3.2.4 is an example of a *single-pass* transpose algorithm because each entry in the external array x is read exactly once.

3.2.8 The Large Buffer Case for Rectangular Matrices

Next we assume that $n_1 = pn_2$ and that $n_2 = Nb$. We continue with the assumption that we can afford a pair of b-by-b main memory buffers. Note that the submatrices in the partitioning

$$x_{n_1 \times n_2} = X = \begin{bmatrix} X_0 \\ \vdots \\ X_{p-1} \end{bmatrix}, \qquad X_j \in \mathbb{C}^{n_2 \times n_2},$$

are *not* contiguous in x. Thus, a permutation is in order if we are to emerge with

$$x_{n_2 \times n_1} = X^T = \left[\; X_0^T \; | \; \cdots \; | \; X_{p-1}^T \; \right].$$

To gain a little intuition, consider the case of $n_2 = 4$, $p = 3$. For clarity set $X_0 = A$, $X_1 = B$, and $X_2 = C$. It follows that

$$x_{4 \times 12} = \left[\begin{array}{ccc|ccc|ccc|ccc} a_{00} & b_{00} & c_{00} & a_{01} & b_{01} & c_{01} & a_{02} & b_{02} & c_{02} & a_{03} & b_{03} & c_{03} \\ a_{10} & b_{10} & c_{10} & a_{11} & b_{11} & c_{11} & a_{12} & b_{12} & c_{12} & a_{13} & b_{13} & c_{13} \\ a_{20} & b_{20} & c_{20} & a_{21} & b_{21} & c_{21} & a_{22} & b_{22} & c_{22} & a_{23} & b_{23} & c_{23} \\ a_{30} & b_{30} & c_{30} & a_{31} & b_{31} & c_{31} & a_{32} & b_{32} & c_{32} & a_{33} & b_{33} & c_{33} \end{array} \right].$$

We see that to make A, B, and C contiguous, we must apply the mod 3 sort permutation to the columns of $x_{4 \times 12}$. This suggests that in the general case we compute

$$x_{n_2 \times n_1} \leftarrow x_{n_2 \times n_1} \Pi_{p,n_1} \qquad\qquad (3.2.4)$$

for then, according to Kron11,

$$x_{n_2 \times n_1} = \left[\; X_0 \; | \cdots | \; X_{p-1} \; \right].$$

We then apply Algorithm 3.2.4 to each of the square (contiguous) blocks and thereby obtain the required transposition. The column scramble (3.2.4) can be accomplished using permutation cycles. (See §2.2.5.) During the shifting associated with each of these cycles, the column associated with the first index of the cycle is temporarily stored in a main-memory workspace. The column shifting then proceeds by successively reading columns into another main-memory workspace and writing them back into their appropriately shifted external-memory positions.

Algorithm 3.2.5 Suppose $x \in \mathbb{C}^n$ resides in an external memory and that $n = n_1 n_2$. Assume that $n_2 = Nb$ and $n_1 = pn_2$ and define g by $\left[\Pi_{p,n_1}^T y \right]_k = y_{g(k)}$ for $k = 0:n_1-1$. If u and v are main-memory buffers, then the following algorithm overwrites $x_{n_1 \times n_2}$ with its transpose.

$$\{ x_{n_2 \times n_1} \equiv X(0:n_2-1, 0:n_1-1) \}$$

$\beta(0:n_1-1) \leftarrow 0$
for $k = 0:n_1 - 1$
    if $\beta_k = 0$
        $j \leftarrow k$; $u(0:n_2-1) \leftarrow X(:,k)$; $next \leftarrow g(k)$
        while $next \neq k$
            $v(0:n_2-1) \leftarrow X(:,next)$; $X(:,j) \leftarrow v(0:n_2-1)$; $\beta_j \leftarrow 1$
            $j \leftarrow next$
            $next \leftarrow g(j)$
        end
        $X(:,j) \leftarrow u(0:n_2-1)$; $\beta_j \leftarrow 1$
    end
end
for $j = 0:p-1$
    $cols = jn_2:(j+1)n_2 - 1$
    $X(0:n_2-1, cols) \leftarrow X(0:n_2-1, cols)^T$ (Algorithm 3.2.4)
end

If length-n_2 vectors do not comfortably fit into main memory, then a block row partitioning of the update $x_{n_2 \times n_1} \leftarrow x_{n_2 \times n_1} \Pi_{p,n_1}$ is required. If

$$x_{n_2 \times n_1} = \begin{bmatrix} Y_0 \\ \vdots \\ Y_{s-1} \end{bmatrix},$$

and the row dimensions of the Y_j are small enough, then we can carry out the update $Y_j \leftarrow Y_j \Pi_{p,n_1}$ for $j = 0{:}s - 1$. Even with this blocking, it is important to recognize that Algorithm 3.2.5 is a 2-pass transposition algorithm. Since each pass corresponds to a permutation of the data, the overall algorithm corresponds to a factorization of the permutation $\Pi_{n_1,n}^T$. It is instructive to dwell upon this point in anticipation of our final and most difficult transposition algorithm.

Recall that if $y = \Pi_{n_1,n}^T x$ with $n = n_1 n_2$, then $y_{n_2 \times n_1} = x_{n_1 \times n_2}^T$. Thus, the transposition problem "merely" requires the application of $\Pi_{n_1,n}^T$ to x. However, because of the underlying data motion constraints, we may be compelled to factor $\Pi_{n_1,n}^T$ into a product of "system-manageable" permutations. In the case of Algorithm 3.2.5, the permutation cycle phase is characterized by

$$x \leftarrow (\Pi_{p,n_1}^T \otimes I_{n_2})x \,,$$

and the phase associated with the X_j transpositions is described by

$$x \leftarrow (I_p \otimes \Pi_{n_2,n_2^2}^T)x \,.$$

Thus, Algorithm 3.2.5 corresponds to the factorization

$$\Pi_{n_1,n}^T = (I_p \otimes \Pi_{n_2,n_2^2}^T)(\Pi_{p,n_1}^T \otimes I_{n_2}), \tag{3.2.5}$$

with each pass corresponding to a factor.

Another way to describe the pass-by-pass transformations that x undergoes in Algorithm 3.2.5 is to identify the original x with $X(0{:}n_2 - 1, 0{:}p - 1, 0{:}n_2 - 1)$ and to trace the motion of component $X(\alpha, \beta, \gamma)$ using Kron9 and Kron11. After the first pass the element $X(\alpha, \beta, \gamma)$ is mapped to $X(\alpha, \gamma, \beta)$, where X is now n_2-by-n_2-by-p. The array is then transposed in its first two dimensions, sending $X(\alpha, \gamma, \beta)$ to $X(\gamma, \alpha, \beta)$. Thus, the two-step process sends $X(\alpha, \beta, \gamma)$ to $X(\gamma, \alpha, \beta)$ and corresponds to the transposition of x as an n_1-by-n_2 array.

3.2.9   The Small Buffer, General Case

We now present a very general external-memory matrix transpose algorithm due to Fraser (1976) and which is nicely described in Bailey (1990). Assume that $n = n_1 n_2$ and that $x \in \mathbb{C}^n$ is stored in external memory. Our goal is the efficient transposition of the matrix $X = x_{n_1 \times n_2}$.

As in the previous two subsections, we work with a pair of length-B main memory buffers (u and v) and assume that data flows to and from the external memory in chunks of length b. However, we do *not* assume that $b^2 \leq B$, which complicates matters considerably. To compensate for this, we assume that there is a length-n external memory workspace y. A schematic of the overall situation is depicted in Fig. 3.2.4. For clarity we assume that

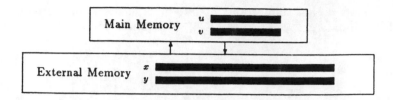

FIG. 3.2.4. *The Fraser transpose setting.*

$$
\begin{aligned}
n_1 &= 2^{t_1}, \\
n_2 &= 2^{t_2}, \\
b &= 2^{\lambda}, \\
B &= 2^{\tau} \quad (B \geq b)
\end{aligned}
$$

and identify two important integers:

$$m = B/b = \text{number of blocks required to fill } u \text{ or } v,$$
$$M = n/B = \text{number of buffer loads required to ``cover'' } X.$$

Within these constraints we seek an algorithm of the following form:

> **Repeat until** (X^T resides in external memory)
>> **for** $k = 0{:}M - 1$
>>> **for** $j = 0{:}m - 1$
>>>> Read a block from x (or y) into the jth block of u.
>>>
>>> **end**
>>> Transfer a permuted version of u into v.
>>> **for** $j = 0{:}m - 1$
>>>> Write the jth block of v into y (or x) .
>>>
>>> **end**
>>
>> **end**
>
> **end**

(3.2.6)

The body of the outermost loop oversees a single pass through the external data. Our goal is to minimize the number of passes, as that statistic more or less determines overall efficiency.

Note that if $b = 1$, then a single pass suffices. We merely read $x(\alpha n_1 + \beta)$ into main memory and write to $y(\beta n_2 + \alpha)$. Upon completion, $y_{n_2 \times n_1} = x_{n_1 \times n_2}^T$. Things get interesting when $b > 1$, because then the entries in a block that has been read are usually not contiguously restored to external memory.

3.2.10   The Structure of a Pass

Assume that the input for the current pass resides in x and that upon completion this data (in permuted form) resides in y. Conceptually, three n-by-n permutations define the movement of data during a pass.

The first permutation, Σ_{read}, determines the order in which the length-b blocks of data are read from x. This implies that Σ_{read} has the form

$$\Sigma_{read} = Q_{read} \otimes I_b, \tag{3.2.7}$$

where Q_{read} is a permutation of order n/b. If

$$z = \Sigma_{read}x ,\qquad\qquad (3.2.8)$$

then

$$z_{b\times(n/b)} = x_{b\times(n/b)}Q_{read}^T .$$

During a pass this array is read into main memory in left-to-right order.

Of course, z cannot be held all at once in main memory. Indeed, it must be processed in chunks of length B, the size of the main memory buffer u. The blocking

$$z = \begin{bmatrix} z_0 \\ \vdots \\ z_{M-1} \end{bmatrix}, \qquad z_k \in \mathbb{C}^B,$$

captures this detail. The act of filling u corresponds to the loading of a subvector z_k. Each z_k is permuted into some w_j in main memory. These are the "u-to-v" mappings in (3.2.6), and the collection of these operations may be expressed as follows:

$$w = \begin{bmatrix} w_0 \\ \vdots \\ w_{M-1} \end{bmatrix} = \Sigma_{main} \begin{bmatrix} z_0 \\ \vdots \\ z_{M-1} \end{bmatrix}, \qquad w_j \in \mathbb{C}^B . \qquad (3.2.9)$$

We assume that during a given pass each transformation of u into v has the form

$$v \leftarrow Q_{main}u,$$

where Q_{main} is a permutation of order B. Since this is performed $n/B = M$ times during a pass, we see that the transition $w = \Sigma_{main}z$ has the form

$$\Sigma_{main} = I_M \otimes Q_{main} . \qquad (3.2.10)$$

Finally we consider the writing of w into the external memory buffer y. Since this involves storing a column-permuted version of $w_{b\times(n/b)}$ into $y_{b\times(n/b)}$, we see that

$$y = \Sigma_{write}w, \qquad\qquad (3.2.11)$$

where Σ_{write} has the form

$$\Sigma_{write} = Q_{write} \otimes I_b \qquad\qquad (3.2.12)$$

and Q_{write} is a permutation of order n/b.

By combining (3.2.8), (3.2.9), and (3.2.11), we see that the transition from x to y is defined by

$$y = \Sigma_{write}\left(\Sigma_{main}\left(\Sigma_{read}\,x\right)\right) .$$

To proceed further, we need to prescribe the Q matrices.

3.2.11   The $\mathcal{P}$ Permutations

Assume that $n = 2^t$ and define the n-by-n permutation $\mathcal{P}_a$ as follows:

$$\mathcal{P}_a = I_{2^{a_4}} \otimes \Pi_{2^{a_2},2^{a_2+a_3}}^T \otimes I_{2^{a_1}} ,$$

where a_1, a_2, a_3, and a_4 are nonnegative and sum to t. To describe the relationship between x and $\tilde{x} = \mathcal{P}_a x$, identify x with $X(0{:}a_1 - 1, 0{:}a_2 - 1, 0{:}a_3 - 1, 0{:}a_4 - 1)$ and $\tilde{x}$ with $\tilde{X}(0{:}a_1 - 1, 0{:}a_3 - 1, 0{:}a_2 - 1, 0{:}a_4 - 1)$. It can be shown using Kron5, Kron6, and Kron9 that $X(\alpha, \beta, \gamma, \delta)$ is mapped to $\tilde{X}(\alpha, \gamma, \beta, \delta)$. In other words, a transpose is performed in the middle two components.

3.2.12   The Σ Permutations

Recall that $b = 2^\lambda$, $B = 2^\tau$, and that Σ_{read}, Σ_{main}, and Σ_{write} have Kronecker structures prescribed by (3.2.7), (3.2.10), and (3.2.12), respectively. These structures are realized with the definitions

$$
\begin{array}{|l|ll|}
\hline
\Sigma_{read} = \mathcal{P}_a & a_1 = \lambda, & a_2 + a_3 + a_4 = t - \lambda \\
\hline
\Sigma_{main} = \mathcal{P}_a & a_4 = t - \tau, & a_1 + a_2 + a_3 = \tau \\
\hline
\Sigma_{write} = \mathcal{P}_a & a_1 = \lambda, & a_2 + a_3 + a_4 = t - \lambda \\
\hline
\end{array}
\qquad (3.2.13)
$$

which imply that

$$
\begin{aligned}
Q_{read} &= I_{2^{a_4}} \otimes \Pi^T_{2^{a_2},\,2^{a_2+a_3}}, & a_2 + a_3 + a_4 = t - \lambda, \\
Q_{main} &= \Pi^T_{2^{a_2},\,2^{a_2+a_3}} \otimes I_{2^{a_1}}, & a_1 + a_2 + a_3 = \tau, \\
Q_{write} &= I_{2^{a_4}} \otimes \Pi^T_{2^{a_2},\,2^{a_3+a_3}}, & a_2 + a_3 + a_4 = t - \lambda.
\end{aligned}
$$

Figures 3.2.5 and 3.2.6 illustrate the action of the Σ permutations in terms of index shifts on t-dimensional arrays.

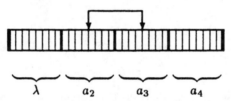

FIG. 3.2.5. *Index movement for* Σ_{read} *and* Σ_{write}.

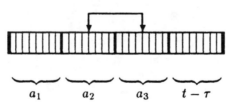

FIG. 3.2.6. *Index movement for* Σ_{main}.

3.2.13   The Overall Algorithm

Through repeated application of the Σ permutations we can carry out the transposition of $x_{n_1 \times n_2}$, where $n_1 = 2^{t_1}$, $n_2 = 2^{t_2}$, and $n = n_1 n_2$. With the identification

$$
x \equiv X(\underbrace{0{:}1, \ldots, 0{:}1}_{t})
$$

we see that the goal of the transposition is to "push" the row indices past the column indices. Consider the case $t_1 = 5$ and $t_2 = 4$:

$$X(\alpha_1, \alpha_2, \alpha_3, \alpha_4, \alpha_5, \alpha_6, \alpha_7, \alpha_8, \alpha_9)$$
$$\downarrow$$
$$X(\alpha_6, \alpha_7, \alpha_8, \alpha_9, \alpha_1, \alpha_2, \alpha_3, \alpha_4, \alpha_5).$$

From this we see that $(\alpha_1, \alpha_2, \alpha_3, \alpha_4, \alpha_5)$ and $(\alpha_6, \alpha_7, \alpha_8, \alpha_9)$ name a row and column of $x_{n_1 \times n_2}$ and that the swapping of these index vectors is exactly the mission of a 32-by-16 transposition. By suitably defining a sequence of Σ permutations, we can carry out this task. Here is a trace indicating the movement of $X(\alpha_1, \alpha_2, \alpha_3, \alpha_4, \alpha_5, \alpha_6, \alpha_7, \alpha_8, \alpha_9)$ as it is moved through a sequence of $\mathcal{P}_a$ permutations under the assumption that $\lambda = 2$ and $\tau = 3$:

	α_1	α_2	α_3	α_4	α_5	α_6	α_7	α_8	α_9	
read	α_1	α_2	α_6	α_7	α_8	α_9	α_3	α_4	α_5	$a = (2,3,4,0)$
main	α_6	α_1	α_2	α_7	α_8	α_9	α_3	α_4	α_5	$a = (0,2,1,6)$
write	α_6	α_1	α_7	α_8	α_9	α_2	α_3	α_4	α_5	$a = (2,1,3,3)$
read	α_6	α_1	α_7	α_8	α_9	α_2	α_3	α_4	α_5	$a = (2,0,0,7)$
main	α_6	α_7	α_1	α_8	α_9	α_2	α_3	α_4	α_5	$a = (1,1,1,6)$
write	α_6	α_7	α_8	α_9	α_1	α_2	α_3	α_4	α_5	$a = (2,1,2,4)$

Thus, this particular problem requires two passes through the external data.

In general, the Fraser algorithm is based on a factorization of the form

$$\Pi^T_{n_1, n_1 n_2} = \mathcal{P}_{a(3p)} \cdots \mathcal{P}_{a(1)}, \tag{3.2.14}$$

where p is the number of passes. The triplet of permutations $(\mathcal{P}_{a(3k-2)}, \mathcal{P}_{a(3k-1)}, \mathcal{P}_{a(3k)})$ are the $(\Sigma_{read}, \Sigma_{main}, \Sigma_{write})$ of the kth pass. Here is a framework for computing the a-vectors in (3.2.14):

$\alpha \leftarrow [1, 2, \ldots, t]$
$\beta \leftarrow [t_1 + 1, \ldots t, 1, \ldots, t_1]$
$p \leftarrow 1$
while $\beta \neq \alpha$

    Determine nonnegative $a = [\lambda, a_2, a_3, a_4]$ subject to $a_2 + a_3 + a_4 = t - \lambda$
        so that if $\Sigma_{read} = \mathcal{P}_a$, then the new index ordering $\tilde{\alpha}$ is as
        close as possible to β.

    $\alpha \leftarrow \tilde{\alpha}$
    $a^{(3p-2)} \leftarrow a$

    Determine nonnegative $a = [a_1, a_2, a_3, t - \tau]$ subject to $a_1 + a_2 + a_3 = \tau$
        so that if $\Sigma_{main} = \mathcal{P}_a$, then the new index ordering $\tilde{\alpha}$ is as
        close as possible to β.

    $\alpha \leftarrow \tilde{\alpha}$
    $a^{(3p-1)} \leftarrow a$

    Determine nonnegative $a = [\lambda, a_2, a_3, a_4]$ subject to $a_2 + a_3 + a_4 = t - \lambda$
        so that if $\Sigma_{write} = \mathcal{P}_a$, then the new index ordering $\tilde{\alpha}$ is as
        close as possible to β.

    $\alpha \leftarrow \tilde{\alpha}$
    $a^{(3p)} \leftarrow a$
    $p \leftarrow p + 1$
end

Upon completion, p houses the number of required passes. The constraints on the a-vectors ensure that the factor permutations in (3.2.14) can be implemented with the given restrictions on the main memory buffer size B and block transfer length b.

Problems

P3.2.1 (a) Work out formulae for the μ_d as they arise in Algorithm 3.2.2. (b) Specialize Algorithm 3.2.2 to the case when $n_1 = n_2$. Arrange the computations so that X is overwritten with X^T.

P3.2.2 Justify the comment after Algorithm 3.2.2 about bank conflict avoidance.

P3.2.3 Trace the path of $X(\alpha_1, \ldots, \alpha_t)$ in the Fraser algorithm for the problems $(t_1, t_2, \lambda, \tau) = (3,7,1,2)$, $(3,7,0,2)$, and $(3,7,4,5)$. Given that $t_1 = 3$ and $t_2 = 7$, choose λ and τ with $(\lambda < \tau)$ to maximize the number of passes.

P3.2.4 Complete the specification of the Fraser algorithm by detailing a method for computing the a-vectors. What can you say about the number of passes required as a function of n_1, n_2, B, and b?

Notes and References for Section 3.2

Believe it or not, there are still other approaches to the transpose problem. A recursive divide-and-conquer algorithm due to

J.O. Eklundh (1972). "A Fast Computer Method for Matrix Transposing," *IEEE Trans. Comput.* *C-21*, 801–803

has attracted considerable attention. We discuss it in the context of distributed computation in §3.5.10. It is based on a nested sequence of 2-by-2 block transpositions. For related work, see

J.O. Eklundh (1981). "Efficient Matrix Transposition," in *Two-Dimensional Digital Signal Processing II. Transforms and Median Filters*, T.S. Huang (ed.), Springer-Verlag, New York, 37–88.
G.C. Goldbogenm (1981). "PRIM: A Fast Matrix Transpose Method," *IEEE Trans. Software Engrg.* *SE-7*, 255–257.
U. Schumann (1973). "Comments on 'A Fast Computer Method for Matrix Transposing and Applications to the Solution of Poisson's Equation'," *IEEE Trans. Comput.* *C-22*, 542–543.
R.E. Twogood and M.P. Ekstrom (1976). "An Extension of Eklundh's Matrix Transposition Algorithm and Its Application in Digital Image Signal Processing," *IEEE Trans. Comput.* *C-25*, 950–952.

Other references for external memory transposition include

D.H. Bailey (1990). "FFTs in External or Hierarchical Memory," *J. Supercomputing 4*, 23–35.
L.G. Delcaro and G.L. Sicuranza (1974). "A Method for Transposing Externally Stored Matrices," *IEEE Trans. Comput.* *C-23*, 967–970.
D. Fraser (1976). "Array Permutation by Index-Digit Permutation," *J. Assoc. Comput. Mach. 23*, 298–309.

Useful connections between transposition and other important permutations are explored in

N. Brenner (1973). "Algorithm 467, Matrix Transposition In-Place," *Comm. ACM 16*, 692–694.
P. Duhamel (1990). "A Connection between Bit Reversal and Matrix Transposition: Hardware and Software Consequences," *IEEE Trans. Acoust. Speech Signal Process. ASSP-38*, 1893–1896.
D.W. Twigg (1983). "Transposition of Matrix Stored on Sequential File," *IEEE Trans. Comput.* *C-32*, 1185–1188.

The organization and analysis of memory hierarchies and cache performance are discussed in

J.L. Hennessy and D.A. Patterson (1990). *Computer Architecture: A Quantitative Approach*, Morgan Kaufmann Publishers, San Mateo, CA.

3.3 The Large Single-Vector FFT Problem

In this section we show how to reduce the single-vector DFT problem to a sequence of multiple DFTs, scalings, and transpositions. We draw heavily upon Bailey (1990). The key idea revolves around (2.1.9), the matrix formulation of the radix-p splitting. Setting $m = n_1$ and $p = n_2$ in that equation we obtain

$$[F_n x]_{n_1 \times n_2} = [F_n(0{:}n_1 - 1, 0{:}n_2 - 1) .* (F_{n_1} x^T_{n_2 \times n_1})]F_{n_2} . \qquad (3.3.1)$$

From this result we see that $F_n x$ can be computed as follows:

$$
\begin{aligned}
x_{n_1 \times n_2} &\leftarrow x^T_{n_2 \times n_1} \\
x_{n_1 \times n_2} &\leftarrow F_{n_1} x_{n_1 \times n_2} \\
x_{n_1 \times n_2} &\leftarrow F_n(0{:}n_1 - 1, 0{:}n_2 - 1) .* x_{n_1 \times n_2} \\
x_{n_1 \times n_2} &\leftarrow x_{n_1 \times n_2} F_{n_2} .
\end{aligned}
\qquad (3.3.2)
$$

This is often referred to as the *twiddle-factor* method because of the *twiddle-factor scaling* that involves the submatrix $F_n(0{:}n_1 - 1, 0{:}n_2 - 1)$. The approach has been known for some time. (See Gentleman and Sande (1966).)

Let us assess the amount of arithmetic in (3.3.2). Assume for clarity that $n_1 = 2^{t_1}$ and $n_2 = 2^{t_2}$. For these values, the multicolumn and multirow DFTs require $5t_1 n_1 n_2$ and $5t_2 n_1 n_2$ flops, respectively, when any standard radix-2 algorithm is used. The arithmetic in these operations dominate the whole process because the twiddle-factor manipulations involve only $O(n_1 n_2)$ flops. Thus, the total number of flops associated with (3.3.2) is given by

$$5t_1 n_1 n_2 + 5t_2 n_1 n_2 = 5(t_1 + t_2)n = 5n \log_2 n ,$$

precisely what is required by a single-vector radix-2 algorithm.

While the twiddle-factor framework is not particularly interesting in terms of flops, it is quite interesting in terms of the re-use of data. To dramatize this point, we consider the problem of computing the DFT of a single vector that is so large it can fit only in external memory. We are therefore going to play the same game that we did with the external memory transpose in §3.2.6 In particular, we have the schematic

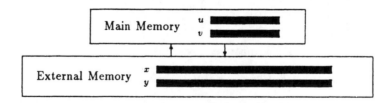

FIG. 3.3.1. *External memory FFT.*

and the rules:

- The data vector x (and perhaps an equally sized workspace y) resides in external memory.

- In a transfer between the two levels of memory, only contiguous data can be referenced. The data in a transfer is moved in blocks of length b.

- The time required for overall execution is proportional to the number of passes over the external data.

- The main memory buffers that are available are too small to house all of x.

Note that if $n = 2^t$ and a standard radix-2 framework is naively applied, then t passes are required. In contrast, the intelligent organization of a twiddle-factor framework can greatly reduce the number of passes, sometimes to just 2 or 3.

Before we begin, it is important to mention that an appreciation of the twiddle-factor approach can also be obtained by examining FFT computations that straddle the cache/main memory interface.

3.3.1   The Four-Step and Six-Step Frameworks

We start by modifying (3.3.2) so that the two multiple DFTs are either column oriented or row oriented. Since different environments may favor different multiple DFT orientations, it is useful to have this flexibility. A simple transpose manipulation of (3.3.1) gives

$$[F_n x]_{n_1 \times n_2} = \left[F_{n_2} \left[F_n(0{:}n_1 - 1, 0{:}n_2 - 1).* \left(F_{n_1} x^T_{n_2 \times n_1} \right) \right]^T \right]^T, \qquad (3.3.3)$$

which is the basis for the *six-step framework*:

$$
\begin{aligned}
x_{n_1 \times n_2} &\leftarrow x^T_{n_2 \times n_1} \\
x_{n_1 \times n_2} &\leftarrow F_{n_1} x_{n_1 \times n_2} \\
x_{n_1 \times n_2} &\leftarrow F_n(0{:}n_1 - 1, 0{:}n_2 - 1).* x_{n_1 \times n_2} \\
x_{n_2 \times n_1} &\leftarrow x^T_{n_1 \times n_2} \\
x_{n_2 \times n_1} &\leftarrow F_{n_2} x_{n_2 \times n_1} \\
x_{n_1 \times n_2} &\leftarrow x^T_{n_2 \times n_1} .
\end{aligned}
\qquad (3.3.4)
$$

It involves three transpositions, two multicolumn DFTs, and a twiddle-factor scaling.

To develop a useful row-oriented twiddle-factor approach we interchange the roles of n_1 and n_2 in (3.3.1) to obtain

$$[F_n x]_{n_2 \times n_1} = [F_n(0{:}n_2 - 1, 0{:}n_1 - 1).* (F_{n_2} x^T_{n_1 \times n_2})] F_{n_1}.$$

Exploiting the symmetry of DFT matrices gives

$$[F_n x]_{n_2 \times n_1} = [F_n(0{:}n_1 - 1, 0{:}n_2 - 1).* (x_{n_1 \times n_2} F_{n_2})]^T F_{n_1}, \qquad (3.3.5)$$

whereupon we get the *four-step framework*:

$$
\begin{aligned}
x_{n_1 \times n_2} &\leftarrow x_{n_1 \times n_2} F_{n_2} \\
x_{n_1 \times n_2} &\leftarrow F_n(0{:}n_1 - 1, 0{:}n_2 - 1).* x_{n_1 \times n_2} \\
x_{n_2 \times n_1} &\leftarrow x^T_{n_1 \times n_2} \\
x_{n_2 \times n_1} &\leftarrow x_{n_2 \times n_1} F_{n_1} .
\end{aligned}
\qquad (3.3.6)
$$

Observe that one transposition, two multirow DFTs, and one twiddle-factor scaling are involved.

From the underlying premise that the n-vector x cannot be completely stored in main memory, we see that it is necessary to break up the steps in (3.3.4) and (3.3.6) into blocks that are small enough to fit in main memory. External memory transposition is covered in §3.2, so we are obliged to show only how to block multiple DFTs and twiddle-factor scalings.

3.3.2 Blocking Multiple DFTs

A multicolumn DFT of the form $F_{n_1}X$, where $X \in \mathbb{C}^{n_1 \times n_2}$ can be handled by partitioning X into block columns. If $n_2 = s_2 m_2$ and we can afford a main-memory buffer $U = U(0{:}n_1 - 1, 0{:}m_2 - 1)$, then

$$X \leftarrow F_{n_1} \left[\; X_0 \; | \; \cdots \; | \; X_{s_2-1} \; \right] = \left[\; F_{n_1}X_0 \; | \; \cdots \; | \; F_{n_1}X_{s_2-1} \; \right],$$

where $X_j \in \mathbb{C}^{n_1 \times m_2}$. It follows that the individual multicolumn DFTs $X_j \leftarrow F_{n_1}X_j$ can be processed in main memory and so we obtain the following one-pass algorithm for $F_{n_1}X$:

$$
\begin{aligned}
&\textbf{for } j = 0{:}s_2 - 1 \\
&\quad cols \leftarrow jm_2{:}(j+1)m_2 - 1 \\
&\quad U \leftarrow X(0{:}n_1 - 1, cols) \\
&\quad U \leftarrow F_{n_1}U \\
&\quad X(0{:}n_1 - 1, cols) \leftarrow U \\
&\textbf{end}
\end{aligned}
\qquad (3.3.7)
$$

We assume here that $n_1 \geq b$. If an autosort framework is used for the DFTs, then an additional main-memory workspace is required. (See §3.1.)

Now consider the multirow DFT problem $X \leftarrow XF_{n_2}$, where $X \in \mathbb{C}^{n_1 \times n_2}$. Suppose that we can afford a main-memory buffer $U = U(0{:}m_1 - 1, 0{:}n_2 - 1)$ and that $n_1 = s_1 m_1$. We assume that $m_1 \geq b$. Consider the following partitioning:

$$
X \leftarrow \begin{bmatrix} X_0 \\ \vdots \\ X_{s_1-1} \end{bmatrix} F_{n_2} = \begin{bmatrix} X_0 F_{n_2} \\ \vdots \\ X_{s_1-1} F_{n_2} \end{bmatrix}, \qquad X_k \in \mathbb{C}^{m_1 \times n_2}.
$$

Since $X_k \leftarrow X_k F_{n_2}$ can be handled in main memory, we obtain the following one-pass algorithm for computing XF_{n_2}:

$$
\begin{aligned}
&\textbf{for } k = 0{:}s_1 - 1 \\
&\quad rows \leftarrow km_1{:}(k+1)m_1 - 1 \\
&\quad U \leftarrow X(rows, :) \\
&\quad U \leftarrow UF_{n_2} \\
&\quad X(rows, :) \leftarrow U \\
&\textbf{end}
\end{aligned}
\qquad (3.3.8)
$$

Again, if an autosort framework is used to carry out the DFTs, an additional main memory workspace is required.

In the above we assumed that $m_1 \geq b$ where b is the block transfer length. The case when we cannot afford a b-by-n_2 main-memory buffer is discussed in §3.3.6.

3.3.3   Blocking the Twiddle-Factor Multiplication

Given an array $X(0{:}n_1 - 1, 0{:}n_2 - 1)$, the twiddle-factor scaling

$$X \leftarrow F_n(0{:}n_1 - 1, 0{:}n_2 - 1){.}{*}\, X \qquad (3.3.9)$$

is a critical step in either the four- or six-step frameworks. Since X does not fit in main memory, it is more sensible to work with a blocking of (3.3.9). To that end, assume that $n_1 = m_1 s_1$ and $n_2 = m_2 s_2$, and write

$$F_n(0{:}n_1, 0{:}n_2 - 1) = \begin{bmatrix} W_{00} & \cdots & W_{0,s_2-1} \\ \vdots & & \vdots \\ W_{s_1-1,0} & \cdots & W_{s_1-1,s_2-1} \end{bmatrix}$$

and

$$X = \begin{bmatrix} X_{00} & \cdots & X_{0,s_2-1} \\ \vdots & & \vdots \\ X_{s_1-1,0} & \cdots & X_{s_1-1,s_2-1} \end{bmatrix},$$

where $W_{kj}, X_{kj} \in \mathbb{C}^{m_1 \times m_2}$. On a block-by-block basis, the scaling (3.3.9) may be computed with a main-memory buffer $U = U(0{:}m_1 - 1, 0{:}m_2 - 1)$ as follows:

$$
\begin{aligned}
&\textbf{for}\ \ k = 0{:}s_1 - 1 \\
&\qquad \textbf{for}\ j = 0{:}s_2 - 1 \\
&\qquad\qquad U \leftarrow X_{kj} \\
&\qquad\qquad U \leftarrow W_{kj}{.}{*}\,U \\
&\qquad\qquad X_{kj} \leftarrow U \\
&\qquad \textbf{end} \\
&\textbf{end}
\end{aligned}
\qquad (3.3.10)
$$

Following Bailey (1990), we show how to "live" with just W_{00} and a pair of small workspaces. The key is the equation

$$
\begin{aligned}
[W_{kj}]_{\alpha,\beta} &= \omega_n^{(km_1+\alpha)(jm_2+\beta)} \\
&= \omega_n^{km_1jm_2}\omega_n^{\alpha jm_2}\omega_n^{\beta km_1}\omega_n^{\alpha\beta} \\
&= \omega_n^{km_1jm_2}\omega_n^{\alpha jm_2}\omega_n^{\beta km_1}[W_{00}]_{\alpha\beta},
\end{aligned}
$$

where $0 \le \alpha \le m_1 - 1$ and $0 \le \beta \le m_2 - 1$. This equation implies

$$W_{kj} = \omega_n^{km_1jm_2}\left\{ [F_n(0{:}m_1 - 1, jm_2)F_n(km_1, 0{:}m_2 - 1)]{.}{*}\,W_{00} \right\}.$$

Thus, if we have precomputed the base block W_{00} and the submatrices

$$
\begin{aligned}
W_{col} &= F_n(0{:}m_1 - 1, 0{:}m_2{:}n_2 - 1), \\
W_{row} &= F_n(0{:}m_1{:}n_1 - 1, 0{:}m_2 - 1),
\end{aligned}
$$

then

$$W_{kj} = \omega_n^{km_1jm_2}\left\{ [W_{col}(:, j)W_{row}(k, :)]{.}{*}\,W_{00} \right\}.$$

Observe that $W_{col}(:, j)W_{row}(k, :)$ is a rank-one matrix and that the storage of the arrays W_{00}, W_{row}, and W_{col} involve $m_1 m_2 + m_1 s_2 + m_2 s_1$ locations. If $s_1 = s_2$ and $m_1 = m_2$, then $W_{col} = W_{row}^T$ and the storage requirement is reduced to just $m_1^2 + n_1$.

If W_{00}, W_{col}, and W_{row} are available, then we can replace the reference to W_{kj} in (3.3.10) with

$$U \leftarrow \omega_n^{km_1jm_2} \{ [W_{col}(:,j)W_{row}(k,:)] .* W_{00} \} .* U .$$

It should be stressed that care must be exercised when computing a twiddle-factor array $F_n(0{:}m_1-1, 0{:}m_2-1)$; otherwise there may be an unacceptable level of accumulated roundoff. Straightforward modifications of the direct call and subvector scaling methods of §1.4 can be applied to generate safely W_{00}, W_{col}, and W_{row}.

3.3.4 The Blocked Six-Step Framework

We now piece together our ideas about blocked multiple DFTs, blocked twiddle-factor scalings, and blocked transpositions.

Algorithm 3.3.1 Suppose $n = n_1 n_2$, $n_1 = s_1 m_1$, and $n_2 = s_2 m_2$. If u is a main memory workspace of length at least $\max\{n_1 m_2, n_2 m_1\}$, then the following algorithm overwrites $x \in \mathbb{C}^n$ with $F_n x$:

$$x_{n_1 \times n_2} \leftarrow x_{n_2 \times n_1}^T$$
$$\{ x_{n_1 \times n_2} \equiv X \}$$
$$\{ u_{n_1 \times m_2} \equiv U \}$$
for $k = 0{:}s_2 - 1$
    $cols \leftarrow km_2{:}(k+1)m_2 - 1$
    $U \leftarrow X(0{:}n_1 - 1, cols)$
    $U \leftarrow F_{n_1} U$
    $U \leftarrow U .* F_n(0{:}n_1 - 1, cols)$
    $X(0{:}n_1 - 1, cols) \leftarrow U$
end
$$x_{n_2 \times n_1} \leftarrow x_{n_1 \times n_2}^T$$
$$\{ x_{n_2 \times n_1} \equiv X \}$$
$$\{ u_{n_2 \times m_1} \equiv U \}$$
for $k = 0{:}s_1 - 1$
    $cols \leftarrow km_1{:}(k+1)m_1 - 1$
    $U \leftarrow X(0{:}n_2 - 1, cols)$
    $U \leftarrow F_{n_2} U$
    $X(0{:}n_2 - 1, cols) \leftarrow U$
end
$$x_{n_1 \times n_2} \leftarrow x_{n_2 \times n_1}^T$$

Excluding the transpositions, this is a two-pass algorithm. The twiddle-factor scaling

$$U \leftarrow U .* F_n(0{:}n_1 - 1, cols)$$

can be based upon a precomputation of the matrices W_{00}, W_{col}, and W_{row}, as described in §3.3.3. If space permits, these blocks should be stored in main memory during the execution of the first k-loop so that the twiddle-factor scaling is processed during the first multicolumn DFT.

3.3.5   The Blocked Four-Step Framework

By combining Algorithm 3.3.1 for the multiple row DFTs and the twiddle-factor blocking scheme of §3.3.3, we obtain a blocked four-step framework.

Algorithm 3.3.2 Suppose $x \in \mathbb{C}^n$ with $n = n_1 n_2$. Assume that $n_1 = s_1 m_1$ and $n_2 = s_2 m_2$. Assume also that a main-memory workspace u of length $\max\{m_2 n_1, m_1 n_2\}$ is available and that m_1 and m_2 are multiples of b. The following algorithm overwrites x with $F_n x$:

$$\{x_{n_1 \times n_2} \equiv X\}$$
$$\{u_{m_1 \times n_2} \equiv U\}$$
$\text{for } k = 0{:}s_1 - 1$
$\quad rows \leftarrow km_1{:}(k+1)m_1 - 1$
$\quad U \leftarrow X(rows, 0{:}n_2 - 1)$
$\quad U \leftarrow U F_{n_2}$
$\quad \text{for } j = 0{:}s_2 - 1$
$\quad\quad cols \leftarrow jm_2{:}(j+1)m_2 - 1$
$\quad\quad U(0{:}m_1 - 1, cols) \leftarrow F_n(rows, cols).* U(0{:}m_1 - 1, cols)\,.$
$\quad \text{end}$
$\quad X(rows, 0{:}n_2 - 1) \leftarrow U$
end
$$x_{n_2 \times n_1} \leftarrow x_{n_1 \times n_2}^T$$
$$\{x_{n_2 \times n_1} \equiv X\}$$
$$\{u_{m_2 \times n_1} \equiv U\}$$
$\text{for } k = 0{:}s_2 - 1$
$\quad rows \leftarrow km_2{:}(k+1)m_2 - 1$
$\quad U \leftarrow X(rows, 0{:}n_1 - 1)$
$\quad U \leftarrow U F_{n_1}$
$\quad X(rows, 0{:}n_1 - 1) \leftarrow U$
end

Notice again that the twiddle-factor scaling and the first multicolumn DFT can be computed together. Precomputation of the twiddle-factor blocks W_{00}, W_{col}, and W_{row} is advantageous, especially if these arrays can be kept in main memory throughout the computation. Algorithm 3.3.2 requires $2 + p$ passes, where p is the number of passes required by the transposition.

If we can afford an external-memory workspace y of length n, then it is possible to hide the cost of the transposition altogether. The central idea revolves around the partitionings

$$x_{n_1 \times n_2} = \begin{bmatrix} X_0 \\ \vdots \\ X_{s_1 - 1} \end{bmatrix}, \qquad F(0{:}n_1 - 1, 0{:}n_2 - 1) = \begin{bmatrix} \tilde{F}_0 \\ \vdots \\ \tilde{F}_{s_1 - 1} \end{bmatrix},$$

where $X_j, \tilde{F}_j \in \mathbb{C}^{m_1 \times n_2}$. During the first pass we compute $Z_j = (X_j F_{n_2}).* \tilde{F}_j$ for $j = 0{:}s_1 - 1$. The *transposes* of these blocks are assembled in y as they are produced:

$$y_{n_2 \times n_1} = \begin{bmatrix} Z_0^T & | & \cdots & | & Z_{s_1 - 1}^T \end{bmatrix}.$$

It follows that

$$y_{n_2 \times n_1} = ((x_{n_1 \times n_2} F_{n_2}).* F_n(0{:}n_1 - 1, 0{:}n_2 - 1))^T\,.$$

We then partition

$$y_{n_2 \times n_1} = \begin{bmatrix} Y_0 \\ \vdots \\ Y_{s_2-1} \end{bmatrix}, \qquad Y_j \in \mathbb{C}^{m_2 \times n_1},$$

where we assume that $n_2 = m_2 s_2$. The final multirow DFT is processed in a second pass:

$$x_{n_2 \times n_1} = \begin{bmatrix} Y_0 F_{n_1} \\ \vdots \\ Y_{s_2-1} F_{n_1} \end{bmatrix}.$$

It follows that x now houses $F_n x$.

3.3.6   Multirow DFTs with a Small Main-Memory Buffer

If we *cannot* afford a main memory buffer of length bn_2, then a modification to Algorithm 3.3.2 is required. The central problem to consider is the multirow DFT of a b-by-n_2 array: $z_{b \times n_2} \leftarrow z_{b \times n_2} F_{n_2}$. A block row partitioning of this problem is not satisfactory because data is read from external memory in blocks of length b. A better approach is to judiciously choose the radix of the underlying FFT. In another setting we have already seen how the proper choice of radix can enhance the re-use of data properties of an algorithm. (See §2.4.7.)

Assume that we have a main-memory buffer $U(0{:}b-1, 0{:}m_2-1)$ at our disposal and that $n_2 = m_2^\lambda$. (The fully general case $n_2 = m_2^\lambda \alpha$ with $1 < \alpha < m_2$ is not that much more difficult to handle.) Our goal is to reduce the application of F_{n_2} to a sequence of main-memory manageable scalings and multirow DFT problems of size b-by-m_2. The vehicle for doing this is the Cooley–Tukey radix-m_2 factorization of F_{n_2}:

$$
\begin{aligned}
F_{n_2} P_{n_2}(\rho) &= A_\lambda \cdots A_1, & \rho &= [\,m_2, \ldots, m_2\,], \\
A_q &= I_r \otimes B_L, & L &= m_2^q, \; r = n_2/L, \\
B_L &= (F_{m_2} \otimes I_{L_*}) D_q, & L_* &= L/m_2, \\
D_q &= \mathrm{diag}(I_{L_*}, \Omega_{L_*}, \ldots, \Omega_{L_*}^{m_2-1}), & \\
\Omega_{L_*} &= \mathrm{diag}(1, \omega_L, \ldots, \omega_L^{L_*-1}). &
\end{aligned}
$$

See §2.3.2 for details. Given this factorization, the task at hand is to compute

$$z \leftarrow (F_{n_2} \otimes I_b)z = (A_\lambda \cdots A_1 P_{n_2}(\rho) \otimes I_b)z = (A_\lambda \otimes I_b) \cdots (A_1 \otimes I_b)(P_{n_2}(\rho) \otimes I_b)z,$$

which can be arranged as follows:

$$
\begin{aligned}
&z \leftarrow (P_{n_2}(\rho) \otimes I_b)z \\
&\textbf{for } q = 1{:}\lambda \\
&\qquad z \leftarrow (A_q \otimes I_b)z \\
&\textbf{end}
\end{aligned}
\tag{3.3.11}
$$

The index reversal $z_{b \times n_2} P_{n_2}(\rho)$ poses no difficulty if we follow the strategy of Algorithm 2.2.2. We require only two vectors of length b in main memory at any one time. A single pass is required for the complete permutation.

Turning our attention to the butterfly operations, we have

$$A_q \otimes I_b = I_r \otimes B_L \otimes I_b = (I_r \otimes F_{m_2} \otimes I_{L_*} \otimes I_b)(I_r \otimes D_q \otimes I_b)$$

and so (3.3.11) transforms into:

$$
\begin{aligned}
&z \leftarrow (P_{n_2}(\rho) \otimes I_b)z \\
&\textbf{for } q = 1{:}\lambda \\
&\qquad L \leftarrow m_2^q; \; r \leftarrow n_2/L; \; L_* \leftarrow L/m_2 \\
&\qquad z \leftarrow (I_r \otimes D_q \otimes I_b)z \\
&\qquad z \leftarrow (I_r \otimes F_{m_2} \otimes I_{L_*} \otimes I_b)z \\
&\textbf{end}
\end{aligned}
\qquad (3.3.12)
$$

We show how to organize efficiently the z updates via the following partitioning:

$$
z_{bL_* \times rm_2} = \begin{bmatrix} Z_{00} & \cdots & Z_{0,r-1} \\ \vdots & & \vdots \\ Z_{L_*-1,0} & \cdots & Z_{L_*-1,r-1} \end{bmatrix}, \quad Z_{kj} \in \mathbb{C}^{b \times m_2} . \qquad (3.3.13)
$$

The update $z \leftarrow (I_r \otimes D_q \otimes I_b)z$ is a scaling and can be shown to have the form

$$
z_{bL_* \times rm_2} \leftarrow \begin{bmatrix} Z_{00}.*\tilde{W}_{00} & \cdots & Z_{0,r-1}.*\tilde{W}_{0,r-1} \\ \vdots & & \vdots \\ Z_{L_*-1,0}.*\tilde{W}_{L_*-1,0} & \cdots & Z_{L_*-1,r-1}.*\tilde{W}_{L_*-1,r-1} \end{bmatrix},
$$

where $\tilde{W}_{kj} \in \mathbb{C}^{b \times m_2}$ with

$$
[\tilde{W}_{kj}]_{\alpha,\beta} = \omega_L^{k\beta}, \qquad \begin{array}{ll} 0 \le k \le L_* - 1, & 0 \le j \le r - 1, \\ 0 \le \alpha \le b - 1, & 0 \le \beta \le m_2 - 1. \end{array} \qquad (3.3.14)
$$

Since $z \leftarrow (I_r \otimes F_{m_2} \otimes I_{L_*} \otimes I_b)z = ((I_r \otimes F_{m_2}) \otimes I_{bL_*})z$ is equivalent to

$$z_{bL_* \times rm_2} \leftarrow z_{bL_* \times rm_2}(I_r \otimes F_{m_2}),$$

the second z-update in (3.3.12) amounts to a multirow DFT of each Z_{kj}:

$$
z_{bL_* \times rm_2} = \begin{bmatrix} Z_{00}F_{m_2} & \cdots & Z_{0,r-1}F_{m_2} \\ \vdots & & \vdots \\ Z_{L_*-1,0}F_{m_2} & \cdots & Z_{L_*-1,r-1}F_{m_2} \end{bmatrix}, \quad Z_{kj} \in \mathbb{C}^{b \times m_2}.
$$

Assuming the availability of the $\tilde{W}_{kj}$, we obtain the following expansion of (3.3.12), which can be used to overwrite $z_{b \times n_2}$ with $z_{b \times n_2}F_{n_2}$:

$$
\begin{aligned}
&z \leftarrow (P_{n_2}(\rho) \otimes I_b)z \\
&\textbf{for } q = 1{:}\lambda \\
&\qquad L \leftarrow m_2^q; \; r \leftarrow n_2/L; \; L_* \leftarrow L/m_2 \\
&\qquad \textbf{for } k = 0{:}L_* - 1 \\
&\qquad\qquad \textbf{for } j = 0{:}r - 1 \\
&\qquad\qquad\qquad U \leftarrow Z_{kj} \\
&\qquad\qquad\qquad U \leftarrow (U.*\tilde{W}_{kj})F_{m_2} \\
&\qquad\qquad\qquad Z_{kj} \leftarrow U \\
&\qquad\qquad \textbf{end} \\
&\qquad \textbf{end} \\
&\textbf{end}
\end{aligned}
$$

Thus, $\lambda + 1$ passes are required. Since $n_2 = m_2^\lambda$, we see the advantage of being able to choose the radix m_2 as large as possible.

In conclusion, we see that the successful organization of a large-scale FFT in a memory hierarchical system may require (1) an intelligent choice of radix, (2) an appropriate application of the four- or six-step frameworks, and (3) a blocking of the underlying multivector DFTs.

Problems

P3.3.1 Prove (3.3.3) and (3.3.5).

P3.3.2 Suppose $x \in \mathbb{C}^n$ and that $n = m^4$. Develop a 10-step "double-twiddle" factor scheme for computing $F_n x$. Your framework should involve four multirow DFTs of the form $x \leftarrow (F_m \otimes I_p)x$, where $p = m^3$, four transpositions, and three twiddle-factor scalings.

P3.3.3 Give an efficient algorithm for computing the twiddle-factor blocks as required in Algorithm 3.3.2.

P3.3.4 Verify (3.3.14).

Notes and References for Section 3.3

Re-use of data is the key to effective external memory FFT computation. The subject has a long history and some of the early papers include

N.M. Brenner (1969). "Fast Fourier Transform of Externally Stored Data," *IEEE Trans. Audio and Electroacoustics AU-17*, 128–132.

H.L. Buijs (1969). "Fast Fourier Transform of Large Arrays of Data," *Applied Optics 8*, 211–212.

M. Drubin (1971b). "Computation of the Fast Fourier Transform Data Stored in External Auxiliary Memory for Any General Radix," *IEEE Trans. Comput. C-20*, 1552–1558.

W.M. Gentleman and G. Sande (1966). "Fast Fourier Transforms for Fun and Profit," *Proc. AFIPS 29*, 563–578.

R.C. Singleton (1967). "A Method for Computing the Fast Fourier Transform with Auxiliary Memory and Limited High-Speed Storage," *IEEE Trans. Audio and Electroacoustics AU-15*, 91–98.

More recent papers include

D.H. Bailey (1990). "FFTs in External or Hierarchical Memory," *J. Supercomputing 4*, 23–35.

D. Fraser (1979). "Algorithm 545, An Optimized Mass Storage FFT," *ACM Trans. Math. Software 5*, 500–517.

M.Y. Kim, A. Nigam, G. Paul, and R. Flynn (1987). "Disk Interleaving and Very Large Fast Fourier Transforms," *International J. Supercomputer Applications 1*, 75–96.

R.C. Singleton (1979). "Two-Dimensional Mixed Radix Mass Storage Fourier Transform," in *Programs for Digital Signal Processing*, Digital Signal Processing Committee (eds.), IEEE Press, New York, 1.9-1–1.9-8.

FFT implementations that address the re-use issue through radix choice and the twiddle-factor approach are discussed in

R.C. Agarwal and J.W. Cooley (1986). "Fourier Transform and Convolution Subroutines for the IBM 3090 Vector Facility," *IBM J. Res. Develop. 30*, 145–162.

R.C. Agarwal and J.W. Cooley (1987). "Vectorized Mixed Radix Discrete Fourier Transform Algorithms," *Proc. IEEE 75*, 1283–1292.

J. Armstrong (1988). "A Multi-Algorithm Approach to Very High Performance 1D FFTs," *J. Supercomputing 2*, 415–434.

M. Ashworth and A.G. Lyne (1988). "A Segmented FFT Algorithm for Vector Supercomputers," *Parallel Comput. 6*, 217–224.

D.H. Bailey (1988). "A High-Performance FFT Algorithm for Vector Supercomputers," *International J. Supercomputer Applications 2*, 82–87.

D.A. Carlson (1991). "Using Local Memory to Boost the Performance of FFT Algorithms on the Cray-2 Supercomputer," *J. Supercomputing 4*, 345–356.

3.4   The Multidimensional FFT Problem

If $n = n_1 \cdots n_d$ and $x \in \mathbb{C}^n$, then

$$y = (F_{n_d} \otimes \cdots \otimes F_{n_1})x \tag{3.4.1}$$

is a *d-dimensional* DFT. If we regard x and y as d-dimensional arrays,

$$\begin{aligned} x &\equiv X(0{:}n_1 - 1, \ldots, 0{:}n_d - 1), \\ y &\equiv Y(0{:}n_1 - 1, \ldots, 0{:}n_d - 1), \end{aligned}$$

then (3.4.1) has the following scalar equivalent:

$$Y(\beta_1, \cdots, \beta_d) \leftarrow \sum_{\alpha_1=0}^{n_1-1} \cdots \sum_{\alpha_d=0}^{n_d-1} \omega_{n_1}^{\beta_1 \alpha_1} \cdots \omega_{n_d}^{\beta_d \alpha_d} X(\alpha_1, \cdots, \alpha_d) . \tag{3.4.2}$$

Multidimensional DFTs require multiple-vector DFTs in each component direction. Indeed, if we define

$$M_\mu = (I_{n_d} \otimes \cdots \otimes I_{n_{\mu+1}}) \otimes F_{n_\mu} \otimes (I_{n_{\mu-1}} \otimes \cdots \otimes I_{n_1}) \tag{3.4.3}$$

for $\mu = 1{:}d$, then we have the factorization

$$F_{n_d} \otimes \cdots \otimes F_{n_1} = M_d \cdots M_1 . \tag{3.4.4}$$

In this section we discuss the computation of multidimensional DFTs, paying close attention to the usual issues of vectorization and data re-use. We begin with specialized remarks for the important cases $d = 2$ and $d = 3$.

3.4.1   Two-Dimensional FFTs

Consider the two-dimensional DFT problem

$$x \leftarrow (F_{n_2} \otimes F_{n_1})x .$$

In identifying $X \in \mathbb{C}^{n_1 \times n_2}$ with $x_{n_1 \times n_2}$, our goal is to compute

$$X \leftarrow F_{n_1} X F_{n_2} = \begin{cases} (F_{n_1} X) F_{n_2} \\ ((X F_{n_2})^T F_{n_1})^T \\ (F_{n_2}(F_{n_1} X)^T)^T . \end{cases} \tag{3.4.5}$$

The most suitable of the three recipes depends upon (a) the relative efficiency of multirow versus multicolumn DFTs and (b) the overhead associated with transposition.

The three frameworks suggested by (3.4.5) do not intermingle the row and column DFTs. In contrast, the row and column DFTs are processed "at the same time," in what is referred to as the *vector-radix* framework. See Rivard (1977). To illustrate the main idea, we assume that $n_1 = n_2 = m = 2^t$ and work with the radix-2 transposed Stockham factorization

$$F_m = S_t \cdots S_1 .$$

(The Cooley–Tukey or Stockham frameworks would also be suitable.) Recall from §1.7.2 that for $q = 1{:}t$

$$S_q \;=\; (I_r \otimes B_L)(\Pi_{2,L_*} \otimes I_{r_*}),$$

$$B_L \;=\; \begin{bmatrix} I_{L_*} & \Omega_{L_*} \\ I_{L_*} & -\Omega_{L_*} \end{bmatrix},$$

$$\Omega_{L_*} \;=\; \mathrm{diag}(1, \omega_L, \ldots, \omega_L^{L_*-1}),$$

with $L = 2^q$, $r = m/L$, $L_* = L/2$, and $r_* = 2r$. Since

$$X \leftarrow F_m X F_m = F_m X F_m^T = (S_t \cdots S_1)X(S_1^T \cdots S_t^T),$$

it follows that

$$
\begin{aligned}
&\textbf{for } q = 1{:}t \\
&\qquad X \leftarrow S_q X S_q^T \\
&\textbf{end}
\end{aligned}
\qquad\qquad (3.4.6)
$$

computes the required transform. Let $X^{(q)}$ denote the matrix housed in X after q steps. If $L = 2^q$ and $r = m/L$, then it is not hard to show that

$$X^{(q)} \;=\; \begin{bmatrix} X_{00}^{(q)} & \cdots & X_{0,r-1}^{(q)} \\ \vdots & & \vdots \\ X_{r-1,0}^{(q)} & \cdots & X_{r-1,r-1}^{(q)} \end{bmatrix},$$

where

$$X_{k_1,k_2}^{(q)} \;=\; F_L X(k_1{:}r{:}m-1, k_2{:}r{:}m-1)F_L^T . \qquad (3.4.7)$$

Thus, the L-by-L blocks of $X^{(q)}$ house intermediate two-dimensional DFTs.

Building on our "subscripting knowledge" of the transposed Stockham procedure (see §1.7.4), we obtain the following expansion for the update $X \leftarrow S_q X S_q^T$:

$$
\begin{aligned}
&Y \leftarrow X \\
&L \leftarrow 2^q; \; r \leftarrow m/L; \; L_* \leftarrow L/2 \\
&\textbf{for } k_2 = 0{:}r-1 \\
&\qquad \textbf{for } k_1 = 0{:}r-1 \\
&\qquad\qquad \alpha_1 \leftarrow k_1 L_*{:}(k_1+1)L_* - 1 \\
&\qquad\qquad \alpha_2 \leftarrow (k_1+r)L_*{:}(k_1+r+1)L_* - 1 \\
&\qquad\qquad \beta_1 \leftarrow k_2 L_*{:}(k_2+1)L_* - 1 \\
&\qquad\qquad \beta_2 \leftarrow (k_2+r)L_*{:}(k_2+r+1)L_* - 1 \\
&\qquad\qquad rows \leftarrow k_1 L{:}(k_1+1)L - 1 \\
&\qquad\qquad cols \leftarrow k_2 L{:}(k_2+1)L - 1 \\
&\qquad\qquad X(rows, cols) \leftarrow B_L \begin{bmatrix} Y(\alpha_1,\beta_1) & Y(\alpha_1,\beta_2) \\ Y(\alpha_2,\beta_1) & Y(\alpha_2,\beta_2) \end{bmatrix} B_L^T \\
&\qquad \textbf{end} \\
&\textbf{end}
\end{aligned}
\qquad (3.4.8)
$$

To complete the derivation, it is necessary to detail the two-sided application of the butterfly matrix B_L, e.g.,

$$
\begin{bmatrix} \tilde{V} & \tilde{W} \\ \tilde{U} & \tilde{Z} \end{bmatrix} \leftarrow \begin{bmatrix} I_{L_*} & \Omega_{L_*} \\ I_{L_*} & -\Omega_{L_*} \end{bmatrix} \begin{bmatrix} V & W \\ U & Z \end{bmatrix} \begin{bmatrix} I_{L_*} & I_{L_*} \\ \Omega_{L_*} & -\Omega_{L_*} \end{bmatrix}. \tag{3.4.9}
$$

The calculation can be organized so that unit stride access is maintained. The number of multiplications can also be reduced by combining the left and right scalings in the (1,1) block of the update. See Rivard (1977).

We conclude our discussion of two-dimensional FFTs with a remark about bit reversal. For clarity, we set $n_1 = n_2 = m = 2^t$ and $n = m^2$. Using Kron8 and the symmetry of $\Pi_{m,n}$, we can express the two-dimensional DFT operator as follows:

$$
F_m \otimes F_m = (F_m \otimes I_m)(I_m \otimes F_m) = \Pi_{m,n}(I_m \otimes F_m)\Pi_{m,n}(I_m \otimes F_m).
$$

If we express the Cooley–Tukey factorization as $F_m = AP_m = P_m A^T$, where A is the product of the butterfly factors and P_m is the bit-reversal permutation, then

$$
\begin{aligned}
F_m \otimes F_m &= \Pi_{m,n}(I_m \otimes AP_m)\Pi_{m,n}(I_m \otimes P_m A^T) \\
&= \Pi_{m,n}(I_m \otimes A)(I_m \otimes P_m)\Pi_{m,n}(I_m \otimes P_m)(I_m \otimes A^T).
\end{aligned}
$$

However, it can be shown that

$$
P_n = (I_m \otimes P_m)\Pi_{m,n}(I_m \otimes P_m). \tag{3.4.10}
$$

For example, if $m = 2^3$ and we identify x with a $2 \times 2 \times 2 \times 2 \times 2 \times 2$ array X, then the three-factor product in (3.4.10) moves $X(\alpha_1, \ldots, \alpha_6)$ as follows:

Operation	Effect
$x \leftarrow (I_m \otimes P_m)x$	$X(\alpha_3, \alpha_2, \alpha_1, \alpha_4, \alpha_5, \alpha_6) \leftarrow X(\alpha_1, \alpha_2, \alpha_3, \alpha_4, \alpha_5, \alpha_6)$
$x \leftarrow \Pi_{m,n}x$	$X(\alpha_4, \alpha_5, \alpha_6, \alpha_3, \alpha_2, \alpha_1) \leftarrow X(\alpha_3, \alpha_2, \alpha_1, \alpha_4, \alpha_5, \alpha_6)$
$x \leftarrow (I_m \otimes P_m)x$	$X(\alpha_6, \alpha_5, \alpha_4, \alpha_3, \alpha_2, \alpha_1) \leftarrow X(\alpha_4, \alpha_5, \alpha_6, \alpha_3, \alpha_2, \alpha_1)$

We therefore obtain the factorization

$$
F_m \otimes F_m = \Pi_{m,n}(I_m \otimes A)P_n(I_m \otimes A^T).
$$

This rearrangement of the two-dimensional DFTs has appeal in certain environments where bit reversal can be implemented at the hardware level. See Duhamel (1990).

3.4.2 Three-Dimensional FFTs

Three-dimensional DFTs are important in many applications. They pose some interesting challenges above and beyond the fact that $n = n_1 n_2 n_3$ is usually very large. Since

$$
F_{n_3} \otimes F_{n_2} \otimes F_{n_1} = (F_{n_3} \otimes I_{n_1 n_2})(I_{n_3} \otimes F_{n_2} \otimes I_{n_1})(I_{n_2 n_3} \otimes F_{n_1}),
$$

it follows that if

$$
\begin{aligned}
x_{n_1 \times n_2 n_3} &\leftarrow F_{n_1} x_{n_1 \times n_2 n_3} \\
x_{n_1 n_2 \times n_3} &\leftarrow (F_{n_2} \otimes I_{n_1}) x_{n_1 n_2 \times n_3} \\
x_{n_1 n_2 \times n_3} &\leftarrow x_{n_1 n_2 \times n_3} F_{n_3},
\end{aligned} \tag{3.4.11}
$$

then x is overwritten by $(F_{n_3} \otimes F_{n_2} \otimes F_{n_1})x$. In this framework, multiple DFTs prevail. If the working environment favors multirow DFTs, then the following reformulation of (3.4.11) is of interest:

$$
\begin{aligned}
x_{n_2 n_3 \times n_1} &\leftarrow x_{n_1 \times n_2 n_3}^T \\
x_{n_2 n_3 \times n_1} &\leftarrow x_{n_2 n_3 \times n_1} F_{n_1} \\
x_{n_1 \times n_2 n_3} &\leftarrow x_{n_2 n_3 \times n_1}^T \\
x_{n_1 n_2 \times n_3} &\leftarrow (F_{n_2} \otimes I_{n_1}) x_{n_1 n_2 \times n_3} \\
x_{n_1 n_2 \times n_3} &\leftarrow x_{n_1 n_2 \times n_3} F_{n_3}.
\end{aligned}
\qquad (3.4.12)
$$

The DFTs associated with F_{n_2} surface in the form of multiple DFTs on *each column* of $x_{n_1 n_2 \times n_3}$. They could be computed as follows:

for $k = 0:n_3 - 1$

$\quad \tilde{x} \leftarrow x(k n_1 n_2 : (k+1) n_1 n_2 - 1)$

$\quad \tilde{x}_{n_1 \times n_2} \leftarrow \tilde{x}_{n_1 \times n_2} F_{n_2}$ $\qquad (3.4.13)$

$\quad x(k n_1 n_2 : (k+1) n_1 n_2 - 1) \leftarrow \tilde{x}$

end

Now suppose that multicolumn DFTs are attractive. This suggests the following column analog of (3.4.12):

$$
\begin{aligned}
x_{n_1 \times n_2 n_3} &\leftarrow F_{n_1} x_{n_1 \times n_2 n_3} \\
x_{n_1 \times n_2 n_3} &\leftarrow x_{n_1 \times n_2 n_3} (I_{n_3} \otimes F_{n_2}) \\
x_{n_3 \times n_1 n_2} &\leftarrow x_{n_1 n_2 \times n_3}^T \\
x_{n_3 \times n_1 n_2} &\leftarrow F_{n_3} x_{n_3 \times n_1 n_2} \\
x_{n_1 n_2 \times n_3} &\leftarrow x_{n_3 \times n_1 n_2}^T.
\end{aligned}
\qquad (3.4.14)
$$

Unfortunately, this poses a stride problem associated with the F_{n_2} applications. Indeed, we must apply $I_{n_3} \otimes F_{n_2}$ to each *row* of $x_{n_1 \times n_2 n_3}$ and the elements in these rows have stride n_1.

This prompts us to consider a different approach to the three-dimensional DFT problem based upon the following factorization.

Theorem 3.4.1 *If $n = n_1 n_2 n_3$, then*

$$
F_{n_3} \otimes F_{n_2} \otimes F_{n_1} = \Pi_{n_2 n_3, n}^T (I_{n_1 n_3} \otimes F_{n_2}) \Pi_{n_2 n_3, n} (F_{n_3} \otimes I_{n_2} \otimes F_{n_1}).
$$

Proof. By setting $A = I_{n_3} \otimes F_{n_2}$ in Kron8 and using Kron7 we conclude that

$$
(I_{n_3} \otimes F_{n_2} \otimes I_{n_1}) = \Pi_{n_2 n_3, n}^T (I_{n_1 n_3} \otimes F_{n_2}) \Pi_{n_2 n_3, n}.
$$

Since

$$
F_{n_3} \otimes F_{n_2} \otimes F_{n_1} = (I_{n_3} \otimes F_{n_2} \otimes I_{n_1})(F_{n_3} \otimes I_{n_2} \otimes F_{n_1}),
$$

the theorem follows. $\square$

Based on this factorization, we obtain the following framework:

$$
\begin{aligned}
x &\leftarrow (F_{n_3} \otimes I_{n_2} \otimes F_{n_1})x \\
x_{n_2 n_3 \times n_1} &\leftarrow x_{n_1 \times n_2 n_3}^T \\
x_{n_2 \times n_1 n_3} &\leftarrow F_{n_2} x_{n_2 \times n_1 n_3} \\
x_{n_1 \times n_2 n_3} &\leftarrow x_{n_2 n_3 \times n_1}^T.
\end{aligned}
\qquad (3.4.15)
$$

At this stage of our understanding, only the first step requires an explanation. Since

$$z = (F_{n_3} \otimes I_{n_2} \otimes F_{n_1})x \quad \Leftrightarrow \quad z_{n_1 n_2 \times n_3} = (I_{n_2} \otimes F_{n_1})x_{n_1 n_2 \times n_3}F_{n_3},$$

it follows that if

$$x_{n_1 n_2 \times n_3} = \begin{bmatrix} X_0 \\ \vdots \\ X_{n_2-1} \end{bmatrix}, \quad X_j \in \mathbb{C}^{n_1 \times n_3},$$

then

$$z = \begin{bmatrix} F_{n_1} X_0 F_{n_3} \\ \vdots \\ F_{n_1} X_{n_2-1} F_{n_3} \end{bmatrix}.$$

Thus, the first step in (3.4.15) involves computing a sequence of two-dimensional DFTs.

3.4.3 d-Dimensional FFTs

We conclude with a few remarks about the d-dimensional DFT problem

$$y = (F_{n_d} \otimes \cdots \otimes F_{n_1})x.$$

Applying Kron7 to (3.4.3) and using the factorization (3.4.4), we obtain the following general framework:

> **for** $\mu = 1{:}d$
> $\quad N_1 \leftarrow n_1 \cdots n_{\mu-1}$
> $\quad N_2 \leftarrow n_\mu$ (3.4.16)
> $\quad N_3 \leftarrow n_{\mu+1} \cdots n_d$
> $\quad x \leftarrow (I_{N_3} \otimes F_{N_2} \otimes I_{N_1})x$
> **end**

The x-update is equivalent to

$$x_{N_1 N_2 \times N_3} \leftarrow (F_{N_2} \otimes I_{N_1})x_{N_1 N_2 \times N_3}$$

and so we have a multiple DFT problem associated with each column of $x_{N_1 N_2 \times N_3}$. Using this, we expand (3.4.16) to obtain

> **for** $\mu = 1{:}d$
> $\quad N_1 \leftarrow n_1 \cdots n_{\mu-1}$
> $\quad N_2 \leftarrow n_\mu$
> $\quad N_3 \leftarrow n_{\mu+1} \cdots n_d$
> $\quad \{x \equiv X(0{:}N_1 - 1, 0{:}N_2 - 1, 0{:}N_3 - 1)\}$
> $\quad$ **for** $j = 0{:}N_1 - 1$ (3.4.17)
> $\quad\quad$ **for** $k = 0{:}N_3 - 1$
> $$\begin{bmatrix} X(j,0,k) \\ \vdots \\ X(j,N_2-1,k) \end{bmatrix} \leftarrow F_{N_2} \begin{bmatrix} X(j,0,k) \\ \vdots \\ X(j,N_2-1,k) \end{bmatrix}$$
> $\quad\quad$ **end**
> $\quad$ **end**
> **end**

Thus, in step μ there are $N_1 N_3 = n/n_\mu$ single-vector DFTs. Note that these DFTs are of vectors that have stride N_1. As we have found in the cases $d = 2$ and $d = 3$, unit stride can be purchased at the expense of transposition. Using Kron8, we have

$$I_{N_3} \otimes F_{N_2} \otimes I_{N_1} = \Pi^T_{N_2 N_3, n}(I_{N_1 N_3} \otimes F_{N_2})\Pi_{N_2 N_3, n}$$

and so we obtain

$$
\begin{aligned}
&\textbf{for } \mu = 1{:}d \\
&\quad N_1 \leftarrow n_1 \cdots n_{\mu-1} \\
&\quad N_2 \leftarrow n_\mu \\
&\quad N_3 \leftarrow n_{\mu+1} \cdots n_d \\
&\quad x_{N_2 N_3 \times N_1} \leftarrow x^T_{N_1 \times N_2 N_3} \\
&\quad x_{N_2 \times N_1 N_3} \leftarrow F_{N_2} x_{N_2 \times N_1 N_3} \\
&\quad x_{N_1 \times N_2 N_3} \leftarrow x^T_{N_2 N_3 \times N_1} \\
&\textbf{end}
\end{aligned}
\qquad (3.4.18)
$$

Let us identify x with $X(0{:}n_1-1, \ldots, 0{:}n_d-1)$ and trace the effect of the transpositions in this algorithm. Each step involves, in sequence, a transpose, a DFT, and another transpose. Here is a trace of the effect of the transpositions for the case $d = 5$:

$\mu = 1$	$X(\alpha_1, \alpha_2, \alpha_3, \alpha_4, \alpha_5)$	$\Pi^T_{1,n}$
	$X(\alpha_1, \alpha_2, \alpha_3, \alpha_4, \alpha_5)$	F_{n_1}
	$X(\alpha_1, \alpha_2, \alpha_3, \alpha_4, \alpha_5)$	$\Pi_{1,n}$
$\mu = 2$	$X(\alpha_2, \alpha_3, \alpha_4, \alpha_5 \alpha_1)$	$\Pi^T_{n_1,n}$
	$X(\alpha_2, \alpha_3, \alpha_4, \alpha_5 \alpha_1)$	F_{n_2}
	$X(\alpha_1, \alpha_2, \alpha_3, \alpha_4, \alpha_5)$	$\Pi_{n_1,n}$
$\mu = 3$	$X(\alpha_3, \alpha_4, \alpha_5, \alpha_1, \alpha_2)$	$\Pi^T_{n_1 n_2,n}$
	$X(\alpha_3, \alpha_4, \alpha_5, \alpha_1, \alpha_2)$	F_{n_3}
	$X(\alpha_1, \alpha_2, \alpha_3, \alpha_4, \alpha_5)$	$\Pi_{n_1 n_2,n}$
$\mu = 4$	$X(\alpha_4, \alpha_5, \alpha_1, \alpha_2, \alpha_3)$	$\Pi^T_{n_1 n_2 n_3,n}$
	$X(\alpha_4, \alpha_5, \alpha_1, \alpha_2, \alpha_3)$	F_{n_4}
	$X(\alpha_1, \alpha_2, \alpha_3, \alpha_4, \alpha_5)$	$\Pi_{n_1 n_2 n_3,n}$
$\mu = 5$	$X(\alpha_5, \alpha_1, \alpha_2, \alpha_3, \alpha_4)$	$\Pi^T_{n_1 n_2 n_3 n_4,n}$
	$X(\alpha_5, \alpha_1, \alpha_2, \alpha_3, \alpha_4)$	F_{n_5}
	$X(\alpha_1, \alpha_2, \alpha_3, \alpha_4, \alpha_5)$	$\Pi_{n_1 n_2 n_3 n_4,n}$

From this it is clear that rather than transforming back to the original array dimensions, it is more sensible just to shift the coordinates once each step, i.e.,

$\mu = 1$	$X(\alpha_1, \alpha_2, \alpha_3, \alpha_4, \alpha_5)$	F_{n_1}
	$X(\alpha_2, \alpha_3, \alpha_4, \alpha_5, \alpha_1)$	$\Pi_{n_1,n}^T$
$\mu = 2$	$X(\alpha_2, \alpha_3, \alpha_4, \alpha_5, \alpha_1)$	F_{n_2}
	$X(\alpha_3, \alpha_4, \alpha_5, \alpha_1, \alpha_2)$	$\Pi_{n_2,n}^T$
$\mu = 3$	$X(\alpha_3, \alpha_4, \alpha_5, \alpha_1, \alpha_2)$	F_{n_3}
	$X(\alpha_4, \alpha_5, \alpha_1, \alpha_2, \alpha_3)$	$\Pi_{n_3,n}^T$
$\mu = 4$	$X(\alpha_4, \alpha_5, \alpha_1, \alpha_2, \alpha_3)$	F_{n_4}
	$X(\alpha_5, \alpha_1, \alpha_2, \alpha_3, \alpha_4)$	$\Pi_{n_4,n}^T$
$\mu = 5$	$X(\alpha_5, \alpha_1, \alpha_2, \alpha_3, \alpha_4)$	F_{n_5}
	$X(\alpha_1, \alpha_2, \alpha_3, \alpha_4, \alpha_5)$	$\Pi_{n_5,n}^T$

We have essentially shown that if $n = n_1 \cdots n_d$, then

$$F_{n_d} \otimes \cdots \otimes F_{n_1} = \tilde{M}_d \cdots \tilde{M}_1, \tag{3.4.19}$$

where

$$\tilde{M}_\mu = \Pi_{n_\mu,n}^T (I_{(n/n_\mu)} \otimes F_{n_\mu}). \tag{3.4.20}$$

Based upon this result, we obtain the following revision of (3.4.17):

$$
\begin{aligned}
&\textbf{for } \mu = 1{:}d \\
&\quad m_\mu \leftarrow n/n_\mu \\
&\quad x_{n_\mu \times m_\mu} \leftarrow F_{n_\mu} x_{n_\mu \times m_\mu} \\
&\quad x_{m_\mu \times n_\mu} \leftarrow x_{n_\mu \times m_\mu}^T \\
&\textbf{end}
\end{aligned}
\tag{3.4.21}
$$

Thus, any d-dimensional DFT problem can be solved as a sequence of unit-stride, multicolumn DFT problems and transpositions. It is also possible to arrange things so that multirow DFTs arise. Indeed, since

$$\tilde{M}_\mu = (F_{n_\mu} \otimes I_{(n/n_\mu)})\Pi_{n_\mu,n}^T$$

by Kron8, we obtain the following row-oriented version of (3.4.21):

$$
\begin{aligned}
&\textbf{for } \mu = 1{:}d \\
&\quad m_\mu \leftarrow n/n_\mu \\
&\quad x_{m_\mu \times n_\mu} \leftarrow x_{n_\mu \times m_\mu}^T \\
&\quad x_{m_\mu \times n_\mu} \leftarrow x_{m_\mu \times n_\mu} F_{n_\mu} \\
&\textbf{end}
\end{aligned}
\tag{3.4.22}
$$

Problems

P3.4.1 Give a detailed unit stride description of (3.4.9).

P3.4.2 Verify (3.4.7).

P3.4.3 Develop a vector-radix framework for the problem $x \leftarrow (F_{n_2} \otimes F_{n_1})x$ for the case when $n_1 = 2n_2$ with $n_2 = 2^{t_2}$.

P3.4.4 Consider the multidimensional problem (3.4.1) for the case when $n_1 = \cdots = n_d = m = 2^{t_1}$. Develop a vector-radix framework for this problem in which step q involves the update

$$x \leftarrow (S_q \otimes \cdots \otimes S_q)x \,.$$

P3.4.5 Prove (3.4.10) and the equivalent formula $P_n = \Pi_{m,n}(P_m \otimes P_m)$.

P3.4.6 Give an inductive proof of (3.4.2).

Notes and References for Section 3.4

References for the vector-radix algorithm include

D.B. Harris, J.H. McClelland, D.S.K. Chan, and H. Schuessler (1977). "Vector Radix Fast Fourier Transform," *Proc. IEEE Int. Conf. on Acoust. Speech Signal Process.*, 548–551.

S. Prakash and V.V. Rao (1982). "Vector Radix FFT Error Analysis," *IEEE Trans. Acoust. Speech Signal Process.* ASSP-30, 808–811.

G.E. Rivard (1977). "Direct Fast Fourier Transform of Bivariate Functions," *IEEE Trans. Acoust. Speech Signal Process.* ASSP-25, 250–52.

See also pages 241ff of

R.E. Blahut (1984). *Fast Algorithms for Digital Signal Processing*, Addison-Wesley, Reading, MA.

Two-dimensional DFTs are crucial in image processing and other areas of signal processing. See

A. Brass and G.S. Pawley (1986). "Two and Three Dimensional FFTs on Highly Parallel Computers," *Parallel Comput. 3*, 167–184.

I. DeLotto and D. Dotti (1975). "Two-Dimensional Transforms by Minicomputer without Transposing," *Computer Graphics and Image Processing 4*, 271–275.

P. Duhamel (1990). "A Connection between Bit Reversal and Matrix Transposition, Hardware and Software Consequences," *IEEE Trans. Acoust. Speech Signal Process.* ASSP-38, 1893–1896.

G. Eden (1979). "Two-Dimensional Fast Transforms Applied to Memory Limited Disk Computers," *Comp. Prog. Biomed. 9*, 258–262.

K. Itano (1979). "Reduction of Page Swaps on the Two-Dimensional Transforms in a Paging Environment," *Inform. Process. Lett. 9*, 137–140.

L.R. Johnson and A.K. Jain (1981). "An Efficient Two-Dimensional FFT Algorithm," *IEEE Trans. Pattern Anal. Machine Intell.* PAMI-3, 698–701.

M. Onoe (1975). "A Method for Computing Large Scale Two-Dimensional Transforms without Transposing the Data Matrix," *Proc. IEEE 63*, 196–197.

Specific comments on three-dimensional transforms may be found in

M. Edwards (1987). "Computation of Fast Fourier Transforms," *Cray Channels, Spring*, 22–25.

S. Lange, U. Stolle, and G. Huttner (1973). "On the Fast Computing of Three-Dimensional Fourier Transforms of Crystallographic Data via External Storage," *Acta Crystallogr. A, A29*, 445–449.

Papers concerned with general, multidimensional DFTs include

G.L. Anderson (1980). "A Stepwise Approach to Computing the Multidimensional Fast Fourier Transform of Large Arrays," *IEEE Trans. Acoust. Speech Signal Process.* ASSP-28, 280–284.

B. Arambepola (1980). "Fast Computation of Multidimensional Discrete Fourier Transforms," *IEE Proc. F, Comm., Radar, and Signal Process. 127*, 49–52.

B. Arambepola and P.J.W. Rayner (1979). "Multidimensional Fast-Fourier-Transform," *Electron. Lett. 15*, 382–383.

L. Auslander, E. Feig, and S. Winograd (1983). "New Algorithms for the Multidimensional Discrete Fourier Transform," *IEEE Trans. Acoust. Speech Signal Process.* ASSP-31, 388–403.

A.A. Belal (1978). "Multidimensional FFT by One and Two Dimensional Array Processing," *Proc. 1978 IEEE Int. Symp., Circuits Systems*, 662–663.

C.S. Burrus (1977). "Index Mappings for Multidimensional Formulation of the DFT and Convolution," *IEEE Trans. Acoust. Speech Signal Process.* ASSP-25, 239–242.

P. Corsini and G. Frosini (1979). "Properties of the Multidimensional Generalized Fourier Transform," *IEEE Trans. Comput.* AC-28, 819–830.

R.M. Mersereau and T.C. Speake (1981). "A Unified Treatment of Cooley–Tukey Algorithms for the Evaluation of the Multidimensional DFT," *IEEE Trans. Acoust. Speech Signal Process.* ASSP-29, 1011–1018.

3.5   Distributed-Memory FFTs

In a distributed-memory computer we have a set of processors that are connected together in some pattern to form a *network*. Typical interconnection patterns include rings, meshes, trees, and hypercubes. A four-processor ring is displayed in Fig. 3.5.1.

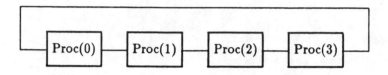

FIG. 3.5.1. *A four-processor ring.*

The act of programming a distributed-memory multiprocessor requires the writing of a *node program* for each of the participating processors. These programs manipulate data that are situated in the processor's *local memory*; they also communicate with other processors through the sending and receiving of messages. We assume that the processor memories are private, meaning that $\text{Proc}(\mu)$ cannot access $\text{Proc}(\lambda)$'s memory. Systems with a physically distributed memory that can be directly accessed by each processor are also possible. See Hennessy and Patterson (1990, pp. 578ff).

The primary objective of this section is to illustrate the kind of algorithmic thinking that is associated with the design of distributed-memory FFTs. As usual, we present computational frameworks and *not* detailed implementations. Various implementations are discussed in the references at the end of the section. We begin with an examination of the two-processor butterfly computation, a simple example that permits the introduction of our message-passing notation and a small handful of tools for performance analysis. We then proceed to a discussion of a general s-processor butterfly. This leads naturally to the development of a distributed-memory, radix-2 Cooley–Tukey procedure. Distributed bit-reversal, transposition, four-step, and six-step methods are also discussed.

3.5.1   The Message-Passing Paradigm

Suppose $L = 2L_*$ and consider the computation of the butterfly

$$\begin{bmatrix} u \\ v \end{bmatrix} \leftarrow \begin{bmatrix} I_{L_*} & \Omega_{L_*} \\ I_{L_*} & -\Omega_{L_*} \end{bmatrix} \begin{bmatrix} u \\ v \end{bmatrix} = \begin{bmatrix} u + w_{L_*}.* v \\ u - w_{L_*}.* v \end{bmatrix} \tag{3.5.1}$$

on a two-processor network, where $u, v \in \mathbb{C}^{L_*}$ and $w_{L_*} = [1, \omega_L, \dots, \omega_L^{L_*-1}]^T$. We make the following assumptions:

- Initially, $u \in \text{Proc}(0)$ and $v \in \text{Proc}(1)$, meaning that u is housed in the local memory of $\text{Proc}(0)$ and v is housed in the local memory of $\text{Proc}(1)$.

- Both processors have a copy of $w_{L_*} = [1, \omega_L, \dots, \omega_L^{L_*-1}]^T$.

- Upon termination, the vector u in $\text{Proc}(0)$ is overwritten by $u + w_{L_*}.* v$ and the vector v in $\text{Proc}(1)$ is overwritten by $u - w_{L_*}.* v$.

Communication between $\text{Proc}(0)$ and $\text{Proc}(1)$ is necessary, since they each require nonlocal data for their computational tasks. To specify messages in a distributed-memory algorithm, we need to extend our algorithmic notation so that we can initiate the sending and receiving of arrays. To that end, we permit commands of the following form:

$$\mathbf{send}(\{local\ array\}, \{destination\ processor\}, \{message\ id\})$$
$$\mathbf{recv}(\{local\ array\}, \{originating\ processor\}, \{message\ id\})$$

In this context, "array" means "complex array." In practice, the real and imaginary portions of an array would probably be stored separately and some preprocessing would be required before invoking the **send**. Likewise, incoming messages, which need not arrive in the order in which they are sent, have to be placed in some kind of buffer before they can be accessed by the receiving node program, a detail that we also suppress. Although these maneuvers can have a great effect on performance, they interfere with the high-level algorithmic mission of this section.

It is necessary to establish the ground rules associated with **send** and **recv**. Because messages need not arrive in the order in which they are sent, we use an integer *message id* that permits the unambiguous deciphering of incoming messages. When a **send** is encountered, the designated local array (= matrix, vector, or scalar) is sent to the named destination processor along with the message id. Execution resumes after the **send** is completed. When a **recv** is encountered, the node waits until the requested array with the designated message id is available from the incoming message buffer. It is then stored in the named array and execution resumes.

3.5.2 Two-Processor Butterfly Computations

We return to the two-processor computation of (3.5.1) and discuss a pair of approaches, the first of which is structured as follows:

Proc(0)	Proc(1)
$\mathbf{send}(u, 1, 0)$	$\mathbf{send}(v, 0, 0)$
$\mathbf{recv}(s, 1, 0)$	$\mathbf{recv}(s, 0, 0)$
$\{s = v\}$	$\{s = u\}$
$u \leftarrow u + w_{L_{\bullet}}.* s$	$v \leftarrow s - w_{L_{\bullet}}.* v$

FIG. 3.5.2. *Two-processor butterfly (Version 1).*

The node program for Proc(0) sends a copy of u to Proc(1) and then waits for a copy of v. Upon receipt of v, it performs the required update of u. Proc(1) proceeds in an analogous fashion. It sends a copy of v to Proc(0) and then waits for u. After u is received, it participates in the update of v. Note that in this distributed butterfly, each processor is required to have a complex buffer of length $L_{\bullet}$ in order to house the "other half" of the input vector. In this simple example, which involves a single **send-recv** pair, the message id is superfluous, but we carry it along for consistency.

It is important to recognize that the node programs in Fig. 3.5.2 do *not* proceed in lock-step fashion. In other words, they do not execute their **send** at the same time, followed by their **recv** at the same time, followed by their butterfly update at the same time. That kind of rigid, highly synchronous computing requires a global clock and is the hallmark of the *systolic paradigm*. Systolic computation is important in practice, but it is more instructive for us to develop our distributed FFTs within an asynchronous, message-passing framework.

An important attribute of a parallel program is whether or not it is *load balanced*, meaning that each participating processor has roughly the same amount of computation and communication. Version 1 is load balanced, but it is also redundant, because each processor computes $w_{L_*}.*v$. The following revision avoids this redundancy at the expense of load balancing:

Proc(0)	Proc(1)
send$(u, 1, 0)$	$v \leftarrow w_{L_*}.* v$
recv$(s, 1, 0)$	**send**$(v, 0, 0)$
$\{s = w_{L_*}.* v\}$	**recv**$(s, 0, 0)$
$u \leftarrow u + s$	$v \leftarrow s - v$

FIG. 3.5.3. *Load-imbalanced two-processor butterfly.*

Note that Proc(1) oversees four times as much arithmetic as Proc(0).

One way to avoid redundancy and to achieve load balancing is to base the computations on the following 4-by-4 blocking of (3.5.1):

$$
\begin{bmatrix} u_0 \\ u_1 \\ v_0 \\ v_1 \end{bmatrix} \leftarrow \begin{bmatrix} I_{L_0} & 0 & D_0 & 0 \\ 0 & I_{L_0} & 0 & D_1 \\ I_{L_0} & 0 & -D_0 & 0 \\ 0 & I_{L_0} & 0 & -D_1 \end{bmatrix} \begin{bmatrix} u_0 \\ u_1 \\ v_0 \\ v_1 \end{bmatrix} = \begin{bmatrix} u_0 + w_{L_*}(top).* v_0 \\ u_1 + w_{L_*}(bot).* v_1 \\ u_0 - w_{L_*}(top).* v_0 \\ u_1 - w_{L_*}(bot).* v_1 \end{bmatrix}.
$$

Here, $L_0 = L_*/2$, $D_0 = \text{diag}(1, \omega_L, \cdots, \omega_L^{L_0-1})$, $D_1 = \text{diag}(\omega_L^{L_0}, \cdots, \omega_L^{L_*-1})$, and the index ranges are prescribed by $top = 0{:}L_0 - 1$, and $bot = L_0{:}L_* - 1$. The algorithmic idea suggested by this blocking is to have Proc(0) compute $w_{L_*}(top).* v_0$ and update u_0 and v_0, and to have Proc(1) compute $w_{L_*}(bot).* v_1$ and update u_1 and v_1. The details are as follows:

Proc(0)	Proc(1)
$m.id \leftarrow 0$	$m.id \leftarrow 0$
send$(u_1, 1, m.id)$	**send**$(v_0, 0, m.id)$
$top \leftarrow 0{:}L_0 - 1$	$bot \leftarrow L_0{:}L_* - 1$
recv$(s, 1, m.id)$	$s \leftarrow w_{L_*}(bot).* v_1$
$\{s = v_0\}$	**recv**$(r, 0, m.id)$
$s \leftarrow w_{L_*}(top).* s$	$\{r = u_1\}$
$t \leftarrow u_0 - s$	$m.id \leftarrow 1$
$m.id \leftarrow 1$	$t \leftarrow r + s$
send$(t, 1, m.id)$	**send**$(t, 0, m.id)$
$u_0 \leftarrow u_0 + s$	$v_1 \leftarrow r - s$
recv$(u_1, 1, m.id)$	**recv**$(v_0, 0, m.id)$

FIG. 3.5.4. *Two-processor butterfly (Version 2).*

There is some flexibility in the placement of the communication primitives. We have followed the guideline of sending as soon as possible and receiving as late as possible–a useful heuristic in the design of efficient distributed algorithms. Note how the message ids resolve a fundamental ambiguity, for without them it would be impossible to determine whether a received message was the result of the first or second **send** in the other processor.

Version 2 of the two-processor butterfly involves no redundant computation, but it does require twice the number of messages as Version 1. To analyze this trade-off, we need to develop a model of execution that captures the cost of communication.

3.5.3 Modeling the Communication Overhead

We adopt a very simple model of distributed program execution that is based upon two assumptions:

- Floating point arithmetic proceeds at a uniform rate of R flops per second within each node in the network.

- The sending or receiving of a message consisting of N complex numbers requires $\alpha + \beta N$ seconds. The constant α reflects a "start-up" overhead, whereas β measures the rate of message transmission, i.e., channel bandwidth.

Despite its simplicity, this model of computation/communication can expose many of the tensions and trade-offs that are associated with the design of a practical distributed FFT. For example, Table 3.5.1 summarizes the key attributes of Versions 1 and 2.

Table 3.5.1
Two-processor butterfly performance.

	Computation Time	Communication Time	Total Time
Version 1	$4L/R$	$2\alpha + \beta L$	$2\alpha + L(\beta + 4/R)$
Version 2	$2.5L/R$	$4\alpha + \beta L$	$4\alpha + L(\beta + 2.5/R)$

Given our model, the choice between Versions 1 and 2 depends upon the values of the system parameters α, β, and R. For example, if the start-up parameter α is very large, then the additional send-receive pair required by Version 2 may dominate the reduction in arithmetic that the extra communication makes possible. Indeed, it is tempting to say that Version 1 is preferable when the inequality

$$2\alpha + L\left(\beta + \frac{4}{R}\right) \; < \; 4\alpha + L\left(\beta + \frac{2.5}{R}\right) \tag{3.5.2}$$

holds, i.e., when $3L < 4\alpha R$. But this level of precision cannot be justified given the crudeness of our model. Indeed, before we proceed, it is vitally important to delineate the various shortcomings of our model.

To begin with, the rate of computation on the nodes may depend upon cache utilization and related factors. Indeed, the organization of the node program may well be driven by the same memory hierarchy concerns addressed earlier in this chapter. Moreover, our model glosses over the fact that the network may be *heterogenous*, meaning that the nodes in the network vary in architecture and hence, performance.

Another suppressed detail concerns the routing of the messages through the network. The overhead associated with a message that is traveling between a pair of processors is likely to be less if the processors are "nearby." Indeed, the time required to transmit a message may be a steeply increasing function of the number of processors that it visits en route to the destination.

Our model also does not capture the fact that a processor may be able to overlap computation and communication. Indeed, what we refer to as a "node" may in fact be a multiprocessor, part of which oversees communication and part of which oversees computation with a minimum of interference between the two activities.

Yet another suppressed overhead in our model concerns the "setting up" of a message. There may be an upper bound N_{max} on message length. Thus, if $N = kN_{max}$, then the sending of a length-N vector may require k messages and time $k(\alpha + \beta N_{max})$. Moreover, the data in the array to be transmitted may have to be made contiguous. Thus, sending a row of an array that is stored in column-major order may require copying that row into a buffer so that its elements are contiguous. This kind of message preprocessing can degrade performance.

Finally, when we try to quantify the communication overhead in a particular node, we have no way of knowing the waiting period associated with each **recv**. This difficulty plagues even more sophisticated models of performance and points to the importance of being able to extract wait-time statistics from the underlying system.

Despite these shortcomings, our model does permit *qualitative* judgments that can be extremely useful during the preliminary derivation of a distributed algorithm. For example, we can look at an inequality of the form (3.5.2) and conclude that Version 1 is more attractive as α grows. The precise identification of "crossover points," where one method becomes preferable to another, requires careful experimentation.

3.5.4   An s-Processor Butterfly

We now consider the application of $s = 2s_*$ processors to the butterfly computation

$$y = \begin{bmatrix} I_{L_*} & \Omega_{L_*} \\ I_{L_*} & -\Omega_{L_*} \end{bmatrix} z, \qquad z \in \mathbb{C}^L, \; L = 2L_* . \tag{3.5.3}$$

Assume that $L = sm$ and that $z \in \mathbb{C}^L$ is *distributed by block*, meaning that

$$z(\mu m : (\mu+1)m - 1) \in \text{Proc}(\mu), \qquad \mu = 0 : s - 1. \tag{3.5.4}$$

To develop an algorithm that overwrites the distributed z with a comparably distributed y, we express

> **for** $j = 0 : L_* - 1$
> $$\begin{bmatrix} z_j \\ z_{j+L_*} \end{bmatrix} \leftarrow \begin{bmatrix} 1 & \omega_L^j \\ 1 & -\omega_L^j \end{bmatrix} \begin{bmatrix} z_j \\ z_{j+L_*} \end{bmatrix}$$
> **end**

as a double loop using the mapping $j = \sigma m + \gamma$ with $0 \leq \sigma \leq s_* - 1$ and $0 \leq \gamma \leq m - 1$:

> **for** $\sigma = 0 : s_* - 1$
> $\quad \tau \leftarrow \sigma + s_*$
> $\quad$ **for** $\gamma = 0 : m - 1$
> $$\begin{bmatrix} z_{\sigma m + \gamma} \\ z_{\tau m + \gamma} \end{bmatrix} \leftarrow \begin{bmatrix} 1 & \omega_L^{\sigma m + \gamma} \\ 1 & -\omega_L^{\sigma m + \gamma} \end{bmatrix} \begin{bmatrix} z_{\sigma m + \gamma} \\ z_{\tau m + \gamma} \end{bmatrix}$$
> $\quad$ **end**
> **end**

Expressing this in vector terms, and bearing in mind the distributed data structure (3.5.4), we obtain

for $\sigma = 0{:}s_* - 1$
$\qquad \tau \leftarrow \sigma + s_*; \ \ top \leftarrow \sigma m{:}(\sigma + 1)m - 1; \ \ bot \leftarrow \tau m{:}(\tau + 1)m - 1$
$\qquad \{\text{Proc}(\sigma) \text{ and } \text{Proc}(\tau) \text{ share this:}\}$

$$\left[\begin{array}{c} z(top) \\ z(bot) \end{array} \right] \leftarrow \left[\begin{array}{c} z(top) \ + \ w_{L_*}(top) .* \ z(bot) \\ z(top) \ - \ w_{L_*}(top) .* \ z(bot) \end{array} \right]$$

end

Anticipating the organization of the distributed algorithm, we see that communication is confined to the processor pairs $\{\,\text{Proc}(\sigma),\ \text{Proc}(\sigma + s_*)\,\}$ for $\sigma = 0{:}s_* - 1$. Moreover, within each pair of communicating processors, the required manipulations are similar to what we developed in the two-processor butterfly computation.

Let us look more carefully at this and consider the node program for $\text{Proc}(\mu)$. The first task is to "figure out" the communication partner λ and the assignment of each processor in the pair to either the top or bottom half of the operation. This requires a few simple integer computations:

if $\mu \leq s_* - 1$
$\qquad \lambda \leftarrow \mu + s_*$
$\qquad top \leftarrow \mu m{:}(\mu + 1)m - 1$
$\qquad bot \leftarrow \lambda m{:}(\lambda + 1)m - 1$
$\qquad$ Communicate with $\text{Proc}(\lambda)$ and compute the top half of

$$\left[\begin{array}{c} z(top) \\ z(bot) \end{array} \right] \leftarrow \left[\begin{array}{c} z(top) \ + \ w_{L_*}(top) .* \ z(bot) \\ z(top) \ - \ w_{L_*}(top) .* \ z(bot) \end{array} \right]$$

else
$\qquad \lambda \leftarrow \mu - s_*$
$\qquad top \leftarrow \lambda m{:}(\lambda + 1)m - 1$
$\qquad bot \leftarrow \mu m{:}(\mu + 1)m - 1$
$\qquad$ Communicate with $\text{Proc}(\lambda)$ and compute the bottom half of

$$\left[\begin{array}{c} z(top) \\ z(bot) \end{array} \right] \leftarrow \left[\begin{array}{c} z(top) \ + \ w_{L_*}(top) .* \ z(bot) \\ z(top) \ - \ w_{L_*}(top) .* \ z(bot) \end{array} \right]$$

end

The updating of $z(top)$ and $z(bot)$ can proceed in either of the two styles that we discussed for the two-processor butterfly problem. Below, we pursue a "Version 1" approach, which involves redundant computation but only entails a single **send-recv** pair.

Before we proceed, we discuss a convention that is useful when describing node program initializations. In particular, we shall encapsulate in a **loc.init** statement all the initializations and assumptions that the node requires before it can execute the "interesting" portion of its code. For example,

$\qquad$ **loc.init** $[\, s = proc.num, \ \mu = proc.id, \ L, \ L_* = L/2, \ m = L/s,$
$\qquad\qquad\qquad\qquad z_{loc} = z(\mu m{:}(\mu + 1)m - 1), \ w_{loc} = w_{L_*} \,]$

sets up local variables s, μ, L, L_*, m, z_{loc}, and w_{loc}. The statements $s = proc.num$ and $\mu = proc.id$ set s to be the total number of processors and μ to be the identification number of the underlying processor. The statements $z_{loc} = z(\mu m{:}(\mu + 1)m - 1)$ and

$w_{loc} = w_L$ indicate that z is distributed by block around the network and that a local copy of the weight vector $w_{L_*} = [\, 1, \, \omega_L, \ldots, \, \omega_L^{L/2-1} \,]$ is housed in w_{loc}.

Algorithm 3.5.1 Suppose we have a network of s processors and that s is even and $z \in \mathbb{C}^L$, with $L = sm$. If the following algorithm is executed in each node, then upon completion Proc(μ) houses $y(\mu m{:}(\mu + 1)m - 1)$ in z_{loc}, where $y = B_L z$. (See (3.5.3).)

> loc.init [$s = proc.num$, $\mu = proc.id$, L, $L_* = L/2$, $m = L/s$, $s_* = s/2$
> $\qquad\qquad\qquad\qquad z_{loc} = z(\mu m{:}(\mu + 1)m - 1)$, $w_{loc} = w_{L_*}$]
> **if** $\mu \leq s_* - 1$
> $\qquad \lambda \leftarrow \mu + s_*$
> $\qquad$ **send**$(z_{loc}, \lambda, 0)$
> $\qquad$ **recv**$(v, \lambda, 0)$
> $\qquad z_{loc} \leftarrow z_{loc} + w_{loc}(\mu m{:}(\mu + 1)m - 1).* v$
> **else**
> $\qquad \lambda \leftarrow \mu - s_*$
> $\qquad$ **send**$(z_{loc}, \lambda, 0)$
> $\qquad$ **recv**$(v, \lambda, 0)$
> $\qquad z_{loc} \leftarrow v - w_{loc}(\lambda m{:}(\lambda + 1)m - 1).* z_{loc}$
> **end**

By applying our simplified computational model of §3.5.3, it is easy to show that each processor spends $8L/(sR)$ seconds computing and $2(\alpha + (\beta L)/s)$ seconds communicating.

3.5.5   Distributed Bit Reversal

In practice, it is possible to avoid the bit-reversal permutation in many applications by making judicious use of the Gentleman–Sande framework. (See §4.2.) However, a discussion of distributed bit reversal is instructive because the underlying logic is very similar to what is required in a distributed Cooley–Tukey framework.

Recall from (1.3.4) that if $n = 2^t$, then the bit-reversal permutation P_n is prescribed by $P_n = R_t \cdots R_2$ where for $q = 2{:}t$

$$R_q = I_r \otimes \Pi_L, \qquad L = 2^q, \; r = n/L\,.$$

Assume that we have $p = 2^d$ processors and that $m = n/p = 2^{t-d} > 1$. Given that x is distributed by block,

$$x(\mu m{:}(\mu + 1)m - 1) \in \text{Proc}(\mu), \qquad \mu = 0{:}p - 1,$$

our goal is to develop a distributed-memory version of the following algorithm, which overwrites x with $P_n x$:

> **for** $q = 2{:}t$
> $\qquad L \leftarrow 2^q; \; r \leftarrow n/L$
> $\qquad$ **for** $k = 0{:}r - 1$ (3.5.5)
> $\qquad\qquad x(kL{:}(k + 1)L - 1) \leftarrow \Pi_L x(kL{:}(k + 1)L - 1)$
> $\qquad$ **end**
> **end**

Note that if $L \leq m$, the perfect shuffle $\Pi_L x(kL:(k+1)L-1)$ is local. Indeed, if $q \leq t-d$ and $s = m/L$, each processor applies $I_s \otimes \Pi_L$ to its local share of x. Looking at (3.5.5), we see that this means that Proc(μ) handles shuffles μs through $(\mu+1)s-1$.

If $q = t - d + 1:t$, then there are more processors than shuffles. Indeed, for q in this range there are $s = L/m = 2^q/2^{t-d} = 2^{q-t+d}$ processors per shuffle. Moreover, Proc(ks),...,Proc($(k+1)s-1$) are assigned to the permutation $\Pi_L x(kL:(k+1)L-1)$. By combining these observations, we can rewrite (3.5.5) as follows:

$$
\begin{aligned}
&m \leftarrow n/p \\
&\textbf{for } q = 2{:}t \\
&\qquad L \leftarrow 2^q; \; r \leftarrow n/L \\
&\qquad \textbf{if } q \leq t-d \\
&\qquad\qquad s \leftarrow m/L \\
&\qquad\qquad \textbf{for } \mu = 0{:}p-1 \\
&\qquad\qquad\qquad \{\text{Proc } (\mu) \text{ does this:}\} \\
&\qquad\qquad\qquad \textbf{for } k = \mu s{:}(\mu+1)s - 1 \\
&\qquad\qquad\qquad\qquad x(kL{:}(k+1)L - 1) \leftarrow \Pi_L x(kL{:}(k+1)L - 1) \\
&\qquad\qquad\qquad \textbf{end} \\
&\qquad\qquad \textbf{end} \\
&\qquad \textbf{else} \\
&\qquad\qquad s \leftarrow L/m \\
&\qquad\qquad \textbf{for } k = 0{:}r - 1 \\
&\qquad\qquad\qquad \{\text{Proc}(ks),\ldots, \text{Proc}((k+1)s - 1) \text{ share this:}\} \\
&\qquad\qquad\qquad x(kL{:}(k+1)L - 1) \leftarrow \Pi_L x(kL{:}(k+1)L - 1) \\
&\qquad\qquad \textbf{end} \\
&\qquad \textbf{end} \\
&\textbf{end}
\end{aligned}
\tag{3.5.6}
$$

From this specification we proceed to derive the μth node program. The cases $q \leq t-d$ and $q \geq t - d + 1$ are handled separately.

The case $q \leq t-d$ is simpler, as there is no interprocessor communication. Assume that Proc(μ) houses $x(\mu m:(\mu + 1)m - 1)$ in a local vector x_{loc}. It follows that for $k = \mu s:(\mu + 1)s - 1$, a reference to subvector $x(kL:(k+1)L - 1)$ is a reference to $x_{loc}((k - \mu s)L:(k - \mu s + 1)L - 1)$. Thus, the first k-loop in (3.5.6) transforms to

$$
\begin{aligned}
&\textbf{for } k = 0{:}s - 1 \\
&\qquad x_{loc}(kL{:}(k+1)L - 1) \leftarrow \Pi_L x_{loc}(kL{:}(k+1)L - 1) \\
&\textbf{end}
\end{aligned}
$$

Focusing next on the case $q \geq t - d + 1$, we observe that there are $s = L/m$ processsors per shuffle. Thus, if Proc(μ) computes the integers $k = \textbf{floor}(\mu/s)$ and $\nu = \mu - ks$, then it "knows" that it is the νth processor in the group of processors that is handling the kth shuffle. To proceed further, we must review the data flow that is associated with the perfect shuffle. If $z \in \mathbb{C}^L$ and $L = 2L_*$, then $z \leftarrow \Pi_L z$ is prescribed by

$$
\begin{aligned}
&y \leftarrow z \\
&L_* \leftarrow L/2 \\
&\textbf{for } j = 0{:}L_* - 1 \\
&\qquad z_{2j} \leftarrow y_j \\
&\qquad z_{2j+1} \leftarrow y_{j+L_*} \\
&\textbf{end}
\end{aligned}
$$

Suppose z is stored by block among eight processors which we designate by $A, B, \ldots, H$. The schematic (3.5.7) shows "where the data come from" in order for each processor to compute its block of the shuffled vector:

$$\Pi_L z \;=\; \begin{array}{|c|} \hline A, E \\ \hline A, E \\ \hline B, F \\ \hline B, F \\ \hline C, G \\ \hline C, G \\ \hline D, H \\ \hline D, H \\ \hline \end{array} \;\longleftarrow\; \begin{array}{|c|} \hline A \\ \hline B \\ \hline C \\ \hline D \\ \hline E \\ \hline F \\ \hline G \\ \hline H \\ \hline \end{array} \;=\; z \; . \tag{3.5.7}$$

Each processor sends the top half of its local portion of z to one processor and the bottom half to another. For example, $\text{Proc}(D)$ must send the top half of its z-block to $\text{Proc}(G)$ and the bottom half to $\text{Proc}(H)$. From the receive point of view, $\text{Proc}(D)$ needs the bottom half of $\text{Proc}(B)$'s block and the bottom half of $\text{Proc}(F)$'s block.

In general, if $z \in \mathbb{C}^L$ is stored by block among $\text{Proc}(0)$, $\ldots$, $\text{Proc}(s-1)$ and $s = 2s_*$, then here are the communication tasks for the νth processor, assuming that s is a power of two and z_{loc} designates the local portion of z:

> $\nu_* \leftarrow \text{floor}(\nu/2)$
> **if** $\nu \le s_* - 1$
> > Send the top half of z_{loc} to $\text{Proc}(2\nu.)$
> > Receive block from $\text{Proc}(\nu_*)$ and put in top half of z_{loc}.
> > Send the bottom half of z_{loc} to $\text{Proc}(2\nu + 1)$.
> > Receive block from $\text{Proc}(\nu_* + s_*)$ and put in bottom half of z_{loc}.
>
> **else**
> > Send the top half of z_{loc} to $\text{Proc}(2(\nu - s_*))$.
> > Receive block from $\text{Proc}(\nu_*)$ and put in top half of z_{loc}.
> > Send the bottom half of z_{loc} to $\text{Proc}(2(\nu - s_*) + 1)$.
> > Receive block from $\text{Proc}(\nu_* + s_*)$ and put in bottom half of z_{loc}.
>
> **end**

Once these maneuvers are complete, and the local shuffle

$$z_{loc} \leftarrow \Pi_m z_{loc}$$

is computed, $\text{Proc}(\mu)$ obtains the μth block of $(\Pi_L x)$. For example, in (3.5.7) we see that G must shuffle the top half of D's block with the top half of H's block.

It is instructive to note that this two-phase approach to $z \leftarrow \Pi_L z$ corresponds to the following factorization:

$$\Pi_L \;=\; (I_s \otimes \Pi_m)(\Pi_{2s} \otimes I_{m/2}), \qquad L = sm. \tag{3.5.8}$$

The first phase involves communication and is characterized by the update

$$z \leftarrow (\Pi_{2s} \otimes I_{m/2})z \; .$$

The second phase involves the shuffling of local data and is described by

$$z \leftarrow (I_s \otimes \Pi_m)z \; .$$

This style of parallel algorithm development through Kronecker manipulation is pursued in Johnson, Johnson, Rodriguez, and Lu (1989).

Before we present the final algorithm, we wish to stress again that message ids are necessary, because in our model we *cannot* assert that messages are received in the order in which they are sent.

Algorithm 3.5.2 Suppose we have a network of $p = 2^d$ processors and $x \in \mathbb{C}^n$, with $n = 2^t \geq p$. If each processor executes the following algorithm, then upon completion, $Proc(\mu)$ houses $y(\mu m:(\mu + 1)m - 1)$ in x_{loc}, where $y = P_n x$ and $m = n/p$.

$loc.init[p = num.proc, \mu = proc.id, n, d, m = n/p, x_{loc} = x(\mu m:(\mu + 1)m - 1)]$
for $q = 2:t - d$
    $L \leftarrow 2^q$
    $s \leftarrow m/L$
    $x_{loc} \leftarrow (I_s \otimes \Pi_L)x_{loc}$
end
$m.id \leftarrow 0$
for $q = t - d + 1:t$
    $s \leftarrow L/m$
    $s_* \leftarrow s/2$
    $top \leftarrow 0:(m/2) - 1; \; bot \leftarrow (m/2):m - 1$
    $k \leftarrow \text{floor}(\mu/s)$
    $\nu \leftarrow \mu - ks$
    $\nu_* \leftarrow \text{floor}(\nu/2)$
    if $\nu \leq s_* - 1$
        $\textbf{send}(x_{loc}(top), ks + 2\nu, m.id)$
        $\textbf{recv}(x_{loc}(top), ks + \nu_*, m.id)$
        $m.id \leftarrow m.id + 1$
        $\textbf{send}(x_{loc}(bot), ks + 2\nu + 1, m.id)$
        $\textbf{recv}(x_{loc}(bot), ks + \nu_* + s_*, m.id)$
        $m.id \leftarrow m.id + 1$
    else
        $\textbf{send}(x_{loc}(top), ks + 2(\nu - s_*), \; m.id)$
        $\textbf{recv}(x_{loc}(top), ks + \nu_*, \; m.id)$
        $m.id \leftarrow m.id + 1$
        $\textbf{send}(x_{loc}(bot), ks + 2(\nu - s_*) + 1, \; m.id)$
        $\textbf{recv}(x_{loc}(bot), ks + \nu_* + s_*, \; m.id)$
        $m.id \leftarrow m.id + 1$
    end
    $x_{loc} \leftarrow \Pi_m x_{loc}$
end

It is not hard to show that each node spends about $\log_2(p)(4\alpha + 2\beta(n/p))$ seconds communicating.

3.5.6 The Distributed Cooley–Tukey Framework

Our next task is to develop a distributed FFT procedure based on Algorithm 3.5.1. Suppose $n = 2^t$ and consider the usual Cooley–Tukey radix-2 framework:

$$x \leftarrow P_n x$$
$$\textbf{for } q = 1{:}t$$
$$\quad L \leftarrow 2^q; \; L_* \leftarrow L/2; \; r \leftarrow n/L$$
$$\quad \textbf{for } k = 0{:}r - 1$$
$$\quad\quad top \leftarrow kL{:}kL + L_* - 1; \; bot \leftarrow kL + L_*{:}(k+1)L - 1 \qquad (3.5.9)$$
$$\quad\quad \begin{bmatrix} x(top) \\ x(bot) \end{bmatrix} \leftarrow \begin{bmatrix} I_{L_*} & \Omega_{L_*} \\ I_{L_*} & -\Omega_{L_*} \end{bmatrix} \begin{bmatrix} x(top) \\ x(bot) \end{bmatrix}$$
$$\quad \textbf{end}$$
$$\textbf{end}$$

Here, $\Omega_{L_*} = \operatorname{diag}(1, \omega_L, \ldots, \omega_L^{L_* - 1})$. Let us distribute this computation among $p = 2^d$ processors. We assume that n is bigger than p and that the vector x is distributed by block, i.e., $x(\mu m{:}(\mu + 1)m - 1) \in \operatorname{Proc}(\mu)$, where $m = n/p = 2^{t-d}$.

We covered distributed bit reversal in the previous subsection. Our focus now is on the butterfly updates. We start our derivation of the node programs by rearranging the q-loop in (3.5.9). Notice that the butterflies are local, provided $L \le m$, i.e., provided $q \le t - d$. Therefore, the first $t - d$ passes through the q-loop may be written as follows:

$$\textbf{for } q = 1{:}t - d$$
$$\quad L \leftarrow 2^q; \; r \leftarrow n/L$$
$$\quad s \leftarrow r/p \quad \{s = \text{number of butterflies per processor.}\}$$
$$\quad \textbf{for } \mu = 0{:}p - 1$$
$$\quad\quad \{\operatorname{Proc}(\mu) \text{ does this:}\}$$
$$\quad\quad \textbf{for } k = \mu s{:}(\mu + 1)s - 1$$
$$\quad\quad\quad top \leftarrow kL{:}kL + L_* - 1; \; bot \leftarrow kL + L_*{:}(k+1)L - 1 \qquad (3.5.10)$$
$$\quad\quad\quad \begin{bmatrix} x(top) \\ x(bot) \end{bmatrix} \leftarrow \begin{bmatrix} I_{L_*} & \Omega_{L_*} \\ I_{L_*} & -\Omega_{L_*} \end{bmatrix} \begin{bmatrix} x(top) \\ x(bot) \end{bmatrix}$$
$$\quad\quad \textbf{end}$$
$$\quad \textbf{end}$$
$$\textbf{end}$$

With this rearrangement, we see that each processor oversees the execution of its own k-loop and that no communication is required.

Things are more complicated for the range $q = t - d + 1{:}t$. For these values of q there are fewer butterflies than processors and so each butterfly is handled by several processors:

$$\textbf{for } q = t - d + 1{:}t$$
$$\quad L \leftarrow 2^q; \; L_* \leftarrow L/2; \; r \leftarrow n/L$$
$$\quad s \leftarrow p/r \quad \{s = \text{number of processors per butterfly.}\}$$
$$\quad \textbf{for } k = 0{:}r - 1$$
$$\quad\quad top \leftarrow kL{:}kL + L_* - 1; \; bot \leftarrow kL + L_*{:}(k+1)L - 1 \qquad (3.5.11)$$
$$\quad\quad \text{Apply } \operatorname{Proc}(ks), \ldots, \operatorname{Proc}((k+1)s - 1) \text{ to}$$
$$\quad\quad \begin{bmatrix} x(top) \\ x(bot) \end{bmatrix} \leftarrow \begin{bmatrix} I_{L_*} & \Omega_{L_*} \\ I_{L_*} & -\Omega_{L_*} \end{bmatrix} \begin{bmatrix} x(top) \\ x(bot) \end{bmatrix}$$
$$\quad \textbf{end}$$
$$\textbf{end}$$

Notice that all communication is concentrated in the s-processor butterfly which we detailed in Algorithm 3.5.1. The complete node program is obtained by combining (3.5.10) and (3.5.11) and observing that

- If $\mu m \leq \tau \leq (\mu + 1)m - 1$, then a global reference to $x(\tau)$ is a reference to $x_{loc}(\tau - \mu m)$ in $\mathrm{Proc}(\mu)$.

- The s-processor butterfly in (3.5.11) can be handled using the techniques that are embodied in Algorithm 3.5.1. Just identify the vector $x(kL:(k+1)L - 1)$ with z and $\mathrm{Proc}(ks), \ldots, \mathrm{Proc}((k+1)s - 1)$ with $\mathrm{Proc}(0), \ldots, \mathrm{Proc}(s)$.

Algorithm 3.5.3 Suppose $n = 2^t$, $p = 2^d$, $d < t$, $x \in \mathbb{C}^n$, and $y = F_n x$. If each processor in a p-processor network executes the following node program, then upon termination x_{loc} is overwritten by $y(\mu m:(\mu + 1)m - 1)$, where $m = n/p$.

> loc.init$[p = num.proc, \mu = proc.id, d, n, m = n/p, x_{loc} = x(\mu m:(\mu + 1)m - 1)]$
> $x_{loc} \leftarrow z(\mu m:(\mu + 1)m - 1)$, where $z = P_n x$ (Algorithm 3.5.2.)
> for $q = 1:t - d$
> $L \leftarrow 2^q$; $r \leftarrow n/L$
> $s \leftarrow r/p$ {s = number of butterflies per processor.}
>   for $k = 0:s - 1$
> $top \leftarrow kL:kL + L_* - 1$; $bot \leftarrow kL + L_*:(k+1)L - 1$
> $\begin{bmatrix} x_{loc}(top) \\ x_{loc}(bot) \end{bmatrix} \leftarrow \begin{bmatrix} I_{L_*} & \Omega_{L_*} \\ I_{L_*} & -\Omega_{L_*} \end{bmatrix} \begin{bmatrix} x_{loc}(top) \\ x_{loc}(bot) \end{bmatrix}$
>   end
> end
> $m\ id \leftarrow 2d$ {To avoid conflict with messages in Algorithm 3.5.2}
> for $q = t - d + 1:t$
> $L \leftarrow 2^q$; $r \leftarrow n/L$; $s \leftarrow p/r$; $s_* \leftarrow s/2$; $k \leftarrow \mathbf{floor}(\mu/s)$; $\nu \leftarrow \mu - ks$
>   {s = number of processors per butterfly.}
>   {k = butterfly number assigned to $\mathrm{Proc}(\mu)$.}
>   {$\mathrm{Proc}(\mu)$ is the ν th processor assigned to the kth butterfly.}
>   if $\nu \leq s_* - 1$
> $\lambda \leftarrow \mu + s_*$ {Communicate with $\mathrm{Proc}(\lambda)$.}
> $\mathbf{send}(x_{loc}, \lambda, m.id)$
> $\mathbf{recv}(v, \lambda, m.id)$
> $m.id \leftarrow m.id + 1$
>   for $j = 0:m - 1$
> $x_{loc}(j) \leftarrow x_{loc}(j) + \omega_L^{\nu m + j} v(j)$
>   end
>   else
> $\lambda \leftarrow \mu - s_*$ {Communicate with $\mathrm{Proc}(\lambda)$.}
> $\mathbf{send}(x_{loc}, \lambda, m.id)$
> $\mathbf{recv}(v, \lambda, m.id)$
> $m.id \leftarrow m.id + 1$
>   for $j = 0:m - 1$
> $x_{loc}(j) \leftarrow v(j) - \omega_L^{(\nu - s_*)m + j} x_{loc}(j)$
>   end
>   end
> end

The computation time required for this algorithm is given by $8n \log_2 n/(pR)$. It is not $5n \log_2 n/(pR)$, because we are relying on the Version 1 butterflies of §3.5.2, which are computationally redundant but communication efficient. Swarztrauber (1987) has shown how to organize the butterfly computation in the Cooley–Tukey context so that there is no redundancy and only a single **send-recv** pair.

If $q \geq t-d+1$, then in step q each processor sends and receives a message of length $m = n/p$. It follows that the time each node spends communicating in Algorithm 3.5.3, including the bit reversal, is approximated by

$$\log_2(p) \left(4\alpha + \frac{2\beta n}{p} \right) + \sum_{q=t-d+1}^{t} 2 \left(\alpha + \beta m \right) = \log_2(p) \left(6\alpha + 4\frac{\beta n}{p} \right). \qquad (3.5.12)$$

3.5.7   Speedup

We pause in our algorithmic development and discuss another performance issue. The *speedup* of a parallel algorithm that requires T seconds to execute on p processors is defined by

$$S_p = \frac{\text{Time Required By Best Single-Processor Algorithm}}{T}.$$

Speedup sheds light on the value of taking a multiprocessor approach to solving the problem on hand. Linear speedup is ideal, i.e., $S_p = p$. However, in practice this cannot be obtained because of communication overheads. For example, if we assume that the best single-processor FFT requires $5n \log n/R$ seconds to execute, then it is not too hard to show that our model predicts the following speedup for Algorithm 3.5.3:

$$S_p = p \frac{1}{1.6 + \dfrac{R \log_2 p}{\log_2 n} \left(1.2\dfrac{\alpha p}{n} + .8\beta \right)}.$$

Note that if $n \rightarrow \infty$, then $S_p \rightarrow \frac{5}{8}p$. Observe also that speedup decreases with increasing R, i.e., it is harder to achieve good speedup with fast processors than with slow processors.

3.5.8   Effect of the Underlying Topology

As we mentioned at the start of this section, our model of execution does not take into account the added cost of sending messages between processors that are far apart in the network. In practice, one tries to design distributed algorithms so that communication is between processors that are physically close in the network.

Looking at Algorithms 3.5.2 and 3.5.3, we see that if $q > t-d$, then communication is between processors whose identification numbers differ by 2^{q-t+d}. Thus, these calculations would be well supported by a network with the property that $\text{Proc}(\mu)$ and $\text{Proc}(\mu \pm 2^j)$ are neighbors in the network.

A popular topology for which this is the case is the *binary n-cube*, often referred to in the literature as the *hypercube*. A hypercube of dimension d has $p = 2^d$ nodes. If each of these nodes is labeled with a d-bit string, then $\text{Proc}(\mu)$ and $\text{Proc}(\lambda)$ are connected whenever their binary addresses differ in exactly one bit position.

3.5.9 Gentleman–Sande Ideas

As in the sequential case, we can avoid reference to the bit-reversal permutation in many important settings through the careful application of the Gentleman–Sande framework. Our development of Algorithms 3.5.1 and 3.5.3 can be easily modified to handle the Gentleman–Sande butterfly:

$$\begin{bmatrix} u \\ v \end{bmatrix} \leftarrow \begin{bmatrix} I_{L_*} & I_{L_*} \\ \Omega_{L_*} & -\Omega_{L_*} \end{bmatrix} \begin{bmatrix} u \\ v \end{bmatrix} = \begin{bmatrix} u + v \\ w_{L_*}.* (u - v) \end{bmatrix}. \tag{3.5.13}$$

Indeed, in the two-processor case with $u \in \text{Proc}(0)$ and $v \in \text{Proc}(1)$ we have

Proc(0)	Proc(1)
send($u, 1, 0$)	send($v, 0, 0$)
recv($s, 1, 0$)	recv($s, 0, 0$)
$\{s = v\}$	$\{s = u\}$
$u \leftarrow u + s$	$v \leftarrow w_{L_*}.* (s - v)$

FIG. 3.5.5. *Load-imbalanced, two-processor Gentleman–Sande butterfly.*

3.5.10 Distributed Transposition Algorithms

The final objective of this section is to develop a distributed-memory framework for the four-step approach to large-scale FFTs. But before we can pursue this, we need a framework for distributed-memory transposition. There are numerous possibilities. For example, suppose $X \in \mathbb{C}^{pm_1 \times pm_2}$ and that we regard X as a p-by-p block matrix $X = (X_{kj})$ with $X_{kj} \in \text{Proc}(\mu)$ whenever $k = \mu$. With this block row distribution of X, $\text{Proc}(\mu)$ must send $X_{\mu\lambda}$ to $\text{Proc}(\lambda)$ for $\lambda = 0:p - 1$. (Actually, there is no need for $\text{Proc}(\mu)$ to send $X_{\mu\mu}$ to itself, but we allow it for the sake of clarity.) Likewise, $\text{Proc}(\mu)$ must receive the block $X_{\lambda,\mu}$ from $\text{Proc}(\lambda)$ for $\lambda = 0:p - 1$. After the blocks have been moved around in this fashion, a final, local transposition is required.

Algorithm 3.5.4 Suppose $X \in \mathbb{C}^{n_1 \times n_2}$ and that $Y = X^T$. If $n_1 = pm_1$, $n_2 = pm_2$, and each processor in a p-processor network executes the following algorithm, then upon completion $\text{Proc}(\mu)$ houses $Y(\mu m_2:(\mu + 1)m_2 + 1, :)$ in Z_{loc} for $\mu = 0:p - 1$.

> **loc.init** $[\, p = num.proc, \ \mu = proc.id, \ m_1, \ m_2, \ X_{loc} = X(\mu m_1:(\mu + 1)m_1 - 1, :) \,]$
> **for** $\lambda = 0:p - 1$
>   **send**($X_{loc}(:, \lambda m_2:(\lambda + 1)m_2 - 1), \ \lambda, \mu$)
> **end**
> **for** $\lambda = 0:p - 1$
>   **recv**($X_{loc}(:, \lambda m_2:(\lambda + 1)m_2 - 1), \ \lambda, \ \lambda$)
> **end**
> **for** $\lambda = 0:p - 1$
> $Z_{loc}(0:m_2 - 1, \lambda m_1:(\lambda + 1)m_1 - 1) \leftarrow X_{loc}(0:m_1 - 1, \lambda m_2:(\lambda + 1)m_2 - 1)^T$
> **end**

Messages are tagged by the processor id of the sender. Note that after the second loop, $X_{loc} = [\, X_{0,\mu} \mid X_{1,\mu} \mid \cdots \mid X_{p-1,\mu} \,]$. The required transpositions of the $X_{k\mu}$ can be approached through the frameworks of §3.2.

Each processor participating in the above distributed transposition procedure spends about $2\alpha p + 2\beta n_1 n_2/p$ seconds communicating. However, because the technique involves "flooding" the network with messages, its performance would be highly dependent upon the quality of the message-routing software and the physical properties of the processor interconnections. This is a polite way of saying that our communication model would probably be a particularly poor predictor of performance for this kind of algorithm.

Some authors have chosen to avoid this dependence upon the whims of the message-routing software by incorporating a more organized swapping of blocks. To convey the spirit of these approaches, we detail a recursive transpose algorithm due to Eklundh (1972) that maps onto the hypercube architecture nicely because of its power-of-two adjacency. It is based upon successive 2-by-2 *block transpositions* of the form

$$\begin{bmatrix} Z_{00} & Z_{10} \\ Z_{01} & Z_{11} \end{bmatrix} \longleftarrow \begin{bmatrix} Z_{00} & Z_{01} \\ Z_{10} & Z_{11} \end{bmatrix}.$$

To illustrate the central idea, suppose we have the following blocking of the original X:

$$X = \begin{bmatrix} X_{00} & X_{01} & X_{02} & X_{03} \\ X_{10} & X_{11} & X_{12} & X_{13} \\ X_{20} & X_{21} & X_{22} & X_{23} \\ X_{30} & X_{31} & X_{32} & X_{33} \end{bmatrix}.$$

Assume that we have reached the stage where these blocks have been overwritten by their respective transposes:

$$X \leftarrow \begin{bmatrix} X_{00}^T & X_{01}^T & X_{02}^T & X_{03}^T \\ X_{10}^T & X_{11}^T & X_{12}^T & X_{13}^T \\ X_{20}^T & X_{21}^T & X_{22}^T & X_{23}^T \\ X_{30}^T & X_{31}^T & X_{32}^T & X_{33}^T \end{bmatrix}.$$

Next, we think of the current X as a 2-by-2 block matrix and perform 2-by-2 block transpositions on each of four blocks:

$$X \leftarrow \begin{bmatrix} X_{00}^T & X_{10}^T & X_{02}^T & X_{12}^T \\ X_{01}^T & X_{11}^T & X_{03}^T & X_{13}^T \\ X_{20}^T & X_{30}^T & X_{22}^T & X_{32}^T \\ X_{21}^T & X_{31}^T & X_{23}^T & X_{33}^T \end{bmatrix}.$$

Finally, we do a 2-by-2 block transpose of the matrix X itself and thereby obtain the required transposition:

$$X \leftarrow \begin{bmatrix} X_{00}^T & X_{10}^T & X_{20}^T & X_{30}^T \\ X_{01}^T & X_{11}^T & X_{21}^T & X_{31}^T \\ X_{02}^T & X_{12}^T & X_{22}^T & X_{32}^T \\ X_{03}^T & X_{13}^T & X_{23}^T & X_{33}^T \end{bmatrix}.$$

In the general case, we assume that $X \in \mathbb{C}^{n_1 \times n_2}$, $n_1 = pm_1$, $n_2 = pm_2$, and $p = 2^d$. Recursive transposition proceeds as follows:

> Write $X = (X_{kj})$ as a p-by-p block matrix with $X_{kj} \in \mathbb{C}^{m_1 \times m_2}$.
> Overwrite each X_{kj} with its transpose.
> **for** $q = 1{:}d$
> $\qquad L_1 \leftarrow 2^q m_1; \; L_2 \leftarrow 2^q m_2; \; r = p/2^q$
> $\qquad$ Write $X = (X_{kj})$ as an r-by-r block matrix with $X_{kj} \in \mathbb{C}^{L_2 \times L_1}$.   (3.5.14)
> $\qquad$ Perform a 2-by-2 block transposition of each X_{kj}.
> **end**

It is not hard to show by induction that this process terminates with the required transpose.

We now consider the execution of (3.5.14) on a p-processor network with $p = 2^d$. Assume that

$$X(\mu m_1{:}(\mu + 1)m_1 - 1, 0{:}n_2 - 1) \in \text{Proc}(\mu).$$

To motivate the basic ideas, assume that $p = 8$, $n_1 = n_2 = 128$, and $m_1 = m_2 = 16$. Regard X as a 2-by-2 block matrix with 64-by-64 blocks. Here a schematic that shows what moves when these blocks are block transposed:

Thus, there are four 32-by-32 swaps. Each swap involves four processors, but they pair up as depicted in the following schematic:

Proc(0){		a		c
Proc(1){		b		e
Proc(2){	a		c	
Proc(3){	b		e	
Proc(4){		f		h
Proc(5){		g		k
Proc(6){	f		h	
Proc(7){	g		k	

In this schematic, blocks with the same letter are swapped. Thus, Proc(1) and Proc(3) swap their b blocks and their e blocks. In general, for $q = 1{:}d$ we set $L_1 = 2^q m_1$, $L_2 = m_2 2^q$, and $r = 2^{d-q}$ and observe that, (a) there are $s = 2^q$ processors per block row, (b) each processor is involved in r swappings, and (c) the swaps involve m_2-by-$(L_1/2)$ blocks.

Algorithm 3.5.5 Suppose $X \in \mathbb{C}^{n_1 \times n_2}$ and that $Y = X^T$. Assume $n_1 = pm_1$, $n_2 = pm_2$, and $p = 2^d$. If each processor in a p-processor network executes the following algorithm, then upon completion Proc(μ) houses $Y(\mu m_2{:}(\mu+1)m_2 + 1, 0{:}n_1 - 1)$ in $[x_{loc}]_{m_2 \times n_1}$.

$$\text{loc.init} \, [\, p = num.proc, \; \mu = proc.id, \; d, \; n_1, \; n_2, \; m_1 = n_1/p, \; m_2 = n_2/p,$$
$$[x_{loc}]_{m_1 \times n_2} = X(\mu m_1{:}(\mu+1)m_1 - 1, 0{:}n_2 - 1)\,]$$

$m \leftarrow m_1 m_2$
for $j = 0{:}p - 1$ {Transpose local blocks.}
    $v(0{:}m - 1) \leftarrow x_{loc}(jm{:}(j+1)m - 1)$
    $v_{m_2 \times m_1} \leftarrow v_{m_1 \times m_2}^T$
    $x_{loc}(jm{:}(j+1)m - 1) \leftarrow v(0{:}m - 1)$
end
$X_{loc}(0{:}m_2 - 1, 0{:}n_1 - 1) \equiv [x_{loc}]_{m_2 \times n_1}$
$m.id \leftarrow 0$
for $q = 1{:}d$
    $L_1 \leftarrow 2^q m_1; \; L_2 \leftarrow 2^q m_2; \; L_* \leftarrow L_1/2; \; r \leftarrow 2^{d-q}$
    {Regard X as an r-by-r block matrix with L_2-by-L_1 blocks.}
    $s \leftarrow 2^q$
    $s_* \leftarrow s/2$
    $k \leftarrow \mathbf{floor}(\mu/s)$
    $\nu \leftarrow \mu - ks$
    {s processors per block row.}
    {Proc(μ) is the νth processor in its group.}
    if $\nu \leq s_* - 1$
        $\lambda \leftarrow \mu + s_*$ {Communicate with Proc(λ).}
        for $j = 0{:}r - 1$
            $\mathbf{send}(X_{loc}(:, jL_1 + L_*{:}(j+1)L_1 - 1), \lambda, m.id)$
            $\mathbf{recv}(X_{loc}(:, jL_1 + L_*{:}(j+1)L_1 - 1), \lambda, m.id)$
            $m.id \leftarrow m.id + 1$
        end
    else
        $\lambda \leftarrow \mu - s_*$ {Communicate with Proc(λ).}
        for $j = 0{:}r - 1$
            $\mathbf{send}(X_{loc}(:, jL_1{:}jL_1 + L_* - 1), \lambda, m.id)$
            $\mathbf{recv}(X_{loc}(:, jL_1{:}jL_1 + L_* - 1), \lambda, m.id)$
            $m.id \leftarrow m.id + 1$
        end
    end
end

There are d communication steps, and during each step half of the data move. For an individual processor, it can be shown that the communication overhead is approximately $2\alpha p + (n\beta/p) \log_2 p$ seconds. For large n this is about the same as Algorithm

3.5.4. The crudeness of our communication model forbids further comparison. However, it is important to note that Algorithm 3.5.5 can be tailored to certain network topologies such as the hypercube giving enhanced performance.

3.5.11 Distributed Four-Step and Six-Step Frameworks

Suppose $n = n_1 n_2$ and assume for clarity that $n_1 = m_1 p$ and $n_2 = m_2 p$. Consider the blocking

$$x_{n_1 \times n_2} = \begin{bmatrix} X_0 \\ \vdots \\ X_{p-1} \end{bmatrix}, \qquad X_\mu \in \mathbb{C}^{m_1 \times n_2}$$

and assume that

$$X_\mu \in \text{Proc}(\mu), \qquad \mu = 0{:}p-1 \,.$$

With this distributed data structure the four-step approach to $x \leftarrow F_n x$ has the form

1. Proc(μ)'s share of $x_{n_1 \times n_2} \leftarrow x_{n_1 \times n_2} F_{n_2}$ is the multirow DFT $X_\mu \leftarrow X_\mu F_{n_2}$.

2. Proc(μ)'s share of $x_{n_1 \times n_2} \leftarrow x_{n_1 \times n_2}.* F_n(0{:}n_1 - 1, 0{:}n_2 - 1)$ is given by

$$X_\mu \leftarrow X_\mu.* F_n(\mu m_1{:}(\mu + 1)m_1 - 1, 0{:}n_2 - 1) \,.$$

3. The distributed transposition $x_{n_2 \times n_1} \leftarrow x_{n_1 \times n_2}^T$ is carried out. Partition the resulting matrix as follows

$$x_{n_2 \times n_1} = \begin{bmatrix} X_0 \\ \vdots \\ X_{p-1} \end{bmatrix}, \qquad X_\mu \in \mathbb{C}^{m_2 \times n_1} \,.$$

and assume that $X_\mu \in \text{Proc}(\mu)$ for $\mu = 1{:}p$.

4. Proc(μ)'s share of $x_{n_2 \times n_1} \leftarrow x_{n_2 \times n_1} F_{n_1}$ is the multirow DFT $X_\mu \leftarrow X_\mu F_{n_1}$.

Thus, there are two local multirow DFTs, a local twiddle-factor scaling, and a distributed transpose.

The communication overheads of the above four-step approach (as predicted by our model) are not significantly different from Algorithm 3.5.3 (distributed Cooley–Tukey). However, the approach does have a number of attractive features which are worth noting in a qualitative way. (1) Because the DFTs are local, existing, optimized, single-processor FFT software can be applied. (2) It may be easier to exploit the underlying topology in a distributed transpose than in a distributed butterfly. (3) There may be less idle waiting in a distributed transpose than in a sequence of distributed butterflies where computation is repeatedly interrupted by the need to communicate.

It should be pointed out that our formulation of the four-step process involves a rather handy distribution of the initial data and the final DFT. In particular, the X_μ blocks are local to Proc(μ). Note that if we begin with $x(\mu m{:}(\mu + 1)m - 1) \in \text{Proc}(\mu)$, where $m = n/p$, then a distributed version of

$$x_{m_1 \times p n_2} \leftarrow x_{m_1 \times p n_2} \Pi_{p, p n_2}$$

is required in order to make the X_μ blocks local as required by step 1 above. A similar distributed sorting is required if each processor is to house a contiguous portion of

$y = F_n x$. With three distributed permutations now part of the process, the six-step framework of §3.3.1 takes on a new interest. A distributed version of that framework involves a pair of local multicolumn DFTs, a local twiddle-factor scaling, and three distributed transpositions.

Problems

P3.5.1   Develop a load-balanced, two-processor butterfly for (3.5.1) that distributes the real and imaginary portions of the scaling $w_{L_*} v$ to Proc(0) and Proc(1), respectively. Compare the communication overheads with those described in Figs. 3.5.2 and 3.5.4, assuming that a length-N real vector can be communicated in time $\alpha + (\beta/2)N$.

P3.5.2   Modify Algorithm 3.5.1 so that it uses Version 2 butterflies.

P3.5.3   Rewrite Algorithm 3.5.2 so that it is based on the factorization $P_n = R_2^T \cdots R_t^T$.

P3.5.4   Modify Algorithm 3.5.3 so that it uses Version 2 butterflies. What is the speedup?

P3.5.5   Prove that 3.5.14 computes the transpose.

P3.5.6   Develop in detail a recursive version of the transpose algorithm (3.5.14).

P3.5.7   Is it worthwhile for each processor to compute the complete weight vector in Algorithm 3.5.3?

P3.5.8   Work out Gentleman–Sande analogs of Algorithms 3.5.1 and 3.5.3. Is there a nonredundant, load-balanced version of the algorithm in Fig. 3.5.5?

P3.5.9   Develop radix-4 analogs for Algorithms 3.5.1 and 3.5.3.

P3.5.10   Modify Algorithm 3.5.3 to handle the case when the number of processors is not a power of two.

P3.5.11   Compare the communication overheads of Algorithm 3.5.3 and the distributed six-step framework.

Notes and References for Section 3.5

One of the earliest papers concerned with parallel FFTs is

M. Pease (1968). "An Adaptation of the Fast Fourier Transform for Parallel Processing," *J. Assocs. Comput. Mach. 15*, 252–264.

Interestingly, the author couches the discussion in Kronecker product language maintaining that it is the proper notation for parallel FFT derivations. This is precisely the premise in

J. Johnson, R.W. Johnson, D. Rodriguez, and R. Tolimieri (1990). "A Methodology for Designing, Modifying, and Implementing Fourier Transform Algorithms on Various Architectures," *Circuits Systems Signal Process. 9*, 449–500.

For general background about distributed-memory systems and a clarification of the attending issues, see

J.L. Hennessy and D.A. Patterson (1990). *Computer Architecture: A Quantitative Approach*, Morgan Kaufman Publishers, Inc., San Mateo, CA.

A great deal of the distributed-memory FFT literature addresses the implementation of the algorithm on the hypercube architecture. A selection of references include

G. Fox, M. Johnson, G. Lyzenga, S. Otto, J. Salmon, and D. Walker (1988). *Solving Problems on Concurrent Processors, Vol. 1, General Techniques and Regular Problems*, Prentice-Hall, Englewood Cliffs, NJ.

S.L. Johnsson, M. Jacquemin, and C.-T. Ho (1989). "High Radix FFT on Boolean Cube Networks," Department of Computer Science Report YALE/DCS/TR-751, Yale University, New Haven, CT. (To appear, *J. Comput. Phys.*)

S.L. Johnsson, R.L. Krawitz, R. Frye, and D. MacDonald (1989). "A Radix-2 FFT on the Connection Machine," *Proceedings Supercomputer 89*, ACM Press, New York, 809–819.

S.L. Johnsson and R.L. Krawitz (1991). "Cooley–Tukey FFT on the Connection Machine," Division of Applied Sciences Report TR-24-91, Harvard University. (To appear in *Parallel Comput.*)

P.N. Swarztrauber (1987). "Multiprocessor FFTs," *Parallel Comput. 5*, 197–210.

C. Tong and P.N. Swarztrauber (1991). "Ordered Fast Fourier Transforms on a Massively Parallel Hypercube Multiprocessor," *J. Parallel and Distributed Computing 12*, 50–59.

In certain applications, the FFT is but one of several parallelizable computational steps. Developing a distributed data structure suitable for the overall computation requires care and compromise. See

R.M. Chamberlain (1988). "Gray Codes, Fast Fourier Transforms, and Hypercubes," *Parallel Comput. 6*, 225–233.

T.F. Chan (1987). "On Gray Code Mappings for Mesh-FFTs on Binary N-Cubes," UCLA CAM Report 87-02, Dept. of Mathematics, University of California, Los Angeles, CA.

Papers that address the communication overhead issue include

S.L. Johnsson (1987). "Communication Efficient Basic Linear Algebra Computations on Hypercube Architecture," *J. Parallel and Distributed Computing 4*, 133–172.

S.L. Johnsson and C.-T. Ho (1991). "Generalized Shuffle Permutations on Boolean Cubes," Report TR-04-91, Center for Research in Computing Technology, Harvard University, Cambridge, MA. (To appear *J. Parallel and Distributed Comput.*)

S.L. Johnsson, C-T. Ho, M. Jacquemin, and A. Ruttenberg (1987). "Computing Fast Fourier Transforms on Boolean Cubes and Related Networks," in *Advanced Algorithms and Architectures for Signal Processing II 826*, Society of Photo-Optical Instrumentation Engineers, 223–231.

S.L. Johnsson, M. Jacquemin, and R.L. Krawitz (1991). "Communication Efficient Multiprocessor FFT," Division of Applied Sciences Report TR-25-91, Harvard University. (To appear in *J. Comput. Phys.*)

Y. Saad and M. Schultz (1989). "Data Communication in Hypercubes," *Parallel Comput. 11*, 131–150.

H. Stone (1971). "Parallel Processing with the Perfect Shuffle," *IEEE Trans. Comput. C-20*, 153–161.

The organization of a distributed matrix transpose and bit reversal has attracted considerable attention. The focus in the following papers is on how to make the best use of the underlying communication channels:

A. Edelman (1991). "Optimal Matrix Transposition and Bit Reversal on Hypercubes: All to All Personalized Communication," *J. Parallel and Distributed Comput. 11*, 328–331.

S.L. Johnsson and C.-T. Ho (1988). "Matrix Transposition on Boolean n-Cube Configured Ensemble Architectures," *SIAM J. Matrix Anal. Appl. 9*, 419–454.

S.L. Johnsson and C.-T. Ho (1989). "Spanning Graphs for Optimum Broadcasting and Personalized Communication," *IEEE Trans. Comput. C-38*, 1249–1268.

S.L. Johnsson and C.-T. Ho (1991a). "Generalized Shuffle Permutations on Boolean Cubes," Division of Applied Sciences Report TR-04-91, Harvard University. (To appear in *J. Parallel and Distributed Comput.*.)

S.L. Johnsson and C.-T. Ho (1991b). "Maximizing Channel Utilization for All-to-All Personalized Communication on Boolean Cubes," *Proc. Sixth Distributed Memory Computing Conference*, IEEE Computer Society Press, New York, 299–304.

O. McBryan and E. Van de Velde (1987). "Hypercube Algorithms and Implementations," SIAM J. Sci. Statist. Comput. 8, s227–s287.

S. Nassimi (1982). "Optimal (BPC) Permutations on a Cube Connected (SIMD) Computer," *IEEE Trans. Comput. C-24*, 338–341.

C. Tong and P.N. Swarztrauber (1991). "Ordered Fast Fourier Transforms on a Massively Parallel Hypercube Architecture," *J. Parallel and Distributed Comput. 1*, 50–59.

As we mentioned, the recursive transposition algorithm that we discussed is presented in

J.O. Eklundh (1972). "A Fast Computer Method for Matrix Transposing," *IEEE Trans. Comput. C-21*, 801–803.

There is a large body of literature concerned with special purpose parallel FFT processors. See the following representative papers:

A.M. Despain, A.M. Peterson, O. Rothaus, and E. Wold (1985). "Fast Fourier Transform Processors Using Gaussian Residue Arithmetic," *J. Parallel and Distributed Comput.* **2**, 219–233.

B. Gold and T. Bially (1973). "Parallelism in Fast Fourier Transform Hardware," *IEEE Trans. Audio and Electroacoustics AU-21*, 5–16.

S.L. Johnsson, U. Weiser, D. Cohen, and A. Davis (1981). "Towards a Formal Treatment of VLSI Arrays," *Proc. Second Caltech Conference on VLSI*, 378–398.

S.L. Johnsson and D. Cohen (1981). "Computational Arrays for the Discrete Fourier Transform," *Proc. Twenty-Second Computer Society International Conference*, COMPCON '81.

S.L. Johnsson and D. Cohen (1982). "An Algebraic Description of Array Implementations of FFT Algorithms," *20th Allerton Conference on Communication, Control, and Computing*, Dept. Electrical Engineering, University of Illinois, Urbana, IL.

W. Shen and A.Y. Oruc (1990). "Systolic Arrays for Multidimensional Discrete Transforms," *International J. Supercomputing* **4**, 201–222.

3.6   Shared-Memory FFTs

Another style of parallel computation is based upon the presence of a shared memory whose contents can be accessed by the individual processors. A schematic that captures the essential idea is given in Fig. 3.6.1. Each processor executes its own

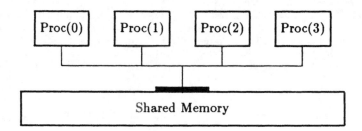

FIG. 3.6.1. *A four-processor shared-memory system.*

node program, which may (a) manipulate data in its own local memory, (b) write data from its own local memory to the shared memory, and (c) read data from the shared memory into its local memory. We assume for simplicity that the shared memory is centralized. However, the reader should note that it is possible to have a shared-memory system in which the shared memory is physically distributed and addressable by all the processors. See Hennessy and Patterson (1990, pp. 578ff).

The nature of the connection between the individual processors and the shared memory is crucial and differs from system to system. See Dongarra, Duff, Sorensen and van der Vorst (1990, pp. 22ff) for a discussion of the more important configurations. However, regardless of the details of the design, it is always the case that a processor can acquire data from its own local memory faster than it can acquire data from the shared memory or from the local memory of another processor. Thus, locality of reference is again of paramount importance, so we can expect shared-memory FFT "thinking" to be very similar to distributed-memory FFT thinking.

We start with the development of our notation and a discussion of the multiple DFT problem. The barrier approach to synchronization is motivated through the two-dimensional DFT problem. We then examine shared-memory frameworks for the transposed Stockham FFT, for matrix transposition, and for the four-step method. Our goal is simply to expose the reader to the broad algorithmic issues associated with the design of shared-memory FFTs. More detailed treatments may be found in Swarztrauber (1987) and Briggs, Hart, Sweet, and O'Gallagher (1987).

3.6.1 Shared-Memory Reads and Writes

As in the distributed-memory setting, the act of designing a parallel algorithm for a shared-memory multiprocessor is tantamount to prescribing a course of action for each of the participating processor nodes. The node algorithms look like ordinary algorithms except that there are occasional references to shared memory of the form

$$\{\text{Local Memory Array}\} \quad \leftarrow \quad \{\text{Shared Memory Array}\},$$

$$\{\text{Shared Memory Array}\} \quad \leftarrow \quad \{\text{Local Memory Array}\}.$$

We have chosen to display explicitly shared-memory reads and writes in order to highlight the importance of locality of reference and to facilitate the quantification of memory traffic overheads. In practice, a good compiler would relieve the programmer of these details.

As a preliminary example of our notation, suppose $X \in \mathbb{C}^{n \times n}$ is a shared-memory array and that $\text{Proc}(\mu)$ houses a local n-by-r array X_{loc}, with $r \leq n$. If $\text{Proc}(\mu)$ executes

$$
\begin{aligned}
X_{loc} &\leftarrow X(:, 0{:}r-1) \\
X_{loc} &\leftarrow c \cdot X_{loc} \\
X(:, 0{:}r-1) &\leftarrow X_{loc}
\end{aligned}
\qquad (3.6.1)
$$

then the first r columns of X are scaled by a factor of c. We assume that movement of data to and from shared memory is an overhead worth monitoring. To that end, if a shared-memory read or write involves an array of N complex numbers, then we assume that $\alpha + \beta N$ seconds are required for the transmission. Here α and β are the latency and bandwidth factors, respectively. We also assume that local computations proceed at a rate of R flops per second. This is the same model of execution that we used in the distributed-memory setting, and it predicts that $2(\alpha + nr\beta) + (6nr/R)$ seconds are required to carry out (3.6.1). As expected, this model is simplistic and ignores a host of practical realities. However, it does an adequate job of exposing the usual tensions between computation and communication.

3.6.2 Multiple Transforms

As a first example of a shared-memory FFT computation, consider the multiple DFT problems $F_n X$ and $X F_n$. We assume that $X \in \mathbb{C}^{n \times n}$ resides in shared memory and is to be overwritten by the desired transform. Let p designate the number of participating processors.

In shared-memory algorithms, the activities assigned to the μth processor are usually a function of μ. For example, an obvious way to handle the computation $F_n X$ is to have $\text{Proc}(\mu)$ compute $F_n X(:, \mu{:}p{:}n-1)$ as follows:

$$
\begin{aligned}
&\textbf{for } k = \mu{:}p{:}n-1 \\
&\qquad x_{loc} \leftarrow X(:, k) \\
&\qquad x_{loc} \leftarrow F_n x_{loc} \\
&\qquad X(:, k) \leftarrow x_{loc} \\
&\textbf{end}
\end{aligned}
\qquad (3.6.2)
$$

Here, x_{loc} is a local one-dimensional array and the DFTs are processed column by column. When the μth processor executes the assignment "$x_{loc} \leftarrow X(:,k)$," it is getting a copy of the kth column of X from shared memory and placing it in its own local memory. The actual FFT operation $x_{loc} \leftarrow F_n x_{loc}$ is local and can be carried out with an appropriate single-processor framework. Finally, the resulting DFT is recorded in shared memory with the execution of $X(:,k) \leftarrow x_{loc}$. Our model predicts that about $2(\alpha + \beta n)(n/p)$ seconds are spent by each processor moving data to and from the shared memory during the execution of (3.6.2). Since each processor oversees about $1/p$th of the overall work, this multicolumn DFT approach is load balanced.

If we can afford a length n^2/p local array, then we rearrange (3.6.2) as follows:

$$X_{loc} \leftarrow X(:,\mu{:}p{:}n-1)$$
$$X_{loc} \leftarrow F_n X_{loc} \qquad\qquad\qquad\qquad (3.6.3)$$
$$X(:,\mu{:}p{:}n-1) \leftarrow X_{loc}$$

The communication overhead here is $2(\alpha + \beta n^2/p)$ seconds per processor. This is less than what we found for (3.6.2), because there is a reduced number of shared-memory references. Moreover, the advantages of having to compute a single multicolumn DFT makes (3.6.3) more attractive than (3.6.2), in which a sequence of single-vector FFTs are executed. However, this advantage may not be realized in practice, because the data in $X(:,\mu{:}p{:}n-1)$ is not contiguous. This may require some copying into a temporary local array or a column-by-column transmission of the data. In either case, additional overheads may be sustained in a way that is not captured by our model.

An alternative approach to the $F_n X$ computation is to partition X into p block columns, $X = \begin{bmatrix} X_0 & | & \cdots & | & X_{p-1} \end{bmatrix}$, and to have $\text{Proc}(\mu)$ handle the calculation of $F_n X_\mu$. For the sake of load balancing, it is important that the block columns have roughly the same width. Thus, if $n = mp$, then we could have $\text{Proc}(\mu)$ compute

$$X_{loc} \leftarrow X(:,\mu m{:}(\mu+1)m-1)$$
$$X_{loc} \leftarrow F_n X_{loc} \qquad\qquad\qquad\qquad (3.6.4)$$
$$X(:,\mu m{:}(\mu+1)m-1) \leftarrow X_{loc}$$

The shared-memory traffic in this approach requires about $2(\alpha + \beta n^2/p)$ seconds per processor.

The multirow DFT problem $X \leftarrow X F_n$ can be handled in a similar fashion. If $n = mp$, then corresponding to (3.6.4) we have

$$X_{loc} \leftarrow X(\mu m{:}(\mu+1)m-1,:)$$
$$X_{loc} \leftarrow X_{loc} F_n \qquad\qquad\qquad\qquad (3.6.5)$$
$$X(\mu m{:}(\mu+1)m-1,:) \leftarrow X_{loc}$$

Again, we mention that if the entries in $X(\mu m{:}(\mu+1)m-1,:)$ are not contiguous, then there may be hidden overheads associated with the movement of data between the shared and local memories.

3.6.3   The Barrier Construct

Now let us put (3.6.4) and (3.6.5) together and develop a complete shared-memory, two-dimensional FFT. The simple concatenation of these two algorithms *does not* result in a correct procedure, because we cannot guarantee that all of the column DFTs are completed when the first processor begins its share of the row DFTs. In short, we need a mechanism for holding up processors that finish their column DFTs early.

The **barrier** is one of several synchronization primitives that can be used to solve this kind of problem. When a **barrier** is encountered in a node program, the executing processor is held up in a "barrier state." If the node programs have been carefully designed, then there will come a time when all the participating processors are in the barrier state. As soon as this happens, each processor is released and control is passed to the next statement beyond the **barrier**. With these properties we see that the organization of a shared-memory, two-dimensional FFT requires a **barrier** in between the column and row DFT segments. What follows is a complete specification that also serves to introduce some new notations:

Algorithm 3.6.1 Suppose $X \in \mathbb{C}^{n \times n}$ resides in a shared memory that is accessible to p processors. If $n = pm$ and each processor executes the following algorithm, then upon completion X is overwritten by $F_n X F_n$.

$$
\begin{aligned}
&\textbf{loc.init}\,[\,p = proc.num,\ \mu = proc.id,\ n\,] \\
&\textbf{global}\,[\,X(0{:}n-1, 0{:}n-1)\,] \\
&m \leftarrow n/p \\
&\tau \leftarrow \mu m{:}(\mu + 1)m - 1 \\
&X_{loc} \leftarrow X(:, \tau) \\
&X_{loc} \leftarrow F_n X_{loc} \\
&X(:, \tau) \leftarrow X_{loc} \\
&\textbf{barrier} \\
&X_{loc} \leftarrow X(\tau, :) \\
&X_{loc} \leftarrow X_{loc} F_n \\
&X(\tau, :) \leftarrow X_{loc}
\end{aligned}
$$

As in the specification of node algorithms in §3.5, we lump all the important (but distracting) local initializations into the **loc.init** statement. We use the **global** statement to designate shared-memory arrays. All other references are to local variables, which are sometimes subscripted with "loc" for emphasis.

In Algorithm 3.6.1, each node must provide a workspace of size n^2/p. About $4(\alpha + \beta n^2/p)$ seconds are spent referencing shared memory and $(10n^2 \log n)/(pR)$ seconds are devoted to floating point arithmetic. Here, we assume that n is a power of two and that (for example) the Stockham radix-2 framework is applied. Because our model does not take into account the idle time spent at the **barrier**, we cannot be more refined in our estimation of the communication overhead.

3.6.4 A Shared-Memory Transposed Stockham Framework

As we discussed in §3.1, multirow DFTs are frequently more attractive than multicolumn DFTs. For this reason, we dwell a little longer on the shared-memory, multirow FFT problem. The framework (3.6.5) has the drawback that the local multirow DFT problems involve vectors of length n/p. Thus, as p grows the benefits of parallelism can be offset by a degradation in nodal performance due to shorter vectors. An alternative approach which does not reduce the effective vector length involves parallelizing the underlying FFT itself. To illustrate this, we assume $n = 2^t$ and reconsider the transposed Stockham radix-2 framework for the problem $X \leftarrow XF_n$, where $X \in \mathbb{C}^{n \times n}$:

> **for** $q = 1{:}t$
> $\qquad L \leftarrow 2^q; \ L_* \leftarrow L/2$
> $\qquad r \leftarrow n/L; \ r_* \leftarrow 2r$
> $\qquad Y \leftarrow X(\Pi_{r_*}^T \otimes I_{L_*})$
> $\qquad X \leftarrow Y(I_r \otimes B_L^T)$
> **end**

The transposed Stockham factorization is developed in §1.7.2. To facilitate the derivation of the shared-memory framework, we express the action of the permutation Π_{r_*} and the butterfly B_L in block form:

> **for** $q = 1{:}t$
> $\qquad L \leftarrow 2^q; \ L_* \leftarrow L/2$
> $\qquad r \leftarrow n/L; \ r_* \leftarrow 2r$
> $\qquad [\, Y_0 \mid Y_1 \mid \cdots \mid Y_{r_*-1} \,] \leftarrow X(\Pi_{r_*}^T \otimes I_{L_*}) \qquad \{Y_k \in \mathbb{C}^{n \times L_*}\}$
> $\qquad$ **for** $k = 0{:}r - 1$
> $\qquad\qquad X_k \leftarrow [\, Y_{2k} \mid Y_{2k+1} \,] B_L^T$
> $\qquad$ **end**
> $\qquad X \leftarrow [\, X_0 \mid \cdots \mid X_{r-1} \,]$
> **end**

Assume that $p = 2^d$ for simplicity. If $q \le t - d$, then each processor can process $r/p = 2^{t-d-q}$ of the butterfly updates. If $q > t - d$, then each butterfly update can be shared among $p/r = 2^{-t+d+q}$ processors. These observations lead to the following framework.

Algorithm 3.6.2 Suppose $X \in \mathbb{C}^{n \times n}$ resides in a shared memory that is accessible to $p = 2^d$ processors. If $n = 2^t > p$ and each processor executes the following algorithm, then upon completion X is overwritten by XF_n.

> loc.init $[\, p = proc.num, \ \mu = proc.id, \ n, \ t, \ d, \ m = n/p, \ m_* = m/2 \,]$
> global $[\, X(0{:}n - 1, 0{:}n - 1) \,]$
> **for** $q = 1{:}t - d$
> $\qquad L \leftarrow 2^q; \ L_* \leftarrow L/2; \ r \leftarrow n/L; \ r_* \leftarrow 2r$
> $\qquad s \leftarrow r/p$
> $\qquad \{s = \text{butterflies per processor.}\}$
> $\qquad \{X = [\, X_0 \mid X_1 \mid \cdots \mid X_{r_*-1} \,], \ X_j \in \mathbb{C}^{n \times L_*}\}$
> $\qquad$ **for** $j{:} = 0{:}s - 1$
> $\qquad\qquad Y_{loc}(0{:}n - 1, jL{:}(j + 1)L - 1) \leftarrow [\, X_{\mu s+j} \mid X_{\mu s+j+r} \,]$
> $\qquad$ **end**
> $\qquad Y_{loc} \leftarrow Y_{loc}(I_s \otimes B_L^T)$
> $\qquad$ **barrier**
> $\qquad X(0{:}n - 1, \mu m{:}(\mu + 1)m - 1) \leftarrow Y_{loc}$
> $\qquad$ **barrier**
> **end**

$$\mathbf{for}\ q = t - d + 1{:}t$$
$$L \leftarrow 2^q;\ L_* \leftarrow L/2;\ r \leftarrow n/L;\ r_* \leftarrow 2r$$
$$\{X = [\,X_0\,|\,X_1\,|\,\cdots\,|\,X_{r_*-1}\,],\ X_j \in \mathbb{C}^{n \times L_*}\}$$
$$s \leftarrow p/r$$
$$\{s = \text{processors per butterfly.}\}$$
$$k \leftarrow \mathbf{floor}(\mu/s);\ \nu \leftarrow \mu - ks$$
$$\{\text{Compute the } \nu\text{th part of } [\,X_k\,|\,X_{k+r}\,]B_L^T.\}$$
$$cols \leftarrow \nu m_*{:}(\nu + 1)m_* - 1$$
$$Y_{loc}(0{:}n - 1, 0{:}m - 1) \leftarrow [\,X_k(:, cols)\,|\,X_{k+r}(:, cols)\,]$$
$$Y_{loc} \leftarrow Y_{loc}\begin{bmatrix} I_{m_*} & \Omega_{L_*}(cols, cols) \\ I_{m_*} & -\Omega_{L_*}(cols, cols) \end{bmatrix}^T$$

barrier

$$X(:, kL + \nu m_*{:}kL + (\nu + 1)m_* - 1) \leftarrow Y_{loc}(0{:}n - 1, 0{:}m_* - 1)$$
$$X(:, kL + L_* + \nu m_*{:}kL + L_* + (\nu + 1)m_* - 1) \leftarrow Y_{loc}(0{:}n - 1, m_*{:}m - 1)$$

barrier

end

It can be shown that each node spends about $(2n\alpha + 2n^2(\log n)\beta)/p$ seconds referencing shared data. For large n the speedup is prescribed by $p/(1 + .4\beta R)$, if we assume that n is so large that latency does not affect performance.

The placement of the barriers in Algorithm 3.6.2 deserves an explanation. During a pass through either of the two q-loops, a **barrier** is placed before and after the write to shared memory. The first barrier prevents one processor from modifying portions of X that are required by another processor during the same q-pass. The second **barrier** ensures that the current q-pass is completely finished before any processor proceeds with its share of the next q-pass.

Our assumption that each processor can accommodate a length n^2/p workspace may not be possible. In this case, $\text{Proc}(\mu)$'s task during the qth pass must be broken down into chunks that can be handled by the local memory. An additional n-by-n shared-memory workspace Y can simplify this endeavor to the extent that only a pair of local, length-n, workspaces u_{loc} and v_{loc} are required. The idea is to have each processor repeat the following cycle of events during each q-pass:

- Two columns from X (Y) are read into $[\,u_{loc}\,|\,v_{loc}\,]$.

- A butterfly of the form $[\,u_{loc}\,|\,v_{loc}\,] \leftarrow [\,u_{loc}\,|\,v_{loc}\,]\begin{bmatrix} 1 & 1 \\ \omega & -\omega \end{bmatrix}$ is computed.

- $[\,u_{loc}\,|\,v_{loc}\,]$ is appropriately stored in Y (X).

The role of X and Y can flip-flop from q-pass to q-pass. In other words, if at the beginning of the pass X houses the intermediate DFTs, then Y can house the double length intermediate DFTs at the end of the pass, and vice versa. For load balancing we merely require each processor to handle $1/p$th of the $n^2/2$ butterflies.

Finally, there is the matter of weight precomputation, which can be handled in several different ways. One possibility is to precompute the weight vector $w_n^{(long)}$ once and for all at the beginning of the algorithm and to maintain a copy in each local memory. If this requires too much space, then the ideas of §3.3.3 may be applicable.

3.6.5 Shared-Memory Transpose: The Square Case

In anticipation of the development of a four-step, shared-memory framework, we look at the problem of shared-memory transposition beginning with the square case. Suppose $n = n_2^2$ and that $x \in \mathbb{C}^n$ resides in shared memory. Our task is to develop parallel algorithms for the transposition of $x_{n_2 \times n_2}$. We work under the assumption that we cannot afford a second shared-memory buffer of length n. Identify X with $x_{n_2 \times n_2}$ and assume that $n_2 = Nb$. Regarding $X = (X_{kj})$ as an N-by-N block matrix with b-by-b blocks, $X = (X_{kj})$, we have:

$$
\begin{aligned}
&\textbf{for } k = 0{:}N - 1 \\
&\quad \textbf{for } j = 0{:}k - 1 \\
&\quad\quad A_{loc} \leftarrow X_{kj}; \; B_{loc} \leftarrow X_{jk} \\
&\quad\quad A_{loc} \leftarrow A_{loc}^T; \; B_{loc} \leftarrow B_{loc}^T \\
&\quad\quad X_{kj} \leftarrow B_{loc}; \; X_{jk} \leftarrow A_{loc} \\
&\quad \textbf{end} \\
&\quad A_{loc} \leftarrow X_{kk}; \; A_{loc} \leftarrow A_{loc}^T; \; X_{kk} \leftarrow A_{loc} \\
&\textbf{end}
\end{aligned}
$$

By assigning each processor an approximately equal fraction of the swap-transpositions, we obtain the algorithm below.

Algorithm 3.6.3 Suppose $x \in \mathbb{C}^n$ resides in a shared memory that is accessible to p processors and that $n = n_2^2$ with $n_2 = Nb$. If each processor executes the following algorithm, then $x_{n_2 \times n_2}$ is overwritten with its transpose:

$$
\begin{aligned}
&\textbf{loc.init}\,[\,p = proc.num, \; \mu = proc.id, \; n = n_2^2, \; b, \; N = n_2/b\,] \\
&\textbf{global}\,[\,x(0{:}n - 1)\,] \\
&\{x_{n_2 \times n_2} \equiv (X_{kj}), \; X_{kj} \in \mathbb{C}^{b \times b}\} \\
&\tau \leftarrow 0 \\
&\textbf{for } k = 0{:}N - 1 \\
&\quad \textbf{for } j = 0{:}k - 1 \\
&\quad\quad \textbf{if } \tau = \mu \bmod p \\
&\quad\quad\quad A_{loc} \leftarrow X_{kj}; \; B_{loc} \leftarrow X_{jk} \\
&\quad\quad\quad A_{loc} \leftarrow A_{loc}^T; \; B_{loc} \leftarrow B_{loc}^T \\
&\quad\quad\quad X_{kj} \leftarrow B_{loc}; \; X_{jk} \leftarrow A_{loc} \\
&\quad\quad \textbf{end} \\
&\quad\quad \tau \leftarrow \tau + 1 \\
&\quad \textbf{end} \\
&\quad \textbf{if } \tau = \mu \bmod p \\
&\quad\quad A_{loc} \leftarrow X_{kk}; \; A_{loc} \leftarrow A_{loc}^T; \; X_{kk} \leftarrow A_{loc} \\
&\quad \textbf{end} \\
&\quad \tau \leftarrow \tau + 1 \\
&\textbf{end}
\end{aligned}
$$

Each processor spends about $2n((\alpha/b^2) + \beta)/p$ seconds communicating with shared memory and is required to have a workspace of length b^2. Note that τ ranges from 0 to $M - 1$ where $M = N(N - 1)/2$ is precisely the total number of swap-transpositions. Each processor handles approximately $1/p$th of these. Of course, if p does not divide M, then some processors are engaged in **floor**(M/p) swap-transpositions; for others the number is $\mathbf{floor}(M/p)+1$. This does not present a serious load-balancing problem, if we assume that $M >> p$. Likewise, for large M there is no danger of load imbalance due to an uneven distribution of the diagonal block problems, which involve half the data movement as the off-diagonal swap-transpositions.

3.6.6 Shared-Memory Transpose: The Case $n_1 = qn_2$

Next we develop a shared-memory algorithm for the transposition of

$$x_{n_1 \times n_2} = \begin{bmatrix} X_0 \\ X_1 \\ \vdots \\ X_{q-1} \end{bmatrix}, \qquad X_j \in \mathbb{C}^{n_2 \times n_2}.$$

A two-pass approach to this problem is discussed in §3.2.8 and it begins with the following permutation:

$$x_{n_2 \times n_1} \leftarrow x_{n_2 \times n_1} \Pi_{q,n_1} .$$

A simple shared-memory approach to this problem is to partition $x_{n_2 \times n_1}$ into (say) s_2 block rows and have $\text{Proc}(\mu)$ oversee the mod q sorting of block rows $\mu{:}p{:}s_2 - 1$. After this manipulation we have $x_{n_2 \times n_1} = \begin{bmatrix} X_0 & | & \cdots & | & X_{q-1} \end{bmatrix}$ in shared memory and by transposing the X_j, we obtain the desired result.

Algorithm 3.6.4 Suppose $x \in \mathbb{C}^n$ resides in a shared memory that is accessible to p processors. Assume that $n = n_1 n_2$, $n_1 = s_1 m_1$, $n_2 = s_2 m_2$, $n_1 = qn_2$, and $p \geq q$. If each processor executes the following algorithm, then $x_{n_2 \times n_1}$ is overwritten with $x_{n_1 \times n_2}^T$.

> **loc.init** $[\, p = proc.num,\ \mu = proc.id,\ n,\ n_1,\ n_2,\ q,\ s_1,\ m_1,\ s_2,\ m_2 \,]$
> **global** $[\, x(0{:}n - 1) \,]$
> **for** $k = \mu{:}p{:}s_2 - 1$
> $\qquad rows \leftarrow km_2{:}(k + 1)m_2 - 1$
> $\qquad [x_{loc}]_{m_2 \times n_1} \leftarrow x_{n_2 \times n_1}(rows, 0{:}n_1 - 1)$
> $\qquad [x_{loc}]_{m_2 \times n_1} \leftarrow [x_{loc}]_{m_2 \times n_1} \Pi_{q,n_1}$
> $\qquad x_{n_2 \times n_1}(rows, 0{:}n_1 - 1) \leftarrow [x_{loc}]_{m_2 \times n_1}$
> **end**
> **barrier**
> $\{ x_{n_2 \times n_1} = [X_0 \,|\, \cdots \,|\, X_{q-1}],\ X_j \in \mathbb{C}^{n_2 \times n_2} \}$
> Let $j = \mu \bmod q$ and participate (via Algorithm 3.6.3) in the transposition
> $\qquad$ of X_j along with all the processors whose $proc.id$ mod q equals j.

3.6.7 The Four-Step Approach

Suppose $x \in \mathbb{C}^n$ and $N = n_1 n_2$. Assume that x resides in global memory and consider the four-step approach:

$$x_{n_1 \times n_2} \leftarrow x_{n_1 \times n_2} F_{n_2}$$
$$x_{n_1 \times n_2} \leftarrow F_n(0{:}n_1 - 1, 0{:}n_2 - 1) .* x_{n_1 \times n_2}$$
$$x_{n_2 \times n_1} \leftarrow x_{n_1 \times n_2}^T$$
$$x_{n_2 \times n_1} \leftarrow x_{n_2 \times n_1} F_{n_1} .$$

The organization of this framework in a shared-memory environment involves piecing together our multiple transform and transposition ideas.

Algorithm 3.6.5 Suppose $x \in \mathbb{C}^n$ resides in a shared memory that is accessible to p processors. Assume that $n = n_1 n_2$, $n_1 = s_1 m_1$, $n_2 = s_2 m_2$, and $n_1 = q n_2$. If each processor executes the following algorithm, then x is overwritten with $F_n x$.

> loc.init $[\, p = proc.num, \ \mu = proc.id, \ n, \ n_1, \ s_1, \ m_1, \ n_2, \ s_2, \ m_2 \,]$
> global $[\, x(0{:}n - 1) \,]$
> for $k = \mu{:}p{:}s_1 - 1$
>> $rows \leftarrow km_1{:}(k+1)m_1 - 1$
>> $X_{loc}(0{:}m_1 - 1, 0{:}n_2 - 1) \leftarrow x_{n_1 \times n_2}(rows, 0{:}n_2 - 1)$
>> $X_{loc} \leftarrow X_{loc} F_{n_2}$
>> $X_{loc} \leftarrow X_{loc} \ .* \ F_n(rows, 0{:}n_2 - 1)$
>> $x_{n_1 \times n_2}(rows, 0{:}n_2 - 1) \leftarrow X_{loc}$
>
> end
>
> **barrier**
>
> Following Algorithm 3.6.4, participate in the transposition $x_{n_2 \times n_1} \leftarrow x_{n_1 \times n_2}^T$.
>
> **barrier**
> for $k = \mu{:}p{:}s_2 - 1$
>> $rows \leftarrow km_2{:}(k+1)m_2 - 1$
>> $X_{loc} \leftarrow x_{n_2 \times n_1}(rows, 0{:}n_1 - 1)$
>> $X_{loc} \leftarrow X_{loc} F_{n_1}$
>> $x_{n_2 \times n_1}(rows, 0{:}n_1 - 1) \leftarrow X_{loc}$
>
> end

A shared-memory, six-step framework is analogous.

3.6.8   A Note on Pool-of-Task Scheduling

A drawback of our §3.6.6 approach to the problem $x_{n_2 \times n_1} \leftarrow x_{n_2 \times n_1} \Pi_{q,n_1}$ is that the length of the vector manipulations may be considerably less than n_2 because of the block row partitioning. This illustrates once again the trade-off between vector length and parallelism.

Alternatively, we could compute the permutation via cycles, as discussed in §3.2.3. This approach enables us to carry out the permutation with a minimum of excess storage and with vectors of length n_2. It also leads to some interesting issues of load balancing. Suppose $q = 2$ and consider Table 3.6.1, in which we report the cycles of the even-odd sort permutation Π_{64}^T. Recall that the columns corresponding to the indices in a cycle are "rotated." Thus, in cycle number five columns 9, 18, and 36 are moved about in the following way:

$$
\begin{array}{rcl}
temp & \leftarrow & \text{col } 9 \\
\text{col } 9 & \leftarrow & \text{col } 18 \\
\text{col } 18 & \leftarrow & \text{col } 36 \\
\text{col } 36 & \leftarrow & temp
\end{array}
$$

TABLE 3.6.1

The cycles of $\Pi_{2,64}^T$.

Cycle Number	Cycle
0	(0)
1	(1, 2, 4, 8, 16, 32)
2	(3, 6, 12, 24, 48, 33)
3	(5, 10, 20, 40, 17, 34)
4	(7, 14, 28, 56, 49, 35)
5	(9, 18, 36)
6	(11, 22, 44, 25, 50, 37)
7	(13, 26, 52, 41, 19, 38)
8	(15, 30, 60, 57, 51, 39)
9	(21, 42)
10	(23, 46, 29, 58, 53, 43)
11	(27, 54, 45)
12	(31, 62, 61, 59, 55, 47)
13	(63)

In a multiprocessor formulation, if p processors are involved in the permutation and c is the total number of cycles, then we can assign cycles $\mu{:}p{:}c - 1$ to Proc(μ). With this strategy, we obtain the following shared-memory version of Algorithm 3.2.5:

Algorithm 3.6.6 Suppose $n = n_1 n_2$ and that $x \in \mathbb{C}^n$ resides in a shared memory that is accessible to p processors. Assume $n_1 = q n_2$ and that the function $g(k)$ is defined by $\left[\Pi_{q,n_1}^T\right]_k = x_{g(k)}$. If each processor executes the following algorithm, then $x_{n_2 \times n_1}$ is overwritten by $x_{n_2 \times n_1} \Pi_{q,n_1}$:

$\quad$ loc.init $[\, p = proc.num, \ \mu = proc.id, \ n, \ n_1, \ n_2 \,]$
$\quad$ global $[\, x(0{:}n - 1) \,]$ $\qquad$ $\{ x_{n_2 \times n_1} \equiv X(0{:}n_2 - 1, 0{:}n_1 - 1) \}$
$\quad$ $\beta(0{:}n_1 - 1) \leftarrow 0; \ cycle.num \leftarrow 0$
$\quad$ **for** $k = 0{:}n_1 - 1$
$\qquad$ **if** $\beta_k = 0$ **and** $cycle.num = \mu \bmod p$
$\qquad\quad$ $j \leftarrow k; \ u_{loc} \leftarrow X(:, k); \ next \leftarrow g(k)$
$\qquad\quad$ **while** $next \neq k$
$\qquad\qquad$ $v_{loc} \leftarrow X(:, next); \ X(:, j) \leftarrow v_{loc}; \ \beta_j \leftarrow 1$
$\qquad\qquad$ $j \leftarrow next; \ next \leftarrow g(j)$
$\qquad\quad$ **end**
$\qquad\quad$ $X(:, j) \leftarrow u_{loc}; \ \beta_j \leftarrow 1; \ cycle.num \leftarrow cycle.num + 1$
$\qquad$ **elseif** $\beta = 0$ **and** $cycle.num \neq \mu \bmod p$
$\qquad\quad$ $j \leftarrow k; \ next \leftarrow g(k)$
$\qquad\quad$ **while** $next \neq k$
$\qquad\qquad$ $\beta_j \leftarrow 1; \ j \leftarrow next; \ next \leftarrow g(j)$
$\qquad\quad$ **end**
$\qquad\quad$ $\beta_j \leftarrow 1; \ cycle.num \leftarrow cycle.num + 1$
$\qquad$ **end**
$\quad$ **end**

Note that although each processor computes all the cycles, they move only the columns in their assigned cycles. The cycle computation redundancy is tolerable because the shared-memory accesses are what typically determine the level of performance.

If a given cycle is assigned to a processor, then that processor proceeds as follows:

- The first column in the cycle is retrieved from shared memory.

- While the first column is held in local memory, the remaining columns in the cycle are processed by reading them into local memory and writing them back to the appropriately shifted locations in the shared-memory array $x_{n_2 \times n_1}$.

- The first column in the cycle is written to the original location of the last column in the cycle.

Let us consider the load-balancing properties of Algorithm 3.6.5. The time required to process a cycle of length ℓ is roughly $2\ell(\alpha + \beta n_2)$ if $\ell > 1$. If $\ell = 1$, then there is no shared-memory traffic. Thus, to achieve load balancing we would like the number of columns that each processor moves to be roughly equal. That is, the sum of the lengths of the cycles assigned to each processor should be approximately the same. In the Table 3.6.1 case, where $n_1 = 64$, we see that the majority of the cycles have length $6 = \log_2 64$. However, there are enough exceptions to create a possible load imbalance. Indeed, if $p = 4$, then the number of columns that must be moved by processors 0, 1, 2, and 3 are, respectively, given by 18, 11, 18, and 15. Thus, the ratio of the heaviest load to the lightest load is given by $18/11 \approx 1.63$. For larger n_1 of the form $n_1 = 2^{t_1}$, the ratio is not so pronounced.

Nevertheless, the problem points to a central difficulty associated with load balancing when the tasks assigned to the individual processors vary in computational intensity. In the case of the Π permutations, there are no ready formulae that tell us the number of cycles and their lengths. Thus, a static, a priori scheduling scheme typified by Algorithm 3.6.6 can result in a serious load imbalance.

One approach that can minimize this difficulty is to renumber the cycles from longest to shortest and with the new ordering, assign cycles $\mu{:}p{:}c - 1$ to Proc(μ). For the $n_1 = 64$, $p = 4$ problem, this reduces the ratio of heaviest to lightest load from 1.63 to to 1.28.

Another idea is to *dynamically schedule* processor activity using the *pool-of-task* idea. Here, a list of remaining tasks is maintained in shared memory. (In our setting, a task would be the processing of a cycle.) When a processor completes a cycle, it queries the list of remaining tasks and if that list is nonempty, it is assigned the next unprocessed cycle. In this way, it is not necessary to work out a load-balanced schedule in advance, as the dynamics of the pool-of-task approach more or less ensure that all the processors are kept busy. To implement this scheme a new set of synchronization primitives is required to ensure that only one processor at a time is involved in the updating of the list of the remaining tasks. As it is somewhat involved, we have chosen not to pursue this matter any further. We refer the reader to Golub and Van Loan (1989) for a discussion of the pool-of-task paradigm as it is used in shared-memory matrix computations.

Problems

P3.6.1 Develop a version of (3.6.4) that can handle the case when n is not a multiple of p, the number of processors.

P3.6.2 Develop a shared-memory, radix-4, transposed Stockham framework for $X \leftarrow X F_n$, assuming that both n and the number of processors are a power of four.

P3.6.3 Write a shared-memory algorithm that computes the vector $w_n^{(long)}$ defined in §1.4.11. Upon completion, $w_n^{(long)}$ should reside in shared memory.

P3.6.4 Detail the butterfly computations in the second q-loop in Algorithm 3.6.2.

Notes and References for Section 3.6

For general background on the organization and exploitation of shared-memory machines, consult

J. Dongarra, I.S. Duff, D.C. Sorensen, and H.A. van der Vorst (1990). *Solving Linear Systems on Vector and Shared Memory Computers*, Society for Industrial and Applied Mathematics, Philadelphia, PA.

J.L. Hennessy and D.A. Patterson (1990). *Computer Architecture: A Quantitative Approach*, Morgan Kaufman Publishers, Inc., San Mateo, CA.

An instructive shared-memory FFT for the Alliant FX/8 is presented in

P.N. Swarztrauber (1987). "Multiprocessor FFTs," *Parallel Comput. 5*, 197–210.

Two different scheduling strategies for single-vector FFTs and three different approaches to the multiple FFTs are discussed in

W.L. Briggs, L. Hart, R. Sweet, and A. O'Gallagher (1987). "Multiprocessor FFT Methods," *SIAM J. Sci. Statist. Comput. 8*, s27–s42.

The above authors also develop models of performance that are consistent with their experiments on the Denelcor HEP. Additional performance studies in the shared-memory FFT setting are pursued in

A. Auerbuch, E. Gabber, B. Gordissky, and Y. Medan (1990). "A Parallel FFT on a MIMD Machine," *Parallel Computing 15*, 61–74.

Z. Cvetanovic (1987). "Performance Analysis of the FFT Algorithm on a Shared-Memory Architecture," *IBM J. Res. Devel. 31*, 419–510.

A. Norton and A. Silberger (1987). "Parallelization and Performance Prediction of the Cooley–Tukey FFT Algorithm for Shared Memory Architectures," *IEEE Trans. Comput. C-36*, 581–591.

The latter paper also points to the value of the Kronecker notation in developing parallel FFTs. To further investigate this, the reader should also review

J. Johnson, R.W. Johnson, D. Rodriguez, and R. Tolimieri (1990). "A Methodology for Designing, Modifying, and Implementing Fourier Transform Algorithms on Various Architectures," *Circuits Systems Signal Process. 9*, 449–500.

Chapter 4

Selected Topics

Surprisingly, we have not yet exhausted the set of all possible factorizations of the DFT matrix F_n. In fact, a case can be made that we are but halfway along in our survey, for until now we have neglected the *prime factor FFTs*. This framework is based upon a number-theoretic splitting of the DFT matrix and a large fraction of the FFT literature is devoted to its implementation and various properties.

Elsewhere in this final chapter we examine two leading application areas that rely heavily upon FFTs: convolution and the numerical solution of the Poisson equation. Methods for one- and two-dimensional convolution are given in §4.2. The duality between fast convolution and FFTs is established and some new FFT frameworks emerge. Fast methods for the product of a Toeplitz matrix and a vector are also discussed.

A real-data FFT framework is derived in §4.3 and comparisons are made with the rival Hartley transform. By exploiting structure, it is possible to halve the amount of required arithmetic. Fast algorithms for various sine and cosine transforms are given in §4.4 and then used in §4.5 to solve the Poisson equation problem. The trigonometric transforms that we develop have many applications and are a fitting tribute to the FFT and its wide applicability.

4.1   Prime Factor Frameworks

The FFT algorithms developed thus far rely in one way or another upon the splitting result

$$F_n \Pi_{n_1,n} = (F_{n_2} \otimes I_{n_1}) \text{diag}(I_{n_2}, \Omega_{n_1,n_2}, \ldots, \Omega_{n_1,n_2}^{n_1-1})(I_{n_2} \otimes F_{n_1}),$$

where $n = n_1 n_2$. In this framework a nontrivial fraction of the work is associated with the twiddle-factor multiplications, i.e., the application of the scaling matrices Ω_{n_1,n_2}^j.

The removal of these scalings is the central feature of the *prime factor FFTs*. This family of algorithms is based upon splittings of the form

$$\Gamma^T F_n \Upsilon = F_{n_2} \otimes F_{n_1}, \qquad (4.1.1)$$

where Γ and Υ are n-by-n permutations. With this reduction the single-vector DFT $F_n x$ becomes a genuine two-dimensional DFT sandwiched in between permutations:

$$x \leftarrow \Upsilon^T x$$
$$x_{n_1 \times n_2} \leftarrow F_{n_1} x_{n_1 \times n_2} F_{n_2}$$
$$x \leftarrow \Gamma x.$$

It turns out that these reductions are possible only if n_1 and n_2 are *relatively prime*, meaning that 1 is the largest integer that divides both n_1 and n_2.

Our presentation of prime factor FFTs begins by motivating the importance of relative primality. We require a handful of related number-theoretic properties for this purpose and some additional notation is handy:

- If $j = <k>_n$, then j equals k modulo n. Thus, $2 = <12>_5$.

- If $p|q$, then p divides q. Thus, $2|6$.

After acquiring the necessary number theory we characterize the permutations Γ and Υ that define the splitting (4.1.1). The splitting leads naturally to a general prime factor factorization and an associated computational framework. Our presentation follows that of Temperton (1983c), (1985), (1988a), (1988b), (1988c).

4.1.1 The Case $n = 6$

Consider the example $(n_1, n_2) = (2, 3)$. We show that $F_3 \otimes F_2$ can be obtained by permuting the rows and columns of F_6. For any scalar w and matrix A, let $B = w.^{**}A$ denote the matrix defined by $[B]_{kj} = w^{a_{kj}}$. Since

$$F_2 = \omega_2.^{**}\begin{bmatrix} 0 & 0 \\ 0 & 1 \end{bmatrix} = \omega_6.^{**}\begin{bmatrix} 0 & 0 \\ 0 & 3 \end{bmatrix},$$

$$F_3 = \omega_3.^{**}\begin{bmatrix} 0 & 0 & 0 \\ 0 & 1 & 2 \\ 0 & 2 & 1 \end{bmatrix} = \omega_6.^{**}\begin{bmatrix} 0 & 0 & 0 \\ 0 & 2 & 4 \\ 0 & 4 & 2 \end{bmatrix},$$

it follows that

$$F_3 \otimes F_2 = \omega_6.^{**}\left[\begin{array}{cc|cc|cc} 0 & 0 & 0 & 0 & 0 & 0 \\ 0 & 3 & 0 & 3 & 0 & 3 \\ \hline 0 & 0 & 2 & 2 & 4 & 4 \\ 0 & 3 & 2 & 5 & 4 & 1 \\ \hline 0 & 0 & 4 & 4 & 2 & 2 \\ 0 & 3 & 4 & 1 & 2 & 5 \end{array}\right].$$

However,

$$F_6 = \omega_6.^{**}\begin{bmatrix} 0 & 0 & 0 & 0 & 0 & 0 \\ 0 & 1 & 2 & 3 & 4 & 5 \\ 0 & 2 & 4 & 0 & 2 & 4 \\ 0 & 3 & 0 & 3 & 0 & 3 \\ 0 & 4 & 2 & 0 & 4 & 2 \\ 0 & 5 & 4 & 3 & 2 & 1 \end{bmatrix}$$

and it is not too hard to show that

$$F_6([\,0,\ 3,\ 4,\ 1,\ 2,\ 5\,],[\,0,\ 3,\ 2,\ 5,\ 4,\ 1\,]) \ = \ F_3 \otimes F_2 \,.$$

In the notation of §1.1.8, if we set $\Gamma = P_v$ and $\Upsilon = P_u$, where

$$v \ = \ [\,0,\ 3,\ 4,\ 1,\ 2,\ 5\,],$$
$$u \ = \ [\,0,\ 3,\ 2,\ 5,\ 4,\ 1\,],$$

then $\Gamma^T F_6 \Upsilon = F_3 \otimes F_2$. From this example we see that the lead item on our agenda is an efficient method for the determination of the "magic vectors" v and u. This requires a little number theory.

4.1.2   Relative Primality

The matrix $F_{n_2} \otimes F_{n_1}$ is an n_2-by-n_2 block matrix with n_1-by-n_1 blocks. Thus, entry (k_1, j_1) of block (k_2, j_2) is given by $\omega_{n_1}^{k_1 j_1} \omega_{n_2}^{k_2 j_2}$. If $n = n_1 n_2$ and $F_{n_2} \otimes F_{n_1}$ is a permutation of F_n, then

$$[F_n]_{11} \ = \ \omega_n \ = \ \omega_{n_2}^{k_2 j_2} \omega_{n_1}^{k_1 j_1} \ = \ \omega_n^{n_1 k_2 j_2} \omega_n^{n_2 k_1 j_1} \ = \ \omega_n^{n_1 k_2 j_2 + n_2 k_1 j_1}$$

for some k_1, j_1, k_2, and j_2 that satisfy $0 \le k_1, j_1 \le n_1 - 1$ and $0 \le k_2, j_2 \le n_2 - 1$. Suppose α is a positive integer that divides both n_1 and n_2. It follows that $n_1 = \alpha \tilde{n}_1$ and $n_2 = \alpha \tilde{n}_2$ and so

$$\omega_n \ = \ \omega_n^{\alpha(\tilde{n}_1 k_2 j_2 + \tilde{n}_2 k_1 j_1)} \,.$$

Thus,

$$\alpha(\tilde{n}_1 k_2 j_2 + \tilde{n}_2 k_1 j_1) \ = \ \beta n + 1 \ = \ \beta \alpha^2 \tilde{n}_1 \tilde{n}_2 + 1$$

for some integer β. But this implies that

$$\alpha(\tilde{n}_1 k_2 j_2 + \tilde{n}_2 k_1 j_1 - \beta \alpha \tilde{n}_1 \tilde{n}_2) \ = \ 1 \,.$$

Since α is positive, we must have $\alpha = 1$. *We have shown that if $F_{n_2} \otimes F_{n_1}$ is a permutation of F_n, then n_1 and n_2 must be relatively prime.*

4.1.3   Facts about Relatively Prime Numbers

The *greatest common divisor* $\gcd(n_1, n_2)$ of a pair of positive integers n_1 and n_2 is the largest positive integer that divides both n_1 and n_2. *Euclid's algorithm* can be used to compute $d = \gcd(n_1, n_2)$:

$$
\begin{aligned}
&r_0 \leftarrow n_1 \\
&r_1 \leftarrow n_2 \\
&j \leftarrow 0 \\
&\textbf{while } r_{j+1} \ne 0 \\
&\qquad j \leftarrow j + 1 \\
&\qquad r_{j+1} \leftarrow <r_{j-1}>_{r_j} \\
&\textbf{end} \\
&d \leftarrow r_j
\end{aligned}
\qquad (4.1.2)
$$

Manipulation of the r_j permits the following characterization of the gcd:

Theorem 4.1.1 *If n_1 and n_2 are positive integers and $d = gcd(n_1, n_2)$, then there exist integers a and b such that $an_1 + bn_2 = d$.*

Proof. See P4.1.1 for hints or Nussbaumer (1981b) for details.

It follows from Theorem 4.1.1 that if $gcd(n_1, n_2) = 1$, $p > 1$, and $p|n_1$, then p *does not* divide n_2. This observation figures heavily in the proof of the next result.

Theorem 4.1.2 *If $n = n_1 n_2$ with $gcd(n_1, n_2) = 1$, then there exist integers α_1, β_1, α_2, and β_2 with $0 \le \alpha_1, \beta_1 \le n_1 - 1$ and $0 \le \alpha_2, \beta_2 \le n_2 - 1$ such that*

$$
\begin{align}
\alpha_2 n_1 &= \beta_1 n_2 + 1, & (4.1.3) \\
\alpha_1 n_2 &= \beta_2 n_1 + 1, & (4.1.4) \\
1 &= gcd(\alpha_1, n_1), & (4.1.5) \\
1 &= gcd(\alpha_2, n_2), & (4.1.6) \\
n + 1 &= \alpha_2 n_1 + \alpha_1 n_2. & (4.1.7)
\end{align}
$$

Proof. Since $gcd(n_1, n_2) = 1$, we know from Theorem 4.1.1 that integers c and d can be found so that $cn_1 + dn_2 = 1$. Define the integer pairs (c_1, c_2) and (d_1, d_2) by

$$
\begin{align}
c &= c_1 n_2 + c_2, & 0 \le c_2 \le n_2 - 1, \\
d &= d_1 n_1 - d_2, & 0 \le d_2 \le n_1 - 1.
\end{align}
$$

It follows that $(c_1 n_2 + c_2)n_1 + (d_1 n_1 - d_2)n_2 = 1$ and therefore,

$$
c_2 n_1 = d_2 n_2 - (c_1 + d_1)n + 1.
$$

Given the bounds on c_2 and d_2, it can be shown that $c_1 + d_1 = 0$. Equation (4.1.3) follows by setting $c_2 = \alpha_2$ and $d_2 = \beta_1$. The proof of (4.1.4) is similar.

To show $gcd(\alpha_1, n_1) = 1$, assume that $\alpha_1 = k_1 d$ and $n_1 = k_2 d$ for positive integers k_1, k_2, and d. Using (4.1.4) we have

$$
1 = \alpha_1 n_2 - \beta_2 n_1 = k_1 d n_2 - \beta_2 k_2 d = d(k_1 n_2 - \beta_2 k_2).
$$

It follows that $d = 1$, thereby confirming (4.1.5). A similar verification establishes (4.1.6).

To verify (4.1.7), write

$$
\alpha_2 n_1 + \alpha_1 n_2 = cn + d,
$$

where $0 \le d \le n - 1$. Since $\alpha_2 n_1 = \beta_1 n_2 + 1$ and $\alpha_1 n_2 = \beta_2 n_1 + 1$, we obtain

$$
\begin{align}
cn + d &= \beta_1 n_2 + 1 + \alpha_1 n_2, \\
cn + d &= \alpha_2 n_1 + \beta_2 n_1 + 1,
\end{align}
$$

from which we conclude that both $n_2|(d - 1)$ and $n_1|(d - 1)$. Since $gcd(n_1, n_2) = 1$, it follows that $n_1 n_2 = n$ divides $d - 1$. But this implies that $d = 1$ since $n > d$. The verification that $c = 1$ is left to the reader. $\square$

The α's and β's for some typical integer pairs are given in Table 4.1.1.

TABLE 4.1.1
Illustrations of Theorem 4.1.2.

(n_1, n_2)	$\alpha_2 n_1 = \beta_1 n_2 + 1$	$\alpha_1 n_2 = \beta_2 n_1 + 1$
(3,2)	$1 \cdot 3 = 1 \cdot 2 + 1$	$2 \cdot 2 = 1 \cdot 3 + 1$
(7,4)	$3 \cdot 7 = 5 \cdot 4 + 1$	$2 \cdot 4 = 1 \cdot 7 + 1$
(27,32)	$19 \cdot 27 = 16 \cdot 32 + 1$	$11 \cdot 32 = 13 \cdot 27 + 1$

4.1.4   Blocking Permutations

Suppose $n = n_1 n_2$ and that the mapping

$$\{0, 1, \ldots, n-1\} \overset{f}{\to} \{0, 1, \ldots, n_1 - 1\} \times \{0, 1, \ldots, n_2 - 1\}$$

is 1:1 and onto. If $x, y \in \mathbb{C}^n$, then the permutation matrix Q_f defined by

$$y = Q_f^T x, \qquad y(j_2 n_1 + j_1) = x(j), \ (j_1, j_2) = f(j)$$

can be thought of as a *blocking permutation*. Indeed, if we think of y as a block vector having n_2 subvectors of length n_1, then $x(j)$ becomes component j_1 of subvector j_2. Equivalently, $x(j)$ is entry (j_1, j_2) of $y_{n_1 \times n_2}$.

Returning to our derivation of the prime factor algorithm, recognize that the task before us is to find a pair of blocking permutations $\Gamma = Q_{f_1}$ and $\Upsilon = Q_{f_2}$ so that (4.1.1) holds. The idea of using blocking permutations to reveal structure in the DFT matrix is not new. If f is defined by $f(j) = (\mathbf{floor}(j/n_2), j - \mathbf{floor}(j/n_2)n_2)$, then $Q_f = \Pi_{n_1, n}$. All of our previous FFT work revolves around the fact that $F_n \Pi_{n_1, n}$ has a rich block structure.

4.1.5   The C Mapping and the Permutation $\Gamma_{n_2, n}$

Suppose $\gcd(n_1, n_2) = 1$ and that $n = n_1 n_2$. The *Chinese Remainder Theorem mapping*

$$\{0, 1, \ldots, n-1\} \overset{C}{\to} \{0, 1, \ldots, n_1 - 1\} \times \{0, 1, \ldots, n_2 - 1\}$$

is defined by

$$C(j) = (\ <j>_{n_1}, \ <j>_{n_2}\ ).$$

This "C mapping" is 1:1. Indeed, if

$$(\ <j>_{n_1}, \ <j>_{n_2}\ ) = (\ <k>_{n_1}, \ <k>_{n_2}\ ),$$

then there exist integers a_1 and a_2 so that $j = k + a_1 n_1$ and $j = k + a_2 n_2$. This implies $a_1 n_1 = a_2 n_2$. Since $\gcd(n_1, n_2) = 1$ and $n_1 | a_2 n_2$, it follows that $n_1 | a_2$. We must have $a_2 = 0$; otherwise $j = k + a_2 n_2 > n$, a contradiction. Thus, $a_1 = a_2 = 0$ and $j = k$. The inverse of the C mapping is simple to prescribe.

Theorem 4.1.3 *Suppose* $\gcd(n_1, n_2) = 1$ *and* $n = n_1 n_2$. *If the integers* j_1 *and* j_2 *satisfy* $0 \le j_1 \le n_1 - 1$ *and* $0 \le j_2 \le n_2 - 1$, *then the function* C^{-1} *defined by*

$$C^{-1}(j_1, j_2) = <\ \alpha_1 n_2 j_1 + \alpha_2 n_1 j_2\ >_n$$

is the inverse of the mapping C, *where* $\alpha_2 n_1 = \beta_1 n_2 + 1$ *and* $\alpha_1 n_2 = \beta_2 n_1 + 1$, *as in Theorem 4.1.2.*

Proof. Suppose $0 \leq j \leq n - 1$. Define the integer a_1 by $j = a_1 n_1 + <j>_{n_1}$ and the integer a_2 by $j = a_2 n_2 + <j>_{n_2}$. Thus,

$$
\begin{aligned}
C^{-1}(C(j)) &= C^{-1}(j - a_1 n_1, j - a_2 n_2) \\
&= <\alpha_1 n_2 (j - a_1 n_1) + \alpha_2 n_1 (j - a_2 n_2) >_n \\
&= <\alpha_1 n_2 j + \alpha_2 n_1 j >_n = <j(\alpha_1 n_2 + \alpha_2 n_1) >_n .
\end{aligned}
$$

But from (4.1.7) we know $\alpha_1 n_2 + \alpha_2 n_1 = n + 1$ and so $C^{-1}(C(j)) = j$. $\quad\square$

Since the C-mapping is invertible, we can use it to define a blocking permutation:

$$
\Gamma_{n_2, n} \equiv Q_C .
$$

In other words,

$$
y = \Gamma_{n_2, n}^T x \quad \Leftrightarrow \quad y(n_1 <j>_{n_2} + <j>_{n_1}) = x(j) . \tag{4.1.8}
$$

In array language, $x(j)$ becomes entry $(<j>_{n_1}, <j>_{n_2})$ of $y_{n_1 \times n_2}$. For example, in the case where $(n_1, n_2) = (3, 5)$

$$
\left[\Gamma_{5,15}^T x \right]_{3 \times 5} = \begin{bmatrix} x_0 & x_6 & x_{12} & x_3 & x_9 \\ x_{10} & x_1 & x_7 & x_{13} & x_4 \\ x_5 & x_{11} & x_2 & x_8 & x_{14} \end{bmatrix} .
$$

Consider the computation of $\Gamma_{n_2, n}^T x$ and set $Y(0:n_1 - 1, 0:n_2 - 1) = \left[\Gamma_{n_2, n}^T x \right]_{n_1 \times n_2}$. Since

$$
Y(j_1, j_2) = x(< \alpha_1 n_2 j_1 + \alpha_2 n_1 j_2 >_n)
$$

and

$$
\begin{aligned}
Y(<j_1 + 1>_{n_1}, <j_2 + 1>_{n_2}) &= x(<\alpha_1 n_2 (j_1 + 1) + \alpha_2 n_1 (j_2 + 1) >_n) \\
&= x(<\alpha_1 n_2 j_1 + \alpha_2 n_1 j_2 + (n + 1) >_n) \\
&= x(<\alpha_1 n_2 j_1 + \alpha_2 n_1 j_2 + 1 >_n)
\end{aligned}
$$

we see that if $x(k) = Y(j_1, j_2)$, then $x(k + 1) = Y(<j_1 + 1>_{n_1}, <j_2 + 1>_{n_2})$. By exploiting this relationship, we obtain the following algorithm:

Algorithm 4.1.1 If $x \in \mathbb{C}^n$ and $n = n_1 n_2$ with $\gcd(n_1, n_2) = 1$, then the following algorithm computes $y = \Gamma_{n_2, n}^T x$. The integer α_1 is defined by Theorem 4.1.2.

```
for j = 0:n₁ - 1
        index(j) ← < α₁n₂j >ₙ
end
for k = 0:n₂ - 1
        y(kn₁:(k + 1)n₁ - 1) ← x(index)
        a ← index(n₁ - 1)
        for j = (n₁ - 1): - 1:1
                index(j) ← index(j - 1) + 1
        end
        index(0) ← a + 1
end
```

The first j-loop generates the zeroth column of $\left[\Gamma_{n_2,n}^T x\right]_{n_1 \times n_2}$. The x-indices associated with the next column involve a shift-add of the current indices.

A discussion of this indexing scheme may be found in Temperton (1985). We remark that if we replace the y-assignment by $y(index) \leftarrow x(kn_1:(k+1)n_1 - 1)$, then the algorithm computes $y = \Gamma_{n_2,n} x$.

4.1.6   The R Mapping and the Permutation $\Upsilon_{n_2,n}$

Suppose $\gcd(n_1, n_2) = 1$ and that $n = n_1 n_2$. The *Ruritanian mapping*

$$\{0, 1 \ldots, n - 1\} \overset{R}{\rightarrow} \{0, 1 \ldots, n_1 - 1\} \times \{0, 1 \ldots, n_2 - 1\}$$

is defined by

$$R(j) = (\; <j\alpha_1>_{n_1}, \; <j\alpha_2>_{n_2}\;),$$

where α_1 and α_2 are defined by $\alpha_2 n_1 = \beta_1 n_2 + 1$ and $\alpha_1 n_2 = \beta_2 n_1 + 1$, as in Theorem 4.1.2. It is easy to verify that the "R mapping" is invertible. The following result gives a recipe for the inverse.

Theorem 4.1.4 *Suppose* $\gcd(n_1, n_2) = 1$ *and* $n = n_1 n_2$. *If the integers* j_1 *and* j_2 *satisfy* $0 \le j_1 \le n_1 - 1$ *and* $0 \le j_2 \le n_2 - 1$, *then the function* R^{-1}, *defined by*

$$R^{-1}(j_1, j_2) = <n_2 j_1 + n_1 j_2>_n,$$

is the inverse of the Ruritanian mapping.

Proof. Suppose $0 \le j \le n - 1$ and let α_1 and α_2 be given by Theorem 4.1.2. Define a_1 by $j\alpha_1 = a_1 n_1 + <j\alpha_1>_{n_1}$ and a_2 by $j\alpha_2 = a_2 n_2 + <j\alpha_2>_{n_2}$. Thus,

$$
\begin{aligned}
R^{-1}(R(j)) &= R^{-1}(j\alpha_1 - a_1 n_1, j\alpha_2 - a_2 n_2) \\
&= <n_2(j\alpha_1 - a_1 n_1) + n_1(j\alpha_2 - a_2 n_2)>_n \\
&= <\alpha_1 n_2 j + \alpha_2 n_1 j>_n \\
&= <(\alpha_1 n_2 + \alpha_2 n_1)j>_n .
\end{aligned}
$$

But from (4.1.7) we know that $\alpha_1 n_2 + \alpha_2 n_1 = n + 1$, and so $R^{-1}(R(j)) = j$.   □

Since the R-mapping is invertible, we can use it to define a blocking permutation $\Upsilon_{n_2,n} \equiv Q_R$. Thus,

$$y = \Upsilon_{n_2,n}^T x \quad \Leftrightarrow \quad y(<j\alpha_2>_{n_2} n_1 + <j\alpha_1>_{n_1}) = x(j).$$

In array terms, $x(j)$ becomes entry $(<j\alpha_1>_{n_1}, <j\alpha_2>_{n_2})$ of $y_{n_1 \times n_2}$, e.g.,

$$\left[\Upsilon_{5,15}^T x\right]_{3 \times 5} = \begin{bmatrix} x_0 & x_3 & x_6 & x_9 & x_{12} \\ x_5 & x_8 & x_{11} & x_{14} & x_2 \\ x_{10} & x_{13} & x_1 & x_4 & x_7 \end{bmatrix}.$$

If

$$Y(0:n_1 - 1, 0:n_2 - 1) = \left[\Upsilon_{n_2,n}^T x\right]_{n_1 \times n_2},$$

then it is not hard to verify that

$$Y(j_1, j_2) = x(k) \quad \Leftrightarrow \quad Y(j_1, j_2 + 1) = x(<k + n_1>_n) .$$

Thus, simple mod n arithmetic is required to generate the x-indices as we move from left to right across $\left[\Upsilon_{n_2,n}^T x\right]_{n_1 \times n_2}$. We therefore obtain the following algorithm.

Algorithm 4.1.2 If $x \in \mathbb{C}^n$ and $n = n_1 n_2$ with $\gcd(n_1, n_2) = 1$, then the following algorithm computes $y = \Upsilon_{n_2,n}^T x$:

$$index(0{:}n_1 - 1) \leftarrow 0{:}n_2{:}n - 1$$
$$\textbf{for } k = 0{:}n_2 - 1$$
$$\quad y(kn_1{:}(k+1)n_1 - 1) \leftarrow x(index)$$
$$\quad \textbf{for } j = 0{:}n_1 - 1$$
$$\quad\quad index(j) \leftarrow <index(j) + n_1>_n$$
$$\quad \textbf{end}$$
$$\textbf{end}$$

See Temperton (1985) for further discussion. In order to obtain an algorithm that computes $y = \Upsilon_{n_2,n} x$, replace the y-assignment with $y(index) \leftarrow x(kn_1{:}(k+1)n_1 - 1)$.

4.1.7 A Prime Factor Splitting

We now show that if we permute the rows and columns of F_n according to the C and R mappings, then a Kronecker block structure emerges.

Theorem 4.1.5 If $n = n_1 n_2$ and $\gcd(n_1, n_2) = 1$, then

$$\Gamma_{n_2,n}^T F_n \Upsilon_{n_2,n} = F_{n_2} \otimes F_{n_1}.$$

Proof. From Theorem 4.1.3 we see that an entry in row $k_2 n_1 + k_1$ of $\Gamma_{n_2,n}^T F_n \Upsilon_{n_2,n}$ is an entry from row $<\alpha_2 n_1 k_2 + \alpha_1 n_2 k_1>_n$ of F_n. Here, $0 \le k_1 \le n_1 - 1$, $0 \le k_2 \le n_2 - 1$, and the α's are defined by Theorem 4.1.2.

Likewise, by invoking Theorem 4.1.4 it can be shown that an entry in column $j_2 n_1 + j_1$ of $\Gamma_{n_2,n}^T F_n \Upsilon_{n_2,n}$ is an entry from column $<j_1 n_2 + j_2 n_1>_n$ of F_n. Here, $0 \le j_1 \le n_1 - 1$ and $0 \le j_2 \le n_2 - 1$. It follows that

$$\begin{aligned} \left[\Gamma_{n_2,n}^T F_n \Upsilon_{n_2,n}\right]_{k_2 n_1 + k_1, j_2 n_1 + j_1} &= \omega_n^{(\alpha_2 n_1 k_2 + \alpha_1 n_2 k_1)(n_1 j_2 + n_2 j_1)} \\ &= \omega_n^{\alpha_2 n_1 k_2 n_1 j_2} \, \omega_n^{\alpha_1 n_2 k_1 n_2 j_1} \\ &= \omega_{n_2}^{\alpha_2 n_1 k_2 j_2} \, \omega_{n_1}^{\alpha_1 n_2 k_1 j_1} \\ &= \omega_{n_2}^{(\beta_1 n_2 + 1)k_2 j_2} \, \omega_{n_1}^{(\beta_2 n_1 + 1)k_1 j_1} \\ &= \omega_{n_2}^{k_2 j_2} \, \omega_{n_1}^{k_1 j_1}. \end{aligned}$$

But this is precisely entry $(k_2 n_1 + k_1, j_2 n_1 + j_1)$ of $F_{n_2} \otimes F_{n_1}$. $\square$

Note that by taking transposes we also have $\Upsilon_{n_2,n}^T F_n \Gamma_{n_2,n} = F_{n_2} \otimes F_{n_1}$.

4.1.8 Prime Factor Framework

Suppose the components of $\rho = (n_1, n_2, n_3)$ are pairwise relatively prime. If $n = n_1 n_2 n_3$ and $m_1 = n_2 n_3$, then by applying the prime factor splitting twice we obtain

$$\Gamma_{m_1,n}^T F_n \Upsilon_{m_1,n} = F_{m_1} \otimes F_{n_1},$$

$$\Gamma_{n_3,m_1}^T F_{m_1} \Upsilon_{n_3,m_1} = F_{n_3} \otimes F_{n_2}.$$

From these formulae it is not too hard to show that

$$\Gamma_\rho^T F_n \Upsilon_\rho \;=\; F_{n_3} \otimes F_{n_2} \otimes F_{n_1} \,,$$

where $\Gamma_\rho = \Gamma_{m_1,n}(\Gamma_{n_3,m_1} \otimes I_{n_1})$ and $\Upsilon_\rho = \Upsilon_{m_1,n}(\Upsilon_{n_3,m_1} \otimes I_{n_1})$. This suggests that if $n = n_1 \cdots n_t$ and the n_j are pairwise relatively prime, then we can permute F_n to a t-fold Kronecker product, thereby reducing the n-point DFT to a t-dimensional DFT.

Theorem 4.1.6 *If the components of $\rho = [\, n_1, \ldots, n_t \,]$ are pairwise relatively prime and $n = n_1 \cdots n_t$, then there exist permutation matrices Γ_ρ and Υ_ρ such that*

$$\Gamma_\rho^T F_n \Upsilon_\rho \;=\; F_{n_t} \otimes \cdots F_{n_1} \,.$$

Proof. We use induction on t, noting that the case $t = 2$ is covered by Theorem 4.1.5. Assume that we have the reduction

$$\Gamma_{\rho_1}^T F_{m_1} \Upsilon_{\rho_1} \;=\; F_{n_t} \otimes \cdots \otimes F_{n_2} \,,$$

where $m_1 = n_2 \cdots n_t$ and Γ_{ρ_1} and Υ_{ρ_1} are m_1-by-m_1 permutations. The theorem follows by substituting this into the factorization

$$F_n \;=\; \Gamma_{m_1,n}(F_{m_1} \otimes F_{n_1})\Upsilon_{m_1,n}^T$$

and defining $\Gamma_\rho = \Gamma_{m_1,n}(\Gamma_{\rho_1} \otimes I_{n_1})$ and $\Upsilon_\rho = \Upsilon_{m_1,n}(\Upsilon_{\rho_1} \otimes I_{n_1})$.   □

We leave it as an exercise to verify that

$$\Gamma_\rho \;=\; U_1 \cdots U_{t-1}, \qquad U_q = \Gamma_{\mu_q,\mu_{q-1}} \otimes I_{n/\mu_{q-1}} \,, \qquad (4.1.9)$$

$$\Upsilon_\rho \;=\; V_1 \cdots V_{t-1}, \qquad V_q = \Upsilon_{\mu_q,\mu_{q-1}} \otimes I_{n/\mu_{q-1}} \,, \qquad (4.1.10)$$

where $\mu_q = n_{q+1} \cdots n_t$ for $q = 0{:}t - 1$.

Algorithm 4.1.3 Suppose $n = n_1 \cdots n_t$ and that the n_q are pairwise relatively prime. If Γ_ρ and Υ_ρ are defined by (4.1.9)–(4.1.10), then the following algorithm overwrites $x \in \mathbb{C}^n$ with $F_n x$:

$$
\begin{aligned}
&x \leftarrow \Upsilon_\rho^T x \\
&\textbf{for}\quad q = 1{:}t \\
&\qquad N_1 \leftarrow n_1 \cdots n_{q-1} \\
&\qquad N_2 \leftarrow n_q \\
&\qquad N_3 \leftarrow n_{q+1} \cdots n_t \\
&\qquad x \leftarrow (I_{N_3} \otimes F_{N_2} \otimes I_{N_1})x \\
&\textbf{end} \\
&x \leftarrow \Gamma_\rho x
\end{aligned}
$$

The prime factor algorithm was first introduced by Good (1958). Important follow-up papers include those by Kolba and Parks (1977) and Winograd (1978). Temperton discusses the implementation of the prime factor framework on vector machines in a series of papers (1983c)–(1988c).

4.1.9 Handling General n

The implementation of the prime factor algorithm requires a library of DFT "modules." In a typical situation, optimized codes for DFTs of length 2, 3, 4, 5, 7, 8, 9, and 16 are crafted. In §4.1.13 we detail the case $p = 5$.

Suppose that we wish to compute the DFT $y = F_n x$ using the prime factor framework "as much as possible." One approach is to factor $n = p_1 \cdots p_t$, where each p_q is a product of relatively prime integers taken from the set of available library modules. For example, if $n = 2^6 \cdot 3^4 \cdot 5 \cdot 7^3 = 8890560$, then we could set $p_1 = 5 \cdot 7 \cdot 9 \cdot 16$, $p_2 = 4 \cdot 7 \cdot 9$, and $p_3 = 7$. We then invoke any of our mixed-radix procedures with $\rho = [\, p_1, \ldots, p_t \,]$ and DFT computations of length $p_1, \ldots, p_t$ arise. For example, in the Cooley–Tukey framework the qth step involves the calculations

$$x \leftarrow \mathrm{diag}(I_{L_*}, \Omega_{p_q, L_*}, \ldots, \Omega_{p_q, L_*}^{p_q-1}) x,$$

$$x_{L \times r} \leftarrow (F_{p_q} \otimes I_{L_*}) x_{L \times r}$$

where $L = p_q L_*$, $L_* = p_1 \cdots p_{q-1}$, and $r = n/L$. (See §2.3.1.) The prime factor framework can thus be used to carry out the length-p_q, multiple DFT computations.

4.1.10 Rotated DFTs

An implication of having both Γ and Υ permutations involved in our prime factor framework is that it precludes the possibility of an in-place implementation. To appreciate this point, consider the case $(n_1, n_2) = (3, 5)$. Since $y = F_{15} x$ implies

$$\Gamma_{5,15}^T y = (F_5 \otimes F_3) \Upsilon_{5,15}^T x ,$$

we have $\left[\Gamma_{5,15}^T y \right]_{3 \times 5} \leftarrow F_3 \left[\Upsilon_{5,15}^T x \right]_{3 \times 5} F_5$, i.e.,

$$\begin{bmatrix} y_0 & y_6 & y_{12} & y_3 & y_9 \\ y_{10} & y_1 & y_7 & y_{13} & y_4 \\ y_5 & y_{11} & y_2 & y_8 & y_{14} \end{bmatrix} \leftarrow F_3 \begin{bmatrix} x_0 & x_3 & x_6 & x_9 & x_{12} \\ x_5 & x_8 & x_{11} & x_{14} & x_2 \\ x_{10} & x_{13} & x_1 & x_4 & x_7 \end{bmatrix} F_5 .$$

It is clear that if we identify y with x, then a length-n workspace would be required.

A way around this problem proposed by Temperton (1985) is to "live" with just the Γ permutation. To that end let us examine the block structure of $\Gamma_{n_2,n}^T F_n \Gamma_{n_2,n}$. From Theorem 4.1.3 we see that an entry in row $k_2 n_1 + k_1$ of $\Gamma_{n_2,n}^T F_n \Gamma_{n_2,n}$ is an entry from row $< \alpha_2 n_1 k_2 + \alpha_1 n_2 k_1 >_n$ of F_n. Here, $0 \le k_1 \le n_1 - 1$, $0 \le k_2 \le n_2 - 1$, and the α's are defined by Theorem 4.1.2.

Likewise, by invoking Theorem 4.1.3 again it can be shown that an entry in column $j_2 n_1 + j_1$ of $\Gamma_{n_2,n}^T F_n \Gamma_{n_2,n}$ is an entry from column $< \alpha_2 n_1 j_2 + \alpha_1 n_2 j_1 >_n$ of F_n. Here, $0 \le j_1 \le n_1 - 1$, $0 \le j_2 \le n_2 - 1$, and the α's are defined by Theorem 4.1.2. Thus,

$$\begin{aligned} \left[\Gamma_{n_2,n}^T F_n \Gamma_{n_2,n} \right]_{k_2 n_1 + k_1, j_2 n_1 + j_1} &= \omega_n^{(\alpha_2 n_1 k_2 + \alpha_1 n_2 k_1)(\alpha_2 n_1 j_2 + \alpha_1 n_2 j_1)} \\ &= \omega_n^{\alpha_2 n_1 k_2 \alpha_2 n_1 j_2} \, \omega_n^{\alpha_1 n_2 k_1 \alpha_1 n_2 j_1} \\ &= \omega_{n_2}^{\alpha_2 k_2 \alpha_2 n_1 j_2} \, \omega_{n_1}^{\alpha_1 k_1 \alpha_1 n_2 j_1} \\ &= \omega_{n_2}^{\alpha_2 k_2 (\beta_1 n_2 + 1) j_2} \, \omega_{n_1}^{\alpha_1 k_1 (\beta_2 n_1 + 1) j_1} \\ &= \omega_{n_2}^{\alpha_2 k_2 j_2} \, \omega_{n_1}^{\alpha_1 k_1 j_1}, \end{aligned}$$

where we have used Theorem 4.1.2. If we define the *rotated DFT matrix* $F_p^{(r)}$ by

$$\left[F_p^{(r)}\right]_{kj} = \omega_p^{kjr},$$

then

$$\omega_{n_2}^{\alpha_2 k_2 j_2} \omega_{n_1}^{\alpha_1 k_1 j_1} = \left[F_{n_2}^{(\alpha_2)} \otimes F_{n_1}^{(\alpha_1)}\right]_{k_2 n_1 + k_1, j_2 n_1 + j_1}$$

and we have established the following result.

Lemma 4.1.7 *If* $\gcd(n_1, n_2) = 1$ *and* $n = n_1 n_2$, *then*

$$\Gamma_{n_2,n}^T F_n \Gamma_{n_2,n} = F_{n_2}^{(\alpha_2)} \otimes F_{n_1}^{(\alpha_1)},$$

where α_1 *and* α_2 *are prescribed by Theorem 4.1.2.*

Let us examine the action of $F_p^{(r)}$, assuming that $\gcd(r, p) = 1$, as is the case in the above splitting. If $y^{(r)} = F_p^{(r)} x$, then it follows that

$$y^{(r)}(k) = [F_p x]_{<kr>_p}.$$

It can be shown that the function $\sigma(k) = <kr>_p$ is a permutation on $\{0, 1, \ldots, p-1\}$. Thus, if $y = F_p x$ then

$$y^{(r)}(k) = y(\sigma(k)),$$

i.e., $y^{(r)}$ is a permutation of y. This is why we refer to $F_p^{(r)}$ as a *rotated* DFT matrix.

Let us return to the $(n_1, n_2) = (3, 5)$ example in which $\alpha_1 = \alpha_2 = 2$. In array form the computation of $y = F_{15} x$ is specified by

$$\left[\Gamma_{5,15}^T y\right]_{3 \times 5} \leftarrow F_3^{(2)} \left[\Gamma_{5,15}^T x\right]_{3 \times 5} F_5^{(2)}$$

i.e.,

$$\begin{bmatrix} y_0 & y_6 & y_{12} & y_3 & y_9 \\ y_{10} & y_1 & y_7 & y_{13} & y_4 \\ y_5 & y_{11} & y_2 & y_8 & y_{14} \end{bmatrix} \leftarrow F_3^{(2)} \begin{bmatrix} x_0 & x_6 & x_{12} & x_3 & x_9 \\ x_{10} & x_1 & x_7 & x_{13} & x_4 \\ x_5 & x_{11} & x_2 & x_8 & x_{14} \end{bmatrix} F_5^{(2)}.$$

An in-place, in-order algorithm could proceed as follows. First compute the column DFTs:

$$\begin{bmatrix} x_0 \\ x_{10} \\ x_5 \end{bmatrix} \leftarrow F_3^{(2)} \begin{bmatrix} x_0 \\ x_{10} \\ x_5 \end{bmatrix}, \ldots, \begin{bmatrix} x_9 \\ x_4 \\ x_{14} \end{bmatrix} \leftarrow F_3^{(2)} \begin{bmatrix} x_9 \\ x_4 \\ x_{14} \end{bmatrix}.$$

Second, compute all the row DFTs:

$$\begin{bmatrix} x_0 \\ x_6 \\ x_{12} \\ x_3 \\ x_9 \end{bmatrix} \leftarrow F_5^{(2)} \begin{bmatrix} x_0 \\ x_6 \\ x_{12} \\ x_3 \\ x_9 \end{bmatrix}, \ldots, \begin{bmatrix} x_5 \\ x_{11} \\ x_2 \\ x_8 \\ x_{14} \end{bmatrix} \leftarrow F_5^{(2)} \begin{bmatrix} x_5 \\ x_{11} \\ x_2 \\ x_8 \\ x_{14} \end{bmatrix}.$$

It turns out that design of a rotated module is only slightly more complicated than the design of "ordinary" DFT modules. (See Temperton (1985).)

4.1.11 A Rotated DFT Factorization

Predictably we derive a generalization of the rotated DFT splitting that handles the case when n is the product of t pairwise relatively prime integers. Two lemmas facilitate the derivation. The first is a slight rearrangement of Lemma 4.1.7.

Lemma 4.1.8 *Suppose* $n = n_1 n_2$ *and that* $\gcd(n_1, n_2) = 1$. *If* $\alpha_1 n_2 = \beta_2 n_1 + 1$ *and* $\alpha_2 n_1 = \beta_1 n_2 + 1$, *as in Theorem 4.1.2, then*

$$F_n = \left(\Gamma_{n_1,n} (I_{n_1} \otimes F_{n_2}^{(\alpha_2)}) \Gamma_{n_1,n}^T \right) \left(\Gamma_{n_2,n} (I_{n_2} \otimes F_{n_1}^{(\alpha_1)}) \Gamma_{n_2,n}^T \right) .$$

Proof. First observe from Lemma 4.1.7 that

$$
\begin{aligned}
F_n &= \Gamma_{n_2,n} (F_{n_2}^{(\alpha_2)} \otimes F_{n_1}^{(\alpha_1)}) \Gamma_{n_2,n}^T \\
&= \left(\Gamma_{n_2,n} (F_{n_2}^{(\alpha_2)} \otimes I_{n_1}) \Gamma_{n_2,n}^T \right) \left(\Gamma_{n_2,n} (I_{n_2} \otimes F_{n_1}^{(\alpha_1)}) \Gamma_{n_2,n}^T \right) .
\end{aligned}
$$

From Kron8

$$(F_{n_2}^{(\alpha_2)} \otimes I_{n_1}) = \Pi_{n_2,n}^T (I_{n_1} \otimes F_{n_2}^{(\alpha_2)}) \Pi_{n_2,n}$$

and so

$$F_n = \left(\Gamma_{n_2,n} \Pi_{n_2,n}^T (I_{n_1} \otimes F_{n_2}^{(\alpha_2)}) \Pi_{n_2,n} \Gamma_{n_2,n}^T \right) \left(\Gamma_{n_2,n} (I_{n_2} \otimes F_{n_1}^{(\alpha_1)}) \Gamma_{n_2,n}^T \right) .$$

The lemma follows, since

$$\left[\Gamma_{n_2,n}^T x \right]_{n_1 \times n_2}^T = \left[\Gamma_{n_1,n}^T x \right]_{n_2 \times n_1}$$

can be used to show that $\Gamma_{n_1,n} = \Gamma_{n_2,n} \Pi_{n_2,n}^T$. $\square$

The next result is an identity involving the Γ permutation.

Lemma 4.1.9 *If* $n = n_1 n_q \tilde{m}_q$ *and the three factors are pairwise relatively prime, then*

$$\left(I_{n_1} \otimes \Gamma_{\tilde{m}_q, m_1}^T \right) \Gamma_{n_1,n}^T = \left(\Gamma_{n_1, m_q}^T \otimes I_{n_q} \right) \Gamma_{m_q, n}^T ,$$

where $m_q = n_1 \tilde{m}_q$ *and* $m_1 = \tilde{m}_q n_q$.

Proof. We use the easily established fact that $<< j >_{ab}>_a = < j >_a$. Let us trace what happens to $x(j)$ when both sides of the above matrix equation are applied to $x \in \mathbb{C}^n$. If $y = \Gamma_{n_1,n}^T x$ and $z = \left(I_{n_1} \otimes \Gamma_{\tilde{m}_q, m_1}^T \right) y$, then by using (4.1.8) we obtain

$$
\begin{aligned}
x(j) &= y(< j >_{n_1} m_1 + < j >_{m_1}) \\
&= z \left(< j >_{n_1} m_1 + << j >_{m_1} >_{\tilde{m}_q} n_q + << j >_{m_1} >_{n_q} \right) \\
&= z \left(< j >_{n_1} m_1 + < j >_{\tilde{m}_q} n_q + < j >_{n_q} \right) .
\end{aligned}
$$

To examine the action of the right-hand side, set $u = \Gamma_{m_q, n}^T x$ and $v = \left(\Gamma_{n_1, m_q}^T \otimes I_{n_q} \right) u$. It follows that

$$
\begin{aligned}
x(j) &= u \left(< j >_{m_q} n_q + < j >_{n_q} \right) \\
&= v \left((<< j >_{m_q} >_{n_1} \tilde{m}_q + << j >_{m_q} >_{\tilde{m}_q}) n_q + < j >_{n_q} \right) \\
&= v \left((< j >_{n_1} \tilde{m}_q + < j >_{\tilde{m}_q}) n_q + < j >_{n_q} \right) \\
&= v \left(< j >_{n_1} m_1 + < j >_{\tilde{m}_q} n_q + < j >_{n_q} \right) .
\end{aligned}
$$

This shows that $v = z$, from which the lemma follows. $\square$

We are now set to establish the main result.

Theorem 4.1.10 *Suppose $n = n_1 \cdots n_t$ and that the n_j are pairwise relatively prime. For $q = 1{:}t$ set $m_q = n/n_q$ and assume from Theorem 4.1.2 that*

$$\alpha_q m_q = \beta_q n_q + 1,$$

where $0 \le \alpha_q \le n_q - 1$, $0 \le \beta_q \le m_q - 1$, and $\gcd(\alpha_q, n_q) = 1$. If

$$T_q = \Gamma_{m_q,n}(I_{m_q} \otimes F_{n_q}^{(\alpha_q)})\Gamma_{m_q,n}^T$$

for $q = 1{:}t$, then $F_n = T_t \cdots T_1$.

Proof. Since $n = n_1 m_1$, we can apply Lemma 4.1.8 with $n_2 = m_1$ and obtain

$$F_n = \left(\Gamma_{n_1,n}(I_{n_1} \otimes F_{m_1}^{(\alpha)})\Gamma_{n_1,n}^T\right) T_1, \tag{4.1.11}$$

where

$$\alpha_1 m_1 = \beta_1 n_1 + 1, \tag{4.1.12}$$
$$\alpha n_1 = \beta m_1 + 1. \tag{4.1.13}$$

By induction on t we may assume that F_{m_1} has the factorization

$$F_{m_1} = S_t \cdots S_2,$$

where for $q = 2{:}t$

$$S_q = \Gamma_{\tilde{m}_q,m_1}(I_{\tilde{m}_q} \otimes F_{n_q}^{(\tilde{\alpha}_q)})\Gamma_{\tilde{m}_q,m_1}^T, \tag{4.1.14}$$
$$\tilde{m}_q = m_1/n_q, \tag{4.1.15}$$
$$\tilde{\alpha}_q \tilde{m}_q = \tilde{\beta}_q n_q + 1, \tag{4.1.16}$$

with $0 \le \tilde{\alpha}_q \le n_q - 1$, $0 \le \tilde{\beta}_q \le \tilde{m}_q - 1$, and $\gcd(\tilde{\alpha}_q, n_q) = 1$. It is easy to verify that

$$F_{m_1}^{(\alpha)} = S_t^{(\alpha)} \cdots S_2^{(\alpha)}, \tag{4.1.17}$$

where

$$S_q^{(\alpha)} = \Gamma_{\tilde{m}_q,m_1}(I_{\tilde{m}_q} \otimes F_{n_q}^{(\alpha\tilde{\alpha}_q)})\Gamma_{\tilde{m}_q,m_1}^T. \tag{4.1.18}$$

It follows that

$$\begin{aligned}
F_n &= \Gamma_{n_1,n}(I_{n_1} \otimes F_{m_1}^{(\alpha)})\Gamma_{n_1,n}^T T_1 \\
&= \Gamma_{n_1,n}(I_{n_1} \otimes S_t^{(\alpha)} \cdots S_2^{(\alpha)})\Gamma_{n_1,n}^T T_1 \\
&= \tilde{T}_t \cdots \tilde{T}_2 T_1,
\end{aligned}$$

where $\tilde{T}_q = \Gamma_{n_1,n}(I_{n_1} \otimes S_q^{(\alpha)})\Gamma_{n_1,n}^T$. We must show that $\tilde{T}_q = T_q$. Using (4.1.14), Lemma 4.1.9, and the fact that $n_1 \tilde{m}_q = m_q$, we have

$$\begin{aligned}
\tilde{T}_q &= \Gamma_{n_1,n}(I_{n_1} \otimes \Gamma_{\tilde{m}_q,m_1})\left(I_{n_1} \otimes I_{\tilde{m}_q} \otimes F_{n_q}^{(\alpha\tilde{\alpha}_q)}\right)(I_{n_1} \otimes \Gamma_{\tilde{m}_q,m_1})^T \Gamma_{n_1,n}^T \\
&= \Gamma_{m_q,n}\left(\Gamma_{n_1,m_q} \otimes I_{n_q}\right)\left(I_{m_q} \otimes F_{n_q}^{(\alpha\tilde{\alpha}_q)}\right)\left(\Gamma_{n_1,m_q} \otimes I_{n_q}\right)^T \Gamma_{m_q,n}^T \\
&= \Gamma_{m_q,n}\left(I_{m_q} \otimes F_{n_q}^{(\alpha\tilde{\alpha}_q)}\right)\Gamma_{m_q,n}^T.
\end{aligned}$$

By multiplying (4.1.13) and (4.1.16) we see that

$$(\alpha n_1)(\tilde{\alpha}_q \tilde{m}_q) = (\beta m_1 + 1)(\tilde{\beta}_q n_q + 1).$$

Since $n_1 \tilde{m}_q = m_q$ and $m_1 = n_q \tilde{m}_q$ we have

$$
\begin{aligned}
(\alpha\tilde{\alpha}_q)m_q &= (\beta m_1 + 1)\tilde{\beta}_q n_q + \beta m_1 + 1 \\
&= \left((\beta m_1 + 1)\tilde{\beta}_q + \beta\tilde{m}_q\right)n_q + 1.
\end{aligned}
$$

The uniqueness of α_q in Theorem 4.1.2 implies that $\alpha\tilde{\alpha}_q = \alpha_q$ and so $\tilde{T}_q = T_q$. $\square$

Based upon this factorization, we have the following in-place, in-order FFT.

Algorithm 4.1.4 Suppose $n = n_1 \cdots n_t$ and that the n_q are pairwise relatively prime. Assume that $\alpha_q m_q = \beta_q n_q + 1$ with $\gcd(\alpha_q, n_q)=1$ for $q = 1{:}t$. The following algorithm overwrites $x \in \mathbb{C}^n$ with $F_n x$:

$$
\begin{aligned}
&\textbf{for } q = 1{:}t \\
&\quad \textbf{for } j = 0{:}n_q - 1 \\
&\quad\quad index(j) \leftarrow \; <\alpha_j n_q j>_n \\
&\quad \textbf{end} \\
&\quad \textbf{for } k = 0{:}m_q - 1 \\
&\quad\quad x(index) \leftarrow F_{n_q}^{(\alpha_q)} x(index) \\
&\quad\quad a \leftarrow index(n_q - 1) \\
&\quad\quad \textbf{for } j = (n_q - 1){:}-1{:}1 \\
&\quad\quad\quad index(j) \leftarrow index(j-1) + 1 \\
&\quad\quad \textbf{end} \\
&\quad\quad index(0) \leftarrow a + 1 \\
&\quad \textbf{end} \\
&\textbf{end}
\end{aligned}
$$

See Temperton (1985) for additional details on implementation.

4.1.12   The Winograd Idea

An alternative way to organize the prime factor algorithm is due to Winograd (1978). This approach involves minimizing the number of multiplications. We say that

$$
F_p = B_p M_p A_p \qquad
\left\{
\begin{aligned}
B_p &\in \mathbb{R}^{p \times s_p} \\
M_p &\in \mathbb{C}^{s_p \times s_p} \\
A_p &\in \mathbb{R}^{s_p \times p}
\end{aligned}
\right.
$$

is a *Winograd factorization* of F_p if the entries of A_p and B_p are taken from the set $\{-1, 0, 1\}$ and if M_p is diagonal with individual diagonal entries that are either pure real or pure imaginary. Winograd factorizations for many prime order DFT matrices have been worked out. Note that if $F_n = \Gamma_\rho(F_{n_t} \otimes \cdots \otimes F_{n_1})\Upsilon_\rho^T$ and we have Winograd factorizations $F_{n_q} = B_{n_q} M_{n_q} A_{n_q}$ for $q = 1{:}t$, then from Kron1

$$F_n = \Gamma_\rho B_\rho M_\rho A_\rho \Upsilon_\rho^T,$$

where

$$A_\rho = A_{n_t} \otimes \cdots \otimes A_{n_1},$$
$$M_\rho = M_{n_t} \otimes \cdots \otimes M_{n_1},$$
$$B_\rho = B_{n_t} \otimes \cdots \otimes B_{n_1}.$$

Note that the nonzero entries in A_ρ and B_ρ are ± 1 and that M_ρ is diagonal with entries that are either real or imaginary. Thus, the computation $x \leftarrow F_n x$ may proceed as follows:

$$x \leftarrow \Upsilon_\rho^T x$$
$$x \leftarrow A_\rho x \quad \text{(Only Additions)}$$
$$x \leftarrow M_\rho x \quad \text{(Only Real Multiplications)}$$
$$x \leftarrow B_\rho^T x \quad \text{(Only Additions)}$$
$$x \leftarrow \Gamma_\rho x.$$

Further factorizations along this line are discussed in Johnson and Burrus (1983).

4.1.13   Prime Order DFT Modules ($p = 5$)

The design of the prime order DFT modules is critical to the success of the prime factor algorithm. It is therefore appropriate to spend a little time to see what is involved. We use the case of $p = 5$ for purposes of illustration. To begin with, we have

$$F_5 = \begin{bmatrix} 1 & 1 & 1 & 1 & 1 \\ 1 & \omega & \omega^2 & \omega^3 & \omega^4 \\ 1 & \omega^2 & \omega^4 & \omega & \omega^3 \\ 1 & \omega^3 & \omega & \omega^4 & \omega^2 \\ 1 & \omega^4 & \omega^3 & \omega^2 & \omega \end{bmatrix},$$

where

$$\omega = c_1 - is_1, \qquad \omega^2 = c_2 - is_2, \qquad \omega^3 = c_2 + is_2, \qquad \omega^4 = c_1 + is_1,$$

with

$$c_1 = \cos(\theta), \qquad s_1 = \sin(\theta), \qquad \theta = \frac{2\pi}{5}.$$
$$c_2 = \cos(2\theta), \qquad s_2 = \sin(2\theta),$$

Since the real and imaginary parts of F_5 are given by

$$F_5^R = \begin{bmatrix} 1 & 1 & 1 & 1 & 1 \\ 1 & c_1 & c_2 & c_2 & c_1 \\ 1 & c_2 & c_1 & c_1 & c_2 \\ 1 & c_2 & c_1 & c_1 & c_2 \\ 1 & c_1 & c_2 & c_2 & c_1 \end{bmatrix}$$

and

$$F_5^I = \begin{bmatrix} 0 & 0 & 0 & 0 & 0 \\ 0 & -s_1 & -s_2 & s_2 & s_1 \\ 0 & -s_2 & s_1 & -s_1 & s_2 \\ 0 & s_2 & -s_1 & s_1 & -s_2 \\ 0 & s_1 & s_2 & -s_2 & -s_1 \end{bmatrix},$$

we see that

$$
u = F_5^R x = \begin{bmatrix}
x_0 + (x_1 + x_4) + (x_2 + x_3) \\
x_0 + (x_1 + x_4)c_1 + (x_2 + x_3)c_2 \\
x_0 + (x_1 + x_4)c_2 + (x_2 + x_3)c_1 \\
x_0 + (x_1 + x_4)c_2 + (x_2 + x_3)c_1 \\
x_0 + (x_1 + x_4)c_1 + (x_2 + x_3)c_2
\end{bmatrix}
$$

and

$$
v = F_5^I x = \begin{bmatrix}
0 \\
-(x_1 - x_4)s_1 - (x_2 - x_3)s_2 \\
-(x_1 - x_4)s_2 + (x_2 - x_3)s_1 \\
(x_1 - x_4)s_2 - (x_2 - x_3)s_1 \\
(x_1 - x_4)s_1 + (x_2 - x_3)s_2
\end{bmatrix}.
$$

It is not too hard to verify that

$$
\lambda \equiv \frac{c_1 + c_2}{2} = -\frac{1}{4}, \qquad \mu \equiv \frac{c_1 - c_2}{2} = \frac{\sqrt{5}}{4} \tag{4.1.19}
$$

and so $c_1 = \lambda + \mu$ and $c_2 = \lambda - \mu$. It follows that if $x_{14}^+ = x_1 + x_4$ and $x_{23}^+ = x_2 + x_3$, then

$$
u = \begin{bmatrix}
x_0 + (x_{14}^+ + x_{23}^+) \\
x_0 + (x_{14}^+ + x_{23}^+)\lambda + (x_{14}^+ - x_{23}^+)\mu \\
x_0 + (x_{14}^+ + x_{23}^+)\lambda - (x_{14}^+ - x_{23}^+)\mu \\
x_0 + (x_{14}^+ + x_{23}^+)\lambda - (x_{14}^+ - x_{23}^+)\mu \\
x_0 + (x_{14}^+ + x_{23}^+)\lambda + (x_{14}^+ - x_{23}^+)\mu
\end{bmatrix}.
$$

Since our task is to compute

$$
y = F_5 x = (F_5^R + iF_5^I)x \equiv u + iv,
$$

we have completed the derivation of the $p = 5$ module.

Algorithm 4.1.5 If $x \in \mathbb{C}^5$, $\mu = \sqrt{5}/4$, $s_1 = \sin(2\pi/5)$, and $s_2 = \sin(4\pi/5)$, then the following algorithm computes $y = F_5 x$:

$x_{14}^+ \leftarrow x_1 + x_4; \quad x_{23}^+ \leftarrow x_2 + x_3$

$a \leftarrow x_{14}^+ + x_{23}^+; \quad b \leftarrow (x_{14}^+ - x_{23}^+)\mu; \quad d \leftarrow x_0 - (a/4)$

$u_0 \leftarrow x_0 + a; \quad u_1 \leftarrow d + b; \quad u_2 \leftarrow d - b; \quad u_3 \leftarrow u_2; \quad u_4 \leftarrow u_1$

$x_{14}^- \leftarrow x_1 - x_4; \quad x_{23}^- \leftarrow x_2 - x_3$

$e \leftarrow x_{14}^- s_1; \quad f \leftarrow x_{14}^- s_2; \quad g \leftarrow x_{23}^- s_1; \quad h \leftarrow x_{23}^- s_2$

$v_1 \leftarrow -e - h; \quad v_2 \leftarrow -f + g; \quad v_3 \leftarrow -v_2; \quad v_4 \leftarrow -v_1$

$y_0 \leftarrow u_0; \quad y_1 \leftarrow u_1 + iv_1; \quad y_2 \leftarrow u_2 + iv_2; \quad y_3 \leftarrow u_3 + iv_3; \quad y_4 \leftarrow u_4 + iv_4$

This algorithm requires 12 real multiplicative operations and 32 real additions.

Very minor modifications of Algorithm 4.1.5 are required to obtain rotated modules for $F_5^{(2)}$, $F_5^{(3)}$, and $F_5^{(4)}$. See Temperton (1988b).

Finally, we mention that the $p = 5$ Winograd factorization is given by $F_5 = B_5 M_5 A_5$ where

$$B_5 = \begin{bmatrix} 1 & 0 & 0 & 0 & 0 & 0 \\ 1 & 1 & 1 & 0 & 1 & 1 \\ 1 & 1 & -1 & -1 & 0 & 1 \\ 1 & 1 & -1 & 1 & 0 & -1 \\ 1 & 1 & 1 & 0 & -1 & -1 \end{bmatrix}, \quad A_5 = \begin{bmatrix} 1 & 1 & 1 & 1 & 1 \\ 0 & 1 & 1 & 1 & 1 \\ 0 & 1 & -1 & -1 & 1 \\ 0 & 1 & 0 & 0 & -1 \\ 0 & 0 & 1 & -1 & 0 \\ 0 & 1 & -1 & 1 & -1 \end{bmatrix},$$

and

$$M_5 = \text{diag}(1, \; -1 + (c_1 + c_2)/2, \; (c_1 - c_2)/2, \; -(s_1 - s_2)i, \; -(s_1 + s_2)i, \; -s_1 i).$$

Problems

P4.1.1 Use induction to prove Theorem 4.1.1. Hint: Show that each r_k is an integral combination of r_{k-1} and r_{k-2}.

P4.1.2 Verify (4.1.17).

P4.1.3 In the proof of Theorem 4.1.2, verify that (a) $c_1 + d_1 = 0$ and (b) $c = 1$.

P4.1.4 Verify (4.1.9) and (4.1.10).

P4.1.5 Give detailed algorithms for the computations $x \leftarrow \Upsilon^T x$ and $x \leftarrow \Gamma x$ in Algorithm 4.1.3.

P4.1.6 Show that if $\gcd(r,p) = 1$, then $\sigma(k) = <kr>_p$ is a permutation on $\{0, 1, \ldots, p-1\}$.

P4.1.7 What can you say about the block structure of the matrix $\Upsilon_{n_2,n}^T F_n \Upsilon_{n_2,n}$ where $n = n_1 n_2$ and $\gcd(n_1, n_2) = 1$?

Notes and References for Section 4.1

A review of the number theory that underpins the prime factor approach can be found in

J.H. McClellan and C.M. Rader (1979). *Number Theory in Digital Signal Processing*, Prentice-Hall, Englewood Cliffs, NJ.

H.J. Nussbaumer (1981b). *Fast Fourier Transform and Convolution Algorithms*, Springer-Verlag, New York.

Classical references for the prime factor algorithm include

I.J. Good (1958). "The Interaction Algorithm and Practical Fourier Analysis," *J. Roy. Statist. Soc. Ser. B. 20*, 361–372.

I.J. Good (1971). "The Relationship between Two Fast Fourier Transforms," *IEEE Trans. Comput. C-20*, 310–317.

The Winograd algorithm with its reduced number of multiplications has attracted a great deal of attention. See

R.C. Agarwal (1983a). "An In-Place and In-order WFTA," *Proc. 1983 IEEE Int. Conf. Acoustics, Speech, and Signal Processing*, 190–193.

J.H. McClellan and H. Nawab (1979). "Complex General-n Winograd Fourier Transform Algorithm (WFTA)," in *Programs for Digital Signal Processing*, Digital Signal Processing Committee (eds.), IEEE Press, New York.

H.F. Silverman (1977). "An Introduction to Programming the Winograd Fourier Transform Algorithm (WFTA)," *IEEE Trans. Acoust. Speech Signal Process. ASSP-25*, 152–164.

S. Winograd (1978). "On Computing the Discrete Fast Fourier Transform," *Math. Comp. 32*, 175–199.

S. Zohar (1979a). "A Prescription of Winograd's Discrete Fourier Transform Algorithm," *IEEE Trans. Acoust. Speech Signal Process. ASSP-27*, 409–421.

S. Zohar (1979b). "Correction to 'A Prescription of Winograd's Discrete Fourier Transform Algorithm'," *IEEE Trans. Acoust. Speech Signal Process. ASSP-27*, 563.

Implementation aspects of the algorithm are discussed in

C.S. Burrus (1981). "A New Prime Factor FFT Algorithm," *Proc. 1981 IEEE Int. Conf. Acoustics, Speech, and Signal Processing,* Atlanta, GA 335–338.

C.S. Burrus and P.W. Eschenbacher (1981). "An In-Place In-Order Prime Factor FFT Algorithm," *IEEE Trans. Acoust. Speech Signal Process. 29,* 806–817.

H.W. Johnson and C.S. Burrus (1983). "The Design of Optimal DFT Algorithms Using Dynamic Programming," *IEEE Trans. Acoust. Speech Signal Process. 31,* 378–387.

D.P. Kolba and T.W. Parks (1977). "A Prime Factor FFT Algorithm Using High-Speed Convolution," *IEEE Trans. Acoust. Speech Signal Process. ASSP-25,* 281–294.

L.R. Morris (1978). "A Comparative Study of Time Efficient FFT and WFTA Programs for General Purpose Computers," *IEEE Trans. Acoust. Speech Signal Process. ASSP-26,* 141–150.

H. Nawab and J.H. McClellan (1979). "Parallelism in the Computation of the FFT and WFTA," *Conf. Record 1979 IEEE Int. Conf. Acoustics, Speech, and Signal Processing,* 514–517.

J.H. Rothweiler (1982). "Implementation of the In-Order Prime Factor Transform for Various Sizes," *IEEE Trans. Acoust. Speech Signal Process. 30,* 105–107.

The implementation of prime factor algorithms on vector machines is discussed in an excellent series of papers by Temperton:

C. Temperton (1983c). "A Note on Prime Factor FFT Algorithms," *J. Comput. Phys. 52,* 198–204.

C. Temperton (1985). "Implementation of a Self-Sorting In-Place Prime Factor FFT Algorithm," *J. Comput. Phys. 58,* 283–299.

C. Temperton (1988a). "A New Set of Minimum-Add Small-*n* Rotated DFT Modules," *J. Comput. Phys. 75,* 190–198.

C. Temperton (1988b). "A Self-Sorting In-Place Prime Factor Real/Half-Complex FFT Algorithm," *J. Comput. Phys. 75,* 199–216.

C. Temperton (1988c). "Implementation of a Prime Factor FFT Algorithm on the Cray-1," *Parallel Comput. 6,* 99–108.

4.2 Convolution

Suppose $\{h_k\}$ and $\{g_k\}$ are bi-infinite sequences with period n, i.e., for all integers k and α we have $h_k = h_{k+\alpha n}$. The *convolution* of these two sequences is another bi-infinite sequence $\{f_k\}$ defined by

$$f_k \;=\; \sum_{j=0}^{n-1} g_j h_{k-j} \;=\; \sum_{j=0}^{n-1} g_j h_{<k-j>_n} \,. \tag{4.2.1}$$

It is easy to show that $\{f_k\}$ has period n as well. In this section we show how FFTs can be used to compute $[\, f_0, \ldots, f_{n-1} \,]$ in $O(n \log n)$ flops. This is one of the most important applications of the FFT, especially in signal processing. In addition, the discussion of fast convolution gives us a chance to illustrate how the proper choice of FFT frameworks can simplify a solution process.

We begin with a matrix treatment of the one-dimensional convolution problem. After deriving a fast FFT-based procedure, we turn the tables and show how an FFT can be based upon fast convolution. The duality between the DFT and convolution is important and opens up a class of new computational frameworks. We conclude with a discussion of two-dimensional convolution.

4.2.1 Discrete Convolution and Circulant Matrices

The computation of $f_0, \ldots, f_{n-1}$ in (4.2.1) amounts to an n-dimensional matrix-vector product, e.g.,

$$\begin{bmatrix} f_0 \\ f_1 \\ f_2 \\ f_3 \end{bmatrix} = \begin{bmatrix} h_0 & h_3 & h_2 & h_1 \\ h_1 & h_0 & h_3 & h_2 \\ h_2 & h_1 & h_0 & h_3 \\ h_3 & h_2 & h_1 & h_0 \end{bmatrix} \begin{bmatrix} g_0 \\ g_1 \\ g_2 \\ g_3 \end{bmatrix} . \tag{4.2.2}$$

Note that each column is a downshifted version of its predecessor. Downshifting in the $n = 4$ case can be accomplished by applying the permutation

$$R_4 = \begin{bmatrix} 0 & 0 & 0 & 1 \\ 1 & 0 & 0 & 0 \\ 0 & 1 & 0 & 0 \\ 0 & 0 & 1 & 0 \end{bmatrix}.$$

The general *downshift permutation matrix* has the form

$$R_n = [\, e_1 \,|\, e_2 \,|\, \cdots \,|\, e_{n-1} \,|\, e_0 \,], \tag{4.2.3}$$

where e_k is the kth column of the n-by-n identity I_n.

The matrix in (4.2.2) is an example of a *circulant matrix*. These matrices have the form

$$H_n(h) = [\, h \,|\, Rh \,|\, R^2 h \,|\, \cdots \,|\, R^{n-1} h \,], \tag{4.2.4}$$

where $h \in \mathbb{C}^n$ and $R = R_n$. Our first result establishes the correspondence between convolution and the product of a circulant matrix and a vector.

Lemma 4.2.1 *If $f \in \mathbb{C}^n$ is the convolution of g and h as prescribed by (4.2.1), then $f = H_n(h)g$.*

Proof. If $u, v \in \mathbb{C}^n$ with $u = R_n^j v$, then $u_k = v_{<k-j>_n}$. Thus, $[H_n(h)]_{kj} = h_{<k-j>_n}$ and

$$[H_n(h)x]_k = \sum_{j=0}^{n-1} h_{<k-j>_n} x_j = g_k,$$

thereby establishing the lemma. $\square$

To develop a fast convolution algorithm, we need to learn more about circulants.

4.2.2 Circulant Matrix Properties

The first property we establish is that a circulant matrix is a polynomial in the downshift operator.

Lemma 4.2.2 $H_n(h) = h_0 I + h_1 R_n + \cdots + h_{n-1} R_n^{n-1}.$

Proof. Write R for R_n and compare the jth columns:

$$(h_0 I + h_1 R + \cdots + h_{n-1} R^{n-1}) e_j =$$
$$h_0 e_j + h_1 e_{<j+1>_n} \cdots + h_{n-1} e_{<n-1+j>_n} = R^j h = H_n(h) e_j.$$

Since this holds for all j, the lemma is established. $\square$

Next, we verify that F_n diagonalizes R_n.

Lemma 4.2.3 $F_n R_n = D_n F_n$, *where* $D_n = \mathrm{diag}(1, \omega, \dots, \omega^{n-1})$ *with* $\omega = \omega_n$.

Proof. $[\, F_n R_n \,]_{kj} = \omega^{k(j+1)}$ and $[\, D_n F_n \,]_{kj} = \omega^k \omega^{kj} = \omega^{k(j+1)}$. $\square$

With these lemmas we can establish that F_n diagonalizes the circulant $H_n(h)$.

Theorem 4.2.4 $F_n H_n(h) = \mathrm{diag}(F_n h) F_n.$

Proof. If $F = F_n$, $R = R_n$, $D = \text{diag}(1, \omega, \ldots, \omega^{n-1})$ with $\omega = \omega_n$, then from Lemma 4.2.3 $FRF^{-1} = D$. Thus, using Lemma 4.2.2

$$FHF^{-1} = \sum_{k=0}^{n-1} h_k FR^k F^{-1} = \sum_{k=0}^{n-1} h_k (FRF^{-1})^k = \sum_{k=0}^{n-1} h_k D^k = p(D).$$

where $p(z) = h_0 + h_1 z + \cdots + h_{n-1} z^{n-1}$. The theorem is established once we observe that $[p(D)]_{kk} = p(\omega^k) = h_0 + h_1 \omega^k + \cdots + h_{n-1} \omega^{k(n-1)} = [Fh]_k$. $\square$

4.2.3   Convolution via the FFT

Since $H_n(h) = F_n^{-1} \text{diag}(F_n h) F_n$, it follows that

$$f = H_n(h)g = F_n^{-1} \text{diag}(F_n h) F_n g = F_n^{-1}((F_n g) .* (F_n h)) . \qquad (4.2.5)$$

If we use FFTs to evaluate $F_n g$ and $F_n h$ and apply an inverse FFT to their pointwise product, then a fast convolution method is obtained. Pursuing this, assume that

$$F_n = (A_t \cdots A_1) P_n^T \equiv A P^T$$

is a Cooley–Tukey factorization of F_n. Here P is the appropriate index-reversal permutation and A is the product of the butterfly operators. (See §2.3.1.) We also have the corresponding DIF and inverse factorizations:

$$F_n = A P^T - (A P^T)^T - P A^T,$$

$$F_n^{-1} = (1/n) \bar{F}_n = (1/n) \bar{A} P^T .$$

By substituting these results into (4.2.5), we obtain

$$
\begin{aligned}
f &= \frac{1}{n} \bar{A} P^T \left((P A^T g) .* (P A^T h) \right) \\
&= \frac{1}{n} \bar{A} P^T \left[P \left((A^T g) .* (A^T h) \right) \right] \\
&= \frac{1}{n} \bar{A} \left[(A^T g) .* (A^T h) \right] .
\end{aligned}
$$

thereby making it possible to avoid entirely the index-reversal operations. In the radix-2 setting we have the following algorithm.

Algorithm 4.2.1 (Fast Convolution) If $g, h \in \mathbb{C}^n$ and $n = 2^t$, then the following algorithm overwrites g with the convolution $H_n(h)g$:

> for $q = t: -1:1$
> $g \leftarrow A_q^T g$
> $h \leftarrow A_q^T h$
> end
> $g \leftarrow g .* h$
> for $q = 1:t$
> $g \leftarrow \bar{A}_q g$
> end
> $g \leftarrow g/n$

This algorithm requires $15n \log_2 n$ flops. The "removal of P" through the judicious combination of the DIF and DIT Cooley–Tukey frameworks is typical in many FFT applications. It is a three-step process:

- A DIF framework is used to transform the given problem into "scrambled" DFT space.

- Simple operations are performed on the scrambled transforms , e.g., pointwise multiplication.

- With data in scrambled form, an inverse DIT framework is used to transform back to the original coordinate space.

The advantage of this approach is that we can completely avoid the workspace overheads associated with the autosort frameworks and the bit-reversal overheads associated with the Cooley–Tukey frameworks.

4.2.4   Toeplitz Matrices

In matrix terms, fast convolution permits the fast evaluation of circulant matrix/vector products. Another matrix/vector product that can be similarly handled involves *Toeplitz* matrices. An n-by-n matrix $T(a) = (t_{kj})$ is *Toeplitz* if there exists a vector

$$a = [\, a_{-n+1}, \ldots, a_{-1}, a_0, a_1, \ldots, a_{n-1} \,] \,,$$

such that $[T]_{kj} = a_{k-j}$ for all k and j. In other words, T is constant along its diagonals. Thus, if $a = [\, a_{-2}, a_{-1}, a_0, a_1, a_2 \,]$, then

$$T = T(a) = \begin{bmatrix} a_0 & a_{-1} & a_{-2} \\ a_1 & a_0 & a_{-1} \\ a_2 & a_1 & a_0 \end{bmatrix}$$

is Toeplitz.

Given a Toeplitz $T \in \mathbb{C}^{n \times n}$, it is possible to construct a circulant $C \in \mathbb{C}^{m \times m}$, with $m \geq 2n - 1$, such that $T = C(0{:}n - 1, 0{:}n - 1)$. For example, the matrix T above is the leading 3-by-3 portion of the circulant

$$C = \begin{bmatrix} a_0 & a_{-1} & a_{-2} & 0 & 0 & 0 & a_2 & a_1 \\ a_1 & a_0 & a_{-1} & a_{-2} & 0 & 0 & 0 & a_2 \\ a_2 & a_1 & a_0 & a_{-1} & a_{-2} & 0 & 0 & 0 \\ 0 & a_2 & a_1 & a_0 & a_{-1} & a_{-2} & 0 & 0 \\ 0 & 0 & a_2 & a_1 & a_0 & a_{-1} & a_{-2} & 0 \\ 0 & 0 & 0 & a_2 & a_1 & a_0 & a_{-1} & a_{-2} \\ a_{-2} & 0 & 0 & 0 & a_2 & a_1 & a_0 & a_{-1} \\ a_{-1} & a_{-2} & 0 & 0 & 0 & a_2 & a_1 & a_0 \end{bmatrix}.$$

In general, we are given an n-by-n Toeplitz matrix $T(a)$ and set

$$c = \begin{bmatrix} a(0{:}n-1) \\ z \\ a(-n+1{:}-1) \end{bmatrix} \in \mathbb{C}^m,$$

where $z \in \mathbb{C}^{m-2n+1}$ is arbitrary. The matrix

$$C = [\, c \mid R_m c \mid R_m^2 c \mid \cdots \mid R_m^{m-1} c \,]$$

is circulant and it can be verified that

$$C(0{:}n-1, 0{:}n-1) \; = \; T(a) \, . \tag{4.2.6}$$

As an application of this result, fast convolution can be used to evaluate the product of a Toeplitz matrix $T \in \mathbb{C}^{n \times n}$ and a vector $u \in \mathbb{C}^n$. In particular, to compute $v = Tu$ we embed T in a circulant $C \in \mathbb{C}^{m \times m}$, as discussed above. If the m-vector $\tilde{u}$ is defined by

$$\tilde{u} \; = \; \left[\begin{array}{c} u \\ 0 \end{array} \right] ,$$

and $\tilde{v} = C\tilde{u}$, then $v = \tilde{v}(0{:}n-1)$ because

$$v \; = \; \tilde{v}(0{:}n-1) \; = \; C(0{:}n-1, :)\tilde{u} \; = \; C(0{:}n-1, 0{:}n-1)u \; = \; Tu \, .$$

Thus, fast evaluation of $C\tilde{u}$ permits fast evaluation of Tu. In this context, one might choose the circulant dimension m so that length-m DFTs are convenient. One possibility is presented in the following algorithm.

Algorithm 4.2.2   If $u \in \mathbb{C}^n$ and $a(-n+1{:}n-1)$ are given, then the following algorithm computes $v = T_n(a)u$.

> Let t be the smallest integer so that $2^t \geq 2n - 1$.
> $m \leftarrow 2^t$
> $h(0{:}n-1) \leftarrow a(0{:}n-1)$
> $h(n{:}m-n) \leftarrow 0$
> $h(m-n+1{:}m-1) \leftarrow a(-n+1{:}-1)$
> $g(0{:}n-1) \leftarrow u$
> $g(n{:}m-1) \leftarrow 0$
> $f \leftarrow H_m(h)g$ (Algorithm 4.2.1)
> $v \leftarrow f(0{:}n-1)$

This algorithm requires $15m \log_2 m$ flops. For further discussion of the connection between Toeplitz matrices, convolution, and the DFT, see Swarztrauber, Sweet, Briggs, Henson, and Otto (1991).

4.2.5   The Chirp-z Factorization and Framework

Using the results of the previous section, it is possible to convert a DFT into a convolution of expanded length. The convolution can be evaluated via FFT techniques, giving us yet another computational framework. (Again, one might chose a particularly convenient expanded length.) The central ideas are due to Bluestein (1970) which we reformulate as the *Chirp-z factorization*:

Theorem 4.2.5 *If $\sigma_j = \omega_{2n}^{j^2}$ for $j = -n+1{:}n-1$, then $F_n = \Sigma_n T_n(a) \Sigma_n$, where*

$$\Sigma_n \; = \; \mathrm{diag}(\sigma_0, \ldots, \sigma_{n-1})$$

and $T_n(a)$ is the n-by-n Toeplitz matrix defined by

$$a_j = \bar{\sigma}_j, \qquad j = -n+1{:}n-1 \, .$$

Proof. Since $2kj = k^2 + j^2 - (k - j)^2$ and

$$[T_n(a)]_{kj} = a_{k-j} = \omega_{2n}^{-(k-j)^2},$$

we have

$$[F_n]_{kj} = \omega_n^{kj} = \omega_{2n}^{2kj} = \omega_{2n}^{k^2}\omega_{2n}^{-(k-j)^2}\omega_{2n}^{j^2} = [\Sigma_n T_n(a)\Sigma_n]_{kj}.$$

The theorem follows since this result holds for all k and j. $\square$

By way of illustration, if $\omega = \omega_8$ then we have

$$F_4 = \begin{bmatrix} 1 & 0 & 0 & 0 \\ 0 & \omega & 0 & 0 \\ 0 & 0 & \omega^4 & 0 \\ 0 & 0 & 0 & \omega \end{bmatrix} \begin{bmatrix} 1 & \omega^7 & \omega^4 & \omega^7 \\ \omega^7 & 1 & \omega^7 & \omega^4 \\ \omega^4 & \omega^7 & 1 & \omega^7 \\ \omega^7 & \omega^4 & \omega^7 & 1 \end{bmatrix} \begin{bmatrix} 1 & 0 & 0 & 0 \\ 0 & \omega & 0 & 0 \\ 0 & 0 & \omega^4 & 0 \\ 0 & 0 & 0 & \omega \end{bmatrix}.$$

To compute $y = F_n x = \Sigma_n T_n(a)\Sigma_n x$, we may proceed as follows:

$$u \leftarrow \Sigma_n x$$
$$v \leftarrow T_n(a)u$$
$$y \leftarrow \Sigma_n v.$$

Filling in some of the details we get the *Chirp-z framework* below.

Algorithm 4.2.3 If $x \in \mathbb{C}^n$, then the following algorithm computes $y = F_n x$.

> **for** $j = 0{:}n - 1$
> $a(j) \leftarrow \exp(j^2 \pi i/n)$
> $a(-j) \leftarrow a(j)$
> $u(j) \leftarrow \bar{a}(j)x(j)$
> **end**
> $v \leftarrow T_n(a)u$ (Algorithm 4.2.2)
> $y \leftarrow \bar{a}(0{:}n - 1).* v$

The work in this algorithm is dominated by the product $T_n(a)u$, which executes at FFT speed.

4.2.6   The Rader Factorization

Another FFT framework that involves conversion of the given DFT to a convolution is due to Rader (1968). It requires n to be prime and is based upon a number-theoretic permutation of F_n that produces a circulant submatrix of order $n - 1$.

The Rader conversion is based on some special properties of mod n arithmetic that hold when n is prime. We summarize these properties in the following lemmas, which we state without proof.

Lemma 4.2.6 *If n is prime, then there exists an integer r with $2 \leq r \leq n - 1$ such that*

$$\{2, \ldots, n - 1\} = \{ <r>_n, <r^2>_n, \ldots, <r^{n-2}>_n \}.$$

The integer r is called a primitive root.

Lemma 4.2.7 *If n is prime and $1 \le \alpha \le n-1$, then there exists a β satisfying $1 \le \beta \le n-1$ such that $<\alpha\beta>_n = 1$. We refer to β as the inverse of α and denote it by α^{-1}.*

Lemma 4.2.8 *If r is a primitive root, then so is r^{-1}. Moreover,*

$$<r^j \cdot (r^{-1})^k >_n = <r^{j-k}>_n .$$

To illustrate these properties, assume $n = 5$. It is easy to verify that 2 and 3 are primitive roots and that the inverses of $2, 3$, and 4 are given by $3, 2$, and 4, respectively. Moreover, in mod 5 arithmetic we see that

$$\{2, 2^2, 2^3\} = \{3, 3^2, 3^3\} = \{2, 3, 4\} .$$

If n is prime and s is a primitive root, then the n-by-n matrix $Q_n(s)$ defined by

$$z = Q_n(s)^T x, \qquad z(k) = \begin{cases} x(k) & \text{if } k = 0, 1 \\ x(<s^{k-1}>_n) & \text{if } 2 \le k \le n-1 \end{cases}$$

is a permutation. This follows from Lemma 4.2.6. The factorization behind the Rader approach depends upon permutations of this type.

Theorem 4.2.9 *If n is prime and r is a primitive root, then*

$$Q_n(r)^T F_n Q_n(r^{-1}) = \begin{bmatrix} 1 & e^T \\ e & C_{n-1} \end{bmatrix}, \tag{4.2.7}$$

where $e \in \mathbb{C}^{n-1}$ is the vector of all ones and C_{n-1} is circulant with

$$C_{n-1}(0{:}n-2, 0) = \begin{bmatrix} 1, & \omega_n^r, & \omega_n^{r^2}, & \dots, & \omega_n^{r^{n-2}} \end{bmatrix}^T .$$

Proof. Since the initial column of both $Q_n(r)$ and $Q_n(r^{-1})$ is the initial column of I_n, it follows that

$$Q_n(r)^T F_n Q_n(r^{-1}) = \begin{bmatrix} 1 & e^T \\ e & C \end{bmatrix},$$

where C is a matrix of order $n-1$. From the definition of the permutations $Q_n(r)$ and $Q_n(r^{-1})$, we have using Lemma 4.2.8 that

$$[C]_{kj} = \omega_n^{(r^k)(r^{-j})} = \omega_n^{r^{k-j}} .$$

It follows that $C = C_{n-1}$ is a circulant matrix whose initial column is prescribed by the theorem. $\square$

As an illustration of the Rader factorization, note that

$$F_5 = \omega_5.** \begin{bmatrix} 0 & 0 & 0 & 0 & 0 \\ 0 & 1 & 2 & 3 & 4 \\ 0 & 2 & 4 & 1 & 3 \\ 0 & 3 & 1 & 4 & 2 \\ 0 & 4 & 3 & 2 & 1 \end{bmatrix}$$

implies

$$Q_5(2)^T F_5 Q_5(3) = F_5([0,1,2,4,3],[0,1,3,4,2])$$

$$= \omega_5.** \begin{bmatrix} 0 & 0 & 0 & 0 & 0 \\ 0 & 1 & 3 & 4 & 2 \\ 0 & 2 & 1 & 3 & 4 \\ 0 & 4 & 2 & 1 & 3 \\ 0 & 3 & 4 & 2 & 1 \end{bmatrix}.$$

In algorithmic terms, the Rader factorization implies that we can compute

$$y = F_n x = Q_n(r) \begin{bmatrix} 1 & e^T \\ e & C \end{bmatrix} Q_n(r^{-1})^T x$$

as follows:

$$
\begin{aligned}
&x(0{:}n-1) \leftarrow Q_n(r^{-1})^T x(0{:}n-1) \\
&h \leftarrow \left[1, \omega_n^r, \omega_n^{r^2}, \ldots, \omega_n^{r^{n-2}} \right]^T \\
&y(0) \leftarrow x(0) + \cdots x(n-1) \\
&y(1{:}n-1) \leftarrow x(0)e + F_{n-1}^{-1}((F_{n-1}x(1{:}n-1)).*(F_{n-1}h)) \\
&y \leftarrow Q_n(r)y.
\end{aligned}
\tag{4.2.8}
$$

We leave the details to the reader. (See P4.2.5.)

4.2.7 Two-Dimensional Convolution

The convolution of a pair of matrices $G, H \in \mathbb{C}^{n_1 \times n_2}$ is another matrix $C \in \mathbb{C}^{n_1 \times n_2}$ defined by

$$c_{pq} = \sum_{k=0}^{n_1-1} \sum_{j=0}^{n_2-1} g_{kj} h_{<p-k>_{n_1},<q-j>_{n_2}}. \tag{4.2.9}$$

See Schakoff (1989, p. 87). If C is computed via these formulae, then $O(n_1^2 n_2^2)$ flops are required. We show how a triplet of two-dimensional DFTs can reduce the amount of work to order $n_1 n_2 \log(n_1 n_2)$.

To that end, we define the matrices $H^{(p,q)} \in \mathbb{C}^{n_1 \times n_2}$ by

$$\left[H^{(p,q)} \right]_{kj} = h_{<p-k>_{n_1},<q-j>_{n_2}}.$$

Recalling the definition of the downshift operator R_m from (4.2.3), we see that

$$H^{(p,q)} = R_{n_1}^p H^{(0,0)} (R_{n_2}^q)^T. \tag{4.2.10}$$

For example, if $(n_1, n_2) = (5,3)$, then

$$H^{(0,0)} = \begin{bmatrix} h_{00} & h_{02} & h_{01} \\ h_{40} & h_{42} & h_{41} \\ h_{30} & h_{32} & h_{31} \\ h_{20} & h_{22} & h_{21} \\ h_{10} & h_{12} & h_{11} \end{bmatrix}, \qquad H^{(2,1)} = \begin{bmatrix} h_{21} & h_{20} & h_{22} \\ h_{11} & h_{10} & h_{12} \\ h_{01} & h_{00} & h_{02} \\ h_{41} & h_{40} & h_{42} \\ h_{31} & h_{30} & h_{32} \end{bmatrix}.$$

We also mention that

$$H^{(0,0)} = \begin{bmatrix} 1 & 0 \\ 0 & E_{n_1-1} \end{bmatrix} H \begin{bmatrix} 1 & 0 \\ 0 & E_{n_2-1} \end{bmatrix}, \qquad (4.2.11)$$

where E_k is I_k with its columns reversed. With these observations we are set to prove the following two-dimensional analog of (4.2.5).

Theorem 4.2.10 *If $C \in \mathbb{C}^{n_1 \times n_2}$ is the convolution of $G, H \in \mathbb{C}^{n_1 \times n_2}$, then*

$$C = F_{n_1}^{-1} \left[(F_{n_1} G F_{n_2}) . * (F_{n_1} H F_{n_2}) \right] F_{n_2}^{-1} .$$

Proof. We make two preliminary observations. First, using Lemma 4.2.3 and the equation $F_m^{-1} = \bar{F}_m / m$, we have

$$R_m = F_m^{-1} D_m F_m = \overline{F_m^{-1} D_m F_m} = F_m \bar{D}_m F_m^{-1},$$

where $D_m = \mathrm{diag}(1, \omega_m, \ldots, \omega_m^{m-1})$. Second, if $Y, Z \in \mathbb{C}^{n_1 \times n_2}$, then

$$\sum_{k=0}^{n_1-1} \sum_{j=0}^{n_2-1} y_{kj} z_{kj} = \mathrm{trace}(Y^T Z),$$

where the *trace* of a square matrix is the sum of its diagonal entries.

The trace of a matrix is equal to the sum of its eigenvalues and is therefore invariant under similarity transformations; so it follows from (4.2.9) and (4.2.10) that

$$
\begin{aligned}
c_{pq} &= \mathrm{trace}(G^T H^{(p,q)}) \\
&= \mathrm{trace}(G^T R_{n_1}^p H^{(0,0)} R_{n_2}^{qT}) \\
&= \mathrm{trace}(G^T (F_{n_1} \bar{D}_{n_1} F_{n_1}^{-1})^p H^{(0,0)} (F_{n_2} \bar{D}_{n_2} F_{n_2}^{-1})^{qT}) \\
&= \mathrm{trace}(G^T F_{n_1} \bar{D}_{n_1}^p F_{n_1}^{-1} H^{(0,0)} F_{n_2}^{-1} \bar{D}_{n_2}^q F_{n_2}) \\
&= \mathrm{trace}((F_{n_2} G^T F_{n_1}) \bar{D}_{n_1}^p (F_{n_1}^{-1} H^{(0,0)} F_{n_2}^{-1}) \bar{D}_{n_2}^q) .
\end{aligned}
$$

Using (4.2.11), it is not hard to verify that

$$
\begin{aligned}
F_{n_1}^{-1} H^{(0,0)} F_{n_2}^{-1} &= F_{n_1}^{-1} \begin{bmatrix} 1 & 0 \\ 0 & E_{n_1-1} \end{bmatrix} H \begin{bmatrix} 1 & 0 \\ 0 & E_{n_2-1} \end{bmatrix} F_{n_2}^{-1} \\
&= \frac{1}{n} F_{n_1} H F_{n_2} . \qquad (4.2.12)
\end{aligned}
$$

Thus, if we define

$$\tilde{G} = F_{n_1} G F_{n_2}, \qquad \tilde{H} = F_{n_1} H F_{n_2},$$

then

$$
\begin{aligned}
c_{pq} &= \frac{1}{n} \mathrm{trace}(\tilde{G}^T \bar{D}_{n_1}^p H \bar{D}_{n_2}^q) = \frac{1}{n} \sum_{k=0}^{n_2-1} \left[\tilde{G}^T \bar{D}_{n_1}^p H \bar{D}_{n_2}^q \right]_{kk} \\
&= \frac{1}{n} \sum_{k=0}^{n_2-1} \sum_{j=0}^{n_1-1} \bar{\omega}_{n_1}^{jp} \bar{\omega}_{n_2}^{kq} \tilde{g}_{jk} \tilde{h}_{jk} .
\end{aligned}
$$

But by using (3.4.2), we see that this is just the recipe for the inverse two-dimensional transform of $\tilde{G} . * \tilde{H}$, i.e., $C = F_{n_1}^{-1} (\tilde{G} . * \tilde{H}) F_{n_2}^{-1}$. $\square$

We can parallel the discussion of one-dimensional convolution in §4.2.3 by designing an in-place FFT method for two-dimensional convolution that avoids index reversal. The idea is again to use the DIF framework when transforming G and H and then a DIT framework for the inverse transforms. For clarity, assume that $n_1 = n_2 = 2^t = m$ and let $F_m = AP = P^T A$ be the Cooley–Tukey factorization, with $A = A_t \cdots A_1$ being the product of the butterfly operators. It follows that

$$
\begin{aligned}
C &= F_m^{-1}\left((F_m G F_m).*(F_m H F_m)\right)F_m^{-1} \\
&= \frac{1}{m^2}\bar{A}P\left((PA^T GAP).*(PA^T HAP)\right)P\bar{A} \\
&= \frac{1}{m^2}\bar{A}\left((A^T GA).*(A^T HA)\right)\bar{A}.
\end{aligned}
$$

Thus, all references to P drop out and we are left with an in-place algorithm that involves nothing but a succession of DIT and DIF butterflies.

Problems

P4.2.1 Show that the sequence $\{f_k\}$ in (4.2.1) has period n.

P4.2.2 Develop a fast algorithm for solving the linear system $H_n(h)x = g$, assuming that $H_n(h)$ is nonsingular and h and g are known.

P4.2.3 Suppose $h \in \mathbb{C}^n$ and define the *Hankel Matrix* $K_n(h) = \left[\, h \mid R^T h \mid \cdots \mid R^{(n-1)T} h \,\right]$. Show that $K_n(h)$ is a column permutation of $H_n(h)$ and develop a fast method for the matrix vector product $f = K_n(h)g$. The vector f is said to be the *correlation* of g and h.

P4.2.4 Verify (4.2.5).

P4.2.5 Detail the computations involving $Q_n(r)$ and $Q_n(r^{-1})$ as they arise in (4.2.8).

P4.2.6 Verify (4.2.12).

Notes and References for Section 4.2

The intimate relation between the FFT and fast convolution is detailed in

C.S. Burrus and T.W. Parks (1985). *DFT/FFT and Convolution Algorithms*, John Wiley & Sons, New York.

H.J. Nussbaumer (1981b). *The Fast Fourier Transform and Convolution Algorithms*, Springer-Verlag, New York.

R. Schakoff (1989). *Digital Image Processing and Computer Vision*, John Wiley & Sons, New York.

Some important algorithmic developments that are a consequence of this interconnection are described in

R.C. Agarwal (1983b). "Comments on 'A Prime Factor FFT Algorithm Using High-Speed Convolution'," *IEEE Trans. Acoust. Speech Signal Process. ASSP-26*, 254.

R.C. Agarwal and C.S. Burrus (1974). "Fast One-Dimensional Digital Convolution by Multidimensional Techniques," *IEEE Trans. Acoust. Speech Signal Process. ASSP-22*, 1–10.

L.I. Bluestein (1970). "A Linear Filtering Approach to the Computation of the Discrete Fourier Transform," *IEEE Trans. Audio and Electroacoustics AU-18*, 451–455.

C.M. Rader (1968). "Discrete Fourier Transforms When the Number of Data Samples Is Prime," *Proc. IEEE 5*, 1107–1108.

C.M. Rader and N.M. Brenner (1976). "A New Principle for Fast Fourier Transformation," *IEEE Trans. Acoust. Speech Signal Process. ASSP-24*, 264–265.

C.M. Rader and S.L. Scharf (1979). "Do Not Use a Chirp to Test a DFT Program," *IEEE Trans. Acoust. Speech Signal Process. ASSP-27*, 430–432.

D.H. Bailey and P.N. Swarztrauber (1990). "The Fractional Fourier Transform and Applications," RNR-90-004, NASA Ames Research Center, Moffett Field, CA. (To appear in *SIAM Rev.*)

P.N. Swarztrauber, R.A. Sweet, W.L. Briggs, V.E. Henson, and J. Otto (1991). "Bluestein's FFT for Arbitrary N on the Hypercube," manuscript.

4.3 FFTs of Real Data

The FFT algorithms that we have developed revolve around recurring block structures that surface when the columns and/or rows of the DFT matrix are permuted. We now reveal additional structure in F_n that permits the efficient evaluation of real-input DFTs. We restrict our attention to radix-2 frameworks and aim to design algorithms that require half of the $5n \log_2 n$ flops that are associated with the fully complex FFT. Real-data FFTs that are based upon mixed-radix, split-radix, or prime factor ideas are referenced at the end of the section.

Before we begin we call attention to a notation change. In this section and the next, the real and imaginary portions of a complex vector x will be denoted by $\text{Re}(x)$ and $\text{Im}(x)$, respectively. The notation x^R and x^I, which we have been using until now, turns out to be rather awkward for the manipulations that follow.

4.3.1 Reflection Patterns

Let $w .* A$ denote the matrix whose kj entry is $w^{a_{kj}}$ and consider the 6-by-6 DFT matrix:

$$F_6 = \omega_6 .** \begin{bmatrix} 0 & 0 & 0 & 0 & 0 & 0 \\ 0 & 1 & 2 & 3 & 4 & 5 \\ 0 & 2 & 4 & 0 & 2 & 4 \\ 0 & 3 & 0 & 3 & 0 & 3 \\ 0 & 4 & 2 & 0 & 4 & 2 \\ 0 & 5 & 4 & 3 & 2 & 1 \end{bmatrix} = \omega_6 .** \begin{bmatrix} 0 & 0 & 0 & 0 & 0 & 0 \\ 0 & 1 & 2 & 3 & 4 & 5 \\ 0 & 2 & 4 & 0 & 2 & 4 \\ 0 & 3 & 0 & 3 & 0 & 3 \\ 0 & -2 & -4 & 0 & -2 & -4 \\ 0 & -1 & -2 & -3 & -4 & -5 \end{bmatrix}.$$

Note that the fifth row is the conjugate of the first row and the fourth row is the conjugate of the second row. The pattern suggested by this example is that the conjugate of F_n can be obtained by reversing the order of the last $n - 1$ rows.

In order to describe this structure in matrix language, we define the *exchange matrix*

$$E_n = I_n(:, n - 1: - 1:0)$$

and the *reflection matrix*

$$T_n = \begin{bmatrix} 1 & 0 \\ 0 & E_{n-1} \end{bmatrix}.$$

Note that E_n is just the n-by-n identity with columns in reverse order, e.g.,

$$E_3 = \begin{bmatrix} 0 & 0 & 1 \\ 0 & 1 & 0 \\ 1 & 0 & 0 \end{bmatrix}.$$

At the matrix-vector level, if $x \in \mathbb{C}^n$, then for $j = 0:n - 1$ we have $[E_n x]_j = x_{n-j-1}$. On the other hand, T_n is the n-by-n identity with its last $n - 1$ columns arranged in reverse order, e.g.,

$$T_4 = \begin{bmatrix} 1 & 0 & 0 & 0 \\ 0 & 0 & 0 & 1 \\ 0 & 0 & 1 & 0 \\ 0 & 1 & 0 & 0 \end{bmatrix}.$$

Observe that if $x \in \mathbb{C}^n$, then $[T_n x]_j = x_{<n-j>_n}$, where $<k>_n$ denotes $k \bmod n$.

Theorem 4.3.1 $\bar{F}_n = T_n F_n = F_n T_n$.

Proof. To verify that $\bar{F}_n = T_n F_n$, observe that

$$[T_n F_n]_{kj} = \omega_n^{(n-k)j} = \omega_n^{-kj} = \bar{\omega}_n^{kj} = [\bar{F}_n]_{kj}$$

for all j and k that satisfy $0 \le j, k < n - 1$. Since F_n and T_n are symmetric, we also have $\bar{F}_n = (T_n F_n)^T = F_n T_n$.   □

This result figures heavily in the design of efficient FFTs for real data.

4.3.2   Conjugate-Even Vectors

We say that $y \in \mathbb{C}^n$ is *conjugate even* if $\bar{y} = T_n y$. Our interest in this pattern stems from the fact that the DFT of a real vector is conjugate even.

Theorem 4.3.2 *If $x \in \mathbb{R}^n$, then $y = F_n x$ is conjugate even.*

Proof. Since x is real, $\bar{y} = \bar{F}_n \bar{x} = \bar{F}_n x = T_n F_n x = T_n y$.   □

If $n = 2m$, then a conjugate-even n-vector y has the form

$$y = \begin{bmatrix} a \\ b + ic \\ d \\ Eb - iEc \end{bmatrix},$$

where a and d are real scalars, b and c are real vectors of length $m-1$, and $E = E_{m-1}$. From the practical point of view, it is attractive to represent y as a single real n-vector:

$$y^{(ce)} = \begin{bmatrix} a \\ b \\ d \\ c \end{bmatrix}. \tag{4.3.1}$$

This *conjugate-even data structure* amounts to a nonredundant stacking of the real and imaginary parts of y. Note that $y^{(ce)}$ is a linear transformation of y, for if we set $I = I_{m-1}$ and $E = E_{m-1}$ and we define the permutation matrix

$$U_n = \begin{bmatrix} 1 & 0 & 0 & 0 \\ 0 & I/2 & 0 & E/2 \\ 0 & 0 & 1 & 0 \\ 0 & -iI/2 & 0 & iE/2 \end{bmatrix}, \tag{4.3.2}$$

then

$$y^{(ce)} = \begin{bmatrix} \text{Re}(y(0{:}m)) \\ \text{Im}(y(1{:}m - 1)) \end{bmatrix} = U_n y.$$

For completeness we define $U_2 = I_2$ and $U_1 = I_1$ and remark that any real 1-vector or 2-vector is conjugate even. The columns of U_n are orthogonal and

$$U_n^{-1} = \begin{bmatrix} 1 & 0 & 0 & 0 \\ 0 & I & 0 & iI \\ 0 & 0 & 1 & 0 \\ 0 & E & 0 & -iE \end{bmatrix} \tag{4.3.3}$$

is its inverse.

4.3.3 The DFT of Two Real Vectors

As an application of conjugate-even vector manipulation, consider the problem of computing the DFT of two real vectors.

Theorem 4.3.3 *If $u_1, u_2 \in \mathbb{R}^n$ and $y_1 + iy_2 = F_n(u_1 + iu_2)$, then*

$$F_n u_1 = [\,(I_n + T_n)y_1 + i(I_n - T_n)y_2\,]/2\,,$$
$$F_n u_2 = [\,(I_n + T_n)y_2 - i(I_n - T_n)y_1\,]/2\,.$$

Proof. Let $I = I_n$, $T = T_n$, and $F = F_n$. By adding and subtracting the equations

$$y_1 + iy_2 = F(u_1 + iu_2),$$
$$T(y_1 + iy_2) = \bar{F}(u_1 + iu_2),$$

we obtain

$$(I + T)(y_1 + iy_2) = (F + \bar{F})(u_1 + iu_2) = 2\,\mathrm{Re}(Fu_1) + 2i\,\mathrm{Re}(Fu_2),$$
$$(I - T)(y_1 + iy_2) = (F - \bar{F})(u_1 + iu_2) = 2i\,\mathrm{Im}(Fu_1) - 2\,\mathrm{Im}(Fu_2).$$

If follows that

$$\mathrm{Re}(Fu_1) = \frac{1}{2}(I + T)y_1\,,$$
$$\mathrm{Im}(Fu_1) = \frac{1}{2}(I - T)y_2\,,$$
$$\mathrm{Re}(Fu_2) = \frac{1}{2}(I + T)y_2\,,$$
$$\mathrm{Im}(Fu_2) = -\frac{1}{2}(I - T)y_1\,,$$

thereby completing the proof. $\square$

After examination of matrix-vector products of the form $(I_n \pm T_n)v$ and consideration of the conjugate-even data structure, we arrive at the algorithm below.

Algorithm 4.3.1 Suppose $u_1, u_2 \in \mathbb{R}^n$ and that $n = 2m$. The following algorithm computes $v_1^{(ce)}$ and $v_2^{(ce)}$, where $v_1 = F_n u_1$ and $v_2 = F_n u_2$.

$$
\begin{aligned}
&y_1 + iy_2 \leftarrow F_n(u_1 + iu_2) \qquad \text{(Via Any Complex FFT)}\\
&v_1^{(ce)}(0) \leftarrow y_1(0)\\
&v_2^{(ce)}(0) \leftarrow y_2(0)\\
&\textbf{for } j = 1{:}m-1\\
&\qquad v_1^{(ce)}(j) \leftarrow [\,y_1(j) + y_1(n-j)\,]/2\\
&\qquad v_1^{(ce)}(m+j) \leftarrow [\,y_2(j) - y_2(n-j)\,]/2\\
&\qquad v_2^{(ce)}(j) \leftarrow [\,y_2(j) + y_2(n-j)\,]/2\\
&\qquad v_2^{(ce)}(m+j) \leftarrow -[\,y_1(j) - y_1(n-j)\,]/2\\
&\textbf{end}\\
&v_1^{(ce)}(m) \leftarrow y_1(m)\\
&v_2^{(ce)}(m) \leftarrow y_2(m)
\end{aligned}
$$

The work in this algorithm is dominated by the n-point complex FFT. It therefore follows that if a standard radix-2 procedure is used, then $5n\log_2 n$ flops are required.

4.3.4   The Conjugate-Even Butterfly

If $x \in \mathbb{R}^n$, then the DFT of any subvector is conjugate even. It follows that during the production of the intermediate DFTs during a radix-2 FFT, the butterflies combine two conjugate-even vectors to produce a single, double-length, conjugate-even vector. To avoid redundant computation, we must examine the action of the radix-2 butterfly in "conjugate-even space."

To that end, assume that $u, v \in \mathbb{C}^{L_*}$ are L_*-point DFTs of real data. Set $L = 2L_* = 4p$ and consider the usual radix-2 synthesis,

$$z = B_L \begin{bmatrix} u \\ v \end{bmatrix} = \begin{bmatrix} I_{L_*} & \Omega_{L_*} \\ I_{L_*} & -\Omega_{L_*} \end{bmatrix} \begin{bmatrix} u \\ v \end{bmatrix},$$

where $\Omega_{L_*} = \mathrm{diag}(1, \omega_L, \ldots, \omega_L^{L_*-1})$. Since z is an L-point DFT of real data, it is conjugate even. It follows from

$$U_L z = \left(U_L B_L (I_2 \otimes U_{L_*}^{-1}) \right) (I_2 \otimes U_{L_*}) \begin{bmatrix} u \\ v \end{bmatrix}$$

that

$$z^{(ce)} = B_L^{(ce)} \begin{bmatrix} u^{(ce)} \\ v^{(ce)} \end{bmatrix},$$

where

$$B_L^{(ce)} = U_L B_L (I_2 \otimes U_{L_*}^{-1}) = U_L \begin{bmatrix} U_{L_*}^{-1} & \Omega_{L_*} U_{L_*}^{-1} \\ U_{L_*}^{-1} & -\Omega_{L_*} U_{L_*}^{-1} \end{bmatrix}. \tag{4.3.4}$$

We call $B_L^{(ce)}$ the *conjugate-even butterfly*. Note that $B_2^{(ce)} = B_2$, since $U_2 = I_2$ and $U_1 = I_1$.

To derive the block structure of U_L, where $L = 2L_* = 4p$, set $I = I_{p-1}$, $E = E_{p-1}$, and $\Delta = \mathrm{diag}(\omega_L, \ldots, \omega_L^{p-1})$. Since $\omega_L^{L_*-j} = \omega_L^{L_*} \omega_L^{-j} = -\bar{\omega}_L^j$, we have

$$\Omega_{L_*} = \begin{bmatrix} 1 & 0 & 0 & 0 \\ 0 & \Delta & 0 & 0 \\ 0 & 0 & -i & 0 \\ 0 & 0 & 0 & -E\bar{\Delta}E \end{bmatrix}.$$

It follows from (4.3.3) that

$$\Omega_{L_*} U_{L_*}^{-1} = \begin{bmatrix} 1 & 0 & 0 & 0 \\ 0 & \Delta & 0 & i\Delta \\ 0 & 0 & -i & 0 \\ 0 & -E\bar{\Delta} & 0 & iE\bar{\Delta} \end{bmatrix}.$$

By substituting this and

$$U_L = \left[\begin{array}{cccc|cccc} 1 & 0 & 0 & 0 & 0 & 0 & 0 & 0 \\ 0 & I/2 & 0 & 0 & 0 & 0 & 0 & E/2 \\ 0 & 0 & 1/2 & 0 & 0 & 0 & 1/2 & 0 \\ 0 & 0 & 0 & I/2 & 0 & E/2 & 0 & 0 \\ \hline 0 & 0 & 0 & 0 & 1 & 0 & 0 & 0 \\ 0 & -iI/2 & 0 & 0 & 0 & 0 & 0 & iE/2 \\ 0 & 0 & -i/2 & 0 & 0 & 0 & i/2 & 0 \\ 0 & 0 & 0 & -iI/2 & 0 & iE/2 & 0 & 0 \end{array} \right]$$

into (4.3.4), we obtain the following block representation for the conjugate-even butterfly:

$$
B_L^{(ce)} = \left[
\begin{array}{cccc|cccc}
1 & 0 & 0 & 0 & 1 & 0 & 0 & 0 \\
0 & I & 0 & 0 & 0 & C & 0 & -S \\
0 & 0 & 1 & 0 & 0 & 0 & 0 & 0 \\
0 & E & 0 & 0 & 0 & -EC & 0 & ES \\
\hline
1 & 0 & 0 & 0 & -1 & 0 & 0 & 0 \\
0 & 0 & 0 & I & 0 & S & 0 & C \\
0 & 0 & 0 & 0 & 0 & 0 & -1 & 0 \\
0 & 0 & 0 & -E & 0 & ES & 0 & EC
\end{array}
\right].
\tag{4.3.5}
$$

Here, $C = \mathrm{diag}(\cos(\theta), \ldots, \cos((p-1)\theta))$ and $S = \mathrm{diag}(\sin(\theta), \ldots, \sin((p-1)\theta))$, with $\theta = -2\pi/n$. Note that $B_L^{(ce)}$ is *real* and if $\alpha_1, \alpha_2, \beta_1, \beta_2 \in \mathbb{R}$ and $a_1, a_2, b_1, b_2 \in \mathbb{R}^{p-1}$, then

$$
B_L^{(ce)}
\left[
\begin{array}{c}
\alpha_1 \\
a_1 \\
\alpha_2 \\
a_2 \\
\beta_1 \\
b_1 \\
\beta_2 \\
b_2
\end{array}
\right]
=
\left[
\begin{array}{c}
\alpha_1 + \beta_1 \\
a_1 + (Cb_1 - Sb_2) \\
\alpha_2 \\
Ea_1 - E(Cb_1 - Sb_2) \\
\alpha_1 - \beta_1 \\
a_2 + (Sb_1 + Cb_2) \\
-\beta_2 \\
-Ea_2 + E(Sb_1 + Cb_2)
\end{array}
\right].
$$

The vectors $Cb_1 - Sb_2$ and $Sb_1 + Cb_2$ require $3p$ flops each. Also required are four length-p vector additions. Thus, the total flop count is $10p = 2.5L$, half that required by a fully complex butterfly of length L.

It is not hard to develop an in-place version of this update. However, for clarity we detail a version of the computation that requires a workspace.

Algorithm 4.3.2 If $x \in \mathbb{R}^L$ and $L = 2^q$ and $q \geq 1$, then the following algorithm overwrites x with $B_L^{(ce)} x$.

$$
\begin{aligned}
&\textbf{if } q \neq 1 \\
&\qquad L_* \leftarrow L/2; \; p \leftarrow L/4 \\
&\qquad \tau \leftarrow x(0); \; x(0) \leftarrow \tau + x(L_*); \; x(L_*) \leftarrow \tau - x(L_*); \; x(3p) \leftarrow -x(3p) \\
&\qquad \textbf{for } j = 1{:}p-1 \\
&\qquad\qquad c \leftarrow \cos(2\pi j/L); \; s \leftarrow \sin(-2\pi j/L) \\
&\qquad\qquad u(j) \leftarrow c \cdot x(L_* + j) - s \cdot x(L_* + p + j) \\
&\qquad\qquad v(j) \leftarrow s \cdot x(L_* + j) + c \cdot x(L_* + p + j) \\
&\qquad \textbf{end} \\
&\qquad y(1{:}p-1) \leftarrow x(1{:}p-1); \; z(1{:}p-1) \leftarrow x(p+1{:}L_*-1) \\
&\qquad \textbf{for } j = 1{:}p-1 \\
&\qquad\qquad x(j) \leftarrow y(j) + u(j) \\
&\qquad\qquad x(p+j) \leftarrow y(p-j) - u(p-j) \\
&\qquad\qquad x(L_* + j) \leftarrow z(j) + v(j) \\
&\qquad\qquad x(L_* + p + j) \leftarrow -z(p-j) + v(p-j) \\
&\qquad \textbf{end} \\
&\textbf{else} \\
&\qquad \tau \leftarrow x(0); \; x(0) \leftarrow \tau + x(1); \; x(1) \leftarrow \tau - x(1) \\
&\textbf{end}
\end{aligned}
$$

This algorithm requires $5L/2$ flops and can be implemented without the work arrays u, v, y, and z.

4.3.5   DFT of a Single Real $2m$ Vector

As an exercise in conjugate-even butterfly manipulation, suppose $n = 2m$ and that we wish to compute $y = F_n x$, where $x \in \mathbb{R}^n$. We can apply Algorithm 4.3.1 to obtain $F_m x(0{:}2{:}n-1)$ and $F_m x(1{:}2{:}n-1)$ and then combine the results using Algorithm 4.3.2 to form y.

Algorithm 4.3.3   If $x \in \mathbb{R}^n$, $n = 2m$, and $y = F_n x$, then the following algorithm overwrites x with $y^{(ce)}$.

> Use Algorithm 4.3.1 to compute $v_1^{(ce)}$ and $v_2^{(ce)}$,
> where $v_1 = F_m x(0{:}2{:}n-1)$ and $v_2 = F_m x(1{:}2{:}n-1)$.
> Use Algorithm 4.3.2 to compute $y^{(ce)} \leftarrow B_n^{(ce)} \begin{bmatrix} v_1^{(ce)} \\ v_2^{(ce)} \end{bmatrix}$.

If $n = 2^t$ and a radix-2 algorithm is used, then this algorithm requires $2.5n \log_2 n$ flops.

4.3.6   The Edson Factorization and Algorithm

We now develop a version of the Cooley–Tukey algorithm that is built upon the conjugate-even butterfly. The idea is attributed to Edson in a paper by Bergland (1968). The key is to obtain a real version of the Cooley–Tukey factorization, which we will refer to as the *Edson factorization*.

Theorem 4.3.4   *If $n = 2^t$, then*

$$ U_n F_n P_n = A_t^{(ce)} \cdots A_1^{(ce)}, \qquad (4.3.6) $$

where

$$ A_q^{(ce)} = I_r \otimes B_L^{(ce)}, \qquad L = 2^q, \qquad r = n/L $$

and P_n is the bit-reversal permutation.

Proof.   We start with the Cooley–Tukey radix-2 factorization $F_n P_n = A_t \cdots A_1$, where for $q = 1{:}t$ we set $L = 2^q$, $r = n/L$, and $A_q = I_r \otimes B_L$. It follows that

$$ U_n F_n P_n = U_n A_t \cdots A_1 = \tilde{A}_t \cdots \tilde{A}_1, $$

where

$$ \tilde{A}_q = (I_r \otimes U_L) A_q (I_{r_*} \otimes U_{L_*}^{-1}), \qquad r_* = 2r, \qquad L_* = L/2 . $$

Thus, $\tilde{A}_q = I_r \otimes \left(U_L B_L (I_2 \otimes U_{L_*}^{-1}) \right) = I_r \otimes B_L^{(ce)} = A_q^{(ce)}$.   □

It is important to stress that each $A_q^{(ce)}$ is *real*. It follows that if $y = F_n x$, then

$$ y^{(ce)} = U_n F_n x = A_t^{(ce)} \cdots A_1^{(ce)} P_n x $$

can be computed as a sequence of conjugate-even butterfly updates on a bit-reversed version of x.

Algorithm 4.3.4 (Edson) If $x \in \mathbb{R}^n$, $y = F_n x$, and $n = 2^t$, then the following algorithm overwrites x with $y^{(ce)}$:

$$x \leftarrow P_n x$$
$$\textbf{for} \quad q = 1{:}t$$
$$\qquad L \leftarrow 2^q; \; r \leftarrow n/L$$
$$\qquad x_{L \times r} \leftarrow B_L^{(ce)} x_{L \times r}$$
$$\textbf{end}$$

This algorithm requires $2.5n \log_2 n$ flops.

4.3.7 Real Autosort FFT Frameworks

Using the U_n permutation we can also develop autosort frameworks for real DFTs. We start by developing a real version of the transposed Stockham factorization.

Theorem 4.3.5 *If $n = 2^t$, then*

$$U_n F_n = S_t^{(ce)} \cdots S_1^{(ce)},$$

where

$$S_q^{(ce)} = (I_r \otimes B_L^{(ce)})(\Pi_{r_*} \otimes I_{L_*}),$$

with $L = 2^q$, $r = n/L$, $L_* = L/2$, and $r_* = 2r$.

Proof. From the radix-2 transposed Stockham factorization (Theorem 1.7.1)

$$F_n = S_t \cdots S_1$$

it follows that

$$U_n F_n = \tilde{S}_t \cdots \tilde{S}_1,$$

where $\tilde{S}_q = (I_r \otimes U_L) S_q (I_{r_*} \otimes U_{L_*}^{-1})$. From the definition of S_q we obtain

$$
\begin{aligned}
\tilde{S}_q &= (I_r \otimes U_L)(I_r \otimes B_L)(\Pi_{r_*} \otimes I_{L_*})(I_{r_*} \otimes U_{L_*}^{-1}) \\
&= (I_r \otimes U_L B_L)(I_{r_*} \otimes U_{L_*}^{-1})(\Pi_{r_*} \otimes I_{L_*}) \\
&= (I_r \otimes U_L B_L)(I_r \otimes (I_2 \otimes U_{L_*}^{-1}))(\Pi_{r_*} \otimes I_{L_*}) \\
&= \left[I_r \otimes U_L B_L (I_2 \otimes U_L^{-1}) \right] (\Pi_{r_*} \otimes I_{L_*}) \\
&= S_q^{(ce)}.
\end{aligned}
$$

Here, we have made use of Kron1 and Kron7.   □

An analogous factorization can be derived for the Stockham factorization.

Theorem 4.3.6 *If $n = 2^t$, then*

$$U_n F_n = G_t^{(ce)} \cdots G_1^{(ce)},$$

where

$$G_q^{(ce)} = B_L^{(ce)} \Pi_L^T \otimes I_r,$$

with $L = 2^q$, $r = n/L$, $L_* = L/2$, and $r_* = 2r$.

Proof. From the radix-2 Stockham factorization (Theorem 1.7.2)

$$F_n = G_t \cdots G_1$$

it follows that

$$U_n F_n = \tilde{G}_t \cdots \tilde{G}_1,$$

where $\tilde{G}_q = (U_L \otimes I_r) G_q (U_{L_\bullet}^{-1} \otimes I_{r_\bullet})$. From the definition of G_q we obtain

$$
\begin{aligned}
\tilde{G}_q &= (U_L \otimes I_r)(B_L \Pi_L^T \otimes I_r)(U_{L_\bullet}^{-1} \otimes I_{r_\bullet}) \\
&= (U_L B_L \otimes I_r)(\Pi_L^T \otimes I_r)((U_{L_\bullet}^{-1} \otimes I_2) \otimes I_r) \\
&= (U_L B_L \otimes I_r)[\Pi_L^T (U_{L_\bullet}^{-1} \otimes I_2) \otimes I_r] \\
&= (U_L B_L \otimes I_r)[(I_2 \otimes U_{L_\bullet}^{-1}) \Pi_L^T \otimes I_r] \\
&= [U_L B_L (I_2 \otimes U_{L_\bullet}^{-1}) \otimes I_r](\Pi_L^T \otimes I_r) \\
&= (B_L^{(ce)} \Pi_L^T \otimes I_r) \\
&= G_q^{(ce)} .
\end{aligned}
$$

Here, we have made use of Kron1, Kron7, and Kron8. □

Note that the factors $S_q^{(ce)}$ and $G_q^{(ce)}$ are real and so, for example,

> **for** $q = 1{:}t$
> $y \leftarrow x$
> $x \leftarrow S_q^{(ce)} x$ (or $x \leftarrow G_q^{(ce)} x$)
> **end**

produces the DFT of x and puts it in conjugate even form.

4.3.8   DFTs of Conjugate Even Data

If $x \in \mathbb{C}^n$ is conjugate even and $y = F_n x$, then

$$\bar{y} = \bar{F}_n \bar{x} = (F_n T_n)(T_n x) = F_n x = y .$$

In other words, the DFT of a conjugate even vector is real. An efficient algorithm for performing this calculation can be obtained by transposing (4.3.6):

$$F_n = P_n (A_1^{(ce)})^T \cdots (A_t^{(ce)})^T U_n^{-T} . \tag{4.3.7}$$

Note from (4.3.3) that

$$
U_n^{-T} = \begin{bmatrix} 1 & 0 & 0 & 0 \\ 0 & I & 0 & E \\ 0 & 0 & 1 & 0 \\ 0 & iI & 0 & -iE \end{bmatrix} .
$$

If $x \in \mathbb{C}^n$ is conjugate even and $n = 2m$, then $U_n^{-T} x$ is real:

$$
U_n^{-T} \begin{bmatrix} a \\ b + ic \\ d \\ Eb - iEc \end{bmatrix} = \begin{bmatrix} a \\ 2b \\ d \\ -2c \end{bmatrix} .
$$

Here, $a, d \in \mathbb{R}$ and $b, c \in \mathbb{R}^{m-1}$. From the Edson factorization (4.3.6)

$$F_n x = P_n (A_1^{(ce)})^T \cdots (A_t^{(ce)})^T U_n^{-T} x$$

and so the DFT of x can proceed on real terms once we have applied U_n^{-T} to x.

Algorithm 4.3.5 Suppose $x \in \mathbb{R}^n$ is conjugate even with $n = 2^t$. If $\tilde{x} \in \mathbb{R}^n$ houses $x^{(ce)}$, then the following algorithm overwrites $\tilde{x}$ with the real vector $y = F_n x$:

> $m \leftarrow n/2$
> $\tilde{x}(1{:}m-1) \leftarrow 2\tilde{x}(1{:}m-1)$
> $\tilde{x}(m+1{:}n-1) \leftarrow -2\tilde{x}(m+1{:}n-1)$
> for $q = t{:}-1{:}1$
> $\tilde{x} \leftarrow (A_q^{(ce)})^T \tilde{x}$
> end
> $\tilde{x} \leftarrow P_n \tilde{x}$

This algorithm requires $2.5 n \log_2 n$ flops.

4.3.9 DIF Frameworks for Real Data

Suppose $n = 2^t$ and abbreviate the Cooley–Tukey factorization $F_n = A_t \cdots A_1 P_n$, with $F = AP$. As shown in §4.2.3, the convolution

$$f = F^{-1}((Fg).*(Fh)) \tag{4.3.8}$$

can be computed using FFTs without reference to P if we use the Gentleman–Sande framework $(F = PA^T)$ for the forward DFTs and the Cooley–Tukey framework $(F^{-1} = \bar{A}P/n)$ for the inverse DFT:

$$f = \frac{1}{n} \bar{A} \left((A^T g).*(A^T h) \right).$$

It is instructive to pursue an analogous approach for the real data convolution problem that is based upon the Edson factorization (4.3.6). By abbreviating this factorization by $UFP = A^{(ce)}$ and substituting

$$F = (U^{-1} A^{(ce)} P)^T = P[A^{(ce)}]^T U^{-T}$$

and

$$F^{-1} = \frac{1}{n} \bar{F} = \bar{U}^{-1}[A^{(ce)}]^T P$$

into (4.3.8), we obtain

$$f = \frac{1}{n} \bar{U}^{-1} A^{(ce)} \left(([A^{(ce)}]^T U^{-T} g).*([A^{(ce)}]^T U^{-T} h) \right).$$

The bit-reversal permutation has dropped out, but the transpose of the real matrix $A^{(ce)} = A_t^{(ce)} \cdots A_1^{(ce)}$ is applied to the *complex* vectors $U^{-T} g$ and $U^{-T} h$. However, these vectors are highly structured and we refer the reader to the work of Briggs (1987) for ideas on how to proceed.

4.3.10   A Real Four-Step Framework

Multicolumn and multirow versions of the Edson algorithm can be effectively arranged for vector computation following the ideas of §3.1.

Suppose $x \in \mathbb{R}^n$ and that $n = n_1 n_2$ with $n_1 = 2^{t_1}$ and $n_2 = 2^{t_2}$. The four-step process begins with the multiple row DFT

$$x_{n_1 \times n_2} \leftarrow x_{n_1 \times n_2} F_{n_2}.$$

An obvious multiple row version of Algorithm 4.3.4 could be applied. The difficulties arise with the twiddle-factor scaling because the data confronting the second multiple DFT has no readily exploitable structure:

$$x_{n_2 \times n_1} \leftarrow ((x_{n_1 \times n_2} F_{n_2}) .* F_n(0{:}n_1 - 1, 0{:}n_2 - 1))^T F_{n_1}.$$

One solution to this problem is to apply the four-step process to the complex DFT that arises in Algorithm 4.3.3. In particular, we compute

$$y = F_{n/2}(x(0{:}2{:}n - 1) + ix(1{:}2{:}n - 1))$$

via the four-step process. The DFTs $F_{n/2}x(0{:}2{:}n - 1)$ and $F_{n/2}x(1{:}2{:}n - 1)$ are then determined in accordance with Theorem 4.3.3 and are combined by the butterfly $B_n^{(ce)}$ to get $F_n x$.

4.3.11   The Hartley Transform

In some real-data applications that require the DFT, some authors have suggested that the Hartley transform provides a viable alternative. In this subsection we briefly describe the fast Hartley transform (FHT) and its connection to the FFT. Readers who want greater detail in matrix/vector notation, should consult the book by Bracewell (1986).

We say that $y \in \mathbb{R}^n$ is the *Hartley transform* $x \in \mathbb{R}^n$ if

$$y_k = \sum_{j=0}^{n-1} \left(\cos\left(\frac{2kj\pi}{n}\right) + \sin\left(\frac{2kj\pi}{n}\right) \right) x_j$$

for $k = 0{:}n - 1$. In matrix-vector terms this means that

$$y = H_n x,$$

where

$$H_n = \text{Re}(F_n) - \text{Im}(F_n).$$

Since $\bar{F}_n = T_n F_n$, we have

$$\text{Re}(F_n) = \frac{F_n + \bar{F}_n}{2} = \frac{1}{2}(I_n + T_n)F_n$$

$$\text{Im}(F_n) = \frac{F_n - \bar{F}_n}{2i} = -\frac{i}{2}(I_n - T_n)F_n$$

and so

$$H_n = \Phi_n F_n, \tag{4.3.9}$$

where

$$\Phi_n = \left(\frac{1}{2}(I_n + T_n) + \frac{i}{2}(I_n - T_n) \right) = \frac{1+i}{2} I_n + \frac{1-i}{2} T_n .$$

Thus, the matrix Φ_n is the connecting link between the Hartley and Fourier transforms. This matrix has a very simple structure, as illustrated by the example

$$\Phi_6 = \begin{bmatrix} 1 & 0 & 0 & 0 & 0 & 0 \\ 0 & \alpha & 0 & 0 & 0 & \beta \\ 0 & 0 & \alpha & 0 & \beta & 0 \\ 0 & 0 & 0 & 1 & 0 & 0 \\ 0 & 0 & \beta & 0 & \alpha & 0 \\ 0 & \beta & 0 & 0 & 0 & \alpha \end{bmatrix}, \qquad \alpha = \frac{1+i}{2}, \beta = \frac{1-i}{2} .$$

We mention that $\Phi_1 = I_1$ and $\Phi_2 = I_2$. In general it can be shown that

$$\Phi_n^{-1} = \frac{1-i}{2} I_n + \frac{1+i}{2} T_n = \bar{\Phi}_n . \qquad (4.3.10)$$

The derivation of a radix-2 Hartley factorization can proceed along the same lines as our derivation of the real Cooley–Tukey factorization once we define the *Hartley butterfly*:

$$B_L^{(Hart)} = \Phi_L \begin{bmatrix} I_{L_*} & \Omega_{L_*} \\ I_{L_*} & -\Omega_{L_*} \end{bmatrix} (I_2 \otimes \Phi_{L_*}^{-1}). \qquad (4.3.11)$$

Here, $L = 2L_*$ and $\Omega_{L_*} = \text{diag}(1, \omega_L, \ldots, \omega_L^{L_*-1})$. Note that $B_2^{(Hart)} = B_2$.

Theorem 4.3.7 *If* $n = 2^t$, *then*

$$H_n P_n = A_t^{(Hart)} \cdots A_1^{(Hart)},$$

where

$$A_q^{(Hart)} = I_r \otimes B_L^{(Hart)}, \qquad L = 2^q, \ r = n/L$$

and P_n *is the bit-reversal permutation.*

Proof. Applying Φ_n to both sides of the Cooley–Tukey factorization $F_n P_n = A_t \cdots A_1$ gives

$$H_n P_n = \tilde{A}_t \cdots \tilde{A}_1,$$

where

$$\tilde{A}_q = (I_r \otimes \Phi_L) A_q (I_{r_*} \otimes \Phi_{L_*}^{-1}), \qquad L_* = L/2, \ r_* = 2r .$$

From the definition of A_q it follows that

$$\begin{aligned} \tilde{A}_q &= (I_r \otimes \Phi_L)(I_r \otimes B_L)(I_r \otimes (I_2 \otimes \Phi_{L_*}^{-1})) \\ &= I_r \otimes (\Phi_L B_L (I_2 \otimes \Phi_{L_*}^{-1})) \\ &= I_r \otimes B_L^{(Hart)} = A_q^{(Hart)}, \end{aligned}$$

thereby completing the proof of the theorem.

To develop a recipe for $B_L^{(Hart)}$, we set $I = I_{L_*-1}$, $E = E_{L_*-1}$, $\alpha = (1+i)/2$, and $\beta = (1-i)/2$ and work with the blockings

$$\Phi_L = \begin{bmatrix} 1 & 0 & 0 & 0 \\ 0 & \alpha I & 0 & \beta E \\ 0 & 0 & 1 & 0 \\ 0 & \beta E & 0 & \alpha I \end{bmatrix},$$

$$\Phi_{L_*}^{-1} = \begin{bmatrix} 1 & 0 \\ 0 & \beta I + \alpha E \end{bmatrix},$$

$$\Omega_{L_*} = \begin{bmatrix} 1 & 0 \\ 0 & \tilde{\Omega} \end{bmatrix},$$

where $\tilde{\Omega} = \mathrm{diag}(\omega_L, \ldots, \omega_L^{L_*-1})$. By substituting these block forms into (4.3.11) and noting that $\alpha^2 + \beta^2 = 0$, $\alpha^2 = i/2$, and $\alpha\beta = 1/2$, we obtain

$$\Phi_L B_L (I_2 \otimes \Phi_{L_*}^{-1}) = \Phi_L \begin{bmatrix} \Phi_{L_*}^{-1} & \Omega_{L_*}\Phi_{L_*}^{-1} \\ \Phi_{L_*}^{-1} & -\Omega_{L_*}\Phi_{L_*}^{-1} \end{bmatrix}$$

$$= \begin{bmatrix} 1 & 0 & 0 & 0 \\ 0 & \alpha I & 0 & \beta E \\ 0 & 0 & 1 & 0 \\ 0 & \beta E & 0 & \alpha I \end{bmatrix} \begin{bmatrix} 1 & 0 & 1 & 0 \\ 0 & \beta I + \alpha E & 0 & \tilde{\Omega}(\beta I + \alpha E) \\ 1 & 0 & -1 & 0 \\ 0 & \beta I + \alpha E & 0 & -\tilde{\Omega}(\beta I + \alpha E) \end{bmatrix}$$

$$= \begin{bmatrix} 1 & 0 & 1 & 0 \\ 0 & I & 0 & (\tilde{\Omega} - E\tilde{\Omega}E)/2 + i(\tilde{\Omega} + E\tilde{\Omega}E)E/2 \\ 1 & 0 & -1 & 0 \\ 0 & I & 0 & -(\tilde{\Omega} - E\tilde{\Omega}E)/2 - i(\tilde{\Omega} + E\tilde{\Omega}E)E/2 \end{bmatrix}.$$

If we index $\tilde{\Omega}$ from 1 to $L_* - 1$, then $\left[E\tilde{\Omega}E\right]_{jj} = \omega_L^{L_*-j} = -\bar{\omega}_L^j = -\left[\tilde{\Omega}\right]_{jj}$ and so

$$\tilde{\Omega} - E\tilde{\Omega}E = 2\,\mathrm{Re}(\tilde{\Omega}),$$

$$\tilde{\Omega} + E\tilde{\Omega}E = 2i\,\mathrm{Im}(\tilde{\Omega}).$$

By defining the vectors

$$c = [\cos(\theta), \ldots, \cos((L_* - 1)\theta)]^T,$$

$$s = [\sin(\theta), \ldots, \sin((L_* - 1)\theta)]^T,$$

with $\theta = -2\pi/L$, we obtain

$$B_L^{(Hart)} = \begin{bmatrix} 1 & 0 & 1 & 0 \\ 0 & I & 0 & \mathrm{diag}(c) - \mathrm{diag}(s)E \\ 1 & 0 & -1 & 0 \\ 0 & I & 0 & -\mathrm{diag}(c) + \mathrm{diag}(s)E \end{bmatrix}. \qquad (4.3.12)$$

The following algorithm is analogous to Algorithm 4.3.4.

Algorithm 4.3.6 If $x \in \mathbb{C}^n$ and $n = 2^t$, then the following algorithm overwrites x with its Hartley transform:

$$x \leftarrow P_n x$$
$$\text{for} \quad q = 1{:}t$$
$$\quad L \leftarrow 2^q; \; r \leftarrow n/L$$
$$\quad x_{L \times r} \leftarrow B_L^{(Hart)} x_{L \times r}$$
$$\text{end}$$

The correspondence between $B_L^{(ce)}$ and $B_L^{(Hart)}$ goes further:

- As in the conjugate-even case, the Hartley butterflies can be implemented in-place.

- Hartley versions of Theorems 4.3.5 and 4.3.6 also exist. (Just replace U_n with Φ_n, $A_q^{(ce)}$ with $A_q^{(Hart)}$, and $B_L^{(ce)}$ with $B_L^{(Hart)}$.) The resulting factorizations can be used to develop autosorted Hartley frameworks.

We refer the reader to the work of Buneman (1986) for further details.

Problems

P4.3.1 Develop an in-place version of Algorithm 4.3.1, assuming that $n = 2^t$.

P4.3.2 Develop an in-place version of Algorithm 4.3.2.

P4.3.3 Develop a complete real-data Stockham algorithm.

P4.3.4 Develop an in-place algorithm for the operation $x \leftarrow (B_L^{(ce)})^T x$.

P4.3.5 Develop an in-place algorithm for the operation $x \leftarrow B_L^{(Hart)} x$.

P4.3.6 Develop an in-place algorithm for $x \leftarrow \Phi_n x$.

P4.3.7 Develop a radix-4, conjugate-even butterfly and formulate a radix-4 version of Algorithm 4.3.4.

P4.3.8 Suppose $X \in \mathbb{R}^{n_1 \times n_2}$ and consider the computation of the two-dimensional DFT $Y = F_{n_1} X F_{n_2}$. Assume that $n_1 = 2m_1$ and $n_2 = 2m_2$. (a) Using the equation $\bar{Y} = T_{n_1} Y T_{n_2}$, show that Y has the form

$$Y = \begin{bmatrix} \alpha & y_{01}^T & \beta & \bar{y}_{01}^T E_{n_2} \\ y_{10} & Y_{11} & y_{12} & E_{n_1} \bar{Y}_{31} E_{n_2} \\ \gamma & y_{21}^T & \delta & \bar{y}_{21}^T E_{n_2} \\ E_{n_1} \bar{y}_{10} & Y_{31} & E_{n_1} \bar{y}_{12} & E_{n_1} \bar{Y}_{11} E_{n_2} \end{bmatrix} \begin{matrix} 1 \\ m_1-1 \\ 1 \\ m_1-1 \end{matrix}$$
$$\quad\quad 1 \quad m_2-1 \quad 1 \quad m_2-1$$

where α, β, γ, and δ are real. (b) Develop a framework for the computation of Y that is based upon the Edson factorization and the vector radix idea in §3.4.1.

P4.3.9 Derive a radix-2, conjugate-even splitting of the form

$$U_n F_n \Pi_n = B_n^{(ce)} (I_2 \otimes U_m F_m).$$

Notes and References for Section 4.3

The approach taken in Algorithm 4.3.3 is detailed in

J.W. Cooley, P.A.W. Lewis, and P.D. Welsh (1970). "The Fast Fourier Transform Algorithm: Programming Considerations in the Calculation of Sine, Cosine, and Laplace Transforms," *J. Sound Vibrations 12*, 315–337.

See also

A.E. Siegman (1975). "How to Compute Two Complex Even Fourier Transforms with One Transform Step," *Proc. IEEE 63*, 544.

R.C. Singleton (1967a). "On Computing Fast Fourier Transforms," *Comm. ACM 10*, 647–654.

The streamlining of the Cooley–Tukey algorithm when x is real is first detailed in

G.D. Bergland (1968). "A Fast Fourier Transform Algorithm for Real-Valued Series," *Comm. ACM 11*, 703–710,

who attributes the idea to Edson. This paper discusses the radix-2 case, but extensions are possible:

G.D. Bergland (1969). "A Radix-8 Fast Fourier Transform Subroutine for Real Valued Series," *IEEE Trans. Audio and Electroacoustics AU-17*, 138–144.

The Edson philosophy, which is to eliminate redundant computation in the conjugate-even butterfly, can be applied to other structured FFTs:

W.L. Briggs (1987). "Further Symmetries of In-Place FFTs," *SIAM J. Sci. and Statist. Comput. 8*, 644–654.

P.N. Swarztrauber (1986). "Symmetric FFTs," *Math. Comp. 47*, 323–346.

Other papers concerned with the computation of real-data DFTs include

C. Temperton (1980a). "Very Fast Real Fourier Transform," in *Special Topics of Applied Mathematics: Functional Analysis, Numerical Analysis, and Optimization*, J. Frehse, D. Pallaschke, and U. Trottenberg (eds.), North Holland, Amsterdam, 165–171.

C. Temperton (1983b). "Fast Mixed-Radix Real Fourier Transforms," *Comput. Phys. 52*, 340–350.

C. Temperton (1988b). "A Self-Sorting In-Place Prime Factor Real/Half-Complex FFT Algorithm," *J. Comp. Phys. 75*, 199–216.

The basic references for the Hartley transformation include

R.N. Bracewell (1986). *The Hartley Transform*, Oxford University Press, New York.

R.N. Bracewell, O. Buneman, H. Hao, and J. Villasenor (1986). "Fast Two-Dimensional Hartley Transforms," *Proc. IEEE 74*, 1282.

O. Buneman (1986). "Conversion of FFT to Fast Hartley Transforms," *SIAM J. Sci. and Statist. Comput. 7*, 624–638 .

O. Buneman (1987a). "Multidimensional Hartley Transforms," *Proc. IEEE 75*, 267.

H. Hao and R.N. Bracewell (1987). "A Three Dimesional DFT Algorithm Using the Fast Hartley Transform," *Proc. IEEE 75*, 264.

H.V. Sorensen, D.L. Jones, M.T. Heideman, C.S. Burrus (1985). "On Computing the Discrete Hartley Transform," *IEEE Trans. Acoust. Speech Signal Process. ASSP-33*, 1231–1238.

The subject of whether the Hartley approach is to be preferred to a real FFT framework is interesting. See

P. Duhamel and M. Vetterli (1987). "Improved Fourier and Hartley Transform Algorithms Application to Cyclic Convolution of Real Data," *IEEE Trans. Acoust. Speech Signal Process. ASSP-35*, 818–824.

H.V. Sorensen, D.L. Jones, M.T. Heideman, C.S. Burrus (1987). "Real-Valued Fast Fourier Transform Algorithms," *IEEE Trans. Acoust. Speech Signal Process. ASSP-35*, 849–863.

These papers discuss very effective real data, split-radix frameworks.

4.4 Fast Trigonometric Transforms

In this section we show how FFTs can be used to compute the following trigonometric transforms:

- *The Inverse Real Periodic Transform:* Given real $x(0{:}n-1)$, with $n = 2m$, compute real $a(0{:}m)$ and $b(1{:}m-1)$ such that

$$x_k = \frac{a_0}{2} + \sum_{j=1}^{m-1} \left(a_j \cos\left(\frac{kj\pi}{m}\right) + b_j \sin\left(\frac{kj\pi}{m}\right) \right) + \frac{(-1)^k a_m}{2} \,. \qquad (4.4.1)$$

- *The Discrete Sine Transform* (DST): Given real $x(1{:}m-1)$, compute $y(1{:}m-1)$ such that

$$y_k = \sum_{j=1}^{m-1} \sin\left(\frac{kj\pi}{m}\right) x_j \,. \qquad (4.4.2)$$

- *The Discrete Cosine Transform* (DCT): Given real $x(0{:}m)$, compute $y(0{:}m)$ such that

$$y_k = \frac{x_0}{2} + \sum_{j=1}^{m-1} \cos\left(\frac{kj\pi}{m}\right) x_j + \frac{(-1)^k x_m}{2} \,. \qquad (4.4.3)$$

- *The Discrete Sine Transform-II* (DST-II): Given real $x(1{:}m)$, compute $y(1{:}m)$ such that

$$y_k = \sum_{j=1}^{m} \sin\left(\frac{k(2j-1)\pi}{2m}\right) x_j \,. \qquad (4.4.4)$$

- *The Discrete Cosine Transform-II* (DCT-II): Given real $x(0{:}m-1)$, compute $y(0{:}m-1)$ such that

$$y_k = \sum_{j=0}^{m-1} \cos\left(\frac{k(2j+1)\pi}{2m}\right) x_j \,. \qquad (4.4.5)$$

These transforms have a wide range of applicability, both in signal processing and in the numerical solution of partial differential equations. *Our goal is to develop FFT-based algorithms for these transforms that require $2.5m \log_2 m$ flops, assuming that m is a power of two.* Much of this section is derived from the papers by Cooley, Lewis, and Welsh (1970) and Swarztrauber (1986).

In order to develop these methods, we need to identify important sine/cosine patterns in the DFT matrix. With these patterns we can show how to obtain the inverse real periodic transform by applying the real-data FFT to x. The other four transforms can be obtained by computing $F_{2m}\tilde{x}$, where $\tilde{x}$ is an "expanded" input vector . Table 4.4.1 illustrates the form of the "tilde" vectors. As the table shows, the tilde vectors are highly structured but have twice the dimension of the original problem. If m is a power of two, then without further economies a real-data FFT such as Algorithm 4.3.4 would require $5m \log_2 m$ to compute $F_{2m}\tilde{x}$, twice our stated goal. To obtain a $2.5m \log_2 m$ algorithm, we must fully exploit all symmetries that arise when computing $F_{2m}\tilde{x}$.

TABLE 4.4.1
The tilde problems ($m = 4$).

Transform	x^T	$\tilde{x}^T$
DST	$[\, x_1,\, x_2,\, x_3\,]$	$[\, 0,\, x_1,\, x_2,\, x_3\ 0,\, -x_3,\, -x_2,\, -x_1\,]$
DCT	$[\, x_0,\, x_1,\, x_2,\, x_3,\, x_4\,]$	$[\, x_0,\, x_1,\, x_2,\, x_3,\, x_4,\, x_3,\, x_2,\, x_1\,]$
DST-II	$[\, x_1,\, x_2,\, x_3,\, x_4]$	$[\, x_1,\, x_2,\, x_3,\, x_4,\, -x_4,\, -x_3,\, -x_2,\, -x_1]$
DCT-II	$[\, x_0,\, x_1,\, x_2,\, x_3]$	$[\, x_0,\, x_1,\, x_2,\, x_3,\, x_3,\, x_2,\, x_1,\, x_0]$

4.4.1   Some Important Matrices

The real and imaginary parts of the DFT matrix are "made up" of cosines and sines. In particular, if we define the real n-by-n *cosine matrix* C_n by

$$[C_n]_{kj} \;=\; \cos\left(\frac{2\pi kj}{n}\right) \tag{4.4.6}$$

and the real n-by-n *sine matrix* S_n by

$$[S_n]_{kj} \;=\; \sin\left(\frac{2\pi kj}{n}\right), \tag{4.4.7}$$

then $F_n \;=\; C_n - iS_n$. Note from Table 4.4.2 that transforms (4.4.2)–(4.4.5) can be specified in terms of the cosine and sine matrices. The tilde vectors enable us to

TABLE 4.4.2
Matrix specification of trigonometric transforms.

Transform	Matrix Specification
DST	$y(1{:}m-1) = S_{2m}(1{:}m-1,1{:}m-1)x(1{:}m-1)$
DCT	$y(0{:}m) = C_{2m}(0{:}m,0{:}m)\left[\; x_0/2 \mid x(1{:}m-1) \mid x_m/2 \;\right]^T$
DST-II	$y(1{:}m) = S_{4m}(1{:}m,1{:}2{:}2m-1)x(1{:}m)$
DCT-II	$y(0{:}m-1) = C_{4m}(0{:}m-1,1{:}2{:}2m-1)x(0{:}m-1)$

"extract" these matrix-vector products from DFT matrix-vector products.

The derivation of these methods relies heavily upon properties of the exchange permutation (E_n), the downshift permutation (R_n), and the reflection permutation (T_n). The definitions of these permutations are worth recalling through example:

$$E_4 = \begin{bmatrix} 0 & 0 & 0 & 1 \\ 0 & 0 & 1 & 0 \\ 0 & 1 & 0 & 0 \\ 1 & 0 & 0 & 0 \end{bmatrix}, \quad R_4 = \begin{bmatrix} 0 & 0 & 0 & 1 \\ 1 & 0 & 0 & 0 \\ 0 & 1 & 0 & 0 \\ 0 & 0 & 1 & 0 \end{bmatrix}, \quad T_4 = \begin{bmatrix} 1 & 0 & 0 & 0 \\ 0 & 0 & 0 & 1 \\ 0 & 0 & 1 & 0 \\ 0 & 1 & 0 & 0 \end{bmatrix}.$$

Here are some useful relationships between these matrices:

$$R_n E_n = T_n, \qquad R_n = T_n E_n, \qquad E_n = T_n R_n. \tag{4.4.8}$$

We leave it to the reader to verify these equalities.

4.4.2 Sine/Cosine Blockings of the DFT Matrix

The sine and cosine matrices have an important block structure that is exploited by all the algorithms to follow.

Theorem 4.4.1 *If we define the vectors* e *and* v *by*

$$e^T = (\underbrace{1, 1, \ldots, 1}_{m-1}), \qquad v^T = (\underbrace{-1, 1 \ldots, (-1)^{m-1}}_{m-1})$$

and the matrices E, C, *and* S *by*

$$E = E_{m-1}, \quad C = C_{2m}(1{:}m-1, 1{:}m-1), \quad S = S_{2m}(1{:}m-1, 1{:}m-1),$$

then

$$F_{2m} = \begin{bmatrix} 1 & e^T & 1 & e^T \\ e & C-iS & v & (C+iS)E \\ 1 & v^T & (-1)^m & v^T E \\ e & E(C+iS) & Ev & E(C-iS)E \end{bmatrix}. \tag{4.4.9}$$

Proof. With C, S, e, and v defined as above, it is easy to confirm from the definition of F_{2m} that

$$F_{2m}(0{:}m, 0{:}m) = \begin{bmatrix} 1 & e^T & 1 \\ e & C-iS & v \\ 1 & v^T & (-1)^m \end{bmatrix}.$$

Recall from Theorem 4.3.1 that $T_n F_n = F_n T_n = \bar{F}_n$, which implies that the columns and rows of F_n are conjugate even. It follows that if

$$F_{2m} = \begin{bmatrix} 1 & e^T & 1 & A_{30}^T \\ e & C-iS & v & A_{31}^T \\ 1 & v^T & (-1)^m & A_{32}^T \\ A_{30} & A_{31} & A_{32} & A_{33} \end{bmatrix}$$

then

$$\begin{aligned} \bar{A}_{30} &= Ee & \Rightarrow & \quad A_{30} = e, \\ \bar{A}_{31} &= E(C-iS) & \Rightarrow & \quad A_{31} = E(C+iS), \\ \bar{A}_{32} &= Ev & \Rightarrow & \quad A_{32} = Ev, \\ \bar{A}_{33} &= EA_{31}^T & \Rightarrow & \quad A_{33} = E(C-iS)E. \end{aligned}$$

From these equations we conclude that the block structure (4.4.9) prevails. □

By using this blocking of the DFT matrix, we can obtain useful characterizations of the DST and DCT.

Theorem 4.4.2 *Suppose $x = x(1{:}m-1)$ is real. If*

$$
\tilde{x} \;=\; \begin{bmatrix} 0 \\ x(1{:}m-1) \\ 0 \\ -E_{m-1}x(1{:}m-1) \end{bmatrix} \in \mathbb{R}^{2m}
$$

and

$$
y(0{:}2m-1) = \frac{i}{2}F_{2m}\tilde{x}\,,
$$

then $y(1{:}m-1)$ is the DST of $x(1{:}m-1)$ defined by (4.4.2).

Proof. From Table 4.4.2 and the notation of Theorem 4.4.1, we see that our task is to compute Sx. Since $E^2 = E$ and $e^T E = e^T$, we have

$$
y(0{:}2m-1) \;=\; \frac{i}{2}\begin{bmatrix} 1 & e^T & 1 & e^T \\ e & C-iS & v & (C+iS)E \\ 1 & v^T & (-1)^m & v^T E \\ e & E(C+iS) & Ev & E(C-iS)E \end{bmatrix}\begin{bmatrix} 0 \\ x \\ 0 \\ -Ex \end{bmatrix}
$$

$$
=\; \frac{i}{2}\begin{bmatrix} e^T x - e^T E x \\ -2iSx \\ v^T x - v^T E^2 x \\ i(ESx + ESE^2 x) \end{bmatrix} = \begin{bmatrix} 0 \\ Sx \\ 0 \\ -ESx \end{bmatrix}
$$

and so $y(1{:}m-1)$ is the desired transform.   □

A corresponding result holds for the DCT.

Theorem 4.4.3 *Suppose $x = x(0{:}m)$ is real. If*

$$
\tilde{x} \;=\; \begin{bmatrix} x_0 \\ x(1{:}m-1) \\ x_m \\ E_{m-1}x(1{:}m-1) \end{bmatrix} \in \mathbb{R}^{2m}
$$

and

$$
y(0{:}2m-1) = \frac{1}{2}F_{2m}\tilde{x}\,,
$$

then $y(0{:}m)$ is the DCT of x defined by (4.4.3).

Proof. The proof is similar to the proof of Theorem 4.4.2 and is omitted.

The DST-II and DCT-II are based upon a blocking of a row-scaled version of F_{2m}. The following lemma is required.

Lemma 4.4.4 *If $\Omega_n = \mathrm{diag}(1, \omega_{2n}, \ldots, \omega_{2n}^{n-1})$, then $\bar{\Omega}_n \bar{F}_n = (\Omega_n F_n) E_n$.*

Proof. Observations about $F_n R_n$ and $F_n T_n$ are required. First, the equation $F_n R_n = \Omega_n^2 F_n$ follows by setting $D_n = \Omega_n^2$ in Lemma 4.2.3. Second, $F_n T_n = \bar{F}_n$ from Theorem 4.3.1. Using (4.4.8) we see that

$$
(\Omega_n F_n)E_n = \Omega_n F_n T_n R_n = \Omega_n \bar{F}_n R_n = \Omega_n \bar{\Omega}_n^2 \bar{F}_n = \bar{\Omega}_n \bar{F}_n,
$$

thereby completing the proof of the lemma.   □

With this lemma we obtain

Theorem 4.4.5 *If*

$$\Omega_{2m} = \text{diag}(1, \omega_{4m}, \ldots, \omega_{4m}^{2m-1}),$$

$$\tilde{C} = C_{4m}(0:2m-1, 1:2:2m-1),$$

$$\tilde{S} = S_{4m}(0:2m-1, 1:2:2m-1),$$

then $\Omega_{2m} F_{2m} = \left[(\tilde{C} - i\tilde{S}) \mid (\tilde{C} + i\tilde{S})E_m \right].$

Proof. Set $G = \Omega_{2m} F_{2m}$. It follows that if $0 \le k, j \le 2m - 1$, then

$$g_{kj} = \omega_{4m}^k \omega_{2m}^{kj} = \omega_{4m}^k \omega_{4m}^{2kj} = \omega_{4m}^{k(2j+1)}$$

$$= \cos\left(\frac{2\pi k(2j+1)}{4m}\right) - i\sin\left(\frac{2\pi k(2j+1)}{4m}\right)$$

$$= [C_{4m}]_{k,2j+1} - i[S_{4m}]_{k,2j+1}.$$

Thus, $G(0:2m-1, 0:m-1) = \tilde{C} - i\tilde{S}$. From the previous lemma we know that $GE_{2m} = \bar{G}$ and so G must have the form $G = \left[(\tilde{C} - i\tilde{S}) \mid (\tilde{C} + i\tilde{S})E \right]$, completing the proof of the theorem. $\square$

With this blocking we are able to obtain useful characterizations of the DST-II and the DCT-II.

Theorem 4.4.6 *Suppose* $x = x(1:m)$ *is real. If*

$$\tilde{x} = \left[\begin{array}{c} x \\ -E_m x \end{array} \right]$$

and

$$y = y(0:2m-1) = \frac{i}{2}\Omega_{2m} F_{2m} \tilde{x},$$

then $y(1:m)$ *is the DST-II of* x *defined by (4.4.4).*

Proof. Using Theorem 4.4.5, if $\tilde{S} = S_{4m}(0:2m-1, 1:2:2m-1)$, then we have

$$y = \frac{i}{2}\left[(\tilde{C} - i\tilde{S}) \mid (\tilde{C} + i\tilde{S})E_m \right]\left[\begin{array}{c} x(1:m) \\ -E_m x(1:m) \end{array} \right] = \tilde{S}x(1:m).$$

However, from Table 4.4.2 we see that the desired transform is given by $\tilde{S}(1:m, 1:m)x$ and so $y(1:m)$ is the DST-II of x. $\square$

An analogous result holds for the DCT-II.

Theorem 4.4.7 *Suppose* $x = x(0:m-1)$ *is real. If*

$$\tilde{x} = \left[\begin{array}{c} x \\ E_m x \end{array} \right]$$

and

$$y = y(0:2m-1) = \frac{1}{2}\Omega_{2m} F_{2m} \tilde{x},$$

then $y(0:m-1)$ *is the DCT-II of* x *defined by (4.4.5).*

Proof. The verification is similar to the proof of Theorem 4.4.6 and is omitted.

4.4.3   Vector Symmetries

The key to the efficient computation of the transforms (4.4.1)–(4.4.5) lies in the systematic exploitation of tilde-vector structure. In Table 4.4.3 we list the important symmetries that arise when attempting to compute trigonometric transforms via the DFT. Note that the tilde vectors that arise in the DST, DCT, DST-II, and DCT-II

TABLE 4.4.3

Important vector symmetries ($n = 6$).

Symmetry	Definition	Example
real even (*re*)	$x = T_n x$	$[\, x_0,\ x_1,\ x_2,\ x_3,\ x_2,\ x_1 \,]$
real odd (*ro*)	$x = -T_n x$	$[\, x_0,\ x_1,\ x_2,\ 0,\ -x_2,\ -x_1 \,]$
quarter wave even (*qe*)	$x = E_n x$	$[\, x_0,\ x_1,\ x_2,\ x_2,\ x_1,\ x_0 \,]$
quarter wave odd (*qo*)	$x = -E_n x$	$[\, x_0,\ x_1,\ x_2,\ -x_2,\ -x_1,\ -x_0 \,]$
conjugate even (*ce*)	$\bar{x} = T_n x$	$[\, x_0,\ x_1,\ x_2,\ x_3,\ \bar{x}_2,\ \bar{x}_1 \,]$
conjugate odd (*co*)	$\bar{x} = -T_n x$	$[\, x_0,\ x_1,\ x_2,\ x_3,\ -\bar{x}_2,\ -\bar{x}_1 \,]$

transforms are, respectively, (*ro*), (*re*), (*qo*), and (*qe*). If x has any of the properties listed in Table 4.4.3, then $F_n x$ has structure itself. Indeed,

$$
\text{if } x \text{ is } \left\{ \begin{array}{c} \text{real} \\ \text{imaginary} \\ \text{real even} \\ \text{real odd} \\ \text{conjugate even} \\ \text{conjugate odd} \end{array} \right\} \text{ then } F_n x \text{ is } \left\{ \begin{array}{c} \text{conjugate even} \\ \text{conjugate odd} \\ \text{real} \\ \text{imaginary} \\ \text{real} \\ \text{imaginary} \end{array} \right\} .
$$

Some of these properties have already been confirmed. They are all easily established. For example,

$$
T_n x = -\bar{x} \ \Rightarrow\ F_n x = -F_n T_n \bar{x} = -\bar{F}_n \bar{x} = -(\bar{F}_n \bar{x})
$$

shows that the DFT of a conjugate-odd vector is imaginary.

The DFT of a (*qo*) or (*qe*) vector does not fit so neatly into the above "option sentence." However, such vectors do produce DFTs of structure.

Theorem 4.4.8 *If* $\Omega_n = \mathrm{diag}(1, \omega_{2n}, \ldots, \omega_{2n}^{n-1})$ *and* $x \in \mathbb{R}^n$, *then*

$$
\begin{aligned}
x = E_n x &\ \Rightarrow\ \Omega_n(F_n x) \ \text{ is real,} \\
x = -E_n x &\ \Rightarrow\ \Omega_n(F_n x) \ \text{ is imaginary.}
\end{aligned}
$$

Proof. If x is (*qe*), then by Lemma 4.4.4

$$
\Omega_n F_n x = (\Omega_n F_n) E_n x = \bar{\Omega}_n \bar{F}_n x = \bar{\Omega}_n \bar{F}_n \bar{x} \,.
$$

The result for (*qo*) vectors is proved similarly.   □

Another set of patterns that we exploit concerns the symmetries that emerge when we perform an even/odd sort of a vector that is either (*re*), (*ro*), (*qe*), or (*qo*). The $n = 8$ examples

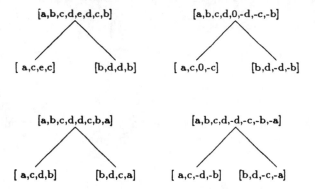

suggest the following result:

Theorem 4.4.9 *Suppose* $x \in \mathbb{R}^n$ *and that* $n = 2m$. *If* $u = x(0{:}2{:}n-1)$ *and* $v = x(1{:}2{:}n-1)$, *then*

$$
\begin{array}{rcllll}
T_n x & = & x & \Rightarrow & T_m u = u \ \text{and} \ E_m v = v, \\
T_n x & = & -x & \Rightarrow & T_m u = -u \ \text{and} \ E_m v = -v, \\
E_n x & = & x & \Rightarrow & E_m u = v, \\
E_n x & = & -x & \Rightarrow & E_m u = -v.
\end{array}
$$

Proof. We establish the first of these results and leave the rest to the reader. If $T_n x = x$, then for $k = 1{:}m-1$ we have $x_{n-k} = x_k$. Since $u_k = x_{2k}$, we have

$$ u_{m-k} = x_{2(m-k)} = x_{n-2k} = x_{2k} = u_k, $$

showing that $T_m u = u$. To show that $v = E_m v$ we must confirm that $v_{m-k-1} = v_k$ for $k = 0{:}m-1$. Since $v_k = x_{2k+1}$, we have

$$ v_{m-k-1} = x_{2(m-k-1)+1} = x_{n-2k-1} = x_{2k+1} = v_k \ . $$

This shows that an (re) vector splits into an (re) and a (qe) vector. $\square$

4.4.4 The Inverse Real Periodic Transform

Algorithmic developments begin with the derivation of a fast method for (4.4.1). Using Theorem 4.4.1 we can make the following interesting observation about the DFT of a (ce) vector.

Theorem 4.4.10 *Suppose* $n = 2m$. *If* $a(0{:}m)$ *and* $b(1{:}m-1)$ *are real and* $x \in \mathbb{R}^n$ *is defined by*

$$
x = \frac{1}{2} F_n \begin{bmatrix} a_0 \\ a(1{:}m-1) + ib(1{:}m-1) \\ a_m \\ E(a(1{:}m-1) - ib(1{:}m-1)) \end{bmatrix},
$$

then

$$
x_k = \frac{a_0}{2} + \sum_{j=1}^{m-1} \left(a_j \cos\left(\frac{kj\pi}{m} \right) + b_j \sin\left(\frac{kj\pi}{m} \right) \right) + \frac{(-1)^k a_m}{2}
$$

for $k = 0{:}n-1$.

Proof. Using the notation of (4.4.9), it is not hard to show that

$$
x = \begin{bmatrix} 1/2 & e^T & 1/2 \\ e/2 & C & v/2 \\ 1/2 & v^T & (-1)^m/2 \\ e/2 & EC & Ev/2 \end{bmatrix} a(0{:}m) + \begin{bmatrix} 0 \\ S \\ 0 \\ -S \end{bmatrix} b(1{:}m-1).
$$

The proof is completed by comparing components.   □

The theorem lays the groundwork for computing the inverse real periodic transform (4.4.1). In particular, if we are given $x \in \mathbb{R}^n$ and compute

$$
2F_n^{-1}x = \begin{bmatrix} a_0 \\ a(1{:}m-1) + ib(1{:}m-1) \\ a_m \\ E(a(1{:}m-1) - ib(1{:}m-1)) \end{bmatrix},
$$

then (4.4.1) holds. Substituting $F_n^{-1} = \bar{F}_n/n$ into this equation and taking conjugates suggests that we compute $a(0{:}m)$ and $b(1{:}m-1)$ via the equation

$$
\frac{2}{n}F_nx = \begin{bmatrix} a_0 \\ a(1{:}m-1) - ib(1{:}m-1) \\ a_m \\ E(a(1{:}m-1) + ib(1{:}m-1)) \end{bmatrix}.
$$

Since x is real, we can ascertain $a(0{:}m)$ and $b(1{:}m-1)$ by applying a real-data FFT.

Algorithm 4.4.1 (Inverse Real Periodic Transform) If $x \in \mathbb{R}^n$ and $n = 2m$, then the following algorithm computes real vectors $a(0{:}m)$ and $b(1{:}m-1)$ so that (4.4.1) holds.

$$y \leftarrow F_nx$$
$$a(0{:}m) \leftarrow (2/n)\mathrm{Re}(y(0{:}m))$$
$$b(1{:}m-1) \leftarrow -(2/n)\mathrm{Im}(y(1{:}m-1))$$

If $n = 2^t$ and Algorithm 4.3.4 is used to compute y, then $2.5n \log_2 n$ flops are required.

4.4.5   The Discrete Sine Transform

If we take Theorem 4.4.2 literally and compute

$$
y = \frac{i}{2}F_{2m}\tilde{x}, \qquad \tilde{x} = \begin{bmatrix} 0 \\ x(1{:}m-1) \\ 0 \\ -E_{m-1}x(1{:}m-1) \end{bmatrix} \tag{4.4.10}
$$

using a real-data FFT, then $5m\log_2 m$ flops are required. This is twice the desired amount of computation. Instead, we pursue an approach that revolves around the framework of §4.3.5:

- *Step 1.* Set $u = \tilde{x}(0{:}2{:}2m-1)$ and $v = \tilde{x}(1{:}2{:}2m-1)$.

- *Step 2.* Compute the complex DFT $z_1 + iz_2 = F_m(v + iu)$.

- *Step 3.* Compute $f = F_m v$ and $g = F_m u$ using the Theorem 4.3.3 formulae

$$\begin{aligned} f &= [(I_m + T_m)z_1 + i(I_m - T_m)z_2]/2 \,, \\ g &= [(I_m + T_m)z_2 - i(I_m - T_m)z_1]/2 \,. \end{aligned}$$

- *Step 4.* If $\Omega_m = \text{diag}(1, \omega_{2m}, \ldots, \omega_{2m}^{m-1})$, then

$$F_{2m}\tilde{x} = \begin{bmatrix} I_m & \Omega_m \\ I_m & -\Omega_m \end{bmatrix} \begin{bmatrix} g \\ f \end{bmatrix}$$

and so from (4.4.10) we have

$$y_k = \frac{i}{2}\left[g_k + \omega_{2m}^k f_k\right], \qquad k = 1{:}m-1 \,. \tag{4.4.11}$$

The cost of this process is dominated by the m-point complex DFT in Step 2. If we assume that m is a power of two, then the overall process requires $5m\log_2 m$ flops, and there is no improvement over the naive approach. Howe·er, the flop count can be halved if we exploit the following result.

Theorem 4.4.11 *Suppose $\tilde{x} \in \mathbb{R}^{2m}$ is (ro). If*

$$\begin{aligned} u &= \tilde{x}(0{:}2{:}n-1), \\ v &= \tilde{x}(1{:}2{:}n-1), \\ \tilde{v} &= (I_m - R_m)\tilde{x}(1{:}2{:}n-1), \end{aligned}$$

then the vector

$$\tilde{z} = \tilde{v} + iu$$

is (ce) and $(I_m - \Omega_m^2)F_m v = F_m \tilde{v}$ where $\Omega_m = \text{diag}(1, \omega_{2m}, \ldots, \omega_{2m}^{m-1})$.

Proof. To show that $\tilde{v} + iu$ is (ce), we must show that $T_m \tilde{v} = \tilde{v}$ and $T_m u = -u$. Since x is (ro), then using Theorem 4.4.9 we know that $E_m v = -v$ and $T_m u = -u$, so we are half done. Making use of the relationships (4.4.8), we find

$$\begin{aligned} T_m \tilde{v} &= T_m(I_m - R_m)v = -T_m(I_m - R_m)E_m v \\ &= (-T_m E_m + T_m R_m E_m)v = (I_m - R_m)v = \tilde{v} \,. \end{aligned}$$

Recall Lemma 4.2.3, which says that $F_m R_m = \Omega_m^2 F_m$. It follows that

$$F_m \tilde{v} = F_m(I_m - R_m)v = (I_m - \Omega_m^2)F_m v,$$

completing the proof of the theorem. □

This result enables us to rewrite the above four-step sine transform as follows:

- *Step $\tilde{1}$.* Set $u = \tilde{x}(0{:}2{:}2m-1)$ and $\tilde{v} = (I_m - R_m)\tilde{x}(1{:}2{:}2m-1)$.

- *Step $\tilde{2}$.* Compute the complex DFT $\tilde{z}_1 + i\tilde{z}_2 = F_m(\tilde{v} + iu)$. Since $\tilde{v} + iu$ is (ce), we may use Algorithm 4.3.5. Note that $\tilde{z}_2 = 0$.

- *Step $\tilde{3}$.* Compute $\tilde{f} = F_m \tilde{v}$ and $g = F_m u$ using the formulae

$$\tilde{f} = F_m \tilde{v} = \frac{1}{2}(I_m + T_m)\tilde{z}_1,$$

$$g = F_m u = -\frac{i}{2}(I_m - T_m)\tilde{z}_1.$$

- *Step $\tilde{4}$.* From Theorem 4.4.11, $(I_m - \Omega_m^2)f = \tilde{f}$ and so for $k = 1{:}m-1$, $f_k = \tilde{f}_k/(1 - \omega_m^k)$. It follows from (4.4.11) and the equation

$$\omega_{2m}^k/(1 - \omega_m^k) = 1/(\bar{\omega}_{2m}^k - \omega_{2m}^k) = -i/(2\sin(k\pi/n))$$

that

$$y_k = \frac{i}{2}(g_k + \omega_{2m}^k f_k) = \left(\frac{i}{2}\right) g_k + \left(\frac{i}{2}\right)\left(\frac{\omega_{2m}^k}{1 - \omega_m^k}\right)\tilde{f}_k$$

$$= \left(\frac{i}{2}\right) g_k + \left(\frac{1}{4\sin(k\pi/m)}\right)\tilde{f}_k.$$

Putting it all together we obtain the following procedure.

Algorithm 4.4.2 (Fast Sine Transform) If $x(1{:}m-1)$ is real, then the following algorithm computes its DST $y(1{:}m-1)$ as defined by (4.4.2):

Define $\tilde{x} \in \mathbb{R}^{2m}$ by (4.4.10).

$u \leftarrow \tilde{x}(0{:}2{:}2m-1)$

$\tilde{v} \leftarrow (I_m - R_m)\tilde{x}(1{:}2{:}2m-1)$

$\tilde{z}_1 \leftarrow F_m(\tilde{v} + iu)$

$a \leftarrow (I_m + T_m)\tilde{z}_1/8$

$b \leftarrow (I_m - T_m)\tilde{z}_1/4$

for $k = 1{:}m-1$

    $y_k \leftarrow b_k + a_k/\sin(k\pi/m)$

end

If m is a power of two and a real-data FFT such as Algorithm 4.3.3 or 4.3.4 is used to compute $\tilde{z}_1$, then $2.5m\log m$ flops are required.

4.4.6   The Discrete Cosine Transform

The derivation of a fast algorithm for the DCT is similar to the derivation in the previous section, so it is necessary to stress only the high points. From Theorem 4.4.3 our goal is to compute $y(0{:}m)$, where

$$y = \frac{1}{2}F_{2m}\tilde{x}, \qquad \tilde{x} = \begin{bmatrix} x_0 \\ x(1{:}m-1) \\ x_m \\ Ex(1{:}m-1) \end{bmatrix} \in \mathbb{R}^{2m}. \qquad (4.4.12)$$

From the definition (4.4.3) we know that

$$y_0 = \frac{1}{2}x_0 + \sum_{j=1}^{m-1} x_j + \frac{1}{2}x_m,$$

$$y_m = \frac{1}{2}x_0 + \sum_{j=1}^{m-1}(-1)^j x_j + \frac{(-1)^m}{2}x_m.$$

It remains to specify $y(1{:}m-1)$.

If $u = \tilde{x}(0{:}2{:}2m-1)$, $v = \tilde{x}(1{:}2{:}2m-1)$, then

$$y = \frac{1}{2}\left[\begin{array}{cc} I_m & \Omega_m \\ I_m & -\Omega_m \end{array}\right]\left[\begin{array}{c} f \\ g \end{array}\right]$$

where $f = F_m u$ and $g = F_m v$. Thus,

$$y_k = \frac{1}{2}(f_k + \omega_{2m}^k g_k)$$

for $k = 1{:}m-1$. If $\tilde{v} = (I_m - R_m)v$, then it is not hard to verify that $u + i\tilde{v}$ is (ce). Therefore, $\tilde{z}_1 = F_m(u + i\tilde{v})$ is real and from Theorem 4.3.3 we have

$$f = F_m u = \frac{1}{2}(I_m + T_m)\tilde{z}_1,$$

$$\tilde{g} = F_m \tilde{v} = -\frac{i}{2}(I_m - T_m)\tilde{z}_1.$$

From Theorem 4.4.11 we know that

$$\tilde{v} = (I_m - R_m)v \quad \Rightarrow \quad \tilde{g} = (I_m - \Omega_{2m}^2)g,$$

where $\Omega_m = \operatorname{diag}(1, \omega_{2m}, \ldots, \omega_{2m}^{m-1})$. Thus,

$$y_k = \frac{1}{2}\left(f_k + \frac{\omega_{2m}^k}{1 - \omega_m^k}\tilde{g}_k\right) = \frac{1}{2}\left(f_k - \frac{i}{2\sin(k\pi/m)}\tilde{g}_k\right).$$

Putting it all together in the style of Algorithm 4.4.2, we obtain the following procedure.

Algorithm 4.4.3 (Fast Cosine Transform) If $x(0{:}m)$ is real, then the following algorithm computes its DCT $y(0{:}m)$ as defined by (4.4.3):

Define $\tilde{x} \in \mathbb{R}^{2m}$ by (4.4.12).

$u \leftarrow \tilde{x}(0{:}2{:}2m-1)$

$\tilde{v} \leftarrow (I_m - R_m)\tilde{x}(1{:}2{:}2m-1)$

$\tilde{z}_1 \leftarrow F_m(u + i\tilde{v})$

$a \leftarrow (I_m + T_m)\tilde{z}_1/4$

$b \leftarrow (I_m - T_m)\tilde{z}_1/8$

$y_0 \leftarrow (x_0 + x_m)/2$

$y_m \leftarrow (x_0 + (-1)^m x_m)/2$

for $k = 1{:}m-1$

$\quad y_0 \leftarrow y_0 + x_k$

$\quad y_m \leftarrow y_0 + (-1)^{k+1} x_k$

$\quad y_k \leftarrow a_k - b_k/\sin(k\pi/m)$

end

If m is a power of two and a real-data FFT is used to compute $\tilde{z}_1$, then $2.5m\log m$ flops are required.

4.4.7   The Inverse Discrete Sine and Cosine Transforms

Recall the matrix U_n and its inverse from §4.3.2:

$$
U_n = \begin{bmatrix} 1 & 0 & 0 & 0 \\ 0 & I/2 & 0 & E/2 \\ 0 & 0 & 1 & 0 \\ 0 & -iI/2 & 0 & iE/2 \end{bmatrix}, \qquad U_n^{-1} = \begin{bmatrix} 1 & 0 & 0 & 0 \\ 0 & I & 0 & iI \\ 0 & 0 & 1 & 0 \\ 0 & E & 0 & -iE \end{bmatrix}.
$$

It is straightforward to confirm that

$$
U_n F_n U_n^{-1} = \begin{bmatrix} 1 & 2e^T & 1 & 0 \\ e & 2C & v & 0 \\ 1 & 2v^T & (-1)^m & 0 \\ 0 & 0 & 0 & 2iS \end{bmatrix}. \tag{4.4.13}
$$

The inverse of the DST and DCT can be deduced from (4.4.13). Since $U_n F_n^{-1} U_n^{-1} = (1/n) U_n \bar{F}_n U_n^{-1}$, we have

$$
U_n F_n^{-1} U_n^{-1} = \frac{1}{n} \begin{bmatrix} 1 & 2e^T & 1 & 0 \\ e & 2C & v & 0 \\ 1 & 2v^T & (-1)^m & 0 \\ 0 & 0 & 0 & -2iS \end{bmatrix}.
$$

By comparing blocks in

$$
\frac{1}{n} \begin{bmatrix} 1 & 2e^T & 1 & 0 \\ e & 2C & v & 0 \\ 1 & 2v^T & (-1)^m & 0 \\ 0 & 0 & 0 & -2iS \end{bmatrix} = \begin{bmatrix} 1 & 2e^T & 1 & 0 \\ e & 2C & v & 0 \\ 1 & 2v^T & (-1)^m & 0 \\ 0 & 0 & 0 & 2iS \end{bmatrix}^{-1},
$$

we may conclude that

$$
[S_n(1{:}m-1, 1{:}m-1)]^{-1} = \frac{2}{m} S_n(1{:}m-1, 1{:}m-1) \tag{4.4.14}
$$

and

$$
\begin{bmatrix} 1/2 & e^T & 1/2 \\ e/2 & C & v/2 \\ 1/2 & v^T & (-1)^m/2 \end{bmatrix}^{-1} = \frac{2}{m} \begin{bmatrix} 1/2 & e^T & 1/2 \\ e/2 & C & v/2 \\ 1/2 & v^T & (-1)^m/2 \end{bmatrix}. \tag{4.4.15}
$$

Thus, apart from a constant factor, the DST and DCT are inverses of themselves. To compute the inverse DST (DCT) transform, we apply Algorithm 4.4.2 (4.4.3), with the roles of x and y reversed and we scale the result by $2/m$.

4.4.8   The Discrete Sine Transform-II

From Theorem 4.4.6 the DST-II of $x(1{:}m)$ is given by $y(1{:}m)$, where

$$
y(0{:}2m-1) = \frac{i}{2} \Omega_{2m} F_{2m} \tilde{x}, \qquad \tilde{x} = \begin{bmatrix} x(1{:}m) \\ -E_m x(1{:}m) \end{bmatrix}. \tag{4.4.16}
$$

Now

$$
F_{2m} \tilde{x} = \begin{bmatrix} I_m & \Omega_m \\ I_m & -\Omega_m \end{bmatrix} \begin{bmatrix} f \\ g \end{bmatrix}, \tag{4.4.17}
$$

where

$$
\begin{array}{ll}
f = F_m u, & u = \tilde{x}(0{:}2{:}2m-1), \\
g = F_m v, & v = \tilde{x}(1{:}2{:}2m-1)
\end{array}
\tag{4.4.18}
$$

and so for $k = 1{:}m-1$

$$
y_k = \frac{i}{2}\omega_{4m}^k \left(f_k + \omega_{2m}^k g_k\right).
\tag{4.4.19}
$$

Since $v = -E_m u$ (Theorem 4.4.9) and $F_m E_m = \bar{\Omega}_m^2 \bar{F}_m$ (Lemma 4.4.4), we have

$$
g = F_m v = -F_m E_m u = -\bar{\Omega}_m^2 \bar{F}_m u = -\bar{\Omega}_m^2 (\bar{F}_m \bar{u}) = -\bar{\Omega}_m^2 \bar{f}.
$$

It follows from (4.4.19) and the equation $\omega_{2m}^k = \omega_{4m}^{2k}$ that

$$
y_k = \frac{i}{2}\omega_{4m}^k (f_k - \omega_{2m}^k \bar{\omega}_m^k \bar{f}_k) = -\mathrm{Im}(\omega_{4m}^k f_k)
\tag{4.4.20}
$$

for $k = 1{:}m-1$. To get an expression for y_m, note from equations (4.4.16) and (4.4.18) that

$$
u = \left[\begin{array}{c} x(1{:}2{:}m) \\ -E_p x(2{:}2{:}m) \end{array} \right]
\tag{4.4.21}
$$

where we assume $m = 2p$. It follows from (4.4.18) and (4.4.4) that

$$
y_m = \sum_{j=1}^{m} \sin\left(\frac{m(2j-1)\pi}{2m}\right) x_j = \sum_{j=1}^{m}(-1)^{j+1} x_j = f_0.
\tag{4.4.22}
$$

Combining the above equations, we obtain the following procedure.

Algorithm 4.4.4 (Fast Sine Transform-II) If $x(1{:}m)$ is real and $m = 2p$, then the following algorithm computes its DST-II, $y(1{:}m)$, as defined by (4.4.4).

$$
f \leftarrow F_m \left[\begin{array}{c} x(1{:}2{:}m) \\ -E_p x(2{:}2{:}m) \end{array} \right]
$$

$$
\textbf{for } k = 1{:}m-1
$$
$$
\qquad y_k \leftarrow -\mathrm{Im}(\omega_{4m}^k f_k)
$$
$$
\textbf{end}
$$
$$
y_m \leftarrow f_0
$$

If m is a power of two and a real-data FFT is used to compute f, then $2.5m \log m$ flops are required.

In the inverse DST-II problem, we are given a real vector $y(1{:}m)$ and seek a real $x(1{:}m)$ so that (4.4.4) holds. The appropriate computations can be derived by "working backwards" through some of the above formulae. In particular, by using y we can obtain f, with f we can retrieve u, and with u we can specify x. Here are some of the details:

We first observe that $f = F_m u$ is (ce) and so from (4.4.20)

$$
y_{m-k} = -\mathrm{Im}\left(\omega_{4m}^{m-k} f_{m-k}\right) = -\mathrm{Im}\left(-i\bar{\omega}_{4m}^k \bar{f}_k\right) = \mathrm{Re}(\omega_{4m}^k f_k)
\tag{4.4.23}
$$

for $k = 1{:}m-1$. Combining (4.4.23) with (4.4.20) gives us

$$
\omega_{4m}^k f_k = y_{m-k} - i y_k, \qquad k = 1{:}m-1,
$$

which means that $f_k = \bar{\omega}_{4m}^k(y_{m-k} - iy_k)$, $k = 1{:}m - 1$. By combining this with (4.4.22), we obtain a complete specification of $f(0{:}m - 1)$:

$$f_k = \begin{cases} y_m, & k = 0, \\ \\ \bar{\omega}_{4m}^k(y_{m-k} - iy_k), & k = 1{:}m - 1. \end{cases}$$

From f we can recover the vector u in (4.4.18) via an IDFT, i.e.,

$$u = F_m^{-1}f = \frac{1}{m}\bar{F}_m f.$$

Since u is real, and f is (ce), we can compute $u = (F_m\bar{f})/m$ via Algorithm 4.3.5. Finally, we observe that x can be recovered from u using (4.4.21). Overall we obtain the following procedure.

Algorithm 4.4.5 (Inverse Sine Transform-II) If $y(1{:}m)$ is real and $m = 2p$, then this algorithm computes real $x(1{:}m)$ such that (4.4.4) holds.

$f_0 \leftarrow y_m$
for $k = 1{:}m - 1$
$\quad f_k \leftarrow \bar{\omega}_{4m}^k(y_{m-k} - iy_k)$
end
$u \leftarrow (F_m\bar{f})/m$
Determine $x(1{:}m)$ from $u = \begin{bmatrix} x(1{:}2{:}m) \\ -E_p x(2{:}2{:}m) \end{bmatrix}$.

If m is a power of two and Algorithm 4.3.5 is used to compute u, then $2.5m \log m$ flops are required.

It can be shown that if $x(1{:}m)$ is produced by Algorithm 4.4.5, then for $k = 1{:}m$

$$x_k = \frac{2}{m}\left(\sum_{j=1}^{m-1}\sin\left(\frac{(2k-1)j\pi}{2m}\right)y_j + \frac{(-1)^k}{2}y_m\right). \qquad (4.4.24)$$

4.4.9   The Discrete Cosine Transform-II

The derivation of the DCT-II and its inverse closely follows the derivation of the DST-II and its inverse. From Theorem 4.4.7 the object is to compute $y(0{:}m - 1)$, where

$$y(0{:}2m - 1) = \frac{1}{2}\Omega_{2m}F_{2m}\tilde{x}, \qquad \tilde{x} = \begin{bmatrix} x(0{:}m - 1) \\ E_m x(0{:}m - 1) \end{bmatrix}. \qquad (4.4.25)$$

Working with

$$\begin{array}{ll} f = F_m u, & u = \tilde{x}(0{:}2{:}2m - 1), \\ g = F_m v, & v = \tilde{x}(1{:}2{:}2m - 1), \end{array} \qquad (4.4.26)$$

and

$$F_{2m}\tilde{x} = \begin{bmatrix} I_m & \Omega_m \\ I_m & -\Omega_m \end{bmatrix}\begin{bmatrix} f \\ g \end{bmatrix},$$

it is not hard to show as we did in (4.4.20) that

$$y_k = \frac{1}{2}\omega_{4m}^k\left(f_k + \omega_{2m}^k g_k\right) = \text{Re}(\omega_{4m}^k f_k). \qquad (4.4.27)$$

If $m = 2p$, then from (4.4.25) and (4.4.26)

$$u = \begin{bmatrix} x(0{:}2{:}m-1) \\ E_p x(1{:}2{:}m-1) \end{bmatrix} \tag{4.4.28}$$

and we obtain the following procedure.

Algorithm 4.4.6 (Fast Cosine Transform-II) If $x(0{:}m-1)$ is real and $m = 2p$, then the following algorithm computes its DCT-II defined by (4.4.5).

$$f \leftarrow F_m \begin{bmatrix} x(0{:}2{:}m-1) \\ E_p x(1{:}2{:}m-1) \end{bmatrix}$$
$$\textbf{for } k = 0{:}m-1$$
$$\qquad y_k \leftarrow \text{Re}(\omega_{4m}^k f_k)$$
$$\textbf{end}$$

If m is a power of two and Algorithm 4.3.4 is used to compute f, then $2.5 m \log m$ flops are required.

In the inverse DCT-II problem we are given a real vector $y(0{:}m-1)$ and seek a real $x(0{:}m-1)$ so that (4.4.5) holds. We start by computing the vector f that is defined by (4.4.26). Since f is (ce),

$$y_{m-k} = \text{Re}\left(\omega_{4m}^{m-k} f_{m-k}\right) = \text{Re}\left(-i\bar{\omega}_{4m}^{k} \bar{f}_k\right) = -\text{Im}(\omega_{4m}^k f_k) \tag{4.4.29}$$

for $k = 1{:}m-1$. Combining this with (4.4.27) gives $\omega_{4m}^k f_k = y_k - i y_{m-k}$ for $k = 1{:}m-1$. The specification of f is complete once we notice from (4.4.26) that $y_0 = f_0$. An inverse DFT prescribes u in terms of f and x is a permutation of u.

Algorithm 4.4.7 (Inverse Cosine Transform-II) If $y(0{:}m-1)$ is real and $m = 2p$, then this algorithm computes real $x(0{:}m-1)$ such that (4.4.5) holds.

$$f_0 \leftarrow y_0$$
$$\textbf{for } k = 1{:}m-1$$
$$\qquad f_k \leftarrow \bar{\omega}_{4m}^k (y_k - i y_{m-k})$$
$$\textbf{end}$$
$$u \leftarrow (F_m \bar{f})/m$$
Determine x from $u = \begin{bmatrix} x(0{:}2{:}m-1) \\ E_p x(1{:}2{:}m-1) \end{bmatrix}$.

If m is a power of two and Algorithm 4.3.5 is used to compute u, then $2.5 m \log_2 m$ flops are required.

It can be shown that if $x(0{:}m-1)$ is produced by Algorithm 4.4.7, then for $k = 0{:}m-1$

$$x_k = \frac{2}{m} \left(\frac{1}{2} y_0 + \sum_{j=1}^{m-1} \cos\left(\frac{(2k+1)j\pi}{2m} \right) y_j \right). \tag{4.4.30}$$

4.4.10 The Structured Splitting Framework

We conclude this section with a brief discussion of the structured splitting approach of Swarztrauber (1986) to solve the tilde-vector DFT problems that are described in Theorems 4.4.2, 4.4.3, 4.4.6, and 4.4.7. The idea is to exploit the redundancies that arise when a structured vector is repeatedly split into its even- and odd-indexed portions. We build upon Theorem 4.4.9, which identifies the structures that emerge when an (re), (ro), (qe), or (qo) vector is split:

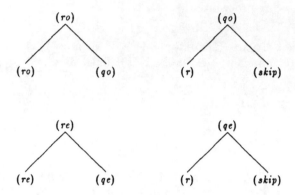

Here, "r" designates a real but otherwise unstructured vector. Note that when a quarter-wave sequence is split, we can "live" with the DFT of the even-indexed portions, as we observed in §§4.4.8 and 4.4.9.

To illustrate how these patterns recur in a repeated splitting, Fig. 4.4.1 illustrates the patterns that emerge during a three-deep splitting of a real-odd vector. Major

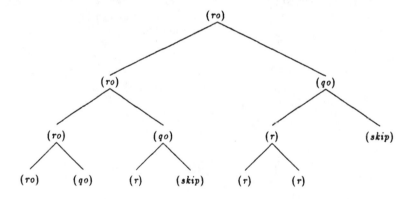

FIG. 4.4.1. *Structured splittings.*

economies result in two ways. First, large portions of the full tree are "clipped" because DFTs of quarter-wave data require only a single half-length DFT. Second, we can essentially apply Algorithm 4.3.4 to any real-data DFT.

Clearly, the repeated splitting of an (re) permits similar economies. The following recursive function captures the key ideas behind this structured FFT framework. It assumes that n is a power of two and that $x \in \mathbb{R}^n$ has one of the structures (ro), (qo), (re), (qe), or (r):

$$\textbf{function } y = \textbf{symdft}(x, n, type)$$

   $\textbf{if } n = 2$

   $$y \leftarrow \begin{bmatrix} 1 & 1 \\ 1 & -1 \end{bmatrix} \begin{bmatrix} x_0 \\ x_1 \end{bmatrix}$$

   $\textbf{else}$

   $m \leftarrow n/2$

   $u \leftarrow x(0{:}2{:}n-1)$

   $v \leftarrow x(1{:}2{:}n-1)$

   $\textbf{if } type = \text{``}ro\text{''}$

   $\quad f \leftarrow \textbf{symdft}(u, m, \text{``}ro\text{''})$

   $\quad g \leftarrow \textbf{symdft}(v, m, \text{``}qo\text{''})$

   $\textbf{elseif } type = \text{``}qo\text{''}$

   $\quad f \leftarrow \textbf{symdft}(u, m, \text{``}r\text{''})$

   $\quad g \leftarrow -\bar{\Omega}_m^2 \bar{f}$

   $\textbf{elseif } type = \text{``}re\text{''}$

   $\quad f \leftarrow \textbf{symdft}(u, m, \text{``}re\text{''})$

   $\quad g \leftarrow \textbf{symdft}(v, m, \text{``}qe\text{''})$

   $\textbf{elseif } type = \text{``}qe\text{''}$

   $\quad f \leftarrow \textbf{symdft}(u, m, \text{``}r\text{''})$

   $\quad g \leftarrow \bar{\Omega}_m^2 \bar{f}$

   $\textbf{elseif } type = \text{``}r\text{''}$

   $\quad f \leftarrow \textbf{symdft}(u, m, \text{``}r\text{''})$

   $\quad g \leftarrow \textbf{symdft}(v, m, \text{``}r\text{''})$

   $\textbf{end}$

   $$y \leftarrow \begin{bmatrix} I_m & \Omega_m \\ I_m & -\Omega_m \end{bmatrix} \begin{bmatrix} f \\ g \end{bmatrix}$$

$\textbf{end}$

The full exploitation of structure in **symdft** would require using the conjugate-even butterfly techniques of §4.3. Note that we assume that n is a power of two in **symdft**.

Problems

P4.4.1 Verify (4.4.8).

P4.4.2 Prove Theorem 4.4.7.

P4.4.3 Complete the proof of Theorem 4.4.9.

P4.4.4 Verify (4.4.21) and (4.4.28).

P4.4.5 Verify (4.4.24) and (4.4.30).

P4.4.6 Write loops to handle all the vector operations that are specified in Algorithms 4.4.2-4.4.7.

Notes and References for Section 4.4

The sine and cosine tilde problems are discussed in

J.W. Cooley, P.A.W. Lewis, and P.D. Welsh (1970). "The Fast Fourier Transform Algorithm: Programming Considerations in the Calculation of Sine, Cosine, and Laplace Transforms," *J. Sound Vibrations 12*, 315–337.

J. Dollimore (1973). "Some Algorithms for Use with the Fast Fourier Transform," *J. Inst. Math. Applic. 12*, 115–117.

See also

P. Swarztrauber (1982). "Vectorizing the FFTs," in *Parallel Computations*, G. Rodrigue (ed.), Academic Press, New York, 490–501.

which also includes a discussion of the vectorization issues.

The DST-II and DCT-II are the inverse *quarter-wave transforms* developed in

P.N. Swarztrauber (1977). "The Methods of Cyclic Reduction, Fourier Analysis, and the FACR Algorithm for the Discrete Solution of Poisson's Equation on a Rectangle," *SIAM Rev. 19*, 490–501.

W.L. Briggs (1987). "Further Symmetries of In-Place FFTs," *SIAM J. Sci. Statist. Comput. 8*, 644–654.

P.N. Swarztrauber (1986). "Symmetric FFTs," *Math. Comp. 47*, 323–346.

The DST-II and DCT-II are but one of several ways in which the basic sine and cosine transforms can be modified. A nice unifying discussion of the possibilities is given in

Z. Wang and B.R. Hunt (1985). "The Discrete *W* Transform," *Appl. Math. Comput. 16*, 19–48.

The computation of sine and cosine transforms is of great importance in signal processing, and numerous algorithmic ideas have evolved from researchers in that field:

N. Ahmed, T. Natarajan, and K.R. Rao (1974). "Discrete Cosine Transform," *IEEE Trans. Comput. C-23*, 90–93.

W.-H. Chen, C.H. Smith, and S.C. Fralick (1977). "A Fast Computational Algorithm for the Discrete Cosine Transform," *IEEE Trans. Comm. COM-25*, 1004–1009.

R.M. Haralick (1976). "A Storage Efficient Way to Implement the Discrete Cosine Transform," *IEEE Trans. Comput. C-25*, 764–765.

F.A. Kamangar and K.R. Rao (1982). "Fast Algorithms for the 2-D Discrete Cosine Transform," *IEEE Trans. Comput. C-31*, 899–906.

H. Kitajima (1980). "A Symmetric Cosine Transform," *IEEE Trans. Comput. C-29*, 317–323.

J. Makhoul (1980). "A Fast Cosine Transform in One and Two Dimensions," *IEEE Trans. Acoust. Speech Signal Process. ASSP-28*, 27–33.

M.J. Narasimha and A.M. Peterson (1978). "On the Computation of the Discrete Cosine Transform," *IEEE Trans. Comm. COM-26*, 934–936.

H. Nussbaumer (1980). "Fast Multidimensional Discrete Cosine Transforms," *IBM Tech. Disclosure Bull. 23*, 1976–1981.

H. Nussbaumer (1981a). "Improved Approach for the Computation of Multidimensional Cosine Transforms," *IBM Tech. Disclosure Bull. 23*, 4517–4521.

L.R. Rabiner (1979). "On the Use of Symmetry in FFT Computation," *IEEE Trans. Acoust. Speech Signal Process. ASSP-27*, 233–239.

B.D. Tseng and W.C. Miller (1978). "On Computing the Discrete Cosine Transform," *IEEE Trans. Comput. C-27*, 966–968.

M.D. Wagh and H. Ganesh (1980). "A New Algorithm for the Discrete Cosine Transformation of Arbitrary Number of Points," *IEEE Trans. Comput. C-29*, 269–277.

Z.D. Wang (1982). A Fast Algorithm for the Discrete Sine Transform Implemented by the Fast Cosine Transform," *IEEE Trans. Acoust. Speech Signal Process. ASSP-30*, 814–815.

Z.D. Wang (1983). "Reconsideration of 'A Fast Computational Algorithm for the Discrete Cosine Transformation'," *IEEE Trans. Comm. COM-31*, 121–123.

Z. Wang and B.R. Hunt (1983). "The Discrete Cosine Transform—A New Version," *Proc. 1983 IEEE Int. Conf. Acoust. Speech Signal Process.*, 1256–1259.

P. Yip and K.R. Rao (1978). "Sparse Matrix Factorization of Discrete Sine Transform," *Conf. Record 12th Asilomar Conf. Circuits, Systems, and Computers*, Pacific Grove, CA, 549–555.

P. Yip and K.R. Rao (1980). "A Fast Computation Algorithm for the Discrete Sine Transform," *IEEE Trans. Comm. COM-28*, 304–307.

The parallel implementation of several fast trigonometric transforms is discussed in

C. Chu (1988). *The Fast Fourier Transform on Hypercube Parallel Computers*, Ph.D. Thesis, Center for Applied Mathematics, Cornell University, Ithaca, NY.

Finally, we mention that the development of structure-exploiting FFTs extends beyond the cases that we have considered in this section. See

L. Auslander and M. Shenefelt (1987). "Fourier Transforms that Respect Crystallographic Symmetries," *IBM J. Research and Development 31*, 213–223.

L.F. Ten Eyck (1973). "Crystallographic Fast Fourier Transforms," *ACTA Crystallogr. A A29*, 183–191.

4.5 Fast Poisson Solvers

Suppose $F(x, y)$ is defined on the rectangle

$$R = \{(x, y) : a \le x \le b, \ c \le y \le d\}.$$

The *Poisson problem* on R involves finding a function $U(x, y)$ that satisfies

$$\frac{\partial^2 U}{\partial x^2} + \frac{\partial^2 U}{\partial y^2} = F(x, y) \qquad (4.5.1)$$

for all $(x, y) \in R$, subject to the constraint that certain *boundary conditions* are satisfied. Sample conditions might be that the value of U is prescribed along the top and bottom of R and the value of its x-partial is prescribed along the sides.

Well-known discretizations of the Poisson problem lead to linear systems of the form

$$[(\mathcal{T}_{row} \otimes I) + (I \otimes \mathcal{T}_{col})]\, u = g, \qquad (4.5.2)$$

where u is a vector of approximate $U(x, y)$ values. The matrices $\mathcal{T}_{row}$ and $\mathcal{T}_{col}$ are low-rank perturbations of appropriately dimensioned "1-2-1" tridiagonal matrices. The nature of the perturbations depends upon the boundary conditions but in all the cases that we consider, the resulting $\mathcal{T}$ matrices in (4.5.2) have highly structured eigensystems that are related to the fast trigonometric transforms of §4.4. Our goal is to establish these eigensystem/transform connections and to show how they can be used to design very effective *fast* Poisson solvers.

Fast Poisson solvers are at the heart of many numerical procedures for partial differential equations and the literature is immense. Our presentation follows the excellent survey by Swarztrauber (1977).

4.5.1 One-Dimensional Problems

We start by examining the one-dimensional Poisson problem

$$\frac{d^2 U}{dx^2} = F(x), \qquad a \le x \le b \qquad (4.5.3)$$

for each of the following possible boundary value specifications:

$$
\begin{array}{lll}
\text{Dirichlet–Dirichlet:} & U(a) = \alpha, \ U(b) = \beta, & \\
\text{Dirichlet–Neumann:} & U(a) = \alpha, \ U'(b) = \beta, & \\
\text{Neumann–Neumann:} & U'(a) = \alpha, \ U'(b) = \beta, & (4.5.4) \\
\text{Periodic:} & U(a) = U(b). &
\end{array}
$$

In each case the discretization leads to a linear system with a coefficient matrix that is a low-rank perturbation of the tridiagonal matrix $\mathcal{T}_m$, which we define as follows:

$$
\mathcal{T}_m = \begin{bmatrix}
-2 & 1 & \cdots & \cdots & 0 \\
1 & -2 & \ddots & & \vdots \\
\vdots & \ddots & \ddots & \ddots & \vdots \\
\vdots & & \ddots & \ddots & 1 \\
0 & 0 & \cdots & 1 & -2
\end{bmatrix} \qquad (m\text{-by-}m). \qquad (4.5.5)
$$

Our first task is to examine the eigenstructure of this matrix.

4.5.2　The Matrix $\mathcal{T}_m$

Let θ be any real number and for any integer k set $c_k = \cos(k\theta)$ and $s_k = \sin(k\theta)$. Consider the following trigonometric identities:

$$
\begin{aligned}
s_{k-1} &= c_1 s_k - s_1 c_k, \\
s_{k+1} &= c_1 s_k + s_1 c_k, \\
c_{k-1} &= c_1 c_k + s_1 s_k, \\
c_{k+1} &= c_1 c_k - s_1 s_k.
\end{aligned}
$$

By adding the first equation to the second and the third equation to the fourth we obtain

$$s_{k-1} - 2c_1 s_k + s_{k+1} = 0, \tag{4.5.6}$$
$$c_{k-1} - 2c_1 c_k + c_{k+1} = 0. \tag{4.5.7}$$

These identities can be used to produce "near-eigenvectors" for $\mathcal{T}_m$.

Lemma 4.5.1 *Suppose $\theta \in \mathbb{R}$. If $c_k = \cos(k\theta)$ and $s_k = \sin(k\theta)$ for $k = 0{:}m+1$, then*

$$
\mathcal{T}_m \begin{bmatrix} s_1 \\ s_2 \\ \vdots \\ s_{m-1} \\ s_m \end{bmatrix} = -4\sin^2(\theta/2) \begin{bmatrix} s_1 \\ s_2 \\ \vdots \\ s_{m-1} \\ s_m \end{bmatrix} - \begin{bmatrix} 0 \\ 0 \\ \vdots \\ 0 \\ s_{m+1} \end{bmatrix} \tag{4.5.8}
$$

and

$$
\mathcal{T}_m \begin{bmatrix} c_0 \\ c_1 \\ \vdots \\ c_{m-2} \\ c_{m-1} \end{bmatrix} = -4\sin^2(\theta/2) \begin{bmatrix} c_0 \\ c_1 \\ \vdots \\ c_{m-2} \\ c_{m-1} \end{bmatrix} - \begin{bmatrix} c_1 \\ 0 \\ \vdots \\ 0 \\ c_m \end{bmatrix}. \tag{4.5.9}
$$

Proof. From the definition of $\mathcal{T}_m$ in (4.5.5) we have

$$
\mathcal{T}_m \begin{bmatrix} s_1 \\ \vdots \\ s_k \\ \vdots \\ s_m \end{bmatrix} = \begin{bmatrix} s_0 - 2s_1 + s_2 \\ \vdots \\ s_{k-1} - 2s_k + s_{k+1} \\ \vdots \\ s_{m-1} - 2s_m \end{bmatrix}.
$$

Since (4.5.6) implies

$$
s_{k-1} - 2s_k + s_{k+1} = \underbrace{s_{k-1} - 2c_1 s_k + s_{k+1}}_{0} + 2(c_1 - 1)s_k,
$$

it follows that

$$
\mathcal{T}_m \begin{bmatrix} s_1 \\ \vdots \\ s_m \end{bmatrix} = 2(c_1 - 1) \begin{bmatrix} s_1 \\ \vdots \\ s_m \end{bmatrix} + \begin{bmatrix} 0 \\ \vdots \\ 0 \\ (s_{m-1} - 2s_m) - 2(c_1 - 1)s_m \end{bmatrix}.
$$

The verification of (4.5.8) follows by noting that $c_1 - 1 = -2\sin^2(\theta/2)$ and

$$(s_{m-1} - 2s_m) - 2(c_1 - 1)s_m = s_{m-1} - 2c_1 s_m = -s_{m+1}.$$

The verification of (4.5.9) proceeds along similar lines. □

We now use this result to identify important properties of the matrices that arise when solving the one-dimensional Poisson problem with each of the four boundary conditions defined in (4.5.4).

4.5.3 The Dirichlet Problem

The simplest finite difference approach to (4.5.3) with Dirichlet–Dirichlet boundary conditions begins with the selection of a uniform mesh,

$$a = x_0 < x_1 < \cdots < x_n = b,$$

where $h = (b - a)/n$ and $x_k = a + kh$ for $k = 0{:}n$. Our goal is to approximate U on the interior meshpoints with a vector $u(1{:}n - 1)$, i.e.,

$$u_k \approx U(x_k), \qquad k = 1{:}n - 1.$$

Set $u_0 = U(0) = \alpha$ and $u_n = U(b) = \beta$. If y_k is the midpoint of $[x_k, x_{k+1}]$, then for $k = 0{:}n - 1$ we have

$$\frac{dU(y_k)}{dx} \approx \frac{U(x_{k+1}) - U(x_k)}{h} \approx \frac{u_{k+1} - u_k}{h},$$

and so

$$\frac{d^2 U(x_k)}{dx^2} \approx \frac{\dfrac{dU(y_k)}{dx} - \dfrac{dU(y_{k-1})}{dx}}{h} \approx \frac{u_{k+1} - 2u_k + u_{k-1}}{h^2}.$$

By stipulating that this second-order divided difference equal $F(x_k)$ at each interior meshpoint, we obtain a set of simple linear equations:

$$(u_{k-1} - 2u_k + u_{k+1})/h^2 = f_k \equiv F(x_k), \qquad k = 1{:}n - 1. \tag{4.5.10}$$

In matrix/vector terms (4.5.10) defines a symmetric, negative definite, tridiagonal, linear system of order $n - 1$. For example, in the case where $n = 5$ we obtain

$$\frac{1}{h^2}\begin{bmatrix} -2 & 1 & 0 & 0 \\ 1 & -2 & 1 & 0 \\ 0 & 1 & -2 & 1 \\ 0 & 0 & 1 & -2 \end{bmatrix}\begin{bmatrix} u_1 \\ u_2 \\ u_3 \\ u_4 \end{bmatrix} = \begin{bmatrix} f_1 - \alpha/h^2 \\ f_2 \\ f_3 \\ f_4 - \beta/h^2 \end{bmatrix}.$$

In general, the discretized version of (4.5.3) with Dirichlet–Dirichlet boundary conditions leads to the linear system

$$\frac{1}{h^2} T_{n-1} u(1{:}n - 1) = \begin{bmatrix} f_1 - \alpha/h^2 \\ f(2{:}n - 2) \\ f_{n-1} - \beta/h^2 \end{bmatrix}. \tag{4.5.11}$$

Tridiagonal systems of this form can be solved in $O(n)$ flops using the Cholesky factorization. See Golub and Van Loan (1989). However, to set the stage for the two-dimensional Poisson problem, we show that (4.5.11) can be solved using a fast diagonalization process based upon the discrete sine transform of §4.4.

Theorem 4.5.2 *Recall from (4.4.7) that* $[S_{2n}]_{kj} = \sin(kj\pi/n)$, $0 \le k, j \le 2n - 1$. *If* $V = S_{2n}(1{:}n - 1, 1{:}n - 1)$ *and*

$$\lambda_j = -4\sin^2\left(\frac{j\pi}{2n}\right)$$

for $j = 1{:}n - 1$, *then*

$$V^{-1}T_{n-1}V = \mathrm{diag}(\lambda_1, \ldots, \lambda_{n-1}).$$

Proof. Setting $m = n - 1$ in (4.5.8) gives

$$T_{n-1}\begin{bmatrix} s_1 \\ s_2 \\ \vdots \\ s_{n-2} \\ s_{n-1} \end{bmatrix} = -4\sin^2(\theta/2)\begin{bmatrix} s_1 \\ s_2 \\ \vdots \\ s_{n-2} \\ s_{n-1} \end{bmatrix} - \begin{bmatrix} 0 \\ 0 \\ \vdots \\ 0 \\ s_n \end{bmatrix}.$$

Note that if $n\theta$ is an integral multiple of π, then $s_n = \sin(n\theta) = 0$. Thus, if we define

$$\theta_j = \frac{j\pi}{n}$$

for $j = 1{:}n - 1$, then

$$T_{n-1}\begin{bmatrix} \sin(\theta_j) \\ \vdots \\ \sin((n-1)\theta_j) \end{bmatrix} = -4\sin^2\left(\frac{j\pi}{2n}\right)\begin{bmatrix} \sin(\theta_j) \\ \vdots \\ \sin((n-1)\theta_j) \end{bmatrix}.$$

The theorem follows because the above eigenvector equals $S_{2n}(1{:}n - 1, j)$. □

Note from Table 4.4.2 that multiplication of a vector by $V = S_{2n}(1{:}n - 1, 1{:}n - 1)$ is tantamount to performing a discrete sine transform. It follows from (4.4.14) that $V^{-1} = (2/n)V$ and thus

$$T_{n-1}^{-1} = V\left(\frac{2}{n}D^{-1}\right)V$$

where $D = \mathrm{diag}(\lambda_1, \ldots, \lambda_{n-1})$. By using the "fast eigensystem" of T_{n-1}, we may solve a linear system of the form $T_{n-1}u = g$ as follows:

$$\begin{aligned} u &\leftarrow Vg \\ u &\leftarrow (2/n)D^{-1}u \\ u &\leftarrow Vu \end{aligned}$$

Note that two DST's and a scaling are required. Normally, one does not solve linear systems via the eigensystem of the coefficient matrix. However, if the action of the eigenvector matrix and its inverse can be realized through a fast transform, then this approach becomes interesting.

4.5.4 Dirichlet–Neumann Conditions

With Dirichlet–Neumann boundary conditions, we solve (4.5.3) with the constraint that $U(a) = \alpha$ and $U'(b) = \beta$. Assuming that $n = 5$, we can approximate $U'(x_5) = \beta$ with

$$\frac{u_5 - u_4}{h} = \beta.$$

This leads to a tridiagonal system

$$\frac{1}{h^2}
\begin{bmatrix}
-2 & 1 & 0 & 0 & 0 \\
1 & -2 & 1 & 0 & 0 \\
0 & 1 & -2 & 1 & 0 \\
0 & 0 & 1 & -2 & 1 \\
0 & 0 & 0 & 2 & -2
\end{bmatrix}
\begin{bmatrix}
u_1 \\ u_2 \\ u_3 \\ u_4 \\ u_5
\end{bmatrix}
=
\begin{bmatrix}
f_1 - \alpha/h^2 \\ f_2 \\ f_3 \\ f_4 \\ -2\beta/h
\end{bmatrix}.
$$

In general we are led to an n-by-n linear system of the form

$$\frac{1}{h^2} T_n^{(DN)} u(1{:}n) = \begin{bmatrix} f_1 - \alpha/h^2 \\ f(2{:}n-1) \\ -2\beta/h \end{bmatrix}, \tag{4.5.12}$$

where

$$T_n^{(DN)} = T_n + e_{n-1}e_{n-2}^T \tag{4.5.13}$$

and $I_n = [\,e_0\mid\cdots\mid e_{n-2}\mid e_{n-1}\,]$. The following result shows that the discrete sine transform-II can be used to solve (4.5.12).

Theorem 4.5.3 *Recall from (4.4.7) that* $[S_{4n}]_{kj} = \sin(kj\pi/(2n))$, $0 \le k, j \le 4n - 1$. *If* $V = S_{4n}(1{:}n, 1{:}2{:}2n - 1)$ *and*

$$\lambda_j = -4\sin^2\left(\frac{2j-1}{4n}\pi\right)$$

for $j = 1{:}n$, *then*

$$V^{-1}T_n^{(DN)}V = \mathrm{diag}(\lambda_1,\ldots,\lambda_n).$$

Proof. Using (4.5.8) with $m = n$ and the definition (4.5.13), we have

$$T_n^{(DN)}
\begin{bmatrix} s_1 \\ \vdots \\ s_n \end{bmatrix}
= -4\sin^2(\theta/2)
\begin{bmatrix} s_1 \\ \vdots \\ s_n \end{bmatrix}
+ (s_{n-1} - s_{n+1})e_{n-1},$$

where $I_n = [\,e_0, e_1,\ldots, e_{n-2}, e_{n-1}\,]$. Note that

$$s_{n-1} - s_{n+1} = \sin((n-1)\theta) - \sin((n+1)\theta) = -2\cos(n\theta)\sin(\theta)$$

is zero if we set $\theta = -(\pi/2) + j\pi$ for any integer j. It follows that if we define θ_j by $\theta_j = (2j-1)\pi/(2n)$ for $j = 1{:}n$, then

$$T_n^{(DN)}
\begin{bmatrix} \sin(\theta_j) \\ \vdots \\ \sin(n\theta_j) \end{bmatrix}
= -4\sin^2\left(\frac{2j-1}{4n}\pi\right)
\begin{bmatrix} \sin(\theta_j) \\ \vdots \\ \sin(n\theta_j) \end{bmatrix}.$$

The theorem follows by noting that these eigenvectors are columns of the matrix $S_{4n}(1{:}n, 1{:}2{:}2n - 1)$. $\square$

With a factorization of the form $T_n^{(DN)} = VDV^{-1}$ a linear system $T_n^{(DN)}u = g$ can be solved as follows:

$$u \leftarrow V^{-1}g$$
$$u \leftarrow D^{-1}u$$
$$u \leftarrow Vu.$$

Note from Table 4.4.2 that the first and third steps involve the discrete sine transform-II and its inverse. See §4.4.9.

4.5.5   Neumann–Neumann Conditions

Here we require $U'(x_0) = \alpha$ and $U'(x_n) = \beta$. Consider the case of $n = 5$. The boundary conditions give us a linear relation between u_0 and u_1 and another linear relation between u_4 and u_5. We obtain a 6-by-6 linear system:

$$\frac{1}{h^2}\begin{bmatrix} -2 & 2 & 0 & 0 & 0 & 0 \\ 1 & -2 & 1 & 0 & 0 & 0 \\ 0 & 1 & -2 & 1 & 0 & 0 \\ 0 & 0 & 1 & -2 & 1 & 0 \\ 0 & 0 & 0 & 1 & -2 & 1 \\ 0 & 0 & 0 & 0 & 2 & -2 \end{bmatrix}\begin{bmatrix} u_0 \\ u_1 \\ u_2 \\ u_3 \\ u_4 \\ u_5 \end{bmatrix} = \begin{bmatrix} 2\alpha/h \\ f_1 \\ f_2 \\ f_3 \\ f_4 \\ -2\beta/h \end{bmatrix}.$$

In general, in the Neumann–Neumann problem we are forced to solve

$$\frac{1}{h^2} T_{n+1}^{(NN)} u(0{:}n) = \begin{bmatrix} 2\alpha/h \\ f(1{:}n-1) \\ 2\beta/h \end{bmatrix}, \tag{4.5.14}$$

where

$$T_{n+1}^{(NN)} = T_{n+1} + e_0 e_1^T + e_n e_{n-1}^T \tag{4.5.15}$$

and $I_{n+1} = [\, e_0, e_1, \ldots, e_{n-1}, e_n \,]$ is a column partitioning of I_{n+1}.

Theorem 4.5.4 *Recall from (4.4.6) that $[C_{2n}]_{kj} = \cos(kj\pi/n)$, $0 \le k, j \le 2n-1$. If $V = C_{2n}(0{:}n, 0{:}n)$ and*

$$\lambda_j = -4\sin^2\left(\frac{j\pi}{2n}\right),$$

for $j = 0{:}n$, then

$$V^{-1} T_{n+1}^{(NN)} V = \mathrm{diag}(\lambda_0, \ldots, \lambda_n).$$

Proof. Using (4.5.9),

$$(T_{n+1} + e_0 e_1^T + e_n e_{n-1}^T)\begin{bmatrix} c_0 \\ c_1 \\ \vdots \\ c_{n-1} \\ c_n \end{bmatrix} = -4\sin^2(\theta/2)\begin{bmatrix} c_0 \\ c_1 \\ \vdots \\ c_{n-1} \\ c_n \end{bmatrix} - \begin{bmatrix} c_1 \\ 0 \\ \vdots \\ 0 \\ c_{n+1} \end{bmatrix} + \begin{bmatrix} c_1 \\ 0 \\ \vdots \\ 0 \\ c_{n-1} \end{bmatrix}.$$

If $n\theta = j\pi$, then

$$c_{n-1} - c_{n+1} = \cos((n-1)\theta) - \cos((n+1)\theta) = 2\sin(\theta)\sin(n\theta) = 0.$$

Thus, if $\theta_j = j\pi/n$, $0 \le j \le n$, then

$$T_{n+1}^{(NN)}\begin{bmatrix} 1 \\ \cos(\theta_j) \\ \vdots \\ \cos(n\theta_j) \end{bmatrix} = -4\sin^2(\theta_j/2)\begin{bmatrix} 1 \\ \cos(\theta_j) \\ \vdots \\ \cos(n\theta_j) \end{bmatrix}.$$

The theorem follows by noting that these eigenvectors are columns of the matrix $C_{2n}(0{:}n, 0{:}n)$. □

Note that the matrix $C_{2n}(0{:}n, 0{:}n)$ does not quite define the discrete cosine transform that we described in §4.4. From Table 4.4.2 we see that the DCT of a vector $x(0{:}n)$ is given by $\tilde{C}x(0{:}n)$, where

$$\tilde{C} = C_{2n}(0{:}n, 0{:}n)\tilde{D}^{-1}, \qquad \tilde{D} = \mathrm{diag}(2, I_{n-1}, 2).$$

Thus, the application of

$$C_{2n}(0{:}n, 0{:}n) = \tilde{C}\tilde{D}$$

or

$$C_{2n}(0{:}n, 0{:}n)^{-1} = \tilde{D}^{-1}\tilde{C}^{-1} = \frac{2}{n}\tilde{D}^{-1}\tilde{C}$$

to a vector may be approached with fast algorithms for the DCT.

4.5.6 Periodic Conditions

With periodic boundary conditions we require that $U(x_0) = U(x_n)$. If we have $n = 5$, then we obtain a system of the form

$$\frac{1}{h^2}\begin{bmatrix} -2 & 1 & 0 & 0 & 1 \\ 1 & -2 & 1 & 0 & 0 \\ 0 & 1 & -2 & 1 & 0 \\ 0 & 0 & 1 & -2 & 1 \\ 1 & 0 & 0 & 1 & -2 \end{bmatrix}\begin{bmatrix} u_1 \\ u_2 \\ u_3 \\ u_4 \\ u_5 \end{bmatrix} = \begin{bmatrix} f_1 \\ f_2 \\ f_3 \\ f_4 \\ f_5 \end{bmatrix}.$$

This is just the collection of the $k = 1{:}5$ instances of (4.5.10), with the assumption (based upon periodicity) that $u_0 = u_5$ and $u_6 = u_1$. For general n, periodic boundary conditions give us

$$\frac{1}{h^2}T_n^{(P)}u(1{:}n) = f(1{:}n) \tag{4.5.16}$$

where

$$T_n^{(P)} = T_n + e_0 e_{n-1}^T + e_{n-1}e_0^T. \tag{4.5.17}$$

Theorem 4.5.5 *If $V = F_n^{-1}$ and*

$$\lambda_j = -4\sin^2\left(\frac{j\pi}{n}\right)$$

for $j = 0{:}n-1$, then

$$V^{-1}T_n^{(P)}V = \mathrm{diag}(\lambda_0, \ldots, \lambda_{n-1}).$$

Proof. Recall from Lemma 4.2.3 that if R_n is the downshift operator, then

$$F_n R_n F_n^{-1} = D_n,$$

where $D_n = \mathrm{diag}(1, \omega, \ldots, \omega^{n-1})$ with $\omega = \omega_n$. Since

$$T_n^{(P)} = R_n - 2I_n + R_n^T = R_n - 2I_n + R_n^{-1}$$

we see that

$$F_n T_n^{(P)} F_n^{-1} = D_n - 2I_n + D_n^{-1} = D_n - 2I_n + \bar{D}_n = 2\mathrm{Re}(D_n) - 2I_n.$$

The theorem follows since $[2\mathrm{Re}(D_n)-2I_n]_{jj} = 2(\cos(2j\pi/n)-1) = -4\sin^2(j\pi/n)$. $\square$

Thus, $T_n^{(P)}$ can be diagonalized by the DFT matrix itself.

4.5.7   Discretizations on a Rectangle

We now consider the discretization of the Poisson equation on a rectangle subject to Dirichlet boundary conditions. In this problem we are given a function $F(x,y)$ defined on

$$R = \{(x,y) : a \le x \le b, \ c \le y \le d\,\}$$

and wish to determine $U(x,y)$ such that

$$\frac{\partial U^2}{\partial x^2} + \frac{\partial U^2}{\partial y^2} = F(x,y) \tag{4.5.18}$$

for all $(x,y) \in R$ subject to the boundary conditions

$$\begin{aligned}
U(x,c) &= south(x), & a \le x \le b, \\
U(x,d) &= north(x), & a \le x \le b, \\
U(a,y) &= west(y), & c \le y \le d, \\
U(b,y) &= east(y), & c \le y \le d.
\end{aligned} \tag{4.5.19}$$

The functions *south*, *north*, *west*, and *east* are given and define the values that U is to assume along the four sides of R. Our goal is to compute an approximation u_{jk} to $U(x_j, y_k)$ at each of the interior meshpoints defined by the partitionings

$$\begin{aligned}
a &= x_0 < x_1 < \cdots < x_{n_1} = b, & x_k = x_0 + kh_1, \\
d &= y_0 > y_1 > \cdots > y_{n_2} = c, & y_k = y_0 - kh_2,
\end{aligned}$$

where $h_1 = (b-a)/n_1$ and $h_2 = (d-c)/n_2$. Figure 4.5.1 depicts the case $(n_1, n_2) = (6,5)$. The ×'s represent meshpoints at which U is known and the dots represent meshpoints at which U is unknown.

By replacing the partials in (4.5.18) with appropriate second-order difference quotients, we obtain the following equation at an interior meshpoint (x_j, y_k):

$$\frac{u_{j,k+1} - 2u_{jk} + u_{j,k-1}}{h_1^2} + \frac{u_{j+1,k} - 2u_{jk} + u_{j-1,k}}{h_2^2} = F(x_j, y_k). \tag{4.5.20}$$

Define the matrix

$$\tilde{U} = \begin{bmatrix} u_{00} & \cdots & u_{0,n_2} \\ \vdots & & \vdots \\ u_{n_1,0} & \cdots & u_{n_1,n_2} \end{bmatrix}$$

and note that $\tilde{U}(1{:}n_1-1, 1{:}n_2-1)$ is comprised of the sought-after unknowns. If we define the vector $u \in \mathbb{R}^{(n_1-1)(n_2-1)}$ by

$$u_{(n_1-1)\times(n_2-1)} = \tilde{U}(1{:}n_1-1, 1{:}n_2-1),$$

then the set of linear equations defined by (4.5.20) can be expressed in matrix-vector form as follows:

$$\left(\frac{1}{h_1^2}(I_{n_2-1} \otimes T_{n_1-1}) + \frac{1}{h_2^2}(T_{n_2-1} \otimes I_{n_1-1}) \right) u = g. \tag{4.5.21}$$

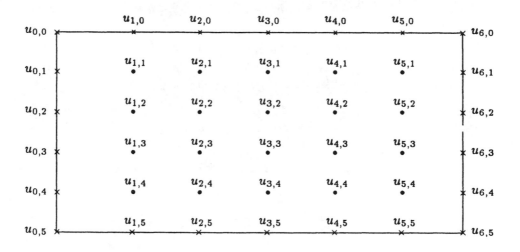

FIG. 4.5.1. *A grid for the Dirichlet problem on a rectangle.*

The right-hand side vector g is made up of F-values from the interior of R and samplings of *south*, *north*, *west*, and *east* around the boundary. For example, if $(n_1, n_2) = (6, 5)$, then at meshpoint $(5,3)$ we have

$$\frac{east(y_3) - 2u_{5,3} + u_{4,3}}{h_1^2} + \frac{u_{5,4} - 2u_{5,3} + u_{5,2}}{h_2^2} = F(x_5, y_3),$$

i.e.,

$$\frac{u_{4,3} - 2u_{5,3}}{h_1^2} + \frac{u_{5,4} - 2u_{5,3} + u_{5,2}}{h_2^2} = F(x_5, y_3) - \frac{east(y_3)}{h_1^2}.$$

The first Kronecker product in (4.5.21) applies the operator T_{n_1-1} to each row of unknowns in the mesh and contributes to the approximation of the x-partial. The second Kronecker product applies T_{n_2-1} to each column of unknowns and contributes to the y-partial. In this way we see how the two-dimensional discretization is built upon copies of the one-dimensional Dirichlet discretization discussed in §4.5.3.

In a similar way, we develop Kronecker systems when other boundary conditions are specified. For example, if we have Dirichlet conditions at $y = d$ and Neumann conditions along the other three sides, then we are seeking a solution to (4.5.1) that satisfies conditions of the form

$$\frac{\partial U(x,c)}{\partial y} = south(x), \qquad a \leq x \leq b,$$

$$U(x,d) = north(x), \qquad a \leq x \leq b,$$

$$\frac{\partial U(a,y)}{\partial x} = west(y), \qquad a \leq x \leq b, \qquad (4.5.22)$$

$$\frac{\partial U(b,y)}{\partial x} = east(y), \qquad a \leq x \leq b.$$

In this case, $\tilde{U}(1{:}n_1+1, 1{:}n_2)$ is the matrix of unknowns and we obtain a Kronecker system of the form

$$\left(\frac{1}{h_1^2}(I_{n_2} \otimes T_{n_1+1}^{(NN)}) + \frac{1}{h_2^2}(T_{n_2}^{(DN)} \otimes I_{n_1+1}) \right) u = g . \qquad (4.5.23)$$

4.5.8   The Fast Poisson Solving Framework

What should be clear from our discussion is that for any mixture of Dirichlet–Dirichlet, Dirichlet–Neumann, Neumann–Neumann, or periodic boundary conditions, we obtain a linear system $Mu = g$, where

$$M = (I_\beta \otimes A) + (B \otimes I_\alpha),$$

A has the form $T_\alpha^{(DD)}$, $T_\alpha^{(DN)}$, $T_\alpha^{(NN)}$, or $T_\alpha^{(P)}$, and B has the form $T_\beta^{(DD)}$, $T_\beta^{(DN)}$, $T_\beta^{(NN)}$, or $T_\beta^{(P)}$. No matter what the combination of boundary conditions, the following theorem tells us that M has a "fast" eigensystem.

Theorem 4.5.6 *Suppose $M = (I_\beta \otimes A) + (B \otimes I_\alpha)$ is nonsingular with $A \in \mathbb{R}^{\alpha \times \alpha}$ and $B \in \mathbb{R}^{\beta \times \beta}$. If $V_A^{-1}AV_A = D_A$, $V_B^{-1}BV_B = D_B$, and $g \in \mathbb{R}^{\alpha\beta}$, then the solution to $Mu = g$ is given by*

$$u = (V_B \otimes V_A)\left[(I_\beta \otimes D_A) + (D_B \otimes I_\alpha)\right]^{-1}(V_B^{-1} \otimes V_A^{-1}).$$

Proof. The theorem follows immediately from

$$\begin{aligned} (V_B^{-1} \otimes V_A^{-1})M(V_B \otimes V_A) &= (I_\beta \otimes V_A^{-1}AV_A) + (V_B^{-1}BV_B \otimes I_\alpha) \\ &= ((I_\beta \otimes D_A) + (D_B \otimes I_\alpha)) \end{aligned}$$

which is easily established from Kron1 and Kron2.   □

Putting this in array format, we obtain the following framework:

$$\begin{aligned} f_{\alpha \times \beta} &\leftarrow V_A^{-1} f_{\alpha \times \beta} V_B^{-1} \\ f_{\alpha \times \beta} &\leftarrow D_A^{-1} f_{\alpha \times \beta} D_B^{-1} \\ f_{\alpha \times \beta} &\leftarrow V_A f_{\alpha \times \beta} V_B. \end{aligned} \qquad (4.5.24)$$

Returning to the discretized Poisson problem (4.5.20), we see that if this framework is applied, then the V operations involve multi-vector trigonometric transforms. For example, with the pure Dirichlet boundary conditions (4.5.19), a pair of multi-vector sine transforms are required. For the mixed-boundary conditions (4.5.22), a multi-vector cosine and a multi-vector sine-II transform arise. As we found in the discussion of multi-vector DFTs in §3.1, multi-vector trigonometric transforms can be very effectively organized to exploit properties of the underlying computer architecture.

We conclude by pointing out that it is not necessary to diagonalize both A and B in the Poisson application. For example, if we set $V_A = I_\alpha$ in (4.5.24), then we obtain

$$
\begin{aligned}
f_{\alpha \times \beta} &\leftarrow f_{\alpha \times \beta} V_B^{-1} \\
f_{\alpha \times \beta} &\leftarrow A^{-1} f_{\alpha \times \beta} D_B^{-1} \\
f_{\alpha \times \beta} &\leftarrow f_{\alpha \times \beta} V_B.
\end{aligned}
\qquad (4.5.25)
$$

If A is tridiagonal, then the middle step entails a multiple tridiagonal system solve, a computation that can be effectively arranged and which is more efficient than a multiple trigonometric problem. See Golub and Van Loan (1989).

Problems

P4.5.1 Verify (4.5.9).

P4.5.2 Develop a computational framework for (4.5.3) subject to the Neumann–Dirichlet condition $U'(a) = \alpha$, $U(b) = \beta$.

P4.5.3 Give a complete specification of the vector g in (4.5.21) and in (4.5.23).

P4.5.4 Show how the cosine transform can be used to compute $C_{2m}(0{:}m, 0{:}m)x(0{:}m)$ in the Neumann–Neumann problem. In particular, show that if $y(0{:}m)$ is the DCT of $x(0{:}m)$, then $\tilde{y}(0{:}m) = C_{2m}(0{:}m, 0{:}m)x(0{:}m)$ is given by

$$
\tilde{y}_k = y_k + \frac{x_0}{2} + \frac{(-1)^k x_m}{2}
$$

for $k = 0{:}m$.

Notes and References for Section 4.5

Overviews of the fast Poisson solving area include

B. Buzbee, G. Golub, and C. Nielson (1970). "On Direct Methods for Solving Poisson's Equation," *SIAM J. Numer. Anal. 7*, 627–656.

F. Dorr (1970). "The Direct Solution of the Discrete Poisson Equation on a Rectangle," *SIAM Rev. 12*, 248–263.

R.W. Hockney (1965). "A Fast Direct Solution of Poisson's Equation Using Fourier Analysis," *J. Assocs. Comput. Mach. 12*, 95–113.

M. Pickering (1986). *Introduction to Fast Fourier Transform Methods for Partial Differential Equations with Applications*, Research Studies Press, Letchworth, England.

C. Temperton (1979). "Direct Methods for the Solution of the Discrete Poisson Equation: Some Comparisons," *J. Comput. Phys. 31*, 1–20.

More specialized papers include

P.N. Swarztrauber (1974). "A Direct Method for the Discrete Solution of Separable Elliptic Equations," *SIAM J. Numer. Anal. 11*, 1136–1150.

R. Sweet (1973). "Direct Methods for the Solution of Poisson's Equation on a Staggered Grid," *J. Comput. Phys. 12*, 422–428.

C. Temperton (1980). "On the FACR(ℓ) Algorithm for the Discrete Poisson Equation," *J. Comput. Phys. 34*, 314.

Some of the more effective techniques involve a combination of FFT techniques and a divide-and-conquer method known as *cyclic reduction*. For a discussion of this method, which is suitable for certain block tridiagonal systems, see

R. Sweet (1977). "A Cyclic Reduction Algorithm for Solving Block Tridiagonal Systems of Arbitrary Dimension," *SIAM J. Numer. Anal. 14*, 706–720.

The derivation of the discretized Poisson problem and the connections with the various trigonometric transforms are discussed in

P.N. Swarztrauber (1977). "The Methods of Cyclic Reduction, Fourier Analysis and Cyclic Reduction-Fourier Analysis for the Discrete Solution of Poisson's Equation on a Rectangle," *SIAM Rev. 19*, 490–501.
P.N. Swarztrauber (1984a). "Fast Poisson Solvers," in *MAA Studies in Numerical Analysis, Vol. 24*, G.H. Golub (ed.), Mathematics Association of America, 319–370.

The design of effective Poisson solvers for parallel architectures is a new and intense area of research. See

W.L. Briggs and T. Turnbull (1988). "Fast Poisson Solvers on MIMD Machines," *Parallel Comput. 6*, 265–274.
B.L. Buzbee (1973). "A Fast Poisson Solver Amenable to Parallel Computation," *IEEE Trans. on Comput. C-22*, 793–796.
R.W. Hockney and C.R. Jesshope (1981). *Parallel Computers*, Adam Hilger Ltd., Bristol, England.
A. Sameh (1984). "A Fast Poisson Solver for Multiprocessors," in *Elliptic Problem Solvers II*, Academic Press, New York, 175–186.

For a discussion of tridiagonal and block tridiagonal system solving, see

G.H. Golub and C. Van Loan (1989). *Matrix Computations, 2nd Ed*, Johns Hopkins University Press, Baltimore, MD.

Bibliography

F. Abramovici (1975). "The Accuracy of Finite Fourier Transforms," *J. Comput. Phys. 17*, 446–449.

R.C. Agarwal (1983a). "An In-Place and In-Order WFTA," *Proc. 1983 IEEE Int. Conf. Acoustics, Speech, and Signal Processing*, 190–193.

R.C. Agarwal (1983b). "Comments on 'A Prime Factor FFT Algorithm Using High-Speed Convolution'," *IEEE Trans. Acoust. Speech Signal Process. ASSP-26*, 254.

R.C. Agarwal and C.S. Burrus (1974). "Fast One-Dimensional Digital Convolution by Multidimensional Techniques," *IEEE Trans. Acoust. Speech Signal Process. ASSP-22*, 1–10.

R.C. Agarwal and J.W. Cooley (1986). "Fourier Transform and Convolution Subroutines for the IBM 3090 Vector Facility," *IBM J. Res. Develop. 30*, 145–162.

R.C. Agarwal and J.W. Cooley (1987). "Vectorized Mixed Radix Discrete Fourier Transform Algorithms," *Proc. IEEE 75*, 1283–1292.

N. Ahmed, T. Natarajan, and K.R. Rao (1974). "Discrete Cosine Transform," *IEEE Trans. Comput. C-23*, 90–93.

R. Alt (1978). "Error Propagation in Fourier Transforms," *Math. Comp. Simul. 20*, 37–43.

G.L. Anderson (1980). "A Stepwise Approach to Computing the Multidimensional Fast Fourier Transform of Large Arrays," *IEEE Trans. Acoust. Speech Signal Process. ASSP-28*, 280–284.

H.C. Andrews and J. Kane (1970). "Kronecker Matrices, Computer Implementation, and Generalized Spectra," *J. Assoc. Comput. Mach. 17*, 260–268.

B. Arambepola (1980). "Fast Computation of Multidimensional Discrete Fourier Transforms," *IEE Proc. F, Comm., Radar, and Signal Process. 127*, 49–52.

B. Arambepola and P.J.W. Rayner (1979). "Multidimensional Fast-Fourier-Transform," *Electron. Lett. 15*, 382–383.

M. Arioli, H. Munthe-Kaas, and L. Valdettaro (1991). "Componentwise Error Analysis for FFT's with Applications to Fast Helmholtz Solvers," CERFACS Report TR/IT/PA/91/55, Toulouse, France.

J. Armstrong (1988). "A Multi-Algorithm Approach to Very High Performance 1D FFTs," *J. Supercomputing 2*, 415–434.

M. Ashworth and A.G. Lyne (1988). "A Segmented FFT Algorithm for Vector Supercomputers," *Parallel Comput. 6*, 217–224.

A. Auerbuch, E. Gabber, B. Gordissky, and Y. Medan (1990). "A Parallel FFT on a MIMD Machine," *Parallel Comput. 15*, 61–74.

L. Auslander, E. Feig, and S. Winograd (1983). "New Algorithms for the Multidimensional Discrete Fourier Transform," *IEEE Trans. Acoust. Speech Signal Process. ASSP-31*, 388–403.

L. Auslander and M. Shenefelt (1987). "Fourier Transforms that Respect Crystallographic Symmetries," *IBM J. Research and Development 31*, 213–223.

L. Auslander and R. Tolimieri (1979). "Is Computing with the Finite Fourier Transform Pure or Applied Mathematics?" *Bull. Amer. Math. Soc.*, 847–897.

D.H. Bailey (1987). "A High-Performance Fast Fourier Transform Algorithm for the Cray-2," *J. Supercomputing 1*, 43–60.

D.H. Bailey (1988). "A High-Performance FFT Algorithm for Vector Supercomputers," *International J. Supercomputer Applications 2*, 82–87.

D.H. Bailey (1990). "FFTs in External or Hierarchical Memory," *J. Supercomputing 4*, 23–35.

D.H. Bailey and P.N. Swarztrauber (1990). "The Fractional Fourier Transform and Applications," RNR-90-004, NASA Ames Research Center, Moffett Field, CA. (To appear in *SIAM Rev.*)

A.A. Belal (1978). "Multidimensional FFT by One and Two Dimensional Array Processing," *Proc. 1978 IEEE Int. Symp., Circuits Systems*, 662–663.

G.D. Bergland (1968a). "A Fast Fourier Transform Algorithm for Real-Valued Series," *Comm. ACM 11*, 703–710.

G.D. Bergland (1968b). "A Fast Fourier Transform Algorithm Using Base 8 Iterations," *Math. Comp. 22*, 275–279.

G.D. Bergland (1969). "A Radix-8 Fast Fourier Transform Subroutine for Real Valued Series," *IEEE Trans. Audio and Electroacoustics AU-17*, 138–144.

S. Bertram (1970). "On the Derivation of the Fast Fourier Transform," *IEEE Trans. Audio and Electroacoustics AU-18*, 55–58.

R.E. Blahut (1984). *Fast Algorithms for Digital Signal Processing*, Addison-Wesley, Reading, MA.

L.I. Bluestein (1970). "A Linear Filtering Approach to the Computation of the Discrete Fourier Transform," *IEEE Trans. Audio and Electroacoustics AU-18*, 451–455.

P. Bois and J. Vignes (1980). "Software for Evaluating Local Accuracy in the Fourier Transform," *Math. Comput. Simul. 22*, 141–150.

R.N. Bracewell (1978). *The Fourier Transform and Its Applications*, McGraw-Hill, New York.

R.N. Bracewell (1986). *The Hartley Transform*, Oxford University Press, New York.

R.N. Bracewell (1989). "The Fourier Transform," *Scientific American, June*, 86–95

R.N. Bracewell, O. Buneman, H. Hao, and J. Villasenor (1986). "Fast Two-Dimensional Hartley Transforms," *Proc. IEEE 74*, 1282.

A. Brass and G.S. Pawley (1986). "Two and Three Dimensional FFTs on Highly Parallel Computers," *Parallel Comput. 3*, 167–184.

N.M. Brenner (1969). "Fast Fourier Transform of Externally Stored Data," *IEEE Trans. Audio and Electroacoustics AU-17*, 128–132.

N.M. Brenner (1973). "Algorithm 467, Matrix Transposition In-Place," *Comm. ACM 16*, 692–694.

W.L. Briggs (1987). "Further Symmetries of In-Place FFTs," *SIAM J. Sci. Statist. Comput. 8*, 644–654.

W.L. Briggs, L. Hart, R. Sweet, and A. O'Gallagher (1987). "Multiprocessor FFT Methods," *SIAM J. Sci. and Statist. Comput. 8*, s27–s42.

W.L. Briggs and V. Henson (1990). "The FFT as Multigrid," *SIAM Rev. 32*, 252–261.

W.L. Briggs and T. Turnbull (1988). "Fast Poisson Solvers on MIMD Machines," *Parallel Comput. 6*, 265–274.

E.O. Brigham (1974). *The Fast Fourier Transform*, Prentice-Hall, Englewood Cliffs, NJ.

E.O. Brigham (1988). *The Fast Fourier Transform and Its Applications*, Prentice-Hall, Englewood Cliffs, NJ.

E.O. Brigham and R.E. Morrow (1967). "The Fast Fourier Transform," *IEEE Spectrum 4*, 63–70.

P. Budnik and D.J. Kuck (1971). "The Organization and Use of Parallel Memories," *IEEE Trans. Comput. C-20*, 1566–1569.

H.L. Buijs (1969). "Fast Fourier Transform of Large Arrays of Data," *Applied Optics 8*, 211–212.

O. Buneman (1986). "Conversion of FFT to Fast Hartley Transforms," *SIAM J. Sci. and Statist. Comput. 7*, 624–638 .

O. Buneman (1987a). "Multidimensional Hartley Transforms," *Proc. IEEE 75*, 267.

O. Buneman (1987b). "Stable On-Line Creation of Sines and Cosines of Successive Angles," *Proc. IEEE 75*, 1434–1435.

C.S. Burrus (1977). "Index Mappings for Multidimensional Formulation of the DFT and Convolution," *IEEE Trans. Acoust. Speech Signal Process. ASSP-25*, 239–242.

C.S. Burrus (1981). "A New Prime Factor FFT Algorithm," *Proc. 1981 IEEE Int. Conf. Acoustics, Speech, and Signal Processing*, Atlanta, GA, 335–338.

C.S. Burrus (1983). "Comments on Selection Criteria for Efficient Implementation of FFT Algorithms," *IEEE Trans. Acoust. Speech Signal Process. ASSP-31*, 206.

C.S. Burrus (1988). "Unscrambling for Fast DFT Algorithms," *IEEE Trans. Acoust. Speech Signal Process. 36*, 1086–1087.

C.S. Burrus and P.W. Eschenbacher (1981). "An In-Place In-Order Prime Factor FFT Algorithm," *IEEE Trans. Acoust. Speech Signal Process. 29*, 806–817.

C.S. Burrus and T.W. Parks (1985). *DFT/FFT and Convolution Algorithms*, John Wiley & Sons, New York.

B.L. Buzbee (1973). "A Fast Poisson Solver Amenable to Parallel Computation," *IEEE Trans. Comput. C-22*, 793–796.

B.L. Buzbee, G. Golub, and C. Nielson (1970). "On Direct Methods for Solving Poisson's Equation," *SIAM J. Numer. Anal. 7*, 627–656.

D.A. Carlson (1991). "Using Local Memory to Boost the Performance of FFT Algorithms on the Cray-2 Supercomputer," *J. Supercomputing 4*, 345–356.

R.M. Chamberlain (1988). "Gray Codes, Fast Fourier Transforms, and Hypercubes," *Parallel Comput. 6*, 225–233.

T.F. Chan (1987). "On Gray Code Mappings for Mesh-FFTs on Binary N-Cubes," UCLA CAM Report 87-02, Dept. of Mathematics, University of California, Los Angeles, CA.

W.-H. Chen, C.H. Smith, and S.C. Fralick (1977). "A Fast Computational Algorithm for the Discrete Cosine Transform," *IEEE Trans. Comm. COM-25*, 1004–1009.

C. Chu (1988). *The Fast Fourier Transform on Hypercube Parallel Computers*, Ph.D. Thesis, Center for Applied Mathematics, Cornell University, Ithaca, NY.

M. Clausen (1989). "Fast Fourier Transforms for Metabelian Groups," *SIAM J. Comput.* 18, 584–593.

W.T. Cochrane, J.W. Cooley, J.W. Favin, D.L. Helms, R.A. Kaenel, W.W. Lang, G.C. Maling, D.E. Nelson, C.M. Rader, and P.D. Welch (1967). "What Is the Fast Fourier Transform?," *IEEE Trans. Audio and Electroacoustics AU-15*, 45–55.

T. Coleman and C.F. Van Loan (1988). *Handbook for Matrix Computations*, Society for Industrial and Applied Mathematics, Philadelphia, PA.

J.W. Cooley (1987). "How the FFT Gained Acceptance," in *History of Scientific Computing*, S. Nash (ed.), ACM Press, New York.

J.W. Cooley, R.L. Garwin, C.M. Rader, B.P. Bogert, and T.G. Stockham Jr. (1969). "The 1968 Arden House Workshop on Fast Fourier Transform Processing," *IEEE Trans. Audio and Electroacoustics AU-17*, 66–76.

J.W. Cooley, P.A. Lewis, and P.D. Welch (1967). "Historical Notes on the Fast Fourier Transform," *IEEE Trans. Audio and Electroacoustics AU-15*, 76–79.

J.W. Cooley, P.A.W. Lewis, and P.D. Welsh (1970). "The Fast Fourier Transform Algorithm: Programming Considerations in the Calculation of Sine, Cosine, and Laplace Transforms," *J. Sound Vibrations 12*, 315–37.

J.W. Cooley and J.W. Tukey (1965). "An Algorithm for the Machine Calculation of Complex Fourier Series," *Math. Comp. 19*, 297–301.

M.J. Corinthios (1971). "The Design of a Class of Fast Fourier Transform Computers," *IEEE Trans. Comput. C-20*, 617–623.

P. Corsini and G. Frosini (1979). "Properties of the Multidimensional Generalized Fourier Transform," *IEEE Trans. Comput. AC-28*, 819–830.

Z. Cvetanovic (1987). "Performance Analysis of the FFT Algorithm on a Shared-Memory Architecture," *IBM J. Res. Devel. 31*, 419–510.

M. Davio (1981). "Kronecker Products and Shuffle Algebra," *IEEE Trans. Comput. C-30*, 116–125.

C.B. de Boor (1979). "Efficient Computer Manipulation of Tensor Products," *ACM Trans. Math. Software 5*, 173–182.

C.B. de Boor (1980). "FFT as Nested Multiplication with a Twist," *SIAM J. Sci. Statist. Comput. 1*, 173–178.

L.G. Delcaro and G.L. Sicuranza (1974). "A Method for Transposing Externally Stored Matrices," *IEEE Trans. Comput. C-23*, 967–970.

I. DeLotto and D. Dotti (1975). "Two-Dimensional Transforms by Minicomputer without Transposing," *Computer Graphics and Image Processing 4*, 271–275.

A.M. Despain, A.M. Peterson, O. Rothaus, and E. Wold (1985). "Fast Fourier Transform Processors Using Gaussian Residue Arithmetic," *J. Parallel and Distributed Comput. 2*, 219–233.

P. Diaconis (1980). "Average Running Time of the Fast Fourier Transform," *J. Algorithms 1*, 187–208.

P. Diaconis (1981). "How Fast Is the Fourier Transform?," in *Computer Science and Statistics: Proceedings of the 13th Symposium on the Interface*, W.F. Eddy (ed.), Springer-Verlag, New York, 43–44.

J. Dollimore (1973). "Some Algorithms for Use with the Fast Fourier Transform," *J. Inst. Math. Applic. 12*, 115–117.

J. Dongarra, I.S. Duff, D.C. Sorensen, and H.A. van der Vorst (1990). *Solving Linear Systems on Vector and Shared Memory Computers*, Society for Industrial and Applied Mathematics, Philadelphia, PA.

F. Dorr (1970). "The Direct Solution of the Discrete Poisson Equation on a Rectangle," *SIAM Rev. 12*, 248–263.

J.R. Driscoll and D.M. Healy Jr. (1989). "Asymptotically Fast Algorithms for Spherical and Related Transforms," Technical Report PCS-TR89-141, Department of Mathematics and Computer Science, Dartmouth College.

M. Drubin (1971a). "Kronecker Product Factorization of the FFT Matrix," *IEEE Trans. Comput. C-20*, 590–593.

M. Drubin (1971b). "Computation of the Fast Fourier Transform Data Stored in External Auxiliary Memory for Any General Radix," *IEEE Trans. Comput. C-20*, 1552–1558.

E. Dubois and A. Venetsanopoulos (1978a). "A New Algorithm for the Radix-3 FFT," *IEEE Trans. Acoust. Speech Signal Process. ASSP-26*, 222–225.

E. Dubois and A.N. Venetsanopoulos (1978b). "The Discrete Fourier Transform over Finite Rings with Application to Fast Convolution," *IEEE Trans. Comput. C-27*, 586–593.

P. Duhamel (1986). "Implementation of the Split-Radix FFT Algorithms for Complex, Real, and Real-Symmetric Data," *IEEE Trans. Acoust. Speech Signal Process. ASSP-34*, 285–295.

P. Duhamel (1990). "A Connection between Bit Reversal and Matrix Transposition, Hardware and Software Consequences," *IEEE Trans. Acoust. Speech Signal Process. ASSP-38*, 1893–1896.

P. Duhamel and H. Hollmann (1984). "Split Radix FFT Algorithms," *Electron. Lett. 20*, 14–16.

P. Duhamel and M. Vetterli (1987). "Improved Fourier and Hartley Transform Algorithms Application to Cyclic Convolution of Real Data," *IEEE Trans. Acoust. Speech Signal Process. ASSP-35*, 818–824.

A. Edelman (1991). "Optimal Matrix Transposition and Bit Reversal on Hypercubes: All to All Personalized Communication," *J. Parallel and Distributed Comput. 11*, 328–331.

G. Eden (1979). "Two-Dimensional Fast Transforms Applied to Memory Limited Disk Computers," *Comp. Prog. Biomed. 9*, 258–262.

M. Edwards (1987). "Computation of Fast Fourier Transforms," *Cray Channels, Spring*, 22–25.

J.O. Eklundh (1972). "A Fast Computer Method for Matrix Transposing," *IEEE Trans. Comput. C-21*, 801–803.

J.O. Eklundh (1981). "Efficient Matrix Transposition," in *Two-Dimensional Digital Signal Processing II. Transforms and Median Filters*, T.S. Huang (ed.) Springer-Verlag, New York, 37–88.

A.C. Elster (1989). "Fast Bit-Reversal Algorithms," *ICASSP '89 Proceedings*, 1099–1102.

D.M.W. Evans (1987). "An Improved Digit-Reversal Permutation Algorithm for the Fast Fourier and Hartley Transforms," *IEEE Trans. on Acoust. Speech Signal Process. 35*, 1120–1125.

W.E. Ferguson Jr. (1982). "A Simple Derivation of the Glassman General-N Fast Fourier Transform," *Comput. Math. Appl. 8*, 401–411.

B.J. Fino and V.R. Algazi (1977). "A Unified Treatment of Discrete Fast Unitary Transforms," *SIAM J. Comput. 6*, 700–717.

B. Fornberg (1981). "A Vector Implementation of the Fast Fourier Transform," *Math. Comp. 36*, 189–191.

G. Fox, M. Johnson, G. Lyzenga, S. Otto, J. Salmon, and D. Walker (1988). *Solving Problems on Concurrent Processors, Vol. 1, General Techniques and Regular Problems*, Prentice-Hall, Englewood Cliffs, NJ.

D. Fraser (1976). "Array Permutation by Index-Digit Permutation," *J. Assoc. Comput. Mach. 23*, 298–309.

D. Fraser (1979). "Algorithm 545, An Optimized Mass Storage FFT," *ACM Trans. Math. Software 5*, 500–517.

E. Garcia-Torano (1983). "FASTF: Fast Fourier Transform with Arbitrary Factors," *Comput. Phys. Comm. 30*, 397–403.

W.M. Gentleman (1968). "Matrix Multiplication and Fast Fourier Transforms," *Bell System Tech. J. 47*, 1099–1103.

W.M. Gentleman (1978). "Some Complexity Results for Matrix Computations on Parallel Processors," *J. Assoc. Comput. Mach. 25*, 112–114.

W.M. Gentleman and G. Sande (1966). "Fast Fourier Transforms for Fun and Profit," *Proc. 1966 Fall Joint Computer Conference AFIPS 29*, 563–578.

J.A. Glassman (1970). "A Generalization of the Fast Fourier Transform," *IEEE Trans. Comput. C-19*, 105–116.

B. Gold and T. Bially (1973). "Parallelism in Fast Fourier Transform Hardware," *IEEE Trans. Audio and Electroacoustics AU-21*, 5–16.

G.C. Goldbogenm (1981). "PRIM: A Fast Matrix Transpose Method," *IEEE Trans. Software Engrg. SE-7*, 255–257.

G.H. Golub and C.F. Van Loan (1989). *Matrix Computations, 2nd Ed.*, Johns Hopkins University Press, Baltimore, MD.

I.J. Good (1958). "The Interaction Algorithm and Practical Fourier Analysis," *J. Roy. Stat. Soc. Ser. B, 20*, 361–372. Addendum, *J. Roy. Stat. Soc. Ser. B, 22*, 372–375.

I.J. Good (1971). "The Relationship between Two Fast Fourier Transforms," *IEEE Trans. Comput. C-20*, 310–317.

A. Graham (1981). *Kronecker Products and Matrix Calculus with Applications*, Ellis Horwood Ltd., Chichester, England.

M.H. Gutknecht (1979). "Fast Algorithms for the Conjugate Periodic Function," *Computing 22*, 79–91.

H. Hao and R.N. Bracewell (1987). "A Three Dimensional DFT Algorithm Using the Fast Hartley Transform," *Proc. IEEE 75*, 264.

R.M. Haralick (1976). "A Storage Efficient Way to Implement the Discrete Cosine Transform," *IEEE Trans. Comput. C-25*, 764–765.

D.B. Harris, J.H. McClelland, D.S.K. Chan, and H. Schuessler (1977). "Vector Radix Fast Fourier Transform," *Proc. IEEE Int. Conf. on Acoust. Speech Signal Process.*, 548–551.

M.T. Heideman and C.S. Burrus (1984). "A Bibliography of Fast Transform and Convolution Algorithms," Department of Electrical Engineering, Technical Report 8402, Rice University, Houston, TX.

M.T. Heideman, D.H. Johnson, and C.S. Burrus (1985). "Gauss and the History of the Fast Fourier Transform," *Arch. Hist. Exact Sci. 34*, 265–277.

H.V. Henderson, F. Pukelsheim, and S.R. Searle (1983). "On the History of the Kronecker Product," *Linear and Multilinear Algebra 14*, 113–120.

H.V. Henderson and S.R. Searle (1981). "The Vec-Permutation Matrix, The Vec Operator and Kronecker Products: A Review," *Linear and Multilinear Algebra 9*, 271–288.

J.L. Hennessy and D.A. Patterson (1990). *Computer Architecture: A Quantitative Approach*, Morgan Kaufmann Publishers, San Mateo, CA.

P. Henrici (1979). "Fast Fourier Methods in Computational Complex Analysis," *SIAM Rev. 21*, 460–480.

R.W. Hockney (1965). "A Fast Direct Solution of Poisson's Equation Using Fourier Analysis," *J. Assoc. Comput. Mach. 12*, 95–113.

R.W. Hockney and C.R. Jesshope (1981). *Parallel Computers*, Adam Hilger Ltd., Bristol, England.

K. Itano (1979). "Reduction of Page Swaps on the Two-Dimensional Transforms in a Paging Environment," *Inform. Process. Lett. 9*, 137–140.

H.W. Johnson and C.S. Burrus (1983). "The Design of Optimal DFT Algorithms Using Dynamic Programming," *IEEE Trans. Acoust. Speech Signal Process. 31*, 378–387.

H.W. Johnson and C.S. Burrus (1984). "An In-Place, In-Order Radix-2 FFT," *Proc. IEEE ICASSP*, San Diego, CA, p. 28A.2.

J. Johnson, R.W. Johnson, D. Rodriguez, and R. Tolimieri (1990). "A Methodology for Designing, Modifying, and Implementing Fourier Transform Algorithms on Various Architectures," *Circuits, Systems, and Signal Processing 9*, 449–500.

L.R. Johnson and A.K. Jain (1981). "An Efficient Two-Dimensional FFT Algorithm," *IEEE Trans. Pattern Anal. Machine Intell. PAMI-3*, 698–701.

S.L. Johnsson (1987). "Communication Efficient Basic Linear Algebra Computations on Hypercube Architecture," *J. Parallel and Distributed Computing 4*, 133–172.

S.L. Johnsson and D. Cohen (1981). "Computational Arrays for the Discrete Fourier Transform," *Proc. Twenty-Second Computer Society International Conference*, COMPCON '81.

S.L. Johnsson and D. Cohen (1982). "An Algebraic Description of Array Implementations of FFT Algorithms," *20th Allerton Conference on Communication, Control, and Computing*, Dept. Electrical Engineering, University of Illinois, Urbana, IL.

S.L. Johnsson and C.-T. Ho (1988). "Matrix Transposition on Boolean n-Cube Configured Ensemble Architectures," *SIAM J. Matrix Anal. Appl. 9*, 419–454.

S.L. Johnsson and C.-T. Ho (1989). "Spanning Graphs for Optimum Broadcasting and Personalized Communication," *IEEE Trans. Comput. C-38*, 1249–1268.

S.L. Johnsson and C.-T. Ho (1991a). "Generalized Shuffle Permutations on Boolean Cubes," Division of Applied Sciences Report TR-04-91, Harvard University. (To appear in *J. Parallel and Distributed Comput.*)

S.L. Johnsson and C.-T. Ho (1991b). "Maximizing Channel Utilization for All-to-All Personalized Communication on Boolean Cubes," *Proc. Sixth Distributed Memory Computing Conference*, IEEE Computer Society Press, New York, 299–304.

S.L. Johnsson, C.-T. Ho, M. Jacquemin, and A. Ruttenberg (1987). "Computing Fast Fourier Transforms on Boolean Cubes and Related Networks," in *Advanced Algorithms and Architectures for Signal Processing II 826*, Society of Photo-Optical Instrumentation Engineers, 223–231.

S.L. Johnsson, M. Jacquemin, and C.-T. Ho (1989). "High Radix FFT on Boolean Cube Networks," Department of Computer Science Report YALE/DCS/TR-751, Yale University, New Haven, CT. (To appear in *J. Comput. Phys.*)

S.L. Johnsson, M. Jacquemin, and R.L. Krawitz (1991). "Communication Efficient Multiprocessor FFT," Division of Applied Sciences Report TR-25-91, Harvard University. (To appear in *J. Comput. Phys.*)

S.L. Johnsson and R.L. Krawitz (1991). "Cooley–Tukey FFT on the Connection Machine," Division of Applied Sciences Report TR-24-91, Harvard University. (To appear in *Parallel Comput.*)

S.L. Johnsson, R.L. Krawitz, R. Frye, and D. MacDonald (1989). "A Radix-2 FFT on the Connection Machine," *Proceedings Supercomputer 89*, ACM Press, New York, 809–819.

S.L. Johnsson, U. Weiser, D. Cohen, and A. Davis (1981). "Towards a Formal Treatment of VLSI Arrays," *Proc. Second Caltech Conference on VLSI*, 378–398.

D.K. Kahaner (1970). "Matrix Description of the Fast Fourier Transform," *IEEE Trans. Audio and Electroacoustics AU-18*, 442–450.

F.A. Kamangar and K.R. Rao (1982). "Fast Algorithms for the 2-D Discrete Cosine Transform," *IEEE Trans. Comput. C-31*, 899–906.

T. Kaneko and B. Liu (1970). "Accumulation of Roundoff Error in Fast Fourier Transforms," *J. Assoc. Comput. Mach.* 17, 637–654.

M.Y. Kim, A. Nigam, G. Paul, and R. Flynn (1987). "Disk Interleaving and Very Large Fast Fourier Transforms," *International J. Supercomputer Applications 1*, 75–96.

H. Kitajima (1980). "A Symmetric Cosine Transform," *IEEE Trans. Comput.* C-29, 317–323.

W.R. Knight and R. Kaiser (1979). "A Simple Fixed Point Error Bound for the Fast Fourier Transform," *IEEE Trans. Acoust. Speech Signal Proc.* ASSP-27, 615–620.

D.P. Kolba and T.W. Parks (1977). "A Prime Factor FFT Algorithm Using High-Speed Convolution," *IEEE Trans. Acoust. Speech Signal Process.* ASSP-25, 281–294.

D.G. Korn and J.J. Lambiotte (1979). "Computing the Fast Fourier Transform on a Vector Computer," *Math. Comp.* 33, 977–992.

T.W. Körner (1988). *Fourier Analysis*, Cambridge University Press, New York.

H.O. Kunz (1979). "On the Equivalence between One-Dimensional Discrete Walsh–Hadamard and Multidimensional Discrete Fourier Transforms, *IEEE Trans. Comput.* C-28, 267–268.

S. Lafkin and M.A. Brebner (1970). "In-situ Transposition of a Rectangular Matrix," *Comm. ACM* 13, 324–326.

S. Lange, U. Stolle, and G. Huttner (1973). "On the Fast Computing of Three-Dimensional Fourier Transforms of Crystallographic Data via External Storage," *Acta Crystallogr. A*, A29, 445–449.

D.H. Lawrie (1975). "Access and Alignment of Data in an Array Processor," *IEEE Trans. Comput.* 24, 99–109.

D.H. Lawrie and C.R. Vora (1982). "The Prime Memory System for Array Access," *IEEE Trans. Comput.* C-31, 1435–1442.

J. Makhoul (1980). "A Fast Cosine Transform in One and Two Dimensions," *IEEE Trans. Acoust. Speech Signal Process.* ASSP-28, 27–33.

O. McBryan and E. Van de Velde (1987). "Hypercube Algorithms and Implementations," *SIAM J. Sci. Statist. Comput.* 8, s227–s287.

J.H. McClellan and H. Nawab (1979). "Complex General-*n* Winograd Fourier Transform Algorithm (WFTA)," in *Programs for Digital Signal Processing*, Digital Signal Processing Committee (eds.), IEEE Press, New York.

J.H. McClellan and C.M. Rader (1979). *Number Theory in Digital Signal Processing*, Prentice-Hall, Englewood Cliffs, NJ.

R.M. Mersereau and T.C. Speake (1981). "A Unified Treatment of Cooley–Tukey Algorithms for the Evaluation of the Multidimensional DFT," *IEEE Trans. Acoust. Speech Signal Process.* ASSP-29, 1011–1018.

M. Metcalf and J. Reid (1990). *Fortran 90 Explained*, Oxford University Press, New York.

L.R. Morris (1978). "A Comparative Study of Time Efficient FFT and WFTA Programs for General Purpose Computers," *IEEE Trans. Acoust. Speech Signal Process.* ASSP-26, 141–150.

M.J. Narasimha and A.M. Peterson (1978). "On the Computation of the Discrete Cosine Transform," *IEEE Trans. Comm.* COM-26, 934–936.

S. Nassimi (1982). "Optimal (BPC) Permutations on a Cube Connected (SIMD) Computer," *IEEE Trans. Comput.* C-24, 338–341.

H. Nawab and J.H. McClellan (1979). "Parallelism in the Computation of the FFT and WFTA," *Conf. Record 1979 IEEE Int. Conf. Acoustics, Speech, and Signal Processing*, 514–517.

P.J. Nicholson (1971). "Algebraic Theory of Finite Fourier Transforms," *J. Comput. System Sci. 5*, 524–527.

A. Norton and A. Silberger (1987). "Parallelization and Performance Prediction of the Cooley–Tukey FFT Algorithm for Shared Memory Architectures," *IEEE Trans. Comput.* C-36, 581–591.

H. Nussbaumer (1980). "Fast Multidimensional Discrete Cosine Transforms," *IBM Tech. Disclosure Bull.* 23, 1976–1981.

H.J. Nussbaumer (1981a). "Improved Approach for the Computation of Multidimensional Cosine Transforms," *IBM Tech. Disclosure Bull.* 23, 4517–4521.

H.J. Nussbaumer (1981b). *Fast Fourier Transform and Convolution Algorithms*, Springer-Verlag, New York.

J. Oliver (1975). "Stable Methods for Evaluating the Points $\cos(i\pi/n)$," *J. Inst. Maths. Applic. 16*, 247–257.

M. Onoe (1975). "A Method for Computing Large Scale Two-Dimensional Transforms without Transposing the Data Matrix," *Proc. IEEE 63*, 196–197.

A. Oppenheim and C. Weinstein (1972). "Effects of Finite Register Length in Digital Filtering and the Fast Fourier Transform," *Proc. IEEE 60*, 957–976.

A.V. Oppenheimer and R.W. Schafer (1975). *Digital Signal Processing*, Prentice-Hall, Englewood Cliffs, NJ.

C.H. Papadimitriou (1979). "Optimality of the Fast Fourier Transform," *J. Assoc. Comput. Mach.* 26, 95–102.

M.C. Pease (1968). "An Adaptation of the Fast Fourier Transform for Parallel Processing," *J. Assoc. Comput. Mach.* 15, 252–264.

M. Pickering (1986). *Introduction to Fast Fourier Transform Methods for Partial Differential Equations with Applications*, Research Studies Press, Letchworth, England.

R.J. Polge and B.K. Bhagavan (1976). "Efficient Fast Fourier Transform Programs for Arbitrary Factors with One Step Loop Unscrambling," *IEEE Trans. Comput.* C-25, 534–539.

R.J. Polge, B.K. Bhagavan, and J.M. Carswell (1974). "Fast Algorithms for Bit-Reversal," *IEEE Trans. Comput.* C-23, 1–9.

S. Prakash and V.V. Rao (1981). "A New Radix-6 FFT Algorithm," *IEEE Trans. Acoust. Speech Signal Process.* ASSP-29, 939–941.

S. Prakash and V.V. Rao (1982). "Vector Radix FFT Error Analysis," *IEEE Trans. Acoust. Speech Signal Process.* ASSP-30, 808–811.

F.P. Preparata and D.V. Sarwate (1977). "Computational Complexity of Fourier Transforms over Finite Fields," *Math. Comp.* 31, 740–751.

L.R. Rabiner (1979). "On the Use of Symmetry in FFT Computation," *IEEE Trans. Acoust. Speech Signal Process.* ASSP-27, 233–239.

L.R. Rabiner and B. Gold (1975). *Theory and Application of Digital Signal Processing*, Prentice-Hall, Englewood Cliffs, NJ.

C.M. Rader (1968). "Discrete Fourier Transforms When the Number of Data Samples Is Prime," *Proc. IEEE* 5, 1107–1108.

C.M. Rader and N.M. Brenner (1976). "A New Principle for Fast Fourier Transformation," *IEEE Trans. Acoust. Speech Signal Process.* ASSP-24, 264–265.

C.M. Rader and S.L. Scharf (1979). "Do Not Use a Chirp to Test a DFT Program," *IEEE Trans. Acoust. Speech Signal Process.* ASSP-27, 430–432.

G.U. Ramos (1971). "Roundoff Error Analysis of the Fast Fourier Transform," *Math. Comp.* 25, 757–768.

D.R. Reddy and V.V. Rao (1982). "Error Analysis of FFT of a Sparse Sequence," *J. Electr. Electron. Eng. Aust.* 2, 169–175.

P.A. Regalia and S. Mitra (1989). "Kronecker Products, Unitary Matrices, and Signal Processing Applications," *SIAM Rev.* 31, 586–613.

A. Rieu (1971). "Matrix Formulation of the Cooley and Tukey Algorithm and Its Extension," *Revue Cethedec* 8, 25–35.

G.E. Rivard (1977). "Direct Fast Fourier Transform of Bivariate Functions," *IEEE Trans. Acoust. Speech Signal Process.* ASSP-25, 250–52.

D. Rodriguez (1987). *On Tensor Product Formulations of Additive Fast Fourier Transform Algorithms and Their Implementations*, Ph.D. Thesis, Department of Electrical Engineering, The City College of New York, CUNY.

D.J. Rose (1980). "Matrix Identities of the Fast Fourier Transform," *Linear Algebra Appl.* 29, 423–443.

P. Rosel (1989). "Timing of Some Bit Reversal Algorithms," *Signal Processing* 18, 425–433.

J.H. Rothweiler (1982). "Implementation of the In-Order Prime Factor Transform for Various Sizes," *IEEE Trans. Acoust. Speech Signal Process.* 30, 105–107.

Y. Saad and M. Schultz (1989). "Data Communication in Hypercubes," *Parallel Comput.* 11, 131–150.

A. Sameh (1984). "A Fast Poisson Solver for Multiprocessors," in *Elliptic Problem Solvers II*, Academic Press, New York, 175–186.

J.E. Savage and S. Swamy (1978). "Space-Time Tradeoffs on the FFT Algorithm," *IEEE Trans. Inform. Theory* IT-24, 563–568.

R. Schakoff (1989). *Digital Image Processing and Computer Vision*, John Wiley & Sons, New York.

U. Schumann (1973). "Comments on 'A Fast Computer Method for Matrix Transposing and Applications to the Solution of Poisson's Equation'," *IEEE Trans. Comput.* C-22, 542–543.

W. Shen and A.Y. Oruc (1990). "Systolic Arrays for Multidimensional Discrete Transforms," *International J. of Supercomputing* 4, 201–222.

A.E. Siegman (1975). "How to Compute Two Complex Even Fourier Transforms with One Transform Step," *Proc. IEEE* 63, 544.

H.F. Silverman (1977). "An Introduction to Programming the Winograd Fourier Transform Algorithm (WFTA)," *IEEE Trans. Acoust. Speech Signal Process.* ASSP-25, 152–164.

H.F. Silverman (1978). "How to Select an Algorithm for the Calculation of the Discrete Fourier Transform," *Proc. 1978 IEEE Int. Symp. Circuits Systems*, 1083–1084.

R.C. Singleton (1967a). "On Computing the Fast Fourier Transforms," *Comm. ACM* 10, 647–654.

R.C. Singleton (1967b). "A Method for Computing the Fast Fourier Transform with Auxiliary Memory and Limited High-Speed Storage," *IEEE Trans. Audio and Electroacoustics* AU-15, 91–98.

R.C. Singleton (1968). "An Algol Procedure for the Fast Fourier Transform with Arbitrary Factors–Algorithm 339," *Comm. ACM 11*, 776–779.

R.C. Singleton (1969). "An Algorithm for Computing the Mixed Radix Fast Fourier Transform," *IEEE Trans. Audio and Electroacoustics AU-17*, 93–103.

R.C. Singleton (1979). "Two-Dimensional Mixed Radix Mass Storage Fourier Transform," in *Programs for Digital Signal Processing*, Digital Signal Processing Committee (eds.), IEEE Press, New York, 1.9-1–1.9-8.

H. Sloate (1974). "Matrix Representations for Sorting and the Fast Fourier Transform," *IEEE Trans. Circuits and Systems CAS-21*, 109–116.

H.V. Sorensen, D.L. Jones, M.T. Heideman, C.S. Burrus (1985). "On Computing the Discrete Hartley Transform," *IEEE Trans. Acoust. Speech Signal Process. ASSP-33*, 1231–1238.

H.V. Sorensen, D.L. Jones, M.T. Heideman, C.S. Burrus (1987). "Real-Valued Fast Fourier Transform Algorithms," *IEEE Trans. Acoust. Speech Signal Process. ASSP-35*, 849–863.

H.V. Sorensen, M.T. Heideman, and C.S. Burrus (1986). "On Calculating the Split-Radix FFT," *IEEE Trans. Acoust. Speech Signal Process. ASSP-34*, 152–156.

H.V. Sorensen, C.A. Katz, and C.S. Burrus (1990). "Efficient FFT Algorithms for DSP Processors Using Tensor Product Decomposition," *Proc. ICASSP-90*, Albuquerque, NM.

H. Stone (1971). "Parallel Processing with the Perfect Shuffle," *IEEE Trans. Comput. C-20*, 153–161.

G. Strang (1987). *Introduction to Applied Mathematics*, Wellesley-Cambridge Press, Wellesley, MA.

G. Strang (1989). "Wavelets and Dilation Equations," *SIAM Rev. 31*, 614–627.

Y. Suzuki, T. Sone, and K. Kido (1986). "A New FFT Algorithm of Radix 3, 6, and 12," *IEEE Trans. Acoust. Speech Signal Process. 34*, 380–383.

P.N. Swarztrauber (1974). "A Direct Method for the Discrete Solution of Separable Elliptic Equations," *SIAM J. Numer. Anal. 11*, 1136–1150.

P.N. Swarztrauber (1977). "The Methods of Cyclic Reduction, Fourier Analysis and Cyclic Reduction-Fourier Analysis for the Discrete Solution of Poisson's Equation on a Rectangle," *SIAM Rev. 19*, 490–501.

P.N. Swarztrauber (1982). "Vectorizing the FFTs," in *Parallel Computations*, G. Rodrigue (ed.), Academic Press, New York, 490–501.

P.N. Swarztrauber (1984a). "Fast Poisson Solvers," in *MAA Studies in Numerical Analysis, Vol. 24*, G.H. Golub (ed.), Mathematics Association of America, 319–370.

P.N. Swarztrauber (1984b). "FFT Algorithms for Vector Computers," *Parallel Comput. 1*, 45–63.

P.N. Swarztrauber (1986). "Symmetric FFTs," *Math. Comp. 47*, 323–346.

P.N. Swarztrauber (1987). "Multiprocessor FFTs," *Parallel Comput. 5*, 197–210.

P.N. Swarztrauber, R.A. Sweet, W.L. Briggs, V.E. Henson, and J. Otto (1991). "Bluestein's FFT for Arbitrary N on the Hypercube," manuscript.

R. Sweet (1973). "Direct Methods for the Solution of Poisson's Equation on a Staggered Grid," *J. Comput. Phys. 12*, 422–428.

R. Sweet (1977). "A Cyclic Reduction Algorithm for Solving Block Tridiagonal Systems of Arbitrary Dimension," *SIAM J. Numer. Anal. 14*, 706–720.

G.C. Temes (1977). "Worst Case Error Analysis for the Fast Fourier Transform," *IEEE J. Electron. Circuits Systems 1*, 110–115.

C. Temperton (1979). "Direct Methods for the Solution of the Discrete Poisson Equation: Some Comparisons," *J. Comput. Phys. 31*, 1–20.

C. Temperton (1980a). "Very Fast Real Fourier Transform," in *Special Topics of Applied Mathematics: Functional Analysis, Numerical Analysis, and Optimization*, J. Frehse, D. Pallaschke, and U. Trottenberg (eds.), North Holland, Amsterdam, 165–171.

C. Temperton (1980b). "On the FACR(ℓ) Algorithm for the Discrete Poisson Equation," *J. Comput. Phys. 34*, 314.

C. Temperton (1983a). "Self-Sorting Mixed Radix Fast Fourier Transforms," *J. Comput. Phys. 52*, 1–23.

C. Temperton (1983b). "Fast Mixed Radix Real Fourier Transforms," *J. Comput. Phys. 52*, 340–350.

C. Temperton (1983c). "A Note on Prime Factor FFT Algorithms," *J. Comput. Phys. 52*, 198–204.

C. Temperton (1984). "Fast Fourier Transforms on the Cyber 205," in *High Speed Computation*, J. Kowalik (ed.), Springer-Verlag, Berlin.

C. Temperton (1985). "Implementation of a Self-Sorting In-Place Prime Factor FFT Algorithm," *J. Comput. Phys. 58*, 283–299.

C. Temperton (1988a). "A New Set of Minimum-Add Small-n Rotated DFT Modules," *J. Comput. Phys. 75*, 190–198.

C. Temperton (1988b). "A Self-Sorting In-Place Prime Factor Real/Half-Complex FFT Algorithm," *J. Comput. Phys. 75*, 199–216.

C. Temperton (1988c). "Implementation of a Prime Factor FFT Algorithm on the Cray-1," *Parallel Comput. 6*, 99–108.

C. Temperton (1991). "Self-Sorting In-Place Fast Fourier Transforms," *SIAM J. Sci. Statist. Comput. 12*, 808–823.

L.F. Ten Eyck (1973). "Crystallographic Fast Fourier Transforms," *ACTA Crystallogr. A A29*, 183–191.

F. Theilheimer (1969). "A Matrix Version of the Fast Fourier Transform," *IEEE Trans. Audio and Electroacoustics AU-17*, 158–161.

T. Thong and B. Liu (1977). "Accumulation of Roundoff Errors in Floating Point FFT," *IEEE Trans. Circuits and Systems CAS-24*, 132–143.

R. Tolimieri, M. An, and C. Lu (1989). *Algorithms for Discrete Fourier Transform and Convolution*, Springer-Verlag, New York.

C. Tong and P.N. Swarztrauber (1991). "Ordered Fast Fourier Transforms on a Massively Parallel Hypercube Multiprocessor," *J. Parallel and Distributed Computing 12*, 50–59.

B.D. Tseng and W.C. Miller (1978). "On Computing the Discrete Cosine Transform," *IEEE Trans. Comput. C-27*, 966–968.

D.W. Twigg (1983). "Transposition of Matrix Stored on Sequential File," *IEEE Trans. Comput. C-32*, 1185–1188.

R.E. Twogood and M.P. Ekstrom (1976). "An Extension of Eklundh's Matrix Transposition Algorithm and Its Application in Digital Image Signal Processing," *IEEE Trans. Comput. C-25*, 950–952.

M. Vetterli and P. Duhamel (1989). "Split-Radix Algorithms for Length p^m DFTs," *IEEE Trans. Acoust. Speech Signal Process. ASSP-34*, 57–64.

V.A. Vlasenko and K.R. Rao (1979). "Unified Matrix Treatment of Discrete Transforms," *IEEE Trans. Comput. C-28*, 934–938.

V.A. Vlasenko (1986). "A Matrix Approach to the Construction of Fast Multidimensional Discrete Fourier Transform Algorithms," *Radioelectron. and Commun. Syst. 29*, 87–90.

M.D. Wagh and H. Ganesh (1980). "A New Algorithm for the Discrete Cosine Transformation of Arbitrary Number of Points," *IEEE Trans. Comput. C-29*, 269–277.

Z. Wang and B.R. Hunt (1985). "The Discrete W Transform," *Appl. Math. Comput. 16*, 19–48.

Z.D. Wang (1982). "A Fast Algorithm for the Discrete Sine Transform Implemented by the Fast Cosine Transform," *IEEE Trans. Acoust. Speech Signal Process. ASSP-30*, 814–815.

Z.D. Wang (1983). "Reconsideration of 'A Fast Computational Algorithm for the Discrete Cosine Transformation'," *IEEE Trans. Comm. COM-31*, 121–123.

Z. Wang and B.R. Hunt (1983). "The Discrete Cosine Transform—A New Version," *Proc. 1983 IEEE Int. Conf. Acoust. Speech Signal Process.*, 1256–1259.

C.J. Weinstein, "Roundoff Noise in Floating Point Fast Fourier Transform Computation," *IEEE Trans. Audio and Electroacoustics AU-17*, 209–215.

S. Winograd (1978). "On Computing the Discrete Fast Fourier Transform," *Math. Comp. 32*, 175–199.

S. Winograd (1979). "On the Multiplicative Complexity of the Discrete Fourier Transform," *Adv. Math. 32*, 83–117.

P. Yip and K.R. Rao (1978). "Sparse Matrix Factorization of Discrete Sine Transform," *Conf. Record 12th Asilomar Conf. Circuits, Systems, and Computers*, Pacific Grove, CA, 549–555.

P. Yip and K.R. Rao (1980). "A Fast Computation Algorithm for the Discrete Sine Transform," *IEEE Trans. Comm. COM-28*, 304–307.

S. Zohar (1979a). "A Prescription of Winograd's Discrete Fourier Transform Algorithm," *IEEE Trans. Acoustics, Speech, and Signal Processing ASSP-27*, 409–421.

S. Zohar (1979b). "Correction to 'A Prescription of Winograd's Discrete Fourier Transform Algorithm'," *IEEE Trans. Acoust. Speech Signal Process. ASSP-27*, 563.

Index